DAUGHTERS, WIVES, AND WIDOWS

Writings by Men about Women
and Marriage in England,
1500–1640

EDITED BY

Joan Larsen Klein

UNIVERSITY OF ILLINOIS PRESS
Urbana and Chicago

Publication of this work has been supported in part
by a grant from the Research Board of the
University of Illinois at Urbana-Champaign.

This book is printed on acid-free paper.

Library of Congress Cataloging-in-Publication Data

Daughters, wives, and widows : writings by men about women and
    marriage in England, 1500–1640 / edited by Joan Larsen Klein.
        p.   cm.
    Includes bibliographical references and index.
    ISBN 0-252-01840-0 (cl). — ISBN 0-252-06206-X (pb)
    1. Women—England—History—16th century.   2. Women—England—
History—17th century.   3. Marriage—England—History—16th
century.   4. Marriage—England—History—17th century.   I. Klein,
Joan Larsen, 1931–
HQ1593.D37   1992
305.4′0942′09031—dc20   91-42373
                                                                        CIP

Daughters, Wives, and Widows

This book is dedicated to the memory of my parents,
William and Eleanor Larsen.

Contents

Preface

In this anthology I have gathered selections of writings about women and marriage which were among those most widely consulted and highly regarded by men and women both in sixteenth- and seventeenth-century England. I have chosen works dealing with women and marriage because marriage was always seen in the period as woman's primary vocation, that for which she was created when God first shaped her out of Adam's rib and that by which the common law of England legally defined her. (As the anonymous author of *The Law's Resolutions of Women's Rights,* following both Scripture and common law, put it, from their birth all women "are understood either married or to be married and their desires are subject to their husband.")[1] In consequence, a woman's sphere was largely private and her voice usually confined to home, family, and neighbors. In fact, recent critics have suggested that the activities of women all over Europe at this time were increasingly more constricted and that even those women who achieved public lives or worked outside the home were increasingly pressured to return to it.[2] Although there were important exceptions, women were rarely able to preach from pulpits or write for publication.[3] Because of the restrictions imposed on their speech and writing by law and custom, we know very little about the ways they understood themselves and their relationships to their husbands, children, other relatives, and neighbors.

What we do possess from this period, however, is a substantial number of books written by men about and often to women. Indeed, as in later periods, women in early modern England were a subject of abiding interest to men. ("Have you any notion how many books are written about women in the course of one year?" asked Virginia Woolf. "Have you any notion how many are written by men?")[4] But nearly all men in the period tended to view women individually and collectively as daughters, wives, mothers, or widows, a viewpoint which they believed was sanctioned, even enforced upon them, by the account of Eve's creation and fall in Genesis and by

customs hardened over time. When men's views of women's place were
embodied in sermon literature or courtesy books, those views were usually
hortatory and prescriptive, often reflecting negatively their authors' per-
ceptions of the daily lives of women. Even when a man wrote about his
own wife, as did Philip Stubbes, his grief over her death and his deter-
mination to portray her as a sainted exemplar of feminine virtue seem to
have colored his vision. We are given additional insights, both positive and
negative, into women and marriage in the drama and the romances of the
period, in pamphlets and broadsides describing witchcraft, murders, and
other felonies, in transcripts of court trials and other sorts of documentary
evidence, and in a few diaries, letters, wills, and account books. But here,
too, playwrights, poets, diarists, court recorders, and the like were usually
men, and the women they described, whether fictive or actual, were often
portrayed as extreme instances of virtue or vice. Nor do the few women
whose writing saw print tell us as much as we would like to know about
themselves and their own accomplishments.[5] We are often forced, as a
result, to fall back upon male authors for glimpses into the lives of women
and their relationships with their husbands and children, in the knowledge
that these glimpses may not provide accurate indices to objective data or
to the private, perhaps more sympathetic, opinions of other men whose
ideas and practices never saw print.[6] But we do not have access to those
private thoughts or to much information about actual relations between
husbands and wives, all of which are ephemeral by their very nature. What
the published works by men about women do tell us is how men publicly
regarded women and taught women to regard themselves. This anthology,
consequently, is as much about men as it is about women, about the way
in which one half of humankind perceived (and usually hoped to order)
the meaning and life of the other.

I have included in this anthology writings which represent the orthodox
Anglican position as it is found in the ceremony of marriage and the homily
on marriage, the very divergent humanist attitudes toward women and
marriage of Erasmus and Vives, two compatible Puritan views of women
in companionate marriages (Philip Stubbes's personal vision of his own
wife and William Perkins's treatise on Christian domestic life), two practical
works on housewifery and midwifery, and two courtesy books written to
instruct and compliment well-born ladies. I have included selections from
the writings of one woman who succeeded in speaking for herself and about
her own marriage, as a partial corrective to the prevailing masculine voices
which dominated the production of books on our subject and hence this
anthology. I thought it important to include Dorothy Leigh's work here
because the discrepancies between her views and masculine views are
significant—even though she never overtly contradicted their main tenets.

Unlike any other book written by a woman in our period, furthermore, hers was extraordinarily popular. It undoubtedly influenced many women and probably did so differently from the ways in which books written by men influenced their female readers.

Nearly all the works represented in this anthology went through numerous editions in sixteenth- and seventeenth-century England, which indicates how widely read and influential they really were. The *Homilies,* for instance, was required to be placed in every church in England, and may have been used in many parishes almost as frequently as the Bible and *The Book of Common Prayer.* (In 1563, not long after Elizabeth ascended the throne, she ordered the new second volume of homilies along with Edward's first volume to be read from every pulpit in England, in all likelihood to effect uniformity of belief. In order to make such a distribution possible, nine separate editions of the second volume were printed at various presses in a single year.)[7] Erasmus's *In Laud and Praise of Matrimony* went through thirteen Latin editions before 1540 and was translated into French and German, twice into English, and was paraphrased in Spanish. Vives's *Instruction of a Christian Woman,* which was written at the request of Catherine, Henry VIII's queen, for her daughter, Mary, was originally composed in Latin and was translated into English, French, German, Italian, and Castilian.[8] Its English translation went through nine editions to 1592, and was probably the most influential Renaissance treatise on the education of women in England and perhaps in Europe. Philip Stubbes's *A Crystal Glass for Christian Women* went through thirty-four editions between 1591 and 1700, and William Perkins's impressive three-volume *Works* (which included *Christian Economy*) went through at least ten editions in England and many others in Europe. His writings were translated variously into Welsh, Irish, Dutch, German, Hungarian, and Spanish. However crabbed in style and misogynist in substance some of these books seem to us now, numbers as high as these are significant. If they do nothing else, they undoubtedly indicate crucial ways in which large segments of a reading public were brought to understand women and their role in marriage. Such numbers also illuminate the importance of the philosophical and religious bases upon which those understandings were built.

Most of the texts in this anthology are relatively inaccessible today, existing in Renaissance editions, on microfilm, in unedited black-letter facsimiles, or in out-of-print nineteenth-century editions. There are, for instance, no modern editions of Taverner's translation of Erasmus's *In Laud and Praise of Matrimony* (although a second contemporary translation can be found buried in a modern edition of Thomas Wilson's *Art of Rhetoric*) or of the homily "On Matrimony," or of Stubbes's *A Crystal Glass,* or indeed of most of these works. This anthology, therefore, not only reflects the

most widely read, predominant male attitudes toward women and marriage
in sixteenth- and early seventeenth-century England, it contains texts which
are hard to obtain and harder, when obtained, to read.

Although all our texts except that written by Dorothy Leigh represent
exclusively male views of women, and although all confine themselves
within the parameters of Christian dogma and common law, they often
differ considerably among themselves. Some of our authors, in particular
Brathwaite and Du Bosc, wrote to and for wealthy gentlewomen whose
lives probably did not reflect those of women in lower social ranks.[9] In
fact, the different social classes to which women belonged and their con-
sequent roles as conduits of wealth seem to have affected male attitudes
and actions differently.[10] Erasmus insisted that his praise of women and
marriage in the *Laud and Praise of Matrimony* was primarily a youthful
rhetorical exercise. But he said so when his book was under attack as
heretical (because in it he praised marriage above celibacy), and he himself
accused of heresy (for which he could have been executed). He escaped
conviction, happily,[11] even though he never retracted the premises upon
which his arguments were based. Other writings like the homily "Of Matrimony" and Vives's two treatises so stress the principle of wifely subordination that their injunctions seem intended to be corrective as well as
prescriptive. But we should also notice that the further our texts move
away from theological assumptions about woman's place and the nearer
they come to describing the actual conditions of women's lives, the less
emphasis we find on notions of women's subordination, inferiority, and
frailty. The principal textbook of obstetrics in our period, *The Birth of
Mankind,* does not even pay lip service to the idea of women's "natural"
inferiority, and Thomas Tusser stresses not their inferiority but their
strengths.

This anthology, therefore, though it cannot be said to describe the real
lives of individual women, does record various positions men took in public
toward women and their place in English family life, most of which were
grounded in the belief that women's subordination was ordained by God
and that their physical and mental inferiority was an attribute of their
creation. Consequently, the body of opinion included in this anthology
records the attempts of men to fashion the lives, characters, and activities
of women they saw as daughters, wives, and widows, and as such, subordinate to themselves. These writers did so according to the dictates of
Scripture, law, and surely their own interests as well. Thus it may have
been only an exceptional woman who was able to escape the restrictions
that her father, her husband, and her society imposed upon her, only an
exceptional woman who became well educated, only exceptional women
whom we now notice in histories and anthologies. But the notes to this

preface, concerned as they are with at least those women and their voices, allow us to hope that the profound silence of the large majority of women in the period does not necessarily reflect adversely upon either their private achievements or their private joys.

Note on the Texts

In transcribing and editing whole texts or selections in this anthology I have used the first editions, except for Thomas Tusser's *The Points of House-wifery*, where I used the edition of W. Payne and Sidney Herrtage (London: Trubner & Co., 1878). In the process I have tried to remain faithful to the original texts. Spelling has been modernized and obsolete words given the preferred spelling in the *Oxford English Dictionary*. Archaic verb endings have been retained, although modern endings are usually indicated in brackets. Punctuation, capitalization, italics, and occasionally paragraphing have been modernized and regularized. Abbreviations have usually been expanded, and obvious printing errors silently corrected. Definitions of difficult or obsolete words are normally taken from the *Oxford English Dictionary*.

NOTES

1. *The Law's Resolutions of Women's Rights: or, The Law's Provision for Women* (London, 1632; facs. rpt., New York: Garland Publishing, 1978), p. 6.
2. In "Women's Defense of Their Public Role," Merry E. Wiesner, following Joan Kelly-Gadol, documents the increase in restrictions imposed upon women in Europe in the Renaissance and the "increasing split between [women's] public and private life" (in *Women in the Middle Ages and the Renaissance: Literary and Historical Perspectives,* ed. Mary Beth Rose [Syracuse: Syracuse University Press, 1986], p. 1). At the same time, she shows that women consistently attempted to defend the public roles they did achieve. Elizabeth I, of course, is the most important exception to the general rule of silence imposed upon women. But Jasper Ridley has suggested that Elizabeth, along with her subjects, believed in the inferiority of women (*Elizabeth I: The Shrewdness of Virtue* [New York: Viking, 1988], p. 91). In her case, however, she also believed that her woman's inferiority "was overruled . . . by the principle of the divine right of Princes." Like men, "lower-class" women worked for pay. But even here they worked mainly as servants in the homes of others or on piecework at home. For a description of women as spinsters (principally in Europe), see Merry E. Wiesner, "Spinsters and Seamstresses: Women in Cloth and Clothing Production," in *Rewriting the Renaissance: The Discourses of Sexual Difference in Early Modern Europe,* ed. Margaret W. Ferguson, Maureen Quilligan, and Nancy J. Vickers (Chicago: University of Chicago Press, 1986), pp. 191–205. For an overview of the difficulties encountered by working women in Florence

and some of the strategies they used to overcome them, see Judith C. Brown, "A Woman's Place Was in the Home: Women's Work in Renaissance Tuscany," in *Rewriting the Renaissance,* pp. 206–22.

3. In several later seventeenth-century sects a few women did preach, as Keith Thomas showed some years ago. See "Women and the Civil War Sects," *Past and Present* 13 (1958), 42–62. Most women who published their writings were high-born, although there were exceptions—for instance, Rachel Speght, Elizabeth Joceline, and Dorothy Leigh. See *The Paradise of Women: Writings by Englishwomen of the Renaissance,* ed. Betty Travitsky (Westport, Conn.: Greenwood Press, 1981); *First Feminists: British Women Writers, 1578–1799,* ed. Moira Ferguson (Bloomington: Indiana University Press; Old Westbury, N.Y.: Feminist Press, 1985); and *Women Writers of the Renaissance and Reformation,* ed. Katharina M. Wilson (Athens: University of Georgia Press, 1987), pp. 481–608.

4. Virginia Woolf, *A Room of One's Own* (1929; rpt., New York: Harcourt Brace Jovanovich, 1989), p. 26.

5. Margaret Roper, one of the most learned women England produced in the sixteenth century, wrote mainly in the form of private letters, exercises, and translations, most of which were never published and are now lost. Her father, Sir Thomas More, counseled her not to seek public esteem or to publish her writings, and to content herself with an audience composed of family and close friends. Even a modern feminist critic who singled her out for notice seems to have been forced to characterize Margaret in terms of her relationship to her father and secondarily her husband—because that was the way in which Margaret apparently understood herself. See Elizabeth McCutcheon, "Margaret More Roper: The Learned Woman in Tudor England," in *Women Writers of the Renaissance and Reformation,* pp. 449–80.

6. Keith Wrightson, following C. L. Powell, has suggested that the evidence of diaries and other admittedly sparse documentary evidence modifies "in some degree the stereotype of marital relations" (*English Society 1580–1680* [New Brunswick, N.J.: Rutgers University Press, 1982], p. 92; C. L. Powell, *English Domestic Relations 1487–1653: A Study of Matrimony and Family Life in Theory and Practice as Revealed by the Literature, Law and History of the Period* [New York, 1917, 1972]). He also suggests that "the picture which emerges indicates the *private* existence of a strong complementary and companionate ethos, side by side with, and often overshadowing, theoretical adherence to the doctrine of male authority and *public* female subordination." See also Alan Macfarlane, *Marriage and Love in England: Modes of Reproduction 1300–1840* (Oxford: Basil Blackwell, 1986), pp. 154–57.

7. In all, twenty-five editions of the *Homilies* were printed between 1563 and 1687. See *The Two Books of Homilies Appointed to be Read in Churches,* ed. John Griffiths (Oxford: Oxford University Press, 1859), pp. xxii–xxiii, lxii–lxvii. See also *Certain Sermons or Homilies (1547) and A Homily against Disobedience and Willful Rebellion (1570),* ed. Ronald B. Bond (Toronto: University of Toronto Press, 1987), pp. 3–18. This welcome new edition contains only the first book of homilies, not the second from which the homily on marriage is taken.

8. Valerie Wayne has counted at least thirty-six English and continental editions of *The Instruction of a Christian Woman* ("Some Sad Sentence: Vives' *Instruction of a Christian Woman*," in *Silent But for the Word: Tudor Women as Patrons, Translators, and Writers of Religious Works,* ed. Margaret Patterson Hannay [Kent, Ohio: Kent State University Press, 1985], p. 15).

9. See Wrightson, *English Society,* p. 71.

10. Recently, scholars have suggested that because of property considerations, many daughters of wealthy men were married earlier and suffered more restrictive lives than their poorer sisters, who were often able, as they grew older, to achieve a measure of independence. See Wrightson, *English Society,* pp. 94–95, and Ralph A. Houlbrooke, *The English Family 1450–1700* (London: Longman, 1984), p. 65.

11. It may be that his accusers felt he had a point. Sara J. Eaton has suggested that many praises and dispraises of women in our period were fashioned according to established rhetorical principles of praise and blame, not everyday realities ("Representations of Women in the English Popular Press," in *Ambiguous Realities: Women in the Middle Ages and Renaissance,* ed. Carole Levin and Jeanne Watson [Detroit: Wayne State University Press, 1987], pp. 166, 169). (She does not mention Erasmus in this context, however.)

Acknowledgments

It is a pleasure to acknowledge the many debts I have incurred while editing the texts for this anthology. I wish to express my gratitude to the Research Board and the Department of English of the University of Illinois at Urbana-Champaign for awards of released time during 1986 and to the Department of English for a graduate student assistant in 1990. In the course of that assistantship, Barbara Sebek patiently read the edited texts against their originals. N. Frederick Nash, Curator of Rare Books at the University of Illinois at Urbana-Champaign, has provided invaluable assistance over the years, as have all the librarians and the staff of the Rare Book and Special Collections Library. The librarians and staff of the Classics Library, the English Library, and the Law Library have also been invariably helpful. I am particularly grateful to Professor Barbara Rosen, Department of English, University of Connecticut, who read the entire manuscript and corrected much that was amiss. I wish to thank Professor Janet Smarr, Program in Comparative Literature, University of Illinois at Urbana-Champaign, who checked my translations from the Latin in *The Law's Resolutions of Women's Rights;* Professor Janet Lyon, Department of English, University of Illinois at Urbana-Champaign, who reviewed the Introduction and annotations of *The Birth of Mankind;* and Professor Carol Neely, Department of English, University of Illinois at Urbana-Champaign, whose reading of the Preface, as always, improved it. I also wish to thank Professors Nori Komorita, College of Nursing, Jan Hinely and Charles Wright, Department of English, and Dr. Joanne Wheeler, University of Illinois at Urbana-Champaign, for points of information. I am grateful to the editors at the University of Illinois Press, especially Carole Appel and Patricia Hollahan, for their careful oversight of the manuscript. I wish to thank, as well, the many other friends and colleagues who have contributed to the completion of this anthology. Last, but never least, I wish to thank my sons, Richard and Roger Klein, for their continual support and encouragement.

PART I

The Orthodox Stance

The Form of
Solemnization of Matrimony from
The Book of Common Prayer
1559

Introduction

English views about women and marriage in the early modern period must be considered in the light of the ceremony of marriage and the prayers relating to it in *The Book of Common Prayer,* relevant statements in the catechism, and the homily, "Of Matrimony," in the second of the two volumes of homilies written to be delivered before the congregations of all churches in England. The authority upon which the ceremony of marriage, the prayers, and the homilies were based, their authors insisted, was Scripture, the revealed word of God, and particularly the account of the creation of man and woman in Genesis. The marriage ceremony and the homily on marriage thus became, because of their authority, the norm in Elizabethan and Jacobean England. All other statements about women and marriage either develop this norm or represent deviations from it. It seems only right, then, that we should begin this anthology of writings about and to women with the texts that women heard most often throughout their lives.

The Book of Common Prayer traces its roots back to the forms and ceremonies of the early Christian church in England as well as the later teachings of Augustine of Canterbury.[1] It was published in English in 1549, in the reign of Edward VI, and ordered to be used thenceforward in all churches. The chief architect of the 1549 *Book of Common Prayer* was Archbishop Cranmer who, together with a committee of revision, translated, simplified, and put in order the many and various Latin forms and rituals then in use throughout the country.[2] Its final form was indebted to the

Use of Sarum (or Salisbury),[3] although it also incorporated into its language and uses other rituals as well. Eight months after it had been established in English churches, Mary acceded to the throne and abolished its use. It was restored by Elizabeth in 1559, after its sharper anti-Roman and extreme Protestant sentiments were excised. Although a few minor alterations in its calendar were made in 1561, *The Book of Common Prayer* remained unchanged from 1559 to 1661.

Like the greater part of *The Book of Common Prayer*, "The Form of Solemnization of Matrimony" is based largely on the Use of Sarum, though it does not differ significantly from other uses. The reasons why matrimony was ordained by God, the priest says, are threefold: first, for the procreation of children; second, as "a remedy against sin and to avoid fornication"; third, "for the mutual society, help, and comfort" of one for the other. In the exchange of vows, although both men and women promise to love, honor, and keep the other, women must promise in addition not only to obey but also to serve their husbands. The principal basis for this long-established vow of subjection enforced upon women in the ceremony of marriage itself is scriptural, and is clearly explained to the whole congregation in the prayers and the directions to newly married wives and husbands following the exchange of vows. Only men were created in the "image and similitude" of God. Women took their "beginning" out of men. Thus a new husband is told to honor his wife "as unto the weaker vessel," and women are told to obey their husbands as they do the Lord God, for their husbands are their heads as Christ is head of the church: "Ye women, submit your selves unto your own husbands as unto the Lord . . . as the Church or congregation is subject unto Christ, so likewise let the wives also be in subjection unto their own husbands in all things." The dominion of husbands over their wives, which shaped the institution of marriage and much of its practice for centuries, is thus explicit in the ceremony of marriage itself.

Our text of the "Form of Solemnization of Matrimony" is from *The Book of Common Prayer*, "Commonly called The first Book of Queen Elizabeth" (Grafton, 1559; rpt., London: William Pickering, 1844), fols. 96–99ᵛ.

NOTES

1. *The Annotated Book of Common Prayer*, ed. John Henry Blunt (London: Rivingtons, 1876), pp. xvii–xix. For a full account of the genesis of the 1549 Prayer Book, see Francis Procter and Walter Howard Frere, *A New History of The Book of Common Prayer* (London: Macmillan and Co., 1951), pp. 3–65.

2. *Annotated Book of Common Prayer*, pp. xxi–ii.

3. Use] The distinctive ritual and ceremonial of a particular church, diocese, community, etc., here of Salisbury.

The Form of Solemnization of Matrimony

First, the banns must be asked three several Sundays or Holy Days in the time of service, the people being present, after the accustomed manner.

And if the persons that would be married dwell in diverse parishes, the banns must be asked in both parishes and the curate of the one parish shall not solemnize matrimony betwixt them, without a certificate of the banns being thrice asked, from the curate of the other parish. At the day appointed for solemnization of matrimony, the persons to be married shall come into the body of the church, with their friends and neighbors. And there the priest shall thus say:

Dearly beloved friends, we are gathered together here in the sight of God and in the face of his congregation, to join together this man and this woman in holy matrimony, which is an honorable state, instituted of God in Paradise, in the time of man's innocence, signifying unto us the mystical union that is betwixt Christ and his Church: which holy state Christ adorned and beautified with his presence and first miracle that he wrought in Cana of Galilee, and is commended of Saint Paul to be honorable among all men, and therefore is not to be enterprised nor taken in hand unadvisedly, lightly, or wantonly, to satisfy men's carnal lusts and appetites, like brute beasts that have no understanding, but reverently, discreetly, advisedly, soberly, and in the fear of God, duly considering the causes for which matrimony was ordained. One was the procreation of children, to be brought up in the fear and nurture of the Lord and praise of God. Secondly, it was ordained for a remedy against sin and to avoid fornication, that such persons as have not the gift of continency might marry and keep themselves undefiled members of Christ's body. Thirdly, for the mutual society, help, and comfort that the one ought to have of the other, both in prosperity and adversity, into the which holy state these two persons present come now to be joined. Therefore if any man can show any just cause why they may not lawfully be joined together, let him now speak or else hereafter for ever hold his peace.

And also speaking to the persons that shall be married, he shall say:

I require and charge you (as you will answer at the dreadful day of judgment, when the secrets of all hearts shall be disclosed) that if either of you do know any impediment, why ye may not be lawfully joined together in matrimony, that ye confess it. For be ye well assured, that so many as be coupled together, otherwise than God's word doeth allow, are not joined together by God, neither is their matrimony lawful.

At which day of marriage, if any man do allege and declare any impediment why they may not be coupled together in matrimony by God's law or the laws of this realm, and will be bound and sufficient sureties with him to the parties, or else put in a caution to the full value of such charges as the persons to be married do sustain to prove his allegation, then the solemnization must be deferred unto such time as the truth be tried. If no impediment be alleged, then shall the curate say unto the man:

N.[1] Wilt thou have this woman to thy wedded wife, to live together after God's ordinance in the holy estate of matrimony? Wilt thou love her, comfort her, honor, and keep her, in sickness and in health? And forsaking all other, keep thee only to her so long as you both shall live?

The man shall answer:

I will.

Then shall the priest say to the woman:

N. Wilt thou have this man to thy wedded husband, to live together after God's ordinance in the holy estate of matrimony? Wilt thou obey him, and serve him, love, honor, and keep him, in sickness and in health? And forsaking all other, keep thee only to him so long as you both shall live?

The woman shall answer:

I will.

Then shall the minister say:

Who giveth this woman to be married unto this man?

And the minister receiving the woman at her father, or friend's hands, shall cause the man to take the woman by the right hand, and so either to give their troth to other, the man first saying:

I, N., take thee, N., to my wedded wife, to have and to hold, from this day forward, for better, for worse, for richer, for poorer, in sickness, and in health, to love and to cherish, till death us depart:[2] according to God's holy ordinance, and thereto I plight thee my troth.

Then shall they loose their hands, and the woman taking again the man by the right hand, shall say:

I, N., take thee, N., to my wedded husband, to have and to hold, from this day forward, for better, for worse, for richer, for poorer, in sickness, and in health, to love, cherish, and to obey, till death us depart, according to God's holy ordinance: and thereto I give thee my troth.

Then shall they again loose their hands, and the man shall give unto the woman a ring, laying the same upon the book, with the accustomed duty to the priest and clerk. And the priest taking the ring, shall deliver it unto the man, to put it upon the fourth finger of the woman's left hand. And the man taught by the priest, shall say:

---

1. Abbreviation for "name." At this point the priest says the given name of the person addressed.

2. Separate. "Depart" was changed to "do part" in 1661.

With this ring I thee wed; with my body I thee worship, and with all my worldly goods I thee endow. In the name of the Father, and of the Son, and of the Holy Ghost. Amen.

Then the man leaving the ring upon the fourth finger of the woman's left hand, the minister shall say:

Let us pray:

O eternal God, creator and preserver of all mankind, giver of all spiritual grace, the author of everlasting life; send thy blessing upon these thy servants, this man and this woman, whom we bless in thy name, that as Isaac and Rebecca lived faithfully together, so these persons may surely perform and keep the vow and covenant betwixt them made, whereof this ring given, and received, is a token and pledge, and may ever remain in perfect love and peace together, and live according unto thy laws, thorough Jesus Christ our Lord. Amen.

Then shall the priest join their right hands together and say:

Those whom God hath joined together, let no man put a sunder.

Then shall the minister speak unto the people:

For as much as N. and N. have consented together in holy wedlock, and have witnessed the same before God and this company, and thereto have given and pledged their troth either to other, and have declared the same by giving and receiving of a ring, and by joining of hands, I pronounce that they be man and wife together. In the name of the Father, of the Son, and of the Holy Ghost. Amen.

And the minister shall add this blessing:

God the Father, God the Son, God the Holy Ghost, bless, preserve, and keep you, the Lord mercifully with his favor look upon you, and so fill you with all spiritual benediction and grace, that you may so live together in this life that in the world to come, you may have life everlasting. Amen.

Then the ministers, or clerks, going to the Lord's table, shall say, or sing this Psalm following, Beati omnes.[3]

Blessed are all they that fear the Lord, and walk in his ways.
For thou shalt eat the labor of thy hands,
O well is thee, and happy shalt thou be.
Thy wife shall be as the fruitful vine upon the walls of thy house.
Thy children like the olive branches round about thy table.
Lo thus shall the man be blessed that feareth the Lord.
The Lord from out of Zion shall bless thee: that thou shalt see Jerusalem in prosperity, all thy life long.
Yea, that thou shalt see thy childers'[4] children, and peace upon Israel. As it was. etc.
Glory be to the. etc.

3. "Blessed [are] all . . ." (Ps. 128).
4. Dialect pl. of child. The text reads "childres."

Or else this Psalm following, Deus misereatur.[5] [Fols. 97ᵛ–98 omitted.]

This prayer next following shall be omitted where the woman is past child birth.

O merciful Lord, and heavenly Father, by whose gracious gift mankind is increased, we beseech thee assist with thy blessing these two persons, that they may both be fruitful in procreation of children, also live together so long in godly love and honesty, that they may see their childers' children, unto the third and fourth generation, unto thy praise and honor; through Jesus Christ our Lord. Amen.

O God, which by thy mighty power hast made all things of naught, which also after other things set in order didest appoint that out of man (created after thine own image and similitude) woman should take her beginning, and knitting them together, didest teach that it should never be lawful to put a sunder those whom thou by matrimony hadest made one. O God which has consecrated the state of matrimony to such an excellent mystery that in it is signified and represented the spiritual marriage and unity betwixt Christ and his Church, look mercifully upon these thy servants, that both this man may love his wife, according to thy word, (as Christ did love his spouse the Church, who gave himself for it, loving and cherishing it, even as his own flesh.) And also that this woman may be loving and amiable to her husband as Rachael, wise as Rebecca, faithful and obedient as Sara, and in all quietness, sobriety, and peace be a follower of holy and godly matrons. O Lord, bless them both and grant them to inherit thy everlasting kingdom, thorough Jesus Christ our Lord. Amen.

Then shall the priest say:

Almighty God, which at the beginning did create our first parents Adam and Eve, and did sanctify and join them together in marriage, pour upon you the riches[6] of his grace, sanctify, and bless you, that ye may please him both in body and soul, and live together in holy love, unto your lives' end, Amen.

Then shall begin the Communion, and after the Gospel shall be said a sermon, wherein ordinarily (so oft as there is any marriage) the office of a man and wife shall be declared, according to holy Scripture, or if there be no sermon, the minister shall read this that followeth:

All ye which be married, or which intend to take the holy estate of matrimony upon you, hear what holy Scripture doth say, as touching the duty of husbands toward their wives, and wives toward their husbands.

Saint Paul (in his Epistle to the Ephesians the v. chapter) doth give this commandment to all married men.

5. "God be merciful [unto us] . . ." (Ps. 67).
6. The text reads "richesse."

"Ye husbands, love your wives, even as Christ loved the Church, and hath given himself for it, to sanctify it, purging it in the fountain of water,[7] through the word, that he might make it unto him self a glorious congregation, not having spot, or wrinkle, or any such thing, but that it should be holy and blameless. So men are bound to love their own wives, as their own bodies. He that loveth his own wife loveth him self. For never did any man hate his own flesh, but nourisheth and cherisheth it, even as the Lord doeth the congregation, for we are members of his body; of his flesh, and of his bones."

For this cause shall a man leave father and mother, and shall be joined unto his wife, and they two shall be one flesh. This mystery is great, but I speak of Christ, and of the congregation. Nevertheless, let every one of you so love his own wife, even as himself.

Likewise the same Saint Paul (writing to the Colossians) speaketh thus to all men that be married.[8] "Ye men love your wives, and be not bitter unto them."

Hear also what Saint Peter, the apostle of Christ, which was him self a married man (saith unto all men) that are married. "Ye husbands, dwell with your wives according to knowledge. Giving honor unto the wife as unto the weaker vessel, and as heirs together of the grace of life, so that your prayers be not hindred."[9]

Hitherto ye have heard the duty of the husband toward the wife.

Now likewise ye wives hear and learn your duty toward your husbands, even as it is plainly set forth in holy Scripture.

Saint Paul (in the forenamed Epistle to the Ephesians)[10] teacheth you thus: "Ye women, submit your selves unto your own husbands as unto the Lord: for the husband is the wives'[11] head, even as Christ is the head of the Church. And he is also the savior of the whole body. Therefore as the Church or congregation is subject unto Christ, so likewise let the wives also be in subjection unto their own husbands in all things." And again he saith: "Let the wife reverence her husband." And (in his Epistle to the Colossians) Saint Paul giveth you this short lesson: "Ye wives submit your selves unto your own husbands as it is convenient in the Lord."

Saint Peter also doeth instruct you very godly thus,[12] saying: "Let wives be subject to their own husbands, so that if any obey not the word, they may be won without the word by the conversation of the wives, while they

7. The 1661 revision reads "and cleanse it with the washing of water."
8. Col. 4.
9. Hindered.
10. Eph. 5.
11. The text reads "wives."
12. 1 Pet. 4.

behold your chaste conversation, coupled with fear, whose apparel let it not be outward, with broided[13] hair, and trimming about with gold, either in putting on of gorgeous apparel, but let the hid man, which is in the heart, be without all corruption, so that the spirit be mild and quiet, which is a precious thing in the sight of God. For after this manner (in the old time) did the holy women which trusted in God apparel themselves, being subject to their own husbands, as Sara obeyed Abraham, calling him Lord, whose daughters ye are made, doing well, and being not dismayed with any fear."

The new married persons (the same day of their marriage) must receive the holy communion.

13. Braided.

An Homily of
the State of Matrimony from
The Second Tome of Homilies
London, 1563

Introduction

The first book of homilies was compiled by Bishop Bonner, Archbishop Cranmer, Nicholas Harpsfield, and others under the authority of Henry VIII. It was not published, however, until July, 1547, seven months after the death of Henry VIII, during the first year of the reign of Edward IV. Then it appeared under the title *Certain Sermons, or Homilies, appointed by the King's Majesty to be declared and read by all parsons, vicars, or curates every Sunday in their churches, where they have cure.* It was placed in churches next to the Bible and *The Book of Common Prayer* and ranked next to them in authority as well. The driving force behind its composition was Archbishop Cranmer, who wrote several of the separate homilies. He hoped they would bring conformity into the newly established Church of England and educate its more uninformed clergymen. (The *Homilies* seemed to have been influenced in some measure by discourses called *Postils* [1540], which had been collected, printed, and in part written by Richard Taverner,[1] who also translated Erasmus's *In Laud and Praise of Matrimony*.) From its first printing, the *Homilies* were continuously revised, sometimes to make them conform to changing tenets of the church of Edward and Elizabeth but more often to make them comprehensible to less-educated parishioners.

The Second Book of Homilies, alternatively titled *The Second Tome of Homilies*, was compiled or composed by Archbishop Parker, Bishop Pilkington, Taverner, and others, and printed separately from the first book in 1563. It is from this edition that the homily "of . . . Matrimony" is taken. (There were in fact at least nine versions of the 1563 first edition of *The Second Book of Homilies,* each of which was somewhat different from the others. Enough copies were printed to furnish texts for every church in the realm.) Like *The First Book of Homilies, The Second Book* was intended "to be read in every parish Church agreeably." *The Second Book of Homilies* was composed mainly under the editorship of Bishop John Jewel who, until Richard Hooker began publishing *Of the Laws of Ecclesiastical Polity* in 1593, was probably the most important voice of the English church. The two books of homilies were not printed as one until 1623, at the behest of King James. This is the latest edition in which changes were made in order to make its language plainer and its message more understandable.

It is impossible to underestimate the influence of the *Homilies* upon the English. Church attendance was obligatory in England until the period of the civil wars in the late seventeenth century. From the last year of Henry's reign (and except for Mary's), an appropriate homily was required to be read in every church each Sunday, although a few learned clergymen as well as other reformers preached their own sermons. The *Homilies,* consequently, must have become over time almost as familiar to English men and women as the Bible and *The Book of Common Prayer.*

Because the *Homilies* were first conceived to inform the unlearned, to rectify the defects of "ignorant preachers,"[2] and to encourage conformity in the church, the first five homilies in Book I were doctrinal in nature and the other seven were concerned with practical morality. *The Second Book of Homilies* also dealt with practical morality. Thomas Becon, for instance, who was one of Cranmer's chaplains, composed a homily against adultery. Pilkington was probably the author of a homily against excesses in apparel as well as a homily against gluttony and drunkenness. John Griffiths notes about the anonymous homily "Of Matrimony" that "Half . . . is translated from a Hortatory Address of Veit Dietrich of Nuremberg, and half from a Homily of St. Chrysostom."[3] Dietrich was born in Nuremberg in 1507 and studied at Wittenberg, where he was influenced by Luther and Melancthon. He was celebrated as a preacher in Nuremberg, and died there about 1549. Whoever compiled the homily on marriage used Erasmus's Latin translation of Chrysostom, and so linked the *Homilies* in yet another way with Erasmus and the humanist traditions as well as with continental protestantism. That the homily "Of Matrimony" was also derived from medieval sources, however, indicates again the conservative nature of male attitudes toward marriage.

The homily on marriage seems to have been intended to be read immediately after the ceremony of marriage. It is addressed to newly married husbands and wives, and describes in racy, colloquial prose the duties of each. Both husbands and wives are exhorted to pray to God that the devil may be hindered from his unceasing attempts to destroy the concord and love that presently exist between them, from his attempts to drive them into adultery and a life of sin, from his attempts to ensnare their souls. The husband is exhorted to cherish and protect his wife because women are frail and inconstant, and to abstain from "rigor in words and stripes." The wife is exhorted to obey and serve her husband because this is the duty laid upon her by God and nature. If a wife is prone to anger, without wit or reason, her husband should bear with her patiently, remembering her weakness. If a husband mistreats his wife, even if he upbraids her or beats her, she should remember that her patience sets an example for others and that her reward is heavenly. Both are exhorted to live in concord and charity, praying to God always for the "better life to come." As this summary indicates, the intent of the homily is to establish patriarchy, commanded by God and instituted in Paradise, as the foundation of family life.

The "Homily . . . of Matrimony" from *The Second Tome of Homilies* (1563), pp. 253–63, *STC* 13666, has been reprinted in its entirety.

NOTES

1. See *The Two Books of Homilies Appointed to be Read in Churches*, ed. John Griffiths (Oxford: Oxford University Press, 1859), p. vii. For a modern edition of and introduction to the first book of homilies (though not the second, from which our homily is taken), see *Certain Sermons or Homilies (1547) and A Homily against Disobedience and Willful Rebellion (1570)*, ed. Ronald B. Bond (Toronto: University of Toronto Press, 1987).

2. *Two Books of Homilies*, p. vii.

3. See *Two Books of Homilies*, p. xxxvi.

An Homily of the State of Matrimony

The word of almighty God doth testify and declare whence the original beginning of matrimony cometh and why it is ordained. It is instituted of God to the intent that man and woman should live lawfully in a perpetual friendly fellowship, to bring forth fruit, and to avoid fornication. By which means a good conscience might be preserved on both parties in bridling the corrupt inclinations of the flesh within the limits of honesty. For God hath straightly forbidden all whoredom and uncleaness and hath from time to time taken grievous punishments[1] of this inordinate lust, as all stories

1. Hath punished grievously.

and ages hath declared.[2] Furthermore, it is also ordained that the Church of God and his kingdom might by this kind of life be conserved and enlarged, not only in that God giveth children by his blessing but also in that they be brought up by the parents godly in the knowledge of God's word, that this,[3] the knowledge of God and true religion, might be delivered by succession from one to another, that finally many might enjoy that everlasting immortality.

Wherefore, forasmuch as matrimony serveth as well to avoid sin and offense as to increase the kingdom of God, you, as all other[s] which enter that state must acknowledge this benefit of God with pure and thankful minds, for that he hath so ruled your hearts that ye follow not the example of the wicked world, who set their delight in filthiness of sin, where both of you stand in the fear of God and abhor all filthiness. For that is surely the singular gift of God, where the common example of the world declareth how the devil hath their hearts bound and entangled in diverse snares so that they in their wiveless state run into open abominations without any grudge[4] of their conscience. Which sort of men that liveth so desperately and filthily, what damnation tarrieth for them Saint Paul describeth it to them, saying: *Neither whoremongers, neither adulterers shall inherit the kingdom of God.*[5] This horrible judgment of God ye be escaped through his mercy, if so be that ye live inseparately[6] according to God's ordinance.

But yet I would not have you careless, without watching. For the devil will assay to attempt all things to interrupt and hinder your hearts and godly purpose, if ye will give him any entry. For he will either labor to break this godly knot once begun betwixt you, or else at the least he will labor to encomber it with diverse griefs and displeasures. And this is his principal craft, to work dissension of hearts of the one from the other, that whereas now there is pleasant and sweet love betwixt you, he will in the stead thereof bring in most bitter and unpleasant discord. And surely that same adversary of ours doth, as it were from above, assault man's nature and condition. For this folly is ever from our tender age grown up with us,

---

2. Griffiths notes that "as much as half of this Homily, namely, all from the beginning of it to the end of the quotation from *Psalm cxxviii*, and the concluding paragraph from 'Whereupon do your best endeavour' is translated with very little alteration from an Address of Veit Dietrich or Theodor, a preacher of great celebrity at Nuremberg; of which there is a Latin Version under the title, *Adhortatio ad Pios Conjuges Germanice scripta a M. Vito Theodoro piae memoriae.* But the address in German has not been found, nor any copy of a Latin Version of it" earlier than 1567 (*Two Books of Homilies*, p. 500).

3. "Thus," after 1571.

4. Pangs.

5. 1 Cor. 6:9–10.

6. Together.

to have a desire to rule, to think highly by ourselves, so that none thinketh it meet to give place to another. That wicked vice of stubborn will and self-love is more meet to break and dissever the love of heart than to preserve concord. Wherefore married persons must apply their minds in most earnest wise to concord, and must crave continually of God the help of his holy spirit so to rule their hearts and to knit their minds together that they be not dissevered by any division or discord.

This necessity of prayer must be oft in the occupying and using of married persons, that ofttime the one should pray for the other lest hate and debate do arise betwixt them. And because few do consider this thing, but more few do perform it (I say to pray diligently) we see how wonderful[ly] the devil deludeth and scorneth this state, how few matrimonies there be without chidings, brawlings, tauntings, repentings, bitter cursings, and fightings. Which things whosoever doth commit, they do not consider that it is the instigation of the ghostly enemy who taketh great delight therein, for else they would with all earnest endeavor strive against these mischiefs not only with prayer, but also with all possible diligence. Yea, they would not give place to the provocation of wrath, which stirreth them either to such rough and sharp words or stripes,[7] which is surely compassed by the devil, whose temptation, if it be followed, must needs begin and weave the web of all miseries and sorrows. For this is most certainly true, that of such beginnings must needs ensue the breach of true concord in heart, whereby all love must needs shortly be banished. Then cannot it be but a miserable thing to behold that yet they are of necessity compelled to live together which yet cannot be in quiet together. And this is most customably every where to be seen. But what is the cause thereof? Forsooth, because they will not consider the crafty trains of the devil and therefore giveth not themselves to pray to God that he would vouchsafe to repress his power. Moreover, they do not consider how they promote the purpose of the devil in that they follow the wrath of their hearts while they threat[en] one another, while they in their folly turn all upside down, while they will never give over their right as they esteem it, yea, while many times they will not give over the wrong part indeed. Learn thou therefore, if thou desirest to be void of all these miseries, if thou desirest to live peaceably and comfortably in wedlock, how to make thy earnest prayer to God that he would govern both your hearts by his holy spirit to restrain the devil's power, whereby your concord may remain perpetually.

But to this prayer must be joined a singular diligence, whereof St. Peter giveth his precept, saying: *You husbands deal with your wives according to knowledge, giving honor to the wife, as unto the weaker vessel, and as unto them*

7. Strokes, blows.

that are heirs also of the grace of life that your prayers be not hindered.[8] This precept doth particularly pertain to the husband. For he ought to be the leader and author of love in cherishing and increasing concord, which then shall take place if he will use measurableness[9] and not tyranny, and if he yield some things to the woman. For the woman is a weak creature, not endued with like strength and constancy of mind. Therefore they be the sooner disquieted and they be the more prone to all weak affections and dispositions of mind more than men be, and lighter they be, and more vain in their fantasies and opinions. These things must be considered of[10] the man, that he be not too stiff, so that he ought to wink at some things and must gently expound all things and to forbear.

Howbeit the common sort of men doth judge that such moderation should not become a man, for they say that it is a token of a womanish cowardness, and therefore they think that it is a man's part to fume in anger, to fight with fist and staff. Howbeit, howsoever they imagine, undoubtedly St. Peter doth better judge what should be seeming to a man and what he should most reasonably perform. For he saith reasoning should be used and not fighting. Yea, he saith more, that the woman ought to have a certain honor attributed to her, that is to say, she must be spared and borne with, the rather for that she is the weaker vessel, of a frail heart, inconstant, and with a word soon stirred to wrath. And therefore, considering these her frailties, she is to be the rather spared. By this means, thou shalt not only nourish concord, but shalt have her heart in thy power and will. For honest natures will sooner be retained to do their duty rather by gentle words than by stripes. But he which will do all things with extremity and severity, and doth use always rigor in words and stripes, what will that avail in the conclusion? Verily nothing but that he thereby setteth forward the devil's work. He banisheth away concord, charity, and sweet amity, and bringeth in dissension, hatred, and irkesomeness, the greatest griefs that can be in the mutual love and fellowship of man's life.

Beyond all this, it bringeth another evil therewith, for it is the destruction and interruption of prayer. For in the time that the mind is occupied with dissension and discord there can be no true prayer used. For the Lord's prayer hath not only a respect to particular persons, but to the whole universal, in the which we openly pronounce that we will forgive them which hath offended against us even as we ask forgiveness of our sins of God. Which thing, how can it be done rightly when their hearts be at dissension? How can they pray each for other when they be at hate betwixt

---

8. 1 Pet. 3:7.
9. Moderation, 1623.
10. By.

themselves. Now, if the aid of prayer be taken away, by what means can they sustain themselves in any comfort? For they can not otherwise either resist the devil or yet have their hearts stayed in stable comfort in all perils and necessities, but by prayer. Thus all discommodities,[11] as well worldly as ghostly,[12] follow this froward testiness and cumbrous[13] fierceness in manners, which be more meet for brute beasts than for reasonable creatures. St. Peter doth not allow these things, but the devil desireth them gladly. Wherefore take the more heed. And yet a man may be a man, although he doth not use such extremity, yea, though he should dissemble some things in his wife's manners. And this is the part of a Christian man which both pleaseth God and serveth also in good use to the comfort of their marriage state.

Now as concerning the wife's duty. What shall become her? Shall she abuse the gentleness and humanity of her husband and at her pleasure turn all things upside down? No surely, for that is far repugnant against God's commandment. For thus doth St. Peter preach to them: *Ye wives, be ye in subjection to obey your own husband.*[14] To obey is another thing then to control or command, which yet they may do to their children and to their family, but as for their husbands, them must they obey and cease from commanding and perform subjection. For this surely doth nourish concord very much when the wife is ready at hand at her husband's commandment, when she will apply herself to his will, when she endeavoreth herself to seek his contentation[15] and to do him pleasure, when she will eschew all things that might offend him. For thus will most truly be verified the saying of the poet: "A good wife, by obeying her husband, shall bear the rule,"[16] so that he shall have a delight and a gladness the sooner at all times to return home to her. But on the contrary part, when the wife be stubborn, froward, and malapert,[17] their husbands are compelled thereby to abhor and flee from their own houses, even as they should have battle with their enemies.

Howbeit, it can scantly[18] be but that some offenses shall sometime chance betwixt them, for no man doth live without fault, specially for that

11. Inconveniences.
12. Of the spirit.
13. Cumbersome.
14. 1 Pet. 3:1.
15. To content him.
16. Griffiths notes that "it does not appear that Dietrich quoted Syrus or any other poet here. . . . And perhaps our English Homilist made his quotation from the *Christiani Matrimonii Institutio* of Erasmus, who . . . cites it thus: *Bona mulier parendo apud virum imperat*" (*Two Books of Homilies,* p. 504–5).
17. Presumptuous, impudent, saucy.
18. Hardly, scarcely; barely.

the woman is the more frail part.[19] Therefore let them beware that they stand not in their faults and willfulness, but rather let them acknowledge their follies and say: "My husband, so it is that by my anger I was compelled to do this or that; forgive it me and hereafter I will take better heed." Thus ought women the more readily to do, the more they be ready to offend. And they shall not do this only to avoid strife and debate, but rather in the respect of the commandment of God as St. Paul expresseth it in this form of words: *Let women be subject to their husbands, as to the Lord; for the husband is the head of the woman, as Christ is the head of the Church.*[20] Here you understand that God hath commanded that ye should acknowledge the authority of the husband and refer to him the honor of obedience. And St. Peter saith in that place afore rehearseth[21] that *holy matrons did sometimes deck themselves,* not with gold and silver, *but in putting their whole hope in God* and in *obeying their husbands, as Sara obeyed Abraham, calling him Lord, whose daughters ye be* (saith he) if ye follow her example. This sentence is very meet for women to print in their remembrance.

Truth it is that they must specially feel the griefs and pains of their matrimony in that they relinquish the liberty of their own rule, in the pain of their travailing,[22] in the bringing up of their children, in which offices they be in great perils and be grieved with great afflictions, which they might be without if they lived out of matrimony. But St. Peter saith that this is the chief ornament of *holy matrons,* in that they *set their hope* and trust *in God,* that is to say, in that they refused[23] not from marriage for the business thereof, for the griefs and perils thereof, but committed all such adventures to God in most sure trust of help, after that they have called upon his aid. O woman, do thou the like, and so shalt thou be most excellently beautified before God and all his angels and saints, and thou needest not to seek further for doing any better works. For, obey thy husband, take regard of his requests, and give heed unto him to perceive what he requireth of thee, and so shalt thou honor God, and live peaceably in thy house. And beyond this, God shall follow thee with his benediction that all things shall well prosper both to thee and to thy husband, as the Psalm saith, *Blessed is the man which feareth God and walketh in his ways. Thou shalt have the fruit of thine own hands, happy shalt thou be, and well shall it go with thee. Thy wife shall be as a vine plentifully spreading about thy house. Thy children shall be as the young springs of the olives about the table. Lo, thus shall that man be blessed* (saith David) *that feareth the Lord.*[24]

19. "Frail party," from 1571.
20. Eph. 5:22–23.
21. 1 Pet. 3.
22. Childbirth.
23. Refrained.
24. Ps. 128:1–4.

This let the wife have ever in mind, the rather admonished thereto by the apparel of her head, whereby is signified that she is under covert[25] and obedience of her husband. And, as that apparel is of nature so appointed to declare her subjection, so biddeth St. Paul that all other of her raiment should express both *shamefastness and sobriety*.[26] For, if it be not lawful[27] for the woman to have her head bare, but to bear thereon the sign of her power[28] wheresoever she goeth, more is it required that she declare the thing that is meant thereby. And therefore these ancient women of the old world called their husbands lords and shewed them reverence in obeying them.

But peradventure she will say that those men loved their wives indeed. I know that well enough and bear it well in mind. But when I do admonish you of your duties, then call not to consideration what their duties be. For when we ourselves do teach our children to obey us as their parents, or when we reform our servants and tell them that they should obey[29] their masters not only at the eye but as to the Lord, if they should tell us again our duties, we would not think it well done. For when we be admonished of our duties and faults, we ought not then to seek what other men's duties be. For though a man had a companion in his fault, yet should not he thereby be without his fault? But this must be only looked on, by what means thou mayest make thy self without blame. For Adam did lay the blame upon the woman and she turned it unto the serpent, but yet neither of them was thus excused. And therefore bring not such excuses to me at this time, but apply all thy diligence to hear thine obedience to thy husband. For when I take in hand to admonish thy husband to love thee and to cherish thee, yet will I not cease to set out the law that is appointed for the woman as well as I would require of the man what is written for his law. Go thou therefore about such things as becometh thee only and shew thyself tractable to thy husband. Or rather, if thou wilt obey thy husband for God's precept, then allege such things as be in his duty to do, but perform thou diligently those things which the Lawmaker hath charged

---

25. Literally 'the cover'; legally 'the protection'. See *The Law's Resolutions of Women's Rights.*

26. 1 Tim. 2:9.

27. Griffiths notes that "so much of this Homily as is comprised within these words, 'For, if it be not lawful,' and these . . . 'in one concord of heart and mind,' is translated, with some abridgements here and there, from the latter part of Chrysost. in Epist. I ad Cor. Homil. xxxi. . . . But the translation was made from the Latin version of his works put forth at Basle in 1530 by Erasmus, in which all the Homilies on I Cor. after the first twenty were done by Fisher, Bishop of Rochester" (*Two Books of Homilies*, p. 506).

28. Her husband's power over her.

29. Eph. 6:5–7.

thee to do. For thus is it most reasonable to obey God if thou wilt not suffer thyself to transgress his law. He that loveth his friend seemeth to do no great thing but he that honoreth him that is hurtful and hateful to him, this man is worthy much commendation. Even so think thou, if thou canst suffer an extreme husband, thou shalt have a great reward therefore. But, if thou lovest him only because he is gentle and courteous, what reward will God give thee therefore? Yet I speak not these things that I would wish the husbands to be sharp towards their wives. But I exhort the women that they would patiently bear the sharpness of their husbands. For, when either parts do their best to perform their duties the one to the other, then followeth thereon great profit to their neighbors for their example's sake. For when the woman is ready to suffer a sharp husband and the man will not extremely entreat his stubborn and troublesome wife, then be all things in quiet as in a most sure haven.

Even thus was it done in old time that every one did their own duty and office and was not busy to require the duty of their neighbors. Consider, I pray thee, that Abraham took[30] to him his brother's son; his wife did not blame him therefore. He commanded him to go with him a long journey; she did not gainsay it, but obeyed his precept. Again, after all those great miseries, labors, and pains of that journey, when Abraham was made as Lord over all, yet did he give place to Lot of his superiority,[31] which matter Sara took so little to grief that she never once suffered her tongue to speak such words as the common manner of women is wont to do in these days when they see their husbands in such rooms to be made underlings and to be put under their youngers.[32] Then they upbraid them with cumbrous talk and call them fools, dastards, and cowards for so doing. But Sara was so far from speaking any such thing that it came never into her mind and thought so to say, but allowed the wisdom and will of her husband. Yea, beside all this, after the said Lot had thus his will and left to his uncle the lesser portion of land, he chanceth to fall into extreme peril.[33] Which chance, when it came to the knowledge of this said patriarch, he incontinently put all his men in harness and prepared himself with all his family and friends against the host of the Persians. In which case, Sara did not counsel him to the contrary, nor did say, as then might have been said, "My husband, whither goest thou so unadvisedly? Why runnest thou thus on head?[34] Why doest thou offer thyself to so great perils, and art thus

30. Gen. 12:4–5.
31. Gen. 13:8–11.
32. Those who are younger then they.
33. Gen. 14:12–14.
34. Ahead.

ready to jeopard thine own life and to peril the lives of all thine, for such a man as hath done thee such wrong? At the least way, if thou regardest not thy self, yet have compassion on me, which for thy love have forsaken my kindred and my country, and have the want both of my friends and kinfolks, and am thus come into so far countries with thee. Have pity on me, and make me not here a widow, to cast me to such cares and troubles." Thus might she have said. But Sara neither said nor thought such words, but she kept herself in silence in all things.

Furthermore, all that time when she was barren and took no pain as other women did by bringing forth fruit in his house, what did he? He complained not to his wife, but to almighty God.[35] And consider how either of them did their duties as became them. For neither did he despise Sara because she was barren, nor never did cast it in her teeth. Consider again how Abraham expelled the handmaid out of the house[36] when she required it. So that by this I may truly prove that the one was pleased and contended[37] with the other in all things.

But yet set not your eyes only on this matter, but look further what was done before this, that Agar[38] used her mistress despitefully, and that Abraham himself was somewhat provoked against her, which must needs be an intolerable matter and a painful to a freehearted woman and a chaste. Let not therefore the woman be too busy to call for the duty of her husband where she should be ready to perform her own, for that is not worthy any great commendation. And even so again let not the man only consider what [be]longeth to the woman and to stand too earnestly gazing thereon, for that is not his part or duty. But as I have said, let either parties be ready and willing to perform that which belongeth specially to themselves. For, if we be bound to hold out our left cheek to strangers which will smite us on the right cheek, how much more ought we to suffer an extreme and unkind husband?

But yet I mean not that a man should beat his wife. God forbid that, for that is the greatest shame that can be, not so much to her that is beaten, as to him that doeth the deed. But, if by such fortune thou chancest upon such an husband, take it not too heavily, but suppose thou that thereby is laid up no small reward hereafter and in this lifetime no small commendation to thee if thou canst be quiet. But yet to you that be men, thus I speak: Let there be none so grievous fault to compel you to beat your wives. But what, say I, your wives? No, it is not to be borne with that an

35. Gen. 15:2, 3; 16:1, 2.
36. Gen. 21:9–14.
37. Misprint. "Contented," from 1570.
38. Gen. 16:4–6.

honest man should lay hands on his maidservant to beat her. Wherefore, if it be a great shame for a man to beat his bondservant, much more rebuke it is to lay violent hands upon his freewoman? And this thing may we well understand by the laws which the paynims[39] hath made which doth discharge her any longer to dwell with such an husband, as unworthy to have any further company with her, that doth smite her. For it is an extreme point thus so vilely to entreat[40] her like a slave that is fellow to thee of thy life and so conjoined unto thee beforetime in the necessary matters of thy living. And therefore a man may well liken such a man (if he may be called a man rather than a wild beast) to a killer of his father or his mother. And whereas we be commanded to forsake our father and mother for our wife's sake, and yet thereby do work them none injury but do fulfill the law of God, how can it not appear then to be a point of extreme madness to entreat her despitefully for whose sake God hath commanded thee to leave parents? Yea, who can suffer such despite? Who can worthily express the inconvenience that is, to see what weepings and wailings be made in the open streets when neighbors run together to the house of so unruly an husband as to a Bedlam man[41] who goeth about to overturn all that he hath at home? Who would not think that it were better for such a man to wish the ground to open and to swallow him in than once ever after to be seen in the market?

But peradventure thou wilt object that the woman provoketh thee to this point. But consider thou again that the woman is a frail vessel and thou art therefore made the ruler and head over her, to bear the weakness of her in this her subjection. And therefore study thou to declare the honest commendation of thine authority, which thou canst no way better do than to forbear to utter[42] her in her weakness and subjection. For even as the king appeareth so much the more noble, the more excellent and noble he maketh his officers and lieutenants, whom, if he should dishonor and despise the authority of their dignity, he should deprive himself of a great part of his own honor. Even so, if thou dost despise her that is set in the next room beside thee, thou dost much derogate and decay the excellency and virtue of thine own authority. Recount all these things in thy mind and be gentle and quiet. Understand that God hath given thee children with her and are made a father and by such reason appease thyself. Dost

39. Pagans. Griffiths notes that it is not clear who were the heathen lawgivers referred to by St. Chrysostom (*Two Books of Homilies*, p. 510).

40. Treat.

41. An inmate of the hospital of St. Mary of Bethlehem in London, used since 1547 as an asylum for the insane.

42. From the French *outrer?* to treat outrageously? as suggested by Griffiths (*Two Books of Homilies*, p. 511).

not thou see the husbandmen, what diligence they use to till that ground which once they have taken to farm, though it be never so full of faults? As for an example, though it be dry, though it bringeth forth weeds, though the soil cannot bear too much wet, yet he tilleth it and so winneth fruit thereof. Even in like manner, if thou wouldest use like diligence to instruct and order the mind of thy spouse, if thou wouldest diligently apply thyself to weed out by little and little the noisome weeds of uncomely manners out of her mind with wholesome precepts, it could not be but in time thou shouldest feel the pleasant fruit thereof to both your comforts.

Therefore, that this thing chance not so, perform this thing that I do here counsel thee. Whatsoever any displeasant matter riseth at home, if thy wife hath done aught amiss, comfort her and increase not the heaviness. For, though thou shouldest be grieved with never so many things, yet shalt thou find nothing more grievous than to want the benevolence of thy wife at home. What offence soever thou canst name, yet shalt thou find none more intollerable than to be at debate with thy wife. And for this cause most of all oughtest thou to have this love in reverence. And if reason moveth thee to bear any burthen at any other men's hands, much more at thy wife's. For if she be poor, upbraid her not; if she be simple, taunt her not, but be the more courteous. For she is thy body and made one flesh with thee.[43]

But thou peradventure wilt say that she is a wrathful woman, a drunkard, and beastly, without wit and reason. For this cause, bewail her the more. Chafe not in anger but pray to almighty God. Let her be admonished and holpen[44] with good counsel, and do thou thy best endeavor that she may be delivered of all these affections. But if thou shouldest beat her, thou shalt increase her evil affections, for frowardness[45] and sharpness is not amended with frowardness but with softness and gentleness. Furthermore, consider what reward thou shalt have at God's hand. For, where thou mightest beat her and yet for the respect of the fear of God thou wilt abstain and bear patiently her great offenses, the rather in respect of that law which forbiddeth that a man should cast out his wife, what fault soever she be combered[46] with, thou shalt have a very great reward and before the receipt of that reward thou shalt feel many commodities, for by this means she shall be made the more obedient and thou for her sake shalt be made the more meek. It is written in a story of a certain strange Philosopher which had a cursed[47] wife, a froward, and a drunkard. When he

43. Gen. 2:24; Eph. 5:28, 31.
44. "Helped," from 1582 (*Two Books of Homilies,* p. 512).
45. Perversity, state of being refractory.
46. Encumbered.
47. Spiteful, ill tempered. Cf. *MND* 3.2.439. The reference is to Socrates and his wife, Xanthippe.

was asked for what consideration he did so bear her evil manners, he made answer: "By this means," said he, "I have at home a schoolmaster and an example how I should behave myself abroad. For I shall," saith he, "be the more quiet with other,[48] being thus daily exercised and taught in the forbearing of her." Surely it is a shame that paynims should be wiser than we, we I say, that be commanded to counterfeit angels or rather God himself through meekness. And for the love of virtue, this said philosopher Socrates would not expel his wife out of his house. Yea, some say that he did therefore marry his wife to learn this virtue by that occasion.

Wherefore, seeing many men be far behind the wisdom of this man, my counsel is that first and before all things that man do his best endeavor to get him a good wife, endued[49] with all honesty and virtue. But, if it so chance that he is deceived, that he hath chosen such a wife as is neither good nor tolerable, then let the husband follow this philosopher and let him instruct his wife in every condition and never lay these matters to sight. For the merchant man, except he first be at composition with his factor[50] to use his interaffairs[51] quietly, he will neither stir his ship to sail, nor yet will lay hands upon his merchandise. Even so let us do all things that we may have the fellowship of our wives, which is the factor of all our doings at home, in great quiet and rest. And by these means all things shall prosper quietly, and so shall we pass through the dangers of the troublous sea of this world. For this state of life will be more honorable and comfortable than our houses, than servants, than money, than lands and possessions, than all things that can be told.[52] As all these, with sedition and discord, can never work us any comfort, so shall all things turn to our commodity and pleasure if we draw this yoke in one concord of heart and mind.

Whereupon do your best endeavor that after this sort ye use your matrimony and so shall ye be armed on every side. Ye have escaped the snares of the devil and the unlawful lusts of the flesh. Ye have the quietness of conscience by this institution of matrimony ordained by God. Therefore use oft prayer to him, that he would be present by you, that he would continue concord and charity betwixt you. Do the best ye can of your parts to custom[53] yourselves to softness and meekness, and bear well in worth such oversights as chance. And thus shall your conversation be most pleasant and comfortable. And although (which can no otherwise be) some

48. "With others," from 1582.
49. Endowed.
50. One who acts for another; an agent, deputy.
51. Affairs between them? "interfairs," from 1582.
52. Counted.
53. Accustom.

adversities shall follow, and otherwhiles now one discommodity, now another, shall appear, yet in this common trouble and adversity, lift up both your hands unto heaven. Call upon the help and assistance of God, the author of your marriage, and surely the promise of relief is at hand. For Christ affirmeth in his Gospel: *Where two or three be gathered together in my name, and be agreed, what matter soever they pray for, it shall be granted them of my heavenly father.*[54] Why therefore shouldest thou be afraid of the danger, where thou hast so ready a promise and so nigh an help? Furthermore, you must understand how necessary it is for Christian folk to bear Christ's cross, for else we shall never feel how comfortable God's help is unto us.

Therefore give thanks to God for his great benefit in that ye have taken upon you this state of wedlock and pray you instantly that almighty God may luckily defend and maintain you therein, that neither ye be overcomed with any temptation nor with any adversity. But before all things take good heed that ye give no occasion to the devil to let and hinder your prayers by discord and dissension. For there is no stronger defense and stay in all our life than is prayer, in the which we may call for the help of God and obtain it, whereby we may win his blessing, his grace, his defense, and protection, so to continue therein to a better life to come. Which grant us he that died for us all, to whom be all honor and praise, for ever and ever.

---

54. Matt. 18:19–20.

The Law's Resolutions of
Women's Rights
London, 1632

Introduction

The Law's Resolutions of Women's Rights: or, The Law's Provision for Women
(London, 1632)[1] is one of the few books excerpted in this anthology which
was not demonstrably popular in its own time. It was issued only once and
never reprinted. But this fact does not help us to know whether the women
for whom it was compiled simply did not wish to read it or whether both
men and women went instead to one of the many other legal handbooks
which were available to them and which were continually reprinted. Nor
do we know who the author was. One T. E. wrote an address to the reader
in which he says he does not know who compiled these laws; he knows
only that the author is dead. T. E. further distances himself from the composition of this law book by insisting that he prepared it for publication
during his Lenten vacation, having, he implies, nothing better to do—even
though he also says he corrected and added to the original manuscript.
(One I. L. wrote a preface to the reader, but he appears to be the book's
printer, not its author.) T. E.'s contention that he is not the author of this
book may be borne out by the fact that the author of *The Law's Resolutions
of Women's Rights* concludes his search of laws in 1597/8, at least thirty years
before its publication.[2]

    The Law's Resolutions of Women's Rights is important to us because it
provides in one convenient place, as it was intended to do, all the laws
regarding women's legal rights and obligations which obtained in England
during the early modern period. Unlike other compilations of English law,
however, and like most sixteenth-century courtesy books written for
women, it begins with the account in Genesis of Eve's role in the fall of

man, which its author understands as the justification for women's subordination: "Eve because she had helped to seduce her husband hath inflicted on her an especial bane," he says as he quotes Genesis 3:16 for the
benefit of his female readers: "thy desires shall be subject to thy husband,
and he shall rule over thee." Speaking both as a man and a lawyer, the
author takes it for granted that in this instance Scripture is the law's ul-
timate authority. Genesis provides an unassailable reason why women are
powerless in public forums, why they have "no voice in parliament," why
"they make no laws, they consent to none, they abrogate none." Common
law "shaketh hand with divinity" in a related way when it decrees that,
married or unmarried, women have no legal existence apart from their
present or future husbands. "Infants" in the eyes of the law from their
birth until the death of their husbands, women "are understood either
married or to be married and their desires are subject to their husband."[3]
Only when a woman is widowed is she free from "subjection."

Perhaps on account of this understanding of the status of woman as
maid/wife/widow, rarely as an individual in her own right, the author of
The Law's Resolution of Women's Rights organizes his handbook in terms of
these three stages of a woman's life. He also constructs his handbook
very nearly as a dialogue in which he addresses women usually in the
third person but sometimes also in the first and second person. In the
process he creates a shadowy fiction, women, or sometimes a single
woman, to whom he addresses his work as he would address himself to
clients. Certainly he seems to see himself in this work as an advocate for
women (even though no married woman could become his client until
she was widowed).[4] His advocacy on behalf of women is directed against
those men who are most empowered to harm women. But, even as he
points out that the law allows a man to beat his wife (though not to
maim or kill her), it is clear that the damage he envisions most often
overtaking her involves depredations to property which is hers by right.
Unlike theologians in our period who instruct women in their moral and
religious duties, he is primarily concerned to safeguard women's material
well-being, by defending them against those men, usually their husbands
or heirs, who would destroy it. It is for this reason he suggests that the
greatest sin "many an honest woman" ever repented was not a spiritual
crime but "her hasty marriage."

Our author takes it for granted that a woman longs to be married as
matter longs for form. He is concerned that her marriage be legal, without
impediments, and, hopefully, with a dower. A husband by himself is a good
thing, he says, but a husband who can endow his wife with worldly goods
is better.[5] That husband is better yet who would in place of dower (in
some instances in addition to dower) make his wife joint tenant[6] with him

in the possession of property. His reason is that joint tenancy is surer than dower. A woman "in her frenzy may cut her husband's throat, and it is no forfeiture of dower, but if she make an elopement (which is a mad trick) dower is forfeited." Dower is chancy in other respects, too: It "must be tarried for till the husband be dead. It must be demanded, sometime sued for, sometime neither with suit or demand obtained. . . . every question in the validity of marriage maketh a scruple of dower." But jointures are a "present possession" and cannot be forfeit.

It is quite otherwise with money or property that a wife brings into a marriage. As far as our author is concerned, the "prerogative of the husband is best discerned in his dominion over all extern things in which the wife by combination"[7] brings to him. Whatever a man had before marriage is "absolutely his own." Whatever is given him by marriage "he taketh it by himself distinctly to himself." "The very goods which a man giveth to his wife are still his own: her chain, her bracelets, her apparel, are all the good-man's goods." But "that which the wife hath is the husband's."

It is only when she is a widow that a woman quite literally comes into her own. There is in consequence a distinctly ironic edge to our author's description of the grief of a newly made widow. "But, alas, when she hath lost her husband, her head is cut off, her intellectual part is gone, the very faculties of her soul are (I will not say) clean taken away, but they are all benumbed, dimmed, and dazzled." He comforts her, none-theless, by urging her to consider her new freedom. "Why mourn you so, you that be widows? Consider how long you have been in subjection under the predominance of parents, of your husbands; now you be free in liberty, and free . . . at your own law." That she may lessen her grief, he tells her to turn to God, who cares for widows, and also to watch over what are at last her own goods: "a sober carefulness . . . in business of profit or disprofit doth mitigate greatly the sorrowing . . . let her look to her affairs as cause and need requireth." For his part, her advocate proceeds to describe in detail the legal processes a widow must follow to secure dower or jointure.

At this point our author suggests that it may be sheer folly, from a financial point of view, to remarry. Certainly the scenario he describes is a worst-case one. If she who is "fair, young, rich, gracious in her carriage" remarries, she is only too likely to marry a man who is equally young and foolish, who might not only within a year dissipate everything she has but also involve himself in a duel, procure his own death, and leave his widow destitute. It is possible, however, for a widow to appeal such a homicide or other felonies committed against her and recover damages—as our author outlines at length. If she does so, she might finally be wise enough to seek consolation in God only, not man. What remains then for our author to describe is what he clearly believes is the other danger men offer women, not material loss but rape. "So drunken are men with their own lusts . . . that if the rampier of laws were not betwixt women and their harms, I verily think none of them being above twelve years of age and under an hundred, being either fair or rich, should be able to escape ravishing." He goes on to outline specifically and in detail the history of the laws concerning rape from before the conquest, concluding with the opinion that Elizabeth, herself a woman, elected to protect women from all rapists by closing the last loophole, the plea of benefit of clergy.

The Law's Resolutions of Women's Rights reveals more than most writings, I think, how public an institution marriage was considered to be in our period (even though it was privately consummated and privately conducted). It reveals as well the period's conviction that marriage was the principal safeguard of the family and society, that, at its heart, marriage and the laws designed to uphold it were fundamentally concerned with the securing and the conservation of property. In fact, whatever tribute this treatise pays to the laws of God, what it obviously considers crucial to the lives of women are the laws governing property and its orderly transfer.

This text is based on *The Law's Resolutions of Women's Rights* (1632; facs. rpt., New York: Garland Publishing, 1978). I have normally placed translations of Latin and law French in brackets in the text itself.

NOTES

1. The title continues: "A methodical collection of such statutes and customs, with the cases, opinions, arguments, and points of learning in the law, as do properly concern women."

2. He ends his book by saying, "Thus have I sailed between the capes of Magna Carta and Quadragesima of Queen Elizabeth" (p. 403). Juliet Dusinberre credits Alice Shalvi with the suggestion that the book was first written by one I. J. "at the turn of the century" (*Shakespeare and the Nature of Women* [New York: Macmillan, 1975], p. 97).

3. In my introductions to authors in this anthology I have occasionally adapted material from my essay, "Women and Marriage in Renaissance England: Male Perspectives" in *Topic: 36 The Elizabethan Woman*, ed. Anne Parten (Washington, Penn.: Washington and Jefferson College, 1982), pp. 20–37, here pp. 20–21.

4. Single women, however, might wish to consult a lawyer, because they could inherit, possess, and, at age twenty-one, convey property.

5. The terms used for these worldly goods are "donements or feoffements."

6. The *OED* defines a jointure as the "holding of property to the joint use of husband and wife for life or in tail, as a provision for the latter during widowhood."

7. combination] By combining herself with her husband in marriage.

The Law's Resolutions of Women's Rights

To the Reader

By whom this following discourse was composed I certainly know not, neither by what inducement the author's pains therein was procured. But if for no other consideration than to make this scattered part of learning in the great volumes of the common law books and there darkly described to be one entire body and more ready and clearer to the view of the reader, his love deserves thanks and his endeavors kind acceptance. The work hath been carefully and with much labor and diligence collected. The theme as the subject is *The Law's Resolutions of Women's Rights,* which comprehends all our laws concerning women, either children in government or nurture of[1] their parents or guardians, maids, wives, and widows, and their goods, inheritances, and other estates. It is profitable and useful learning to be well known. I am sure it will please all them whose actions are guided *virtutis amore*[2] [by the love of virtue] and offend none but those ill manners[3] who can have no other antidote made them than *formidine poenae* [by the fear of punishment], for it sets forth law and justice, things honest and things convenient. I had such good conceit of the matter and frame of the whole work that having a copy thereof lying by me sometimes, within the compass of a Lent vacation, I pluckt my intentions from my own course of studies and cast them upon this. And those *vitia scriptoris,* and *authoris* [faults of a writer and author] which I found, I amended, and have added many reasons, opinions, cases and resolutions of cases to the author's store; wherefore those oversights or neglects that thou mayst impose upon the printer or me (which I suppose will be some if not many) thou shalt have thanks to supply or amend, which is all I expected and more than the author, as I believe, had (or now being dead can receive) and perhaps thou mayst have a better reward, for the old adage is true *pretium non vile laboris* [the reward of labor is not worthless].

Vale, T. E.

1. By.
2. Where appropriate, in order to translate particularly Renaissance Latin usages, I consulted Thomas Cooper, *Thesaurus Linguae Romanae et Britannicae* (London, 1565).
3. Those persons of ill manners.

Book I [Of Maids [Sigs. B–B2ᵛ omitted]]

Sect. ii. Now man and woman are one

Now because Adam hath so pronounced that man and wife shall be but one flesh, and our law is that if a feofment[4] be made jointly to John at Stile and to Thomas Noke[5] and his wife, of three acres of land, that Thomas and his wife get no more but one acre and a half, *quia una persona* [because they are one person], . . . and by this a married woman perhaps may either doubt whether she be either none or no more than half a person. But let her be of good cheer, though, for the near conjunction which is between man and wife and to tie them to a perfect love, agreement, and adherence, they be by intent and wise fiction of law, one person, yet in nature and in some other cases by the law of God and man, they remain diverse. For, as Adam's punishment was several from Eve's, so in criminal and other special causes our law argues them several persons. You shall find that *persona* is an *individuum* spoken of anything which hath reason and therefore of nothing but *vel de angelo, vel de homine* [either of angel or of man],[6] fol. 154 in Dyer,[7] who citeth no worse authority for it than Callepinus'[8] own self, seeing therefore I list not to doubt with Plato whether women be reasonable or unreasonable creatures, I may not doubt but every woman is a temporal person, though no woman can be a spiritual vicar. . . .

Sect. iii. The punishment of Adam's sin

Return a little to Genesis, in the third chapter whereof is declared our first parents' transgression in eating the forbidden fruit, for which Adam, Eve, the serpent first, and lastly, the earth itself is cursed; and besides, the participation of Adam's punishment, which was subjection to mortality, exiled from the garden of Eden, enjoined to labor. Eve because she had helped to seduce her husband hath inflicted on her an especial bane. *In sorrow shalt thou bring forth thy children, thy desires shall be subject to thy husband, and he shall rule over thee.* See here the reason of that which I touched before, that women have no voice in parliament. They make no laws, they consent to none, they abrogate none. All of them are understood either married or to be married and their desires are[9] subject to their husband. I know no remedy, though some women can shift it well enough.

4. The action of granting a feudal estate or fee.
5. Sixteenth-century equivalents of John Doe.
6. Some authors believed that only men and angels were rational creatures.
7. Sir James Dyer (1512–82), chief justice of the English Court of Common Pleas from 1559.
8. Ambrogio Calepino of Bergamo, Italy (1440–1510), the lexicographer?
9. The text reads "or"—an apparent misprint.

The common law here shaketh hand with divinity, but because I am come too soon to the title of baron and feme,[10] and Adam and Eve were the first and last that were married so young, it is best that I run back again to consider of the things (which I might seem to have lost by the way) that are fit to be known concerning women before they be fit for marriage.

Sect. iv. The ages of a woman

The learning is 35. Hen[ry] 6. fol. 40 that a woman hath diverse special ages.[11] At the seventh year of her age, her father shall have aid of his tenants to marry her. At nine years age, she is able to deserve and have dower. At twelve years to consent to marriage. At fourteen to be *hors du guard* [outside wardship]. At sixteen to be past the Lord's tender of a husband. At twenty one to be able to make a feoffement. And *per Ingelton*[12] therein the end of the case. A woman married at twelve cannot disagree

10. French law term for husband and wife. When translating law French, I consulted J. H. Baker, *Manual of Law French* ([Aldershot]: Avebury, 1979).

11. The following passage appears to mean that at seven a girl may be married on the authority of her father or guardian (though such marriages were normally not consummated until after a girl attained puberty); at nine she was entitled to dower if her husband died—even if the marriage was not consummated; at twelve she could herself consent to marriage although she still needed the consent of her father or guardian (Juliet's case) for the marriage to be valid; at fourteen she could consent to marriage without the additional consent of her father or her guardian if she were not a ward; at sixteen if still a ward she could not be compelled to marry; at twenty-one if single she could convey lands. It is clear from this description of a woman's legal "ages" that the older she becomes the more control over her affairs she has. For an extended analysis of the problems involved in wardship see Joel Hurstfield, *The Queen's Wards: Wardship and Marriage under Elizabeth I*, 2d ed. (London: Frank Cass, 1973). I have not, however, been able to trace the reference to 35 Henry 6. fol. 40. There were no statutes enacted in a parliamentary session of the thirty-fifth year of the reign of Henry VI, even though a sidenote to the statute, "A woman at 14 years of age at the death of her ancestor shall have livery of her land," made at Westminster in the thirty-ninth year of the reign of James VI (39 Hen. VI. Cap. 2) refers to "35 H. 6. F 40 Fitz. Gard. 7 Bro Livery, 66." See *The Statutes at Large, from the Magna Charta to the End of the Reign of Henry VI*, vol. 1 of *The Statutes at Large, from the Magna Charta to the End of the Last Parliament*, 1761 by Owen Ruffhead (London: Baslett, Woodfall, and Strahan, 1769), p. 635. See Robert Brooke, *La Graunde Abridgement* (1586), fol. 18, "Age," 6, which also refers to "35. H. 6. 4." Nor does this citation appear to refer to a case in the Court of Exchequer. See *The English Reports*, vol. 145, "Exchequer Division" (Edinburgh: W. Green and Son, 1914). On the other hand, William Blackstone, in his *Commentaries on the Laws of England*, without citing a source and with some discrepancies, summarizes these "ages" of women (3d ed. [Oxford: Clarendon Press, 1768], pp. 463–64). (I am indebted to Jane Williams, reference librarian, Law Library, University of Illinois at Urbana-Champaign, and Charlotte Wager, visiting instructor, School of Law, University of Illinois at Urbana-Champaign, for assistance in my attempts to track down this citation.)

12. I have not been able to trace this reference.

afterward. But if she be married younger, she may dissent till she be fourteen. [Pp. 8–50 omitted.]

Book II [Of Coming to Marriage]

Now that I have brought up a woman and made her an inheritrix, taken her out of ward, helped her to make partition, etc., methinks she should long to be married. *Foemina appetit virum, sicut materia formam* [A woman longs for man as matter (longs for) form].[13] And I did not mean when I begun to produce any vestal virgin, nun, or new Saint Bridget. Following therefore my first intention, I will begin to instruct women grown, first such as are or shortly shall be wives and then widows.

Sect. i. Of marriage, according to the civil and common law[14]

Marriage is defined to be a conjunction of man and woman, containing an inseparable connection and union of life. But as there is nothing that is begotten and finished at once, so this contract of coupling man and woman together hath an inception first and then an orderly proceeding. The first beginning of marriage (as in respect of contract and that which law taketh hold on) is when wedlock by words in the future tense is promised and vowed, and this is but *sponsio*[15] or *sponsalia* [those things which are promised]. The full contract of matrimony is when it is made by words *de praesenti* [in the present (tense)] in a lawful consent, and thus two be made man and wife existing without lying together. Yet matrimony is not accounted consummated until there go with the consent of mind and will conjunction of body.

Sect. ii. Of sponsion or first promising

The first promising and inception of marriage is in two parts. Either it is plain, simple, and naked, or confirmed and born by giving of something. The first is when a man and woman bind themselves simply by their word only to contract matrimony hereafter. The second, when there is an oath made or somewhat taken as an earnest or pledge betwixt them on both parts or on one part to be married hereafter. There is not here to be stood upon the age definitively set down for making of marriage irrevocable, but all that are seven years old (betwixt whom matrimony may consist) may

13. Aristotle's definition of relations between form and unformed matter, cf. *Metaphysics* 9.6–8.
14. Common law refers to English case law and the commentaries on it. Civil law refers to Roman law.
15. Sponsions, a solemn or formal betrothal.

make sponsion and promise. But if any that is under the age of seven begin this vow and betrothing, it is esteemed as a mist and vanisheth to nothing.

Sect. iii. Of public sponsion

This sponsion (in which as it stands, is no full contract of matrimony, nor any more save only an obligation or being bound in a sort to marry hereafter) may be public or secret: public, either by the parties themselves present together, or by message or letters when they be distant one from another. Neither is there herein any curious form of paction[16] or stipulation required, but only by words, howsoever expressed, a plain consent and agreement of the parties, and by the civil law (with which the ancient canons concorded) of their parents, if the contractors were *sub potestate parentum* [under the power of parents].[17] The like reason seemeth to be for consent of tutors, etc. But it is now received a general opinion that the good-will of parents is required in regard of honesty, not of necessity, according to the canons which exact necessarily none other consent but only of the parties themselves, whose conjunction is in hand, without which the conclusion of parents is of none effect. Note further, that *sponsalia* may be made pure or conditional, and whatsoever is else adjected (as earnest, pledge, or such like) is but accidental.

Sect. iv. Of secret sponsion

Those spousals which are made when a man is without witness, *solus cum sola* [he alone with her], are called secret promising or desponsation, which though it be tolerated when by liquid[18] and plain probation it may appear to the judge, and there is not any lawful impediment to hinder the contract, yet it is so little esteemed of (unless it be very manifest) that another promise public made after it shall be preferred and prevail against it. The cause why it is misliked is the difficulty of proof for avoiding[19] of it when for offense her just cause of refusal, the one or other party might seek to go loose and perhaps cannot, but must stand haltered from any other marriage and the judge in suspense what to determine. [Pp. 54–56 omitted.]

Sect. x. Of matrimony contracted in the present time, and who may contract

Those which the *Latins* call *puberes,* that is, they which are come once to such state, habit, and disposition of body that they may be deemed able

16. The act of making a bargain or pact.

17. "Parens" usually referred to a mother or a father, but sometimes it could also refer to a grandfather or to ancestors.

18. Clear, manifest.

19. Canceling.

to procreate, may contract matrimony by words of the time present, for in contract of wedlock, *pubertas* is not strictly esteemed by number of years as it is in wardship, but rather by the maturity, ripeness, and disposition of body. There is further required in them which contract matrimony a sound and whole mind to consent, for he that is mad, without intermission of fury, cannot marry. But he that is deaf and dumb may contract matrimony, *quia non verbis tantum sed nuta & signis sentia mentis exprimuntur* [because not only by words, but also by a nod and signs the feelings of the mind are expressed], and as they which are *impuberes* cannot for infirmity of age make any firm knot of wedlock, so likewise they which by coldness of nature, or by enchantment[20] are impotent, be forbidden to contract. . . .

Sect. xiii. Diversity of religion
Amongst the hindrances of marriage, note this also, that by constitution of holy church, marriage is forbidden betwixt persons of diverse religions, as Jews and Christians.

Sect. xiv. Of fear and constraint
Also matrimony holdeth not when it is extorted by force, or by such a fear as may *cadere in constantem virum, quia matrimonia debent esse libera* [(happen) to befall a constant man, because marriages ought to be free].

Sect. xv. Of marriage detestable made
Also marriage holdeth not when it is sought or made with wickedness, and if a man promise to a woman which[21] he hath adulterously polluted that he will marry her when his wife dieth, etc., or if a man have sought to abridge the days of his lawful wife to marry another. These villainies are such perpetual cankers in marriage that they do not only hinder it to be made, but also rend it in sunder when it is made.

There are other crimes *quia distrahunt matrimonia contracta* [which tear apart contracted marriages] as incest *cum cognata* [with a relative] and ravishment, yet if any man ravish a maid or other unmarried woman, the canons do admit him to marry with her if she consent. But otherwise she shall be rendered to her father, upon whose suit and accusation the ravisher is put to capital punishment. . . .

20. By a magic spell.
21. Whom.

Sect. xviii. What words are requisite

There needs no stipulation or curious form of contract in wedlock making, but such words as prove a mutual consent are sufficient. And it may be made by letters. . . .

Sect. xix. The accidents of marriage

Those things which are of solemnity or benevolence, as provision of dower, earnest, giving pledges, nuptial benediction, etc., are not of the essence of matrimony, which is made by consent. For though dower cannot consist without marriage, yet marriage may very well stand without dower. And so it is of all donations *propter nuptias* [on account of marriage]. In only one case, written instruments are required in making of marriage, and that is where a man marrieth her whom he hath holden a long time as concubine. Here *instrumenta dotalia*[22] are behoveful, that the children had before marriage may be esteemed legitimate. But this holdeth not in England. . . .

Sect. xxi. The consummation and individuity of marriage

When to the consent of mind there is added copulation of body, matrimony is consummate[d], the principal end whereof is propagation or procreation. But where the course after going[23] is not observed, there riseth no lawful offspring. The children which are had are not in power and commandment of them which beget or bear them. Neither are they taken by law for any other than *vulgo quesiti*.[24] Otherwise it is in lawful wedlock the knot whereof is so straight and indissoluble that they which are yoked therein cannot the one without the consent of the other (neither was it ever permitted) abdicate themselves, or enter into religion, for Saint Paul in the above titled epistle and chapter saith plainly that the husband hath not power of his own body, etc. And there cannot chance any fedity[25] or uncleanness of body so great as that for it a man and wife ought perpetually to be segregated, yea, so unpartable be they that law saith they may not utterly leave *conjugalem consuetudinem* [conjugal relations], though one of them have the very leprosy itself. And here is moved a question not impertinent, that is, whether a woman be bound to follow her husband where-

22. Instruments relating to dower.
23. I.e., when there is no marriage ceremony (course).
24. Those [children] claimed by the public. Children who are at the disposition of society?
25. Foulness, moral or physical.

soever he goeth, if he require it, whereunto it is answered by Bartall[26] and by some other that if the wife before she married knew the negotiations and occasions of her husband would be such that he must of necessity ever be traveling, she is bounded and in the contract seemeth to have consented to go with him at commandment. But if, after the bargain made, he take up a new trick of *circumnagari*[27] she may let him go when he list and tarry at home when she will.

Sect. xxii. Of divorce

... And as no man can be compelled by any convention of pain or penalty to contract matrimony, so is it impossible, when it is once lawfully and evidently contracted, to distract[28] it by any partition, covenant, or human traction, *Quos Deus conjunxit, homo non separet* [Those whom God has joined, man may not separate], yet there are causes for which diverse[29] are permitted. But divorce, that only separateth *a consuetudine conjugali* [from conjugal relations] taketh not away the bond of matrimony and therefore divorces are sometimes perpetual, as long as the parties live, sometimes for a season limited, and sometime till reconcilement be had. And he that maketh divorce with his wife being only separated *a toro* [from the marriage couch] is forbidden to take another wife.

Sect. xxiii. Causes of divorce

The civil law hath many causes of divorce, but by divine and common law the only sufficient cause is adultery and fornication, which by the canons is carnal and spiritual. The spiritual is heresy and idolatry. They dissolve matrimony for spiritual fornication only where one of the parties is converted to Christian faith and the other for hatred of his religion will not cohabit etc. And this is taken also from Saint Paul I *ad Corinth.* 7 where he saith, "If the unbelieving depart, let him depart, a brother or sister is not in subjection."

Sect. xxiv. Impotency or disability of procreation

There is admitted also in dissolution of marriage the complaint of impotency. And Justinian[30] very discreetly willed that in that exploration or

26. Also spelled Bartol in our text. Bartolus of Saxoferrato (1314–57), lawyer and commentator on civil (Roman) law at Perugia.

27. *Circumnavigari?* lit. sailing around [the earth].

28. Pull it apart.

29. Divorces?

30. The reference is to the Code of Justinian, the collection of laws and legal interpretations developed under the sponsorship of the Byzantine emperor, Justinian I, from A.D. 529 to 565.

proof of the defect there should be expected three years. But the canons ordain that matrimony is dissolved by probation of impotency without mention or[31] limits of time. And this is more than a bare divorce or separation *a toro,* for it dissolveth marriage, avoiding[32] it as it had never been. So that he or she whose fellow is convicted of impotency may choose a new friend and presently marry again. But this is to be understood of impotency which was before the marriage made. For, indeed, where the impediment was so precedent, there could not any matrimony exist or have being, etc.

Otherwise it is when this disability betideth after marriage perfected and consummate[d], for in that case, he or she which remaineth potent shall not leave and depart from the impotent, but be compelled to bear the discommodity as well as any other ill fortune. And that which is here taught of conjugal impotency stretcheth to all impediments of marriage which are perpetual.

Sect. xxvi. Captivity or long absence of one which is married

It falleth out not seldom, the one of them which are married to be taken captive or otherwise so detained that it is uncertain if he live or no. Therefore because it is in some sort dangerous to expect long the uncertain return of an absent yoke-fellow, here the civil law did ordain that after a husband had been gone five years and nothing known whether he lived or no, the wife might marry again and so might the husband that had expected his wife, etc. But the common law commandeth simply to forbear marriage till the death of him or her that is missing be certainly known. [Pp. 67–71 omitted.]

Sect. xxxii. Of wooing

I am afraid my feminine acquaintance will say I write as I live. I talk much of marriage, but I came not forward. Stay a while yet, I pray you. I know many an honest woman more repenting her hasty marriage ere she was wooed than all the other sins that ever she committed. It were good reason we speak a little of wooing, but to handle that matter, *per genus & species* would take up as much room as the Indian fig tree, every thread whereof, when it falleth to the ground, groweth to a body. I will slip by it, only observing that the giving of gloves, rings, bracelets, chains, or anything that is *ex sponsaliorum largitate* [(given) from the bounty of the betrothal] (as a man would say, of love's liberality) or as a pledge of future marriage betwixt them that are promised, have a condition (silent for the

31. Of?
32. Canceling.

most part) annexed unto them, that if matrimony do not ensue, the things may be demanded back and recovered. . . .

Sect. xxxii.[33] *The condiments of love*

There are with us, as well as with the civilians,[34] many kinds of donations *propter nuptias* [on account of nuptials], and some *ex sponsaliorum largitate* [out of the bounty of the betrothal]. Good meats are the better for good sauce. Venison craveth wine and wedlock hath certain condiments which come best in season in the wooing time and serve (as Breton[35] saith) *pour doner fees come melier talent d'aymor matrimonie.*[36] A husband *per se* [of itself] is a desirable thing. But donements or feoffements, etc., better the stomach, though of itself it be good and eager. And because the first marriage made in paradise, if you mark it well, had a jointure,[37] I cannot but allow the circumspection which is had. [Pp. 73–79 omitted.]

Sect. xl. *The courtesy of England*[38]

For Sir, in the married life, children are some token of true love, and honest life and kindness in a husband breedeth increase of liking in a wife, and where affection hath her right repercussion (if secret imperfection be none inpediment) there is like to follow fecundity which hath this privilege: whosoever taketh a wife fiefed[39] of lands or tenements in fee-simple,[40] fee-

---

33. Misprint for xxxiii.

34. Lawyers who practice civil law.

35. Sir John Breton (d. 1275), bishop of Hereford, author of the law book now known as *Britton*. It is mainly a condensation of Bracton's treatise on English law.

36. "To give money to increase the desire of wanting matrimony." The original phrase from *Britton* V.i as quoted in the *OED* (under talent) reads: "Pur doner meillour talent a femmes de amer matrimoigne," "to give women a greater desire to like matrimony." I am indebted to Prof. James W. Marchand, Department of Germanic Languages and Literatures, University of Illinois at Urbana-Champaign, for assistance in translating these phrases of law French.

37. This passage seems to refer to Genesis 1:26–29: "And God said, Let us make man [i.e., man and woman? the sense in the entire passage is plural] in our image, after our likeness; and let them [i.e., man and woman] have dominion over the fish of the sea, and over the fowl of the air, and over the cattle, and over the earth, and over every creeping thing that creepeth upon the earth. So God created man in his own image, in the image of God created he him: male and female created he them . . . And God blessed them, and God said unto them . . . Behold, I have given you every herb bearing seed, which is upon the face of the earth, and every tree in the which is the fruit of a tree yielding seed, to you it shall be meat" (King James Version, London, 1625).

38. A tenure by which a husband, after his wife's death, holds certain kinds of property which she has inherited.

39. Invested with a fief or fee, an estate of inheritance in land.

40. An estate in land [held] in absolute possession.

tail[41] general, or as the heir of fee-tail special, and hath issue by her, a child born alive that by possibility might be heir of the estate which the mother hath though the child die afterward, he [i.e., the husband] shall have and hold his wife's inheritance after her death, in estate of frank tenement[42] during his life. And this is called an estate by the law and courtesy of England because it is this realm's privilege peculiar. I give it place in my book because it is taken out of the inheritance of woman and in this part because it resembleth the donations that are *propter nuptias,* the doctrine of it being something like that of dower. [Pp. 80–89 omitted.]

Sect. liv. Of dower

I have hitherto handled only those gifts, *causa matrimonii* [by reason of matrimony], which come from women or their ancestors, as if Englishmen were so dainty and coy that they must be enticed, or our women so un-amiable, that unless it were by purchase, they could have no husbands. But I could never hear of any woman that needed buy new boots to ride on wooing. Contrariwise, so sweet, fair and pleasing are they, or so very good and prudent . . . that though some men get lands by them, most men are fain to assure part or all of such lands as they have (in jointure or otherwise) to them ere they can win their love. And where there is no such assurance, the Christian custom and law of the realm giveth every good wife part of her husband's lands to live on when he is dead, which we call dower, and of which we come now to speak.

Sect. lv. What dower is

The word in Latin imports no more but a bringing, giving, or bestowing. And with the Civilians *Dos* [a gift] is no other thing than that which a wife or some other body in her name, or for her sake, giveth to her husband to be his during coverture. Though Bartol more fine will have it to be *ipsum ius rebus vi[v]endi* [the right to the necessities of life], *dos profectitia* [dower (given) at the (bride's) departure (from her father's house)] (with them) is that which cometh from the bride's father or her father's father; *adventitia dos* [dower coming from other sources (than from her father)] is from her mother or other kindred of their liberality. And *paraphernalia bona,*[43] or such things as the wife bringeth in *aedes mariti propter dotem* [into the home of (her) husband as dower] [is brought] as it were instead of dower

41. An estate of inheritance entailed or limited to some particular class of heirs.

42. Freehold.

43. Those articles of personal property which the law allowed a married woman to keep and, to a certain extent, to deal with as her own.

and into the husband's custody, but not into his full dominion. For unless she make a gift of them, she may ask them and have them again.

Bracton saith, *dos profectitia* is the land given for frank marriage by the woman's ancestors, *adventitia* the lands which some other kinsman giveth, and *paraphernalia* that which is given to a man or woman before or after marriage for other considerations than marriage. There is further with the civilians a gift *pro dore*[44] [as dower], given in recompense of security of dower, and this doth somewhat resemble our dower[45] because it proceedeth from the husband, as Homer, Tully, and St. Paul are called, the poet, the doctor, the apostle, carrying a name of generality for their special excellency. So in my opinion for the like excellency among the estates which are made *causa matrimonii*, that which women claim in their husband's inheritances when they be dead, by a special and universal largeness of the law is called dower, concerning which the plainest and most plentiful rule is that of . . . Littleton,[46] viz. where the husband is seised of lands or tenements of such estate, that the issue which by possibility his wife may bear him, may by possibility be heir of that estate *si le possession le baron ne soit loyalment anient* [as long as the possessions (of) the baron are not legally reduced to nothing]. As addeth Parkins,[47] the wife shall be endowed.

Sect. lvi. The husband must be seised[48]

Dower is of the possession of a husband. The ground of it therefore is marriage. A concubine then shall have no dower. No more shall she which is but only contracted. And it was holden by some, 10. H[enry] 3,[49] that she which was married in a parlor or chamber should have no dower, but it is now taken otherwise. Also, where marriage is clearly void and unlawful, there groweth no title of dower. But if a woman first contracted to E. I.

44. Misprint for *pro dote?*

45. The author seems to be distinguishing between dowry defined in Roman law (i.e., civil law) as property coming to a husband from his wife's father and/or other relatives and dower understood in common law as a life interest in property to which a widow is entitled (usually one-third of her husband's estate) at his death.

46. The reference is to the *Tenures* of Sir Thomas Littleton (1422–81).

47. John Perkins alias Parkins (d. 1545). "Author of the law-French *Perutilis tractatus magistri Johannis Parkins interioris Templi socii* (1528), better known as Perkins' *Profitable Book*. The most successful early sixteenth-century discussion of land and testamentary law, it had three more editions in Henry VIII's reign and remained in print until 1827" (*Biographical Dictionary of the Common Law*, ed. A. W. B. Simpson [London: Butterworths, 1984], pp. 412–13).

48. Put in possession, as of a freehold.

49. I was not able to discover any parliamentary statutes enacted in the tenth year of the reign of Henry III. See vol. 1 of *Statutes at Large*. Brooke does not mention this citation in his section on "Dower" in *La Graunde Abridgement*, fols. 252–56.

intermarry afterwards with T. K., this marriage is voidable but not clearly void, and if it be not frustrated otherwise than by death of T. K., the wife shall have dower of his land. Here ye may perceive that which destroyeth an absolute true marriage, destroyeth dower also. For though by Bracton there may be by special constitution a dower appointed that shall stand good against the tempest of diverse assaults, yet by ground of the common law: *matrimonium est fulcimentum dotis*[50] [matrimony is the prop of dower]. And Bracton saith in his second book and 39 chapter, *Ubi nullum omnino matrimonium, ibi nulla dos igitur, ubi matrimonium, ibi dos, quod verum est si matrimonium in facie ecclesiae contrahatur* [where there is no marriage at all, there is therefore no dower; where there is marriage, there is dower, which is true as long as the marriage is brought about through the countenance of the church].

Sect. lvii. Matrimony may be, and yet no dower

Though matrimony dò always proceed dower, yet doth not dower always follow matrimony. For first, where the husband had no land, the wife can have no dower by the common law. Bracton[51] and Breton which give a woman dower in a certain sum of money or in other chattels[52] speak rather as civil lawyers than mere English. Also dower is not granted unless the husband is above seven years old, and the wife above nine. . . . Also if a man marry his bond-woman in gross and die, she shall not recover dower against the heir, for she is his bond-woman, but against the feoffee[53] of her husband she shall recover dower, unless she be *regardant*[54] to the manor whereof the feoffement was made. [Pp. 93–107 omitted.]

Sect. lxv. Less or more than a third part

Though by the common law a woman is to have no less than a third part, yet if a widow will be so foolish as to accept a fourth or fifth part or moiety[55] of her husband's inheritance assigned in allowance of all his frank tenement, it is a good[56] assignment. And by custom in some places, a

---

50. The text reads "dosis."

51. The reference is to *De Legibus et Consuetudinibus Angliae,* a comphrensive treatise on the laws of England by Henry de Bracton (Bratton, Bretton) (d. 1268).

52. Any piece of property other than real estate or a freehold.

53. The person to whom a feoffment is made; the action of investing with a fief or fee.

54. Belonging. See Thomas Littleton, *Lyttleton, His Treatise of Tenures,* ed. T. E. Tomlins (1841; rpt., n.p.: Russell and Russell, 1970), p. 219: "Such things which are regardant or appendant to a manor . . ." (A bond-woman "in gross" belongs solely to her master.)

55. Usually a half, but here perhaps a smaller part.

56. Legal and binding.

woman shall claim and have of right a moiety of her husband's lands, and
in some town or borough, she shall have the entirety in dower. . . . [Pp.
108–10 omitted.]

Sect. lxix. Of dower at the church door

The old kind of endowment at the church door cometh now-a-days
seldom in use. But for all that I would have women better learned than
to be ignorant of it. It is when a man seised in fee-simple, being of full
age, coming to the church door to be married doth there affirm affiance
and endow his spouse of all his lands or of part as of half or a less quantity
openly and with certainty. The woman thus endowed may enter into her
dower after the husband's death without assignment and this dower may
be at the church door in one county, of lands in another county and without
deed. . . . Also a son and heir apparent, when he is espoused by consent
of his father, may endow his wife at the church door in part of such lands
and tenements as are the father's in fee-simple, and the son's wife after
his death (the father living) may enter presently without further assignment
into the parcels thus certainly appointed. But if she enter after her husband's death and agree to any of these endowments *ad ostium ecclesiae* [at
the door of the church], she is concluded from claiming any other dower.
. . . yet here in England it[57] must be in lands and not in goods. All moveable
treasure which the wife or husband hath are the husband's to spend as he
list *dum vilem redigatur ad assem*[58] [until it is reduced to worthlessness]. . . .

I have held young maids now indeed somewhat long in the old endowments, and I would proceed to instruct them in the dower of the new
learning jointures. I mean, for my desire is that they should be able to
have when they are widows a coach or at the least an ambler[59] and some
money in their purses. But they are of the mind for themselves, I perceive,
that Themistocles[60] was in for his daughter. He desired a man rather without
money than money without a man. Here is a wise ado, ye say. I tell you
of dower, of the widow's estate, and God knows whether ye shall ever have
the grace to be widows or no. Ye would know what belongeth to wives.
On then in a good way, I have brought you to the church door. If ye be
not shortly well married, I pray God I may.

Book III [Of Wives]

As soon as a man and woman are knit and fast linked together in bands
of wedlock, they are become in common parlance *coniuges & consores*[61]

57. Dower.
58. Misprint?
59. Horse or mule.
60. Athenian statesman and naval commander (ca. 525–ca. 460 B.C.).
61. Misprint for *consortes?*

[spouses and equal-sharers], yoke-fellows, that in a[n] even participation must take all fortunes equally. Yet law permits not so great an *intervallum* [interval] betwixt them as society, which must alway[s] consist among two or more. Rather it affirms them to be *una caro* [one flesh], regarded to many intents merely as one undivided substance.

Sect. i. When or how soon baron et feme are said to be one person

If Titus and Sempronia by words *de praesenti* in a lawful consent contract marriage, they are man and wife before God. But they cannot do all that married couples may, ye know my meaning, *id possumus quod de iure possumus* [we are able to do that which we can do legally], but they may (saith Parkins) infeoffe one another, for they are not yet *una persona* [one person] in the eye of the law.

If it fall out that the woman chance to die before nuptials celebrated, he which is no more but betrothed shall not have her goods, unless it be by her last will and testament, which she might without craving license of any body have ordained according to her pleasure. If a man affianced to Sempronia know her carnally, infeoffe her of a carve[62] of land, and then marry her *in facie ecclesiae,* the old world would have judged this feoffement void coming *post fidem datum et carnalem copulam* [after faith (had been) pledged and flesh joined], but at this day it is good enough. Public celebration therefore according to law is it which maketh man and wife in plain view of law, *consensus non concubitus facit matrimonium* [an agreement, not copulation, makes marriage]. But one nail keepeth out another and a firm betrothing forbiddeth any new contract. Yet they which dare play man and wife only in the view of heaven and closet of conscience, let them be advised how they shall take the advantages or emoluments of marriage in conscience or in heaven. For on earth if the priest see no celebrated marriage, the judge saith no legitimate issue, nor the law any reasonable or constituted dower. How if Titus and Sempronia were Christianly married *in facie ecclesiae,* but Titus soon after dinner or a little before night, leaving his wife a virgin, took his way *ad campos Elysios* [to the Elysian fields], shall Sempronia have a child[63] of his body? *Videtur quod sic* [it seems so because] . . . in a writ of dower, the tenant saith the demandant was not of age to deserve dower, *tempore mortis viri sui, viz.* 9 *annorum etc.* [at the time of the death of her husband, (she having) nine years (of age) etc.], . . . for Littleton is plain in the affirmative, a woman shall have dower if she were past the age of nine years, the third part of that which the husband had during coverture, and ye shall not take coverture here like a master stallion or breeder of colts, but a woman is covert baron as soon as she is

62. Subdivision.
63. Dower?

overshadowed with her husband's protection and supereminency. Now the law that giveth dower to her that is able to deserve it and enableth at so green years knoweth well enough that women are at their husband's commandment. If Titus being dead have left his wife her maidenhead, *inmunis a culpa, a poena immunis erit* [she shall be immune from blame or punishment]. . . . Yet in case of dower and the privilege thereof, they are extended to matrimony consummate[d]. . . . here ye say was the law as clear as crystal on your side, when supper is done, dance a while, leave out the long measures till you be in bed, get you there quickly, and pay the minstrels tomorrow. [Pp. 119–28 omitted.]

Sect. vii. The baron may beat his wife

. . . if a man beat an out-law, a traitor, a pagan, his villein, or his wife, it is dispunishable, because by the Law Common these persons can have no action.[64] God send the gentlewoman better sport or better company. But it seemeth to be very true that there is some kind of castigation which law permits a husband to use, for if a woman be threatened by her husband to be beaten, mischieved, or slain . . . she may sue out of chancery to compel him to find surety of honest behavior toward her, and that he shall neither do nor procure to be done to her (mark, I pray you) any bodily damage, otherwise than appertains to the office of a husband for lawful and reasonable correction. How far that extendeth I cannot tell, but herein the sex feminine is at no very great disadvantage, for first for the lawfulness: if it be in none other regard lawful to beat a man's wife than because the poor wench can sue no other action for it, I pray why may not the wife beat the husband again? What action can he have if she do? Where two tenants in common be on a horse, and one of them will travel and use this horse, he may keep it from his companion a year, two, or three, and so be even with him; so the actionless woman beaten by her husband hath retaliation left to beat him again, if she dare. . . .

Sect. viii. That which a husband hath is his own

But the prerogative of the husband is best discerned in his dominion over all extern things in which the wife by combination divesteth herself of propriety in some sort and casteth it upon her governor, for here practice everywhere agrees with the theoric of law, and forcing necessity submits women to the affection thereof. Whatsoever the husband had before coverture either in goods or lands, it is absolutely his own; the wife hath therein no seisin at all. If any thing when he is married be given him, he taketh it by himself distinctly to himself. If a man have right and title to enter into lands, and the tenant enfeoffe the baron and feme, the wife

---

64. Action at law for redress.

taketh nothing. The very goods which a man giveth to his wife are still his own: her chain, her bracelets, her apparel, are all the good-man's goods. . . . A wife how gallant soever she be, glistereth but in the riches of her husband, as the moon hath no light but it is the sun's. . . .

Sect. ix. That which the wife hath is the husband's

For thus it is, if before marriage the woman were possessed of horses, neat, sheep, corn, wool, money, plate, and jewels, all manner of moveable substance is presently by conjunction the husband's, to sell, keep, or bequeath if he die. And though he bequeath them not, yet are they the husband's executor's and not the wife's which brought them to her husband. [Pp. 130–41 omitted.]

Sect. xiii. Of acts done by a feme covert[65]

Every feme covert is *quodammodo* [in a certain way] an infant, for see her power even in that which is most her own. A wife may be seised in her own right with her husband in estate of inheritance. But if she make livery[66] and seisin to another in any parcel of this inheritance by herself alone without gree[67] of her husband, it is void. Yea, her husband and she together may maintain an assize upon the entry, but where only the baron is seised, and the feme maketh livery, the assize must be only by the baron in his own name. Likewise . . . where a man is seised in the right of his wife and the wife grants a rent charge out of her own land, the husband not knowing it or the husband knowing but not consenting, but the deed is only in the name of the wife, this grant is void. . . .

Sect. xiv. Of elopement

Amongst the acts of a feme covert, I must not forget to admonish her that she take heed of elopements. A woman shall not forfeit dower by not suing appeal of her husband's death, or by not visiting her husband, or not coming to comfort him when he is wounded or exceeding sick in a foreign shire. But if he be in his home county where he dwelleth, *quaere* [that is the question]. A woman in her frenzy may cut her husband's throat, and it is no forfeiture of dower, but if she make an elopement (which is a mad trick) dower is forfeited. [Pp. 145–82 omitted.]

Sect. xxx. Of jointures

. . . all husbands are not so unkind or untrusty as to endamage their wives by alienation[68] of their lands. But contrariwise, the greatest part of

---

65. A married woman.
66. The legal delivery.
67. Goodwill, consent.
68. The act of transferring ownership to another.

honest, wise, and sober men are of themselves careful to purchase some-what for their wives. If they be not, yet they stand sometimes bound by the woman's parents to make their wives some jointure. . . . Many of our English women have with their singular virtue so much wisdom of their own as to foresee for themselves and discern the difference between that which we call dower and jointure. Jointures . . . are made for the most part to baron and feme jointly, or to the feme only. This also is comprehended under the term jointure before marriage or after, for sustentation of the charge and necessities of espousals; and they are made *causa matrimonii &* *gratis* [on account of marriage and freely] without the consideration of money bargain or any thing, saving for love and affection of the baron or his ancestors, and these jointures are a present possession. But dower must be tarried for till the husband be dead. It must be demanded, sometime sued for, sometime neither with suit or demand obtained. Again, dower was subject to forfeiture in times past by felony done and proved in the baron, by the baron's treason, by the wife's elopement, and every question in the validity of marriage maketh a scruple of dower. All which incon-veniences being wisely foreseen, women did learn to become joint pur-chasers with their husbands of such estates as would avoid all weathers, and a good while they did enjoy jointures and dowers after their husbands were dead.

Sect. xxxi. A part of 27 H[enry] 8. Cap. 10[69]

[But] . . . the woman having such a jointure etc. shall not claim any dower of the residue of any hereditaments that were her husband's, by whom she had such a jointure . . . provided that if any woman be lawfully expulsed or evicted from her said jointure or from any part thereof without fraud or covin,[70] by lawful entry, action, or discontinuance of her husband, that every such woman shall be endowed of as much of the residue of her husband's hereditaments as the lands or tenements so evicted shall amount or extend unto. [Pp. 184–204 omitted.]

Sect. xlii. When a wife may sue or be sued alone

It is seldom, almost never, that a married woman can have any action to use her writ only in her own name. Her husband is her stern, her *primus*

---

69. I.e., the tenth act or statute, referred to as Chapter 10 (abbreviated C., Ca., or Cap.), "to receive the Royal Assent during the parliamentary session taking place" in the twenty-seventh year of the reign of Henry VIII. See *Manual of Law Librarianship: The Use of and Organization of Legal Literature,* ed. Elizabeth M. Moys (Boulder, Colo.: Westview Press, 1976), pp. 114–15. See also *Statutes at Large,* especially Cap. 10: "An act concerning uses and wills" in vol. 2, *The Statutes at Large, from the First Year of King Edward the Fourth to the End of the Reign of Queen Elizabeth* (1770), pp. 226–29.

70. A privy agreement between two or more to the prejudice of another.

motor [first mover] without whom she cannot do much at home and less abroad. But if her husband commit felony, take the church and abjure the realm,[71] she is now in case as a widow enabled to make alienation of her own land as a feme sole. . . .

Sect. xliii. Of felonies

In matters criminal and capital causes, a feme covert shall answer without her husband. And note, if a feme covert steal any thing by coercion of her husband, this is not felony in her. . . . If a man and wife commit felony jointly, it seemeth the wife is no felon, but it shall be wholly judged the husband's fact. . . . But a woman by herself without the privity of her husband may commit felony to become either principal or accessory, as if she steal goods or receive thieves to her house, etc., and if the husband so soon as he perceive it waive and forsake their company and his own house, in this case the woman's offense makes not felony in the baron. But if the baron commit felony, his wife not ignorant of it may keep his company still notwithstanding, and not be deemed accessory, for a woman cannot be accessory to her husband, insomuch as she is forbidden by the law of God to betray him. Note also that a woman cannot be thief of her husband's goods. If she take and give them away, the receiver is no felon. . . . If a woman be arraigned of felony, it is no plea to say she is with child. But she must plead to the felony and, if she be found guilty, she may then claim the benefit of her womb. Whereupon, the marshall or vicount shall be commanded to put her in a chamber and cause some women to examine and try her whether she be *ensoint de infant* [pregnant], which if she be not, she shall be hanged *maintenant* [immediately]. And though she be quick with child, yet judgment shall not be delayed, but only execution deferred. [Pp. 208–30 omitted.]

Book IV [Regarding Widows]

Death . . . hath called the husband hence, left the house full of mourning, and specially the wife cannot chuse but sorrow and lament. If my four-legged beast should fall into halves, the one-half stark dead without motion or spirit, and the other half standing still upright, scenting, seeing, feeling, gazing, must it not, think you, be wonderfully astonished? If an elephant, in whom (as some do write) is understanding of his country's speech, a wonderful memory and retenting of things past, a great delight in love and glory, besides prudence, equity, and religion, should have his head cut off, his body remaining still for all that vegetable and sensitive,[72] would he not

71. Become a Roman Catholic priest and (of necessity) leave England?

72. Plato believed that the soul was divided into three parts: rational, sensible or passionate, and vegetative. Cf. *Timaeus*, 69D–72C.

(trow ye) be exceeding sorrowful for the forgoing such an ornament? I dare be bold to give a woman as much as Pliny gave the elephant. She hath understanding and speech, firm memory, love natural, and kindness, desire of glory and reputation, with the accomplishment of many meritorious virtues. But, alas, when she hath lost her husband, her head is cut off, her intellectual part is gone, the very faculties of her soul are (I will not say) clean taken away, but they are all benumbed, dimmed, and dazzled, so that she cannot think or remember when to take rest or recreation for her weak body. And though her spirits and natural moisture being inwardly exhausted with sorrow and extreme grief, she be called and enforced to seek restauration[73] by such aliments[74] as life is prolonged by, yet is she nothing desirous of life, having lost a moiety of herself, yea the principal moiety now best prized and esteemed, but never best loved. Time must play the physician, and I will help him a little. Why mourn you so, you that be widows? Consider how long you have been in subjection under the predominance of parents, of your husbands; now you be free in liberty, and free . . . at your own law; you may see . . . that maidens' and wives' vows made upon their souls to the Lord himself of heaven and earth were all disavowable and infringable by their parents or husbands unless they ratified and allowed them, either express or by silence at the day when such vows came first to their notice and knowledge. But the vow of a widow or of a woman divorced, no man had power to disallow of, for her estate was free from controlment. Must a woman needs weep thus for the loss of her buckler, shield, and defence in the person of him with whom she held daily commutation of all offices proceeding from love and superlative kindness? Let her learn to cast her whole love and devotion on him that is better able to love and defend her than all the men in the world. Him I mean that hath forbidden to afflict widows or orphans, with promise to hear their cries and vindicate their wrongs, by killing them by the sword and making the wives widows and their children fatherless of them which break this commandment.[75] Then, because a sober carefulness and moderate sedulity in business of profit or disprofit doth mitigate greatly the sorrowing for such actions, as opinion or fancy makes thus grievous, let her look to her affairs as cause and need requireth. . . .

Sect. ii. A reasonable part of the goods
If there be a will proved, the widow must take such goods as were bequeathed her by delivery from the executors, but whether there were a

73. The restoration of a person to a former status or position.
74. That which nourishes or feeds.
75. See Exod. 22:21.

will or none, in some places she shall have a third part of all her late husband's goods. For this there is an ordinary writ to the sheriff, where she cannot have a third part of that which remains after funerals discharged and legacies paid and performed, to summon the executors to appear and make answer why she should not have, as the custom of the court is, that women ought to have *rationabilem partem de bonis & catallis virorum* [a reasonable part of the goods and chattels of (her) husband]. The like writ for is children, whether they be sons or daughters, or both. And this writ speaketh of a custom in the county that children which are not heirs nor promoted in the father's lifetime, shall have their reasonable part. . . . The custom was that where the baron died sans issue, the wife should have a moiety of his goods after debts and funerals discharged, but if there were issue, she should have but a third part. . . . A woman that is at her own commandment may make a will, and dispose the fruits and corn growing on her dower lands, whether they be severed from the soil or not severed. . . . she that is *sub potestate viri* [under the power of her husband] can make no will without her husband's ratification. . . .

Though our law may seem somewhat rigorous towards wives, yet for the most part, they can handle their husbands so well and doucely,[76] specially when they be sick, that where the law gives them nothing, their husbands at their death of their good will give them all, and few there be that be not either made sole or chief executor of the husband's last will and testament, having for the most part the government of the children and their portions, except it be in London, where a peculiar order is taken by the city much after the fashion of the law civil.

Sect. iii. Of quarantine

All this while the widow remains still in the house where her husband dwelt. . . . Therefore Magna Charta, Cap. 7,[77] giveth a widow quarantine or forty days abode in the capital messuage[78] of her husband after his decease, except the house be a castle. If she must leave it because it is a castle, there must presently a competent habitation be provided for her, in which she may honestly dwell till dower be assigned her, and in the mean season she shall be allowed reasonable estovers[79] in the common, etc. . . .

76. Sweetly.

77. "A widow shall have her marriage inheritance and quarentine," *Statutes at Large,* vol. 1, p. 3.

78. A dwelling house with its outbuildings and curtilage and the adjacent land assigned to its use.

79. Necessaries allowed by law.

Sect. iv. Assignment[80] of dower

Now to the assignment of dower, it is true that when it appears certain what it is that a woman shall have in dower, she may enter presently[81] when her husband is dead and tarry for none assignment. . . .

Sect. v. Who may assign dower

Sometime dower is assignable by the husband's heir, as if a man seised of two acres of land in one county make a feoffement of one acre with warranty and die, the heir may endow the widow with parcel of the acre remaining in allowance and full satisfaction of the whole dower. . . . And if the heir make a lease for life of part of such lands as are to him descended, and endow his mother of the parcel remaining in allowance of all, etc., it is good. Yet in this case in a writ of dower against the lessee, if he vouch his lessor, the recovery shall not be against the vouchee, because he is not bound to warranty as the heir of his father. But if he had been generally vouched the heir, and had generally entered into warranty, judgment perhaps should be conditionally against him. [Pp. 245–74 omitted.]

Sect. xvii. Judgment

Judgment in a writ of dower is framed according to the substance of the title, and circumstance of the pleading. . . . Dower . . . shall be assigned by the heir if he be of full age, or by the Lord in the heir's name, if he be underage. And this within forty days after the husband's death, for otherwise *occurit tempus & sequantur damna, nisi rationabilis causa excuset* [time runs on and harms follow, unless some reasonable cause excuses (the delay)]. This assignation must be made of the land, as it was by the husband, tilled or untilled, with the fruits growing upon it, allowing nothing to the heir or executor for manuring, husbanding, or culture of it, for of old time it was observed that in what case or plight a woman had received her dower, whether it were tilled or untilled, she must restore in like plight to the heir, etc. She might not make her will of any corn growing or fruit not separated from the frank tenement. . . . [But] a woman may now ordain her testament of corn or fruit growing on her dowry or severed growing, all is one. If the husband alien all his lands, and the tenants need not yield dower to the widow as soon as she demandeth it, if there be just cause of calling to warranty, one or more, successively till the heir be vouched, and all that time the tenants are not charged with damages or costs. But when

80. Legal transference of a right or property.
81. At once. This passage appears to mean that a widow may take possession of her dower rights and properties as soon as they are determined and before they have been legally transferred.

the heir entreth into warranty, if he do not presently yield dower, but stand out obstinately, he shall pay damages, as much as dower might have been worth to the woman from the time of the husband's death to the day wherein she hath judgment, and the heir shall be amerced.[82] In like manner is it, if a widow without any assignation enter into her dower that was certainly nominated to her *ad ostium ecclesiae* and which she findeth empty at her husband's death, if she be ejected or put to suit and delays, she shall recover damages. So shall she if she be ejected the tenement assigned for quarantine during the forty days, or before dower assigned after the forty days. So likewise is it if she have no place at all assigned to dwell in, *ubi reclinet caput suum* [where she may lay her head], etc. . . . [Pp. 278–314 omitted.]

Sect. xxxiii. The Statute of 11 H[enry] 7. Cap. 20[83]

The common law restrictive of itself and helped something by the statute of Gloucester was sufficient, a great while, to bridle women from making alienations for any land that they held in dower or jointure, as arguments of their own good deserts and testimonies of their husband's love. But time, which made the art of fencing more fine than it was at the first when combatants fought all at heads and shoulders and it was greater shame to strike under the girdle than it is now, made law also more subtle than in the beginning it was when lands went altogether or for the most part by livery of seisin.[84] And women, witty of themselves, instructed by crafty men, grew cunning at the last, that they could alien lands holden for life or in tail[85] to whom they listed in fee.[86] And he which suffereth disinheritance should not easily help himself by writ of entry . . . for remedy whereof was made this severe statute in effect as followeth. 11 H[enry] 7.

If any woman, which hath had or hereafter shall have any estate in dower, or for life or in tail, jointly with her husband or only to her self, or to her use in any manors, lands, tenements, or other hereditaments of the inheritance, or purchase of her husband, or given to the husband and wife in tail, or for term of life by any ancestors of the husband, or by any other person seised[87] to the use of the husband or of his ancestors, and have or shall hereafter being sole or with any other after taken to husband, dis-

---

82. Fined arbitrarily.

83. "What estates or alienations made by the wife, of the lands of her deceased husband, shall be void," in *Statutes at Large,* vol. 2, p. 89.

84. The delivery of a token of possession.

85. The limitation or destination of a freehold estate or fee to a person and the heirs of his body.

86. An estate of heritance in land.

87. Put in possession of.

continued, or discontinue, aliened, released or confirmed, alien, release, or confirm, with warranty or by covin suffered or suffer any recovery of the same against them or any of them or any other seised to their use or to the use of either of them, after the form aforesaid, that all such recoveries, discontinuances, alienations, releases, confirmations, and warranties, so had and made and from henceforth to be had and made, be utterly void, etc. And that it shall be lawful to every person and persons to whom the interest, title, or inheritance, after the decease of the said woman, of the said manors, lands, or tenements, or other hereditaments being discontinued, aliened, or suffered to be recovered, after the first day of December next coming in the form aforesaid should appertain, to enter into all and every of the premises and peaceably to possess and enjoy the same, in such manner and form as he or they should have done if no such discontinuance, warranty, or recovery, had been had or made. [Pp. 316–30 omitted.]

Book V [Widows Who Have Remarried]

The widow married again to her own great liking, though not with applause of most friends and acquaintance. But, alas, what would they have her to have done? She was fair, young, rich, gracious in her carriage, and so well became her mourning apparel that when she went to church on Sundays, the casements opened of their own accord on both sides the streets that bachelors and widowers might behold her. . . . Her man[88] at home kissed her pantables[89] and served diligently; her late husband's physician came and visited her often. The lawyer to whom she went for counsel took opportunity to advise for himself. . . . Therefore to set men's hearts and her own at rest, she chuse amongst them, one not of the long robe, not a man macerate and dried up with study, but a gallant gulburd[90] lad, that might well be worthy of her had he been as thrifty, as kindhearted, or half so wise as hardy and adventurous. . . . Within less than a year . . . the bags[91] were all empty, the plate was all at pawn, all to keep the square bones in their amble and to relieve companions. One of which notwithstanding, that had cost him many a pound, for none other quarrel but *vous mentes* [you lie] challenged him one day in the field which was appointed, and there my new married man was slain. Now his wife will bring her appeal.

Sect. i. Appeal of the husband's death

A woman can have an appeal, but only in two cases . . . as in case where injury and force is committed against her person by ravishment, or when

---

88. Man-servant.
89. Pantofles? slippers? not listed in *OED*.
90. Gullible? not listed in *OED*.
91. Moneybags.

her husband is killed *inter brachia sua* [between her arms]. [Pp. 333–76 omitted.]

Sect. xx. Of Rape

Chuse now whether ye will imagine that the widow hath agreed with him which was her husband's bane or that she hath pursued him to death. She remaineth from henceforth a widow, giving herself to alms and deeds of charity, and of this good mind are many of our widows which purpose constantly to live out the residue of their days in a devout remembrance of their dear husbands departed, to whom perhaps they made vows never to marry again after their deaths. But to what purpose is it for women to make vows, when men have so many millions of ways to make them break them? And when sweet words, fair promises, tempting, flattering, swearing, lying will not serve to beguile the poor soul, then with rough handling, violence, and plain strength of arms, they are or have been heretofore rather made prisoners to lust's thieves than wives and companions to faithful honest lovers. So drunken are men with their own lusts and the poison of Ovid's false precept, "*Vim licet appellant, vis est ea grata puellis*" ["It is allowed to call it force, (but) it is a force which pleases girls"][92] that if the rampier of laws were not betwixt women and their harms, I verily think none of them being above twelve years of age and under an hundred, being either fair or rich, should be able to escape ravishing. This is therefore a matter concerning maids, wives, widows, and women of all degrees and conditions, if either they be or possess any thing worth the having, and because the ignorance of law may here turn a mollifying heart to harm, I were to blame if I left my scholars without warning to take heed.

Sect. xxi. Ravishment is in two sorts

There are two kinds of rape, of which though the one be called by the common people and by the law itself, ravishment, yet in my conceit it borroweth the name from *rapere,* but unproperly, for it is no more but . . . a hideous hateful kind of whoredom in him which committeth it when a woman is enforced violently to sustain the fury of brutish concupiscence, but she is left where she is found, as in her own house or bed as Lucrece was and not hurried away as Helen by Paris or as the Sabine women were by the Romans, for that is both by nature of the word and definition of the matter. The second and right ravishment, *Cum quis honestae famae foeminam, sive virgo, sive vidua, sive sanctimonialis, sit invitis illis in quorum est potestate, abducit* [(is) when anyone abducts a woman of honest fame,

---

92. *Ars Amatoria (Art of Love)* 1.673. The text in Ovid reads: "Vim licet appelles, gratast vis ista puellis."

whether she be a virgin, a widow, or a nun, (and) it is (done) against the will of them in whose power she is]. It seemeth the first kind of rape deserved always death by God's laws, unless the woman ravished were unbetrothed, so that the ravisher might marry her, as you may read Deut. 22:23 and by the civil law. *Raptores* [rapists] in the second kind *subjiciebantur poenae mortis rapta si fuerit ingenua* [were thrown to the punishment of death, if she was honest]. How heinous they be both and have a long time been, by the laws of England ye shall now perceive.

Sect. xxii. *The old law of libidinous rape*

Bracton in the eight and twentieth chapter of his third book sheweth that by the antique law of King Adelstan, he that meeting a virgin sole or with company did but touch her unhonestly was guilty of breaking the king's edict. . . . If against her will he threw her on the ground, he lost the king's favor; if he discovered[93] her and cast himself upon her, he lost all his possessions; if he lay with her, he suffered judgement of life and member; yea, if he were an horseman, his horse lost his tail and mane. . . . His hawk likewise lost her beak, talons, and train. And the virgin had in recompence all his land and money by the king's warrant. This was in King Adelstan's days, at least an hundred and twenty years before the Conquest, when *corruptores virginitatis & castitatis* [corrupters of virginity and chastity] were hanged, and their fautors[94] also. But in Bracton's time it seemeth that these kind of ravishers were otherwise punished; they lost their eyes and were gelt.[95]

She that brought an appeal was to complain herself presently to the next neighbor or to the chief men of the hundred, or to the coroner, or viscount, shewing her garments bloody and torn and in the first county to enter her appeal and pursue it, at coming of the king's justices. Before whom, unless the offender aid himself by exception that the appellant was still a virgin (which was tried by inspection of women) and if she were found a virgin, the appellant was imprisoned for her slander, or that he held her before time as his concubine, or that she consented to his embracements, or some other like plea, he lost his eyes and stones. . . . Except the woman before judgment given demanded him for her husband, for that was only in the woman's election and not in the man's, because of the inconvenience which otherwise might have happened if some hardy, strong lecher had ravished a dame noble or of great birth, he should either go

93. Uncovered, i.e., took her clothes off her.
94. Partisans, abettors.
95. Gelded.

away unpunished or else by means of one pollution, perpetually desire her, to the disgrace of her whole stock. . . .

It is set down for a law made by King William the Conqueror, . . . "I command that from henceforth no man be hanged, or put to death for any transgression, but let the offender's eyes be pulled out or his stones, feet, or hands cut away, that the trunk or mutilate[d] body still left alive may remain as a testimony of his prodition[96] and lewdness." Now if this mangling law of King William were still in force in Bracton's time against ravishers, was it Magna Charta, Cap. 29,[97] or what was it that made the law so meek in Edward the first his time, that the first Statute against rape speaketh of it so mildly, as if it had been at common law a very small trespass?

Sect. xxiii. West. I. Cap. 14. Anno 3 E[ward]. I[e98]

The king commands that no man ravish or take by force any damsel within age, either with her consent or without, nor any dame or damsel (of full age) or other man's wife against her will. If any do, the king will do justice and common right at his or her suit that shall sue within 40 days. If none commence suit within 40 days, the king shall have the suit; they which are culpable shall be imprisoned two years and be ransomed at the king's pleasure. And if they have not[99] to satisfy the ransom, they shall suffer a longer imprisonment as the trespass shall require. A man may well suspect that there was something which had allayed the rigor of former law before this statute was made. It may be the importation of clergymen urging satisfaction according to Moses' law, if the woman ravished were unmarried and otherwise the bashfulness of those which are betrothed and espoused, kept in the truculent Law of King William. Howsoever it were, this statute of West. I (in my poor opinion) being rather affirmative than otherwise, runneth not in favor of ravishers to abrogate their old punishment, but inflicteth a greater punishment upon them than that which had lately been put in practice. Or it may be very well that the common right, which King Edward promised here to do for them that would pursue within forty days, was according to the severity which Bracton speaketh of.

96. Betrayal, treason, treachery.

97. *Statutes at Large,* vol. 1, p. 7: "None shall be condemned without trial. Justice shall not be sold or deferred."

98. The author of *The Law's Resolutions of Women's Rights* mistakenly set down Cap. 14 instead of Cap. 13: "The punishment of him that doth ravish a woman." See the thirteenth Statute of Westminster the First (1275) in the parliamentary session of the third year of the reign of Edward I, *Statutes at Large,* vol. 1, p. 45.

99. Have not the means.

Sect. xxiv. West 2. Cap. 35[100]

The mitigation of the old Law, one day or other, in a few years brought forth so many enormities that at the next parliament which King Edward held ten years after, it was ordained as followeth: It is ordained that if any man ravish any woman espoused or damsel or other woman which consenteth not afore nor after, that he shall have judgment of life and member. And whosoever ravisheth any woman by force, though she consent afterward, shall have judgment as afore is said, if he be attainted[101] at the king's suit. And if any woman be carried away with the goods of their husband, the king shall have the suit for goods so carried away. . . .

Sect. xxv. 6 Richard 2. Cap. 6

A man would have thought that this statute should have repressed for ever all violence towards the persons of women, but *quantos motos scies, reclamante ratione, Priape* ["You shall know how many motions, despite reason's loud disapprobation, O Priapus"]. In the first year of King Richard's reign, and about the 16th of his age, this villany of rape was so increased and women so little offended with the injury or so ashamed to confess the outrage that a new law was made to punish women which consented to their ravishers, *ut sequitur* [as follows]: against ravishers of ladies and daughters of noblemen and other women in every part of the realm nowadays more violently offending and oftener than was wont, it is ordained that wheresoever and whensoever such ladies, daughters, or other women be ravished and after rape do consent to such ravishers, that as well the ravishers as they which be ravished be from henceforth disabled to have or challenge heritage, dower, or joint feoffement after the death of their husbands and ancestors. . . . And that the husbands of such women, if they have husbands, or if they have no husband living, the father or other next of the blood have from henceforth the suit to pursue against the offenders and ravishers in this behalf, and to have them thereof convict[ed] of life and member, though the woman after such rape do consent to the ravisher. . . .

This is a shrewd statute. Till this time, he that had ravished a woman might hope for a clemency, at the least at her hands, because he had ventured his life for her sake, but what shall lusty lechers now do? The more a woman is worthy to be won, because she hath or shall have wherewith to keep a man, the more danger it is to meddle with her. . . .

100. The Statute of Westminster the Second (1285), Chapter 35.
101. Convicted.

Sect. xxvii. 3 H[enry] 7. Cap. 2[102]

But 3 Hen[ry] 7. Cap. 2 beginning with a better complaint against takers for lucre of maids, widows, or wives having substance of lands or goods, or being heirs apparent, which takers sometimes married them, and sometimes deflowered them, to the breach of God's law and the king's, the disparagement of such women, and utter heaviness and discomfort of their friends ordaineth that whosoever taketh against her will unlawfully any maid, widow, or wife, shall together with the procurers, abetters, and receivers of any such woman (knowing her to be so taken against her will), be felons and every of them been reputed and judged as felons principal. But this extendeth not to taking where a woman is claimed as a ward or bondwoman. . . .

Sect. xxviii. 4 & 5 Phi[lip] & Mar[y] Cap. 8[103]

Therefore to supply what hitherto was wanting against takers and also enticers, ravishing by allurements, and flatterers, 4 & 5 Phil[lip] and Mar[y], Cap. 8 saith that for want of sufficient law . . . maidens and women, children of noble men, gentlemen, and others, which were heirs apparent, or had lands in great substance left by their ancestors or friends, by flattery, trifling gifts, or fair promises of light persons, and also by subtlety of such as bought and sold them for reward, were many times allured to contract matrimony with unthrifty persons and thereupon oftentimes with sleight or force were taken from their parents, friends, or kinfolk, to the high displeasure of God, the disparagement of the children, and perpetual condolence of their friends. Therefore it is ordained that it shall not be lawful to convey any maid or woman child, unmarried or under the age of sixteen years, out of the possession and against the will of her father or of such person to whom by his will or otherwise in his lifetime he shall have appointed the keeping, education, and governance of her. . . . And if any person that is above the age of fourteen years shall convey or cause to be conveyed any such maid being within the age of sixteen years out of the possession and against the will of the father or mother or any other person which then shall have by lawful means the order, keeping, education, or governance of her, the offender duly attainted or convicted (other than such, of whom she shall hold by knight's service) shall suffer two years

---

102. "The penalty of carrying a woman away against her will" (*Statutes at Large*, vol. 2, p. 69).

103. "An act for the punishment of such as shall take away maidens that be inheritors being within the age of 16 years, or that marry them without consent of their parents" (*Statutes at Large*, vol. 2, p. 515).

imprisonment without bail or mainprize,[104] or pay such fine as shall be assessed by the Queen's Council in the Starchamber.

And if any shall take away and deflower any such maid or woman child, or shall against the will of her father or he not knowing (if the father be in life) or without the assent or knowledge of the mother having custody and governance of the child, the father being dead, by letters, messages, or otherwise, contract matrimony with any such maid (except it be by the consent of the person or persons by interest of wardship entitled to have the marriage) he shall suffer (being lawfully convicted) five years imprisonment without bail or mainprize, and pay such fine as shall be assessed in the Starchamber etc., the one moiety of all which fines shall be to the Queen and her successors and the other to the grieved. . . . Moreover, if any woman-child or maiden, being above the age of twelve years and under sixteen do at any time consent to such person as shall make contract of matrimony contrary to the form of this statute, the next of kin to whom the inheritance should come after her death shall from time of such assent have and enjoy all such lands, tenements, and hereditaments as she had in possession, reversion, or remainder at the time of assent, during the life of such person so contracting matrimony, and after her decease so contracting, etc. then the said lands shall descend, revert, remain, and come to such person or persons (other than to him that shall so contract matrimony) as they should have done in case this statute hath never been made.[105] [Pp. 387–400 omitted.]

Sect. xxxviii. The Statute 18 Eliz[abeth]. Cap. 7[106]

I am at the end of my voyage, but before I take shore, I will shew you how our late most excellent lawgiver, renowned Queen Elizabeth (whose vigilent care hath always been that all her people might live under her in peace and without oppression) hath given strength and perfection to the former functions of other princes to make them a firm bulwark against all manner of injurers that possibly might oppress women, and I can but marvel that when so damnable a crime as rape had given so often to the whole realm such cause of bitter complaint and men in sundry ages had beaten their brains so carefully in finding out remedy against it, how it was possible, so long space together to leave such a privilege to him that could read the

104. Surety.

105. The example that follows makes it clear that this statute does not prohibit the children of such a marriage from inheriting from their mother. It does prohibit either the mother or father from benefiting from her inheritance.

106. "An act to take away clergy from the offenders in rape or burglary" (*Statutes at Large*, vol. 2, p. 615).

blessed psalm of Miserere, etc.,[107] that though he had ravished the fairest lady in the land, he might almost go away without touch of breast for it. Therefore the eighteenth of Queen Elizabeth, for repressing of felonious rapes and ravishments of women and of felonious burglaries, it was enacted that they which were found guilty by verdict, or by confession, or outlawed of or for such felonious rapes or burglary, they should suffer death and forfeit as in cases of felony had been used by the laws of the realm, without allowance of privilege, or benefit of clergy. Further, that they which were in other cases to have benefit of clergy should immediately after burning in the hand, according to the statute in that case provided, be forthwith enlarged by the justices and not be delivered to the ordinary.[108] But yet that the justices before whom the clergy shall be allowed may detain such persons in prison for correction as long as they shall think convenient, so it be not above a year. Then because in the fourteenth year of her majesty's reign . . . in the case of a Scot which had ravished a girl being not past seven years old, the justices were in doubt whether rape could be of a child of such tender years, not yet nine years old, and therefore they went not to judgment of the Scot, though by evidence of diverse matrons he seemed guilty. This statute ordaineth that if any person unlawfully and carnally know and abuse any woman child under age of ten years, every such unlawful and carnal knowledge shall be felony, and the offender being duly convicted shall suffer as a felon, without allowance of clergy. . . .

Sect. xl. The conclusion

Thus have I sailed betwixt the capes of Magna Charta and Quadragesima of Queen Elizabeth, collected the statutes principally belonging to women. . . . They to whom my travels are chiefly addressed are women, so many as bear the title of honest women, how good and virtuous soever they be. . . .

107. Men accused of certain crimes could plead benefit of clergy by reading the psalm "Miserere mei" ("Have mercy on me"), and thereby escape punishment.

108. As used in ecclesiastical or common law, one who has, of his own right and not by deputation, immediate jurisdiction in ecclesiastical cases, as the archbishop in a province, or the bishop or bishop's deputy in a diocese.

PART II

Humanist Traditions

ERASMUS

A Right Fruitful Epistle . . . in Laud and Praise of Matrimony
1518, trans. Richard Taverner, London [1536?] and
Defense of His Declamation in Praise of Marriage
1519, trans. David Sider, 1991

Introduction

Richard Taverner's translation of Erasmus's *Encomium Matrimonii* was published about 1536,[1] some eighteen years after Erasmus first published it, in 1518, in Latin along with three other pieces. The timing of its publication in English is important because Henry VIII, by 1536, had divorced himself from Catherine and separated the English Church from the Roman Catholic Church. (Henry had been declared "Supreme Head" of the Church of England "as far as the laws of Christ allow" in 1530, was divorced from Catherine in 1532, and in 1534 signed the acts of Succession and Supremacy, by which his daughter Mary was declared a bastard and he was made unconditional head of the Church of England.) That Taverner dedicated his translation to Thomas Cromwell is significant, because Cromwell was counselor to Henry and was instrumental in Henry's efforts from 1536 onwards to dissolve the monasteries and eradicate their cloistered, celibate religious orders. Taverner appears to have seen Erasmus's *Praise of Matrimony* as a tract which would forward the cause of the nascent protestant church in England, and he singles out Erasmus's opposition to the celibacy

of the clergy for special mention in his dedication to Cromwell: "he considered the blind superstition of men and women, which cease not day by
day to profess and vow perpetual chastity before or they sufficiently know
themselves and the infirmity of their nature. Which thing (in my opinion)
hath been and is yet unto this day the root and very cause original of
innumerable mischiefs" (Sig. Aii).

Taverner's translation was faithful to its Latin original. That is, it did
not stretch Erasmus's deliberately ambiguous language to suit the new
protestantism as the French translation of Louis de Berquin was thought,
perhaps wrongly, to have done.[2] Taverner was elliptical where Erasmus
was elliptical, unambiguous where Erasmus was unambiguous. Indeed
many of the awkwardnesses in Taverner's text appear to be the result of
a literal translation of Erasmus's Latin. This fidelity was less well maintained in the second English translation of the *Encomium Matrimonii,* by
Thomas Wilson, who published it as an example of the exhortation (actually
"an oration deliberative")[3] in his *Art of Rhetoric* in 1553. There, Erasmus's
Latin forms are explicitly Christianized ("all the devils," for instance, in
place of Erasmus's pagan "manes").

The *Encomium Matrimonii* was constructed as an imaginary argument
against a young man who has dedicated himself to celibacy. In it Erasmus
sets himself to convince the young man that he should abandon virginity,
marry the girl his friends have found for him, and raise a family. The epistle
begins by suggesting that matrimony is the holiest of all the sacraments
because it was instituted by God in Paradise and because it follows God's
command to increase and multiply. Erasmus goes on to argue that although
Christ praised marriage in the first of his miracles, nowhere did he suggest
that celibacy is a virtue. If all men were to remain virgin, who would people
the earth? asks Erasmus. Why was woman created if not to be a companion
to man and to give him children? Erasmus sums up his argument thus:
"Wherefore, if the sense of nature, if honesty, if natural affection, if devotion, if gentleness, if virtue anything move you, why abhor you from that
which God ordaineth, nature enacteth, reason enticeth, the Scriptures both
of God and man praise, the laws command, the whole consent of all nations
approve, to which the ensample of every good man provoketh?"

In 1523, Erasmus said that he wrote his *Encomium Matrimonii* about
twenty years before its 1518 publication as an exercise in the style of a
"persuasive" declamation—like his *Praise of Folly*—in order to amuse himself and give pleasure to his English pupil, William Blount, Lord Mountjoy.
But, as Margolin points out,[4] Erasmus seems to have composed his *Encomium Matrimonii* before he met Mountjoy; certainly he makes no mention
of Mountjoy in his text. Erasmus may have made light of the genesis of
his *Encomium Matrimonii* in order to deflect the charge of heresy leveled

against it soon after its first publication, a charge which Erasmus was never able to put to rest.

Catholic theologians called Erasmus's treatise heretical mainly because it elevated marriage above celibacy. Erasmus ranked the sacrament of marriage above celibacy because he believed it took precedence: "Now Sir, if the other sacraments of Christ's church be had in great veneration, who seeth not that much worship ought to be given to this, which was both ordained of God, and first of all other? And the other [sacraments] in earth, this in Paradise, the other for remedy [of sin], this for solace, the other were put to in help of nature, which was fallen, only this was given to nature at the first creation." Accordingly, Erasmus claimed that the holiest manner of life was not the cloistered life of monks and nuns, but rather the secular life of married men and women: "Let the swarms of monks, friars, canons, and nuns avaunce their profession as much as them lust. Let them boast as much as they will their ceremonies and disguised coats (whereby they be chiefly known from the temporal); surely the most holy kind of life is wedlock purely and chastely kept." At the same time, Erasmus contradicted many of the church fathers who claimed that sexual union was sinful in itself, indeed a cause and the result of sin. Erasmus's arguments in favor of the naturalness of sexual union follow from his arguments in favor of the holiness and primacy of marriage. The natural act of sexual union, Erasmus suggests, must also have been sanctified by God in Paradise before the Fall: "Nor I hear not him which will say unto me that the foul itching and pricks of carnal lust have come not of nature, but of sin. What is more unlike the truth? As though matrimony (whose office cannot be executed without these pricks) was not before sin. . . . Wonder it is, if not of nature. And as touching the foulness, surely we make that by our imagination to be foul, which of the self nature is fair and holy."

On account of statements like these, churchmen accused Erasmus of heresy—a crime that was punishable by death. In 1519, the vice-chancellor of the University of Louvain, Jan Briart d'Ath, suggested indirectly that Erasmus was guilty of heresy when he elevated marriage above celibacy. In his *Defense of His Declamation in Praise of Marriage,* Erasmus defended himself by saying first, that his work was the product of his youth; second, that it was only a rhetorical exercise meant to instruct pupils in the proper way to compose a "declamation"; and third, that he was not writing generally about marriage but rather attempting to persuade only one particular young man to marry in order to preserve his lineage—although his identification of the young man is by no means clear.[5] In order to clinch his argument, Erasmus said he had included in his as-yet-unpublished *De Conscribendis Epistolis* (*On the Writing of Letters*) not only his praise of marriage but also the short outline of a dispraise of marriage. That Erasmus continued to take pains to deflect the charge of heresy, however, may be evident from the subsequent publishing history of the *Encomium Matrimonii*.[6] In 1521, a truncated version of the text appeared as an example of a letter of persuasion in an abbreviated and apparently early version of the *De Conscribendis Epistolis* printed without Erasmus's permission by John Siberch in Cambridge.[7] Siberch entitled this work *Libellus de Conscribendis Epistolis* (*The Little Book on the Writing of Letters*). The following year, 1522, Erasmus brought out a significantly revised and enlarged version of his *De Conscribendis Epistolis*. There, in the short outline of arguments against marriage, Erasmus appears to have added at least one sentence praising virginity ("What true worth and what happiness in virginity!"),[8] which supports the notion that he felt it necessary to continue to counter accusations of heresy levied against him. But the brevity and the offhand nature of the section disparaging marriage lend credence to Fantazzi's suggestion that the "recantation" in the *De Conscribendis Epistolis* can only be called "supposed" and its arguments "specious."[9]

Theologians at the Sorbonne continued to levy charges of heresy against Erasmus and his French translator, Berquin, who was burned as a heretic in 1529. That Luther, a monk, married a nun in 1526 exacerbated their suspicions of Erasmus. But Erasmus did not then retract any part of his argument in favor of marriage or any part of his argument against the clergy; nor did he ever do so. Afterwards, Erasmus went on to write yet more works praising marriage and to defend his position in much the same way as in his *Encomium Matrimonii*. The most important of these works were various colloquies, for instance, "Coniugium," "A Merry Dialogue, declaring the Properties of Shrewd Wives and Honest Wives," "The Wooer and the Maiden," and, in 1526, his *Institutio Christiani Matrimonii* (*Institution of Christian Marriage*), dedicated to Catherine of Aragon. This last was translated into English by Nicholas Leigh in 1568 as *A Modest Mean to Marriage* and considerably broadened the scope of the debate. Erasmus also wrote a piece on divorce, "Whether divorce between man and wife standeth with the law of God," and published it in his *Annotationes in Novum Testamentum*. It was translated into English in 1550. As late as 1532 Erasmus was forced once more to defend his *Encomium Matrimonii* (in the *Dilutio eorum quae Iodocus Clichtoveus scripsit adversus declamationem Des. Erasmi Roterodami suasoriam matrimonii* [*A refutation of those things which Josse Clichtove wrote against the declamation of Des. Erasmus in praise of matrimony*]). Here too Erasmus argued for the merely rhetorical form of his *Encomium Matrimonii* and retracted nothing of its substance.

The *Praise of Marriage* is central to Erasmus's Christian humanism and, despite his arguments about the innocence of the rhetoric, it also became central to reformist groups in Europe and in England. That it was eagerly and widely read is obvious from the number of reprints, new editions, and translations; it went through thirteen editions in Latin up to 1540; it was translated into French, German, and English, and paraphrased in Spanish. After 1522, the version of the *Encomium Matrimonii* included in *De Conscribendis Epistolis* reached even more readers. Sowards, following F. Vander Haeghen in the *Bibliotheca Erasmiana*, notes that twenty-eight editions of *De Conscribendis Epistolis* were printed in Erasmus's lifetime and that sixty additional editions were published before the end of the sixteenth century; Margolin believed that the actual number of editions was larger yet.[10]

Taverner's English translation has not been reprinted since the sixteenth century, although Wilson's translation has been included in modern editions of the *Art of Rhetoric*. Erasmus's first defense of the *Encomium Matrimonii* has not, to my knowledge, been translated from the Latin to the English until Professor David Sider, Department of Classics, Fordham University, made his translation for inclusion in this anthology. Professor Sider's translation is based on the Latin text of the *Apologia Pro Declamatione Matrimonii*, in Desiderii Erasmi, *Opera Omnia,* cura et impensis Petri Vander Aa, Tomus Nonus (Lugduni Batavorum [Leyden], 1706), pp. 106–11. Erasmus's *In Laud and Praise of Matrimony* and his *Defense of His Declamation in Praise of Marriage* have both been reprinted in their entirety.

NOTES

1. I am following the dating which was revised from [1530?] (*STC,* 1926) to [1536?] in *A Short-Title Catalogue of Books Printed in England, Scotland, and Ireland . . . 1475–1640,* first compiled by A. W. Pollard and G. R. Redgrave (2d ed., rev. and enlarged, begun by W. A. Jackson and F. S. Ferguson, completed by Katherine F. Pantzer, vol. 1 [London: Bibliographical Society, 1986]).

2. See *Encomium Matrimonii,* ed. J.-C. Margolin, in *Opera Omnia Desiderii Erasmi Roterodami,* Ordinis Primi, Tomus Quintus (Amsterdam: North-Holland Publishing Company, 1975), pp. 355–57. I am indebted to Margolin for much of the information contained in this introduction.

3. See Thomas Wilson, *Art of Rhetoric,* ed. Thomas J. Derrick (New York: Garland Publishing, 1982), p. 76.

4. *Encomium Matrimonii,* pp. 337–38.

5. In a private letter to Thomas More in 1520, Erasmus was far more open about his praise of marriage: "I have praised marriage so highly in my published treatise that theologians have regarded my excessive tribute to marriage as an error smacking of heresy." See *Erasmus and His Age: Selected Letters of Desiderius Erasmus,* ed. Hans J. Hillerbrand, trans. Marcus A. Haworth, S.J. (New York: Harper and Row, 1970), pp. 154–55.

6. Even the early publishing history of the *Encomium Matrimonii* is complex. It was published originally by Dirk Martens in March, 1518, as one of four

declamations under the general title *Declamationes Aliquot*. On the title page it is called simply *Exhortatoria ad Matrimonium* (*Encouragements toward Marriage*). See *Encomium Matrimonii*, pp. 334–35. Another edition printed by Nicholas Caesar appeared in May, 1518, and a third was published by Froben in August, 1518, under the title *Encomium Matrimonii*. See the notes to page 129 of the *De Conscribendis Epistolis*, which appears in volume 25 of the *Collected Works of Erasmus* (ed. J. K. Sowards, trans. and annotated by Charles Fantazzi, notes printed in vol. 26 [Toronto: University of Toronto Press, 1985], pp. 528–29).

7. Sowards, "Introduction" to *De Conscribendis Epistolis* (*Collected Works*, vol. 25, pp. li–lii). Fantazzi, in his note to page 129 of volume 25, follows Margolin's suggestion that Siberch's edition represents a version written by Erasmus in 1498–99 (vol. 26, p. 529).

8. *De Conscribendis Epistolis*, ed. Sowards, *Collected Works*, vol 25, p. 147. I am indebted to Professor N. Frederick Nash, Curator of Rare Books, Rare Book and Special Collections Library, University of Illinois at Urbana-Champaign, for assistance in translating sections of the *Libellus*.

9. Fantazzi's note to page 129 of *De Conscribendis Epistolis*, volume 25 of *Collected Works* (vol. 26, p. 529).

10. See Sowards's "Introduction" to *De Conscribendis Epistolis* (*Collected Works*, vol. 25, pp. li–lii).

A Right Fruitful Epistle . . . in Laud and Praise of Matrimony[1]

The Preface

To the right honorable Master Cromwell, one of the king's most honorable council, his humble servant, Richard Taverner sendeth greeting.

Our daily orator (most honorable sir), pondering with himself your gratuite[2] bounty towards him, began busily to revolve in mind how he, again on his part, might somewhat declare his fervent zeal of heart towards you. Which he thus revolving, lo, suddenly (as God wolde) a certain Epistle of Doctor Erasmus, devised in commendation of wedlock, offered it self unto his

1. The full title reads as follows: "A Right Fruitful Epistle devised by the most excellent clerk, Erasmus, in laud and praise of matrimony. Translated into English by Richard Taverner, which translation he hath dedicate[d] to the right honorable Master Thomas Cromwell, most worthy counselor to our sovereign lord, King Henry the eight."

2. Gratuitous, freely bestowed. In 1536, Cromwell made Taverner Clerk of the Privy Seal.

sight. Which so soon as he began to read, he thought it a thing full necessary and expedient to translate it into our vulgar tongue, and so under your noble protection to communicate it to the people, namely when he considered the blind superstition of men and women which cease not[3] day by day to profess and vow perpetual chastity before or they sufficiently know themselves and the infirmity of their nature. Which thing (in my opinion) hath been and is yet unto this day the root and very cause original of innumerable mischiefs. I pray our lord Jesu of his infinite goodness to provide some speedy reformation,[4] when it shall be his pleasure. In the mean season, please it your goodness (right honorable sir) to accept this rude and simple translation of your servant, and ye so doing shall not a little encourage him to greater things in time coming. And thus Christ have you always in his keeping. Amen.

Although, sweet cousin, ye be wise enough of yourself, nor need not other men's counsel, yet for the old friendship continued from our childhood betwixt us, and also for your kindness towards me, and finally because of the straight alliance betwixt us, I thought it my duty (if I would be the man whom ye always have take[n] me for, that is to say, your friend and lover) of such things as I judged to belong most to the preservation and dignity of you and yours, gladly and freely to advertise[5] you. Other men's profit sometime we espy better than our own. I have often followed your counsel, which I have found no less profitable than friendly. Now if ye again will follow mine, I trust it shall repent neither me of my counselling nor you of your following. Our friend, Antony Bald[6] supped with me the last night, one that is (as ye know well enough) your great friend and near kinsman—an heavy fest[7] and full of tears. He shewed me (which was a great sorrow to us both) that the good gentlewoman, your mother, is departed,[8] that your sister for sorrow and desire is entered into a house of barren nuns,[9] that the hope of your stock is turned only unto you, that

3. Taverner uses the obsolete form "nat" throughout. I have regularized it to "not."
4. The "reformation" Taverner looks to may well be the dissolution of the monasteries, undertaken mainly by Cromwell from 1536 onwards.
5. Advise.
6. Probably a fictive name.
7. Feast.
8. Departed this life.
9. Margolin makes the point that Erasmus not only argues for marriage in this tract, but argues against celibacy of the clergy (*Opera Omnia, Desiderii Erasmi Roterodami, Encomium Matrimonii*, ed. J.-C. Margolin, Ordinis Primi, Tomus Quintus [Amsterdam: North-Holland Publishing Company, 1975], p. 387, ll. 17–18). I am indebted to M.

your friends with whole assent have offered you a wife of great substance,[10] of noble blood, of excellent beauty, of gentle manners, and finally which beareth great love towards you. That ye yet, this notwithstanding, for some immoderate sorrow, or else some superstitious holiness, have so determined to live a chaste life and never to marry, that neither[11] for the care of your stock, nor love of issue, nor for any requests, prayers, or tears of your friends ye can be plucked away from your purpose. But ye by mine advice shall change this mind, and leaving bachelorship, a form of living both barren and unnatural, shall give yourself to most holy wedlock. In which matter I covet that neither the love of your friends which else ought to overcome your mind, nor mine authority anything should aid my cause, if I shew not that by clear reasons that this shall be for you both most honest, most profitable, and most pleasant. Yet what will ye say if (as this time require)[12] also most necessary?

For, first of all, if the regard of honesty moveth you, which with good men is highly considered, what thing is more honest than matrimony, whereunto Christ himself did great honor and worship, which vouchsafed not only to be present with his mother at the marriages[13] but also consecrated the marriage [it]self with the first fruits of his miracles? What is more holy than that which the creator of all things hath ordained, coupled, sanctified? which Dame Nature herself hath enacted? What is more laudable than it, which who reprehendeth, is condemnable of heresy?[14] So honorable is matrimony, as is the name of heretic slanderous. What is a thing of more equity, than to render that to the posterity which we ourselves received of our ancestry? What act on the contrary side is done with less consideration, then under the zeal of holiness to flee that, as unholy and ungodly, which God, the well and father of all holiness, would have counted most holy? What thing is farther[15] from all humanity, then man to abhor from[16] the

---

Margolin for many classical and biblical references. I have also consulted the text and notes to the version of the *Encomium Matrimonii* found as an "example of a letter of persuasion" in *De Conscribendis Epistolis*, ed. J. K. Sowards, trans. and annotated by Charles Fantazzi (*Collected Works*, vol. 25, pp. 129–48; vol. 26, pp. 528–34).

10. Wealth.

11. Taverner uses the obsolete form "nouther" throughout. I have regularized it.

12. The sense of "require" here is "seek to learn," or ask about.

13. The marriage at Cana, where Christ worked his first miracle by changing water into wine (John 2:1–12).

14. Because marriage was ordained by God in Eden, to condemn it is to commit heresy.

15. Here and occasionally elsewhere, Taverner uses the obsolete form "farder," which I have regularized.

16. To shrink from.

laws of man's estate?[17] What is a more unkind act than to deny that to our youngsters[18] which if ye took not of your elders, ye could not be he that might deny? Now if we require the Author of matrimony, it was founded and ordained not of Lycurgus, not of Moses, not of Solon,[19] but of the high and mighty worker of all things, of Him it was also praised, enhonested,[20] and consecrate[d]. For at the beginning when He had made man of the slime of the earth, he thought that his life should be utterly miserable and unpleasant, if he joined not Eve, a companion, unto him. Wherefore He brought forth the wife not of the earth, as he did man, but out of the ribs of Adam, whereby it is to be understood that nothing ought to be more dear to us than the wife, nothing more conjoined, nothing more fast glued unto us. The self same God after the flood, when he was at one again with mankind, enacted (as we read in Scripture) this law first, not that we should love bachelorship, but to [in]crease, to multiply, to replenish the earth. But how could that be, unless men would give their labor to wedlock? And lest we should here find cavilations, alleging the liberty of the old law of Moses, or the necessity of that season, I pray you what meaneth that sentence repeated also in the new law of Christ, ratified and confirmed by Christ's own mouth? *For this cause* (saith he) *shall man leave father and mother and stick to his wife.*[21] What thing is more holy than the natural love of the child to his father? And yet the faith of wedlock is preferred above it. By whose authority? by God's. At what time? When not only the old law flourished, but also when the new law of Christ began to spring. The father is forsaken; the mother is forsaken; and the wife is sticked to.[22] The son (in the civil law) emancipate[d], that is to say enfranchised and out of his father's bonds, beginneth to be his own man and at liberty. The son, in the same law, abdicate, that is to say, forsaken and disinherited of his father, ceaseth to be his son. But only death undo wedlock, if yet that death undo it. Now Sir, if the other sacraments of Christ's church be had in great veneration, who seeth not that much worship ought to be given to this, which was both ordained of God, and first of all other? And the other [sacraments] in earth, this in Paradise, the other for remedy,[23] this for solace, the other were put to in help of nature, which was fallen, only this was given to nature at the first creation. If we count the laws holy

---

17. "Ab humanae conditionis legibus abhorrere": literally, "to shrink from the laws of the human condition," probably natural law.

18. Taverner normally uses the obsolete form "yongers," which I have regularized.

19. Biblical and classical lawgivers.

20. Made honest.

21. Mark 10:7.

22. Matt. 19:5.

23. Of sins.

which be institute[d] of men, shall not the law of wedlock be most holy which we have received of him of whom we have received life? and which began in manner even at one time with mankind? To be short, because he would confirm this law by some example, when he was a young man, and bidden (as said is) to the bridal, he came thither gladly with his mother, and not contended[24] with so doing, did also great honor to the feast with his wonderful work, making none otherwhere the prosperous commencement and beginning of his miracles?

Why then (ye will say) did Christ himself abstain from wedlock? As though there be not very many things in Christ which we ought rather to marvel at than follow. He was born without carnal father, he proceeded without pain of his mother,[25] he arose from death to live when the sepulcher was closed; what is not in him above nature? Let such things be appropriate to him. Let us (living within the law of nature) wonder and praise the things that be above nature, but follow those works that be[26] for our capacity. But he would be born of a virgin. Truth it is, of a virgin, but yet wedded. A virgin to his mother became him that was God, but that she was wedded, she signified unto us what we ought to do. Virginity became her which, (by the divine inspiration of the Holy Ghost) being pure and immaculate, brought forth him which was most pure and unspotted; but yet Joseph was her husband, which thing setteth forth unto us the commendation of the laws of wedlock.[27] How could he more commend wedlock, than when he, willing to declare the privy and wonderful conjunction of the divine nature with the human body and soul, and willing to declare his ineffable and eternal love toward his church (that is to say, the company of Christian people), calleth himself the bridegroom and the church his spouse? *Great* (saith Paul) *is the mystery of matrimony: in Christ and in the church.*[28] If there had been any couple in earth more holy, if there had be[en] any bond of love and concord more religiously to be kept than wedlock, undoubtedly he had fetched his similitude from thence. What like thing do ye ever read in all Scripture of bachelorship? *Honorable wedlock and the immaculate bride* both [? illegible] is spoken of.[29] Bachelorship is not once named. Now, Sir, Moses' law abhoreth barren wedlock, and therefore we read that some were put out of the communality for the same

24. Contented.

25. Mary bore Christ without pain.

26. Be ordained.

27. Erasmus seems to suggest that the marriage between Mary and Joseph was consummated, that Mary was a "chaste" wife. Vives, on the other hand, seems to suggest that Mary lived a virgin throughout her life.

28. Eph. 5:21–33.

29. Heb. 13:4.

cause. And why so? Surely because they, living unprofitably to the commonweal and for their own singular avail, did not multiply the people with any issue. If then the law damneth barren matrimony, much more it damneth bachelors. If the infirmity of nature escapeth not punishment, certes the froward will shall not eschape.[30] If they were punished whose nature failed to their will, what have they deserved, which will not so much as put to their good will, that they be not barren? The laws of the Hebrews gave this honor to matrimony, that he that married a new wife should not be compelled that year to go forth to the battle.[31] The city is in great jeopardy if there be not men of arms to defend it, but needs it must decay if there be not wedded men, by whom the youth continually sailing may be supplied. Also the laws of the Romans punished them that were bachelors in removing them from all promotions of the city.[32] But such as had increased with children the commonweal, to them they ordained a reward openly to be given as it were for their well deserving. The law of the three children is a sufficient proof for this matter.[33] For I will not here rehearse all the rest. Lycurgus made a law that they which married not wives, should in summer season be driven from the interludes[34] and other sights and in winter go about the market-place all naked and curse themselves, saying they suffered just punishment because they would not obey the laws.[35]

Now will ye know how much matrimony was set by in old time? Consider the punishment for the desoiling of it. The Greeks once thought it expedient to revenge the breech of matrimony by continual wars enduring the space of ten years.[36] Furthermore, by the laws, not only of the Romans but also of the Hebrews and other nations, adulterers should lose their lives.[37] The thief was delivered by paying four times so much as he had stolen; the sin of adultery was punished with the ax. Also among the Hebrews he was stoned to death with the people's hands which defiled that, without which the people should not be. And the rigor of their laws not contented therewith, suffered also that he which was found in adultery should be put to death without judgment, without laws, giving that liberty

30. Escape.

31. Deut. 20:5–7.

32. Plutarch, *Cato maior* 21. Fantazzi identifies the Roman laws as "the *lex Julia de maritandis ordinibus* (18 B.C.) and the *lex Papia Poppaea* (A.D. 9), both passed under the emperor Augustus," *De Conscribendis Epistolis, Collected Works*, vol. 26, p. 530.

33. Or *ius liberorum*, the right conferred on the woman who brought into the world three or four full-term children who were born living. Cf. Julius Paulus, *Sententiae* IV.9.1–2.

34. "Games," athletic and otherwise.

35. See Plutarch, *Lycurgus* 15; *Apophethegmata Laconica* 14.

36. Erasmus refers to the Trojan war.

37. Deut. 22:22.

to the grief of the wedded men, which unneath[38] is granted to him that in jeopardy of life defendeth himself. Doubtless wedlock must needs seem a right holy thing which defiled cannot be repurged without man's blood, and the revenging whereof is neither compelled to abide the laws nor the judge, the which severity and rigor of law is neither in murder nor in treason.

But what stand we all day in written laws? This is the law of nature not graven in tables of brass, but inwardly fixed in our hearts, which who will not obey, he is not so much as to be esteemed a man, much less a good citizen. For if (as the Stoics, men of sharp judgments do dispute)[39] to live well is nothing else but to follow the guide of nature, what thing is so agreeable to nature as matrimony? For nothing is so naturally given neither to men, nor yet to any other kind of brute beasts as that every one should preserve his kind from destruction and by propagation of posterity to make it as it were immortal, which without carnal copulation (as every man knoweth) cannot be brought to pass. And it seemeth a foul shame dumb beasts to obey the laws of nature, and men (after the manner of giants) to bid battle against nature, whose work if we will behold with eyes not dazzling, we shall perceive that her will is that there be in every kind of things a certain spice of wedlock. For I omit to speak of trees, in whom yet by the authority of Pliny, wedlock is found with so manifest diversity of the male and female, that if the male tree should not with his boughs lie upon the female trees that stand about him coveting as it were a meddling together, they should abide barren and fruitless.[40] I hold my peace of precious stones, in which the same author writeth (but not he alone) that there is found both male and female.[41] I pray you, hath not God so knit all things together with certain bonds, that one thing doth need another's help? What think ye to the heaven which turneth about with continual moving? I pray you, while it maketh the earth lying[42] underneath, which is mother of all, with sundry kind of things fruitful, pouring seed (as it were) upon it, doth it not the office of an husband? But to run through each thing were overlong. Now, to what purpose have we spoken this? Surely, that ye may understand by such natural commixtions, everything to have his being and continuance, without which all things to be dissolved, to perish and to fall away.

It is feigned by the old and wise poets[43] (whose study was to cover the precepts of philosophy under mystical fables) that giants, the sons of the

38. With difficulty, hardly.
39. Argue for.
40. Pliny, *Natural History* XIII.13.
41. Pliny, *Natural History* XXXVI.25.
42. Taverner uses the obsolete "leying."
43. Homer, Hesiod, Pindar, Virgil, Ovid, among others. Cf. Ovid, *Metamorphoses* I.184.

earth, having feet like serpents, did cast mountains upon mountains that reached unto heaven, and so standing upon them, warred against the gods. What signifieth this fable? Surely that certain ungodly persons, wild and of an ungentle nature, did greatly abhor from matrimonial concord, and therefore they were cast down headlong with Jupiter's thunderbolt, that is to say, they utterly decayed and came to nought, sith they eschewed the thing whereby mankind is only preserved. But the selfsame poets have feigned that Orpheus being a poet and a minstrel did move with the sweet note of his musical instrument the hard rocks of stone. What meaned they hereby? Nothing else, but that a wise and an eloquent man did first prohibit the stony men and which lived after the manner of wild beasts from lying at large and brought them to the holy laws of matrimony. Wherefore it appeareth evidently that whosoever is not touched with desire of wedlock seemeth to be no man, but a stone, an enemy to nature, a rebel to God, by his own folly seeking his decay and undoing.

But go to, sith we be fallen into fables nothing fabulous nor vain, the same Orpheus when he descended down to hell and there moved Pluto, lord of hell, and the souls there abiding on such wise that he might easily lead away with him Euridice his wife, what other thing suppose we that the poets thought, than that they would commend unto us the love of wedlock, which also in hell is counted holy and religious? Hereunto also belongeth, that the antiquity made Jupiter lord of wedlock, and named him for the same purpose Gamelius and made Juno the lady of women in childbed, calling her *pronuba* and *Lucina*,[44] superstitiously erring (I grant well) in the names of the gods, but not erring in this, that they judged matrimony a thing holy and worthy to be regarded of the gods.

Surely there have been diverse laws, ceremonies, and usages among diverse peoples and nations. But there was never nation so barbarous, so far from all humanity, with whom the name of wedlock hath not be[en] recounted holy, hath not be[en] recounted worshipful. This the Thracian, this the Sarmate, this the man of Inde, this the Greek, this the Italian, this the Britain furthest of all the world,[45] or if there be any further than they, have had in high reverence. And why so? For of necessity that thing must needs be common, which the common parent of all hath imprinted, and so inwardly imprinted, that the sense and feeling of it hath not only pierced the turtles[46] and the doves, but also the most cruel wild beasts.

---

44. *Pronuba* refers to Juno's function as the goddess of marriage; *Lucina* refers to her role as goddess of childbirth.

45. If Jerusalem is taken to be the center of the world, as it often was, then Britain is a country far from that center. But Erasmus may also be indulging in a joke aimed at William Blount, Lord Mountjoy, his English pupil and friend.

46. Turtledoves, emblems of undying love.

For the lions be gentle and meek to their lionesses. The tigers fight for
their whelps. The asses stick not to run through fires lying in their way
for the safeguard and defense of their foals.[47] And this they call the law
of nature, which as it is most strong, so it is most large.[48] Wherefore like
as he is no diligent husband which contented with the things present,
tendeth full curiously the trees ready grown, but hath little regard either
of setting or of grafting, because that of necessity within few years those
orchards (be they never so well kept) must decay and become desolate.
So in like wise he is to be judged an undiligent citizen in the public weal
which contented with the company present, hath no respect nor consideration to supply new in place of the old. No man therefore have been
counted a noble and worthy citizen which hath not bestowed his diligence
in begetting children and bringing them virtuously up.

Among the Hebrews and Persians he was most highly commended that
had most plenty of wives, as though the country were most bound to him,
that with most children had enriched it. Do ye study to be more holy than
was Abraham? He should never have been called *pater multarum gentium,*
that is to say, the father of many peoples and that of God's own mouth,[49]
if he had fled the company of his wife. Do ye labor to be reputed more
religious than Jacob? He sticked not[50] to buy his wife, Rachel, with so long
apprenticehood and bondage. Be ye wiser than Solomon? But what a flock
of wives kept he at home? Be ye chaster than Socrates? which suffered at
home in his house Zantippe, that wayward woman, not only (as he was
wont to jest himself) because he might learn patience at home, but because
he would seem not to halt in the offices of nature. For he, a man (whom
the divine answer of Apollo only judged wise)[51] understood full well, that
under this law and condition he was begotten, to this he was born, this he
did owe to nature. For if it have been well said of the old philosophers, if
it have been not without cause confirmed of our divines, if it have been
rightly everywhere pronounced as a proverb, that *God not nature have made
no thing frustrate nor in vain,* why (I pray you) hath God given us these
members? why these pricks and provocations? why hath He added the
power of begetting, if bachelorship be taken for a praise? If one would
give you a precious gift, as a bow, a garment, or a sword, ye should seem
unworthy the thing that ye have received if either ye would not or ye could
not use it. Whereas all other things be ordained by nature with most high

47. Pliny, *Natural History* VIII.16, 19, 25, 68.
48. Bountiful, open-handed, extensive, widespread.
49. Gen. 12:2–3.
50. He did not hesitate; he was not reluctant.
51. Plato, *Apology* 21A.

reason, it is not likely that she slumbered and slept in making only this privy member. Nor I hear not him which will say unto me that the foul itching and pricks of carnal lust have come not of nature, but of sin. What is more unlike the truth? As though matrimony (whose office can not be executed without these pricks) was not before sin. Moreover in other beasts, I pray you, from whence cometh those pricks and provocations? of nature or of sin? Wonder it is, if not of nature. And as touching the foulness, surely we make that by our imagination to be foul, which of the self nature is fair and holy. Else, if we would weigh the thing not by the opinion of the people, but by the very nature, how is it less foul (after the manner of wild beasts) to eat, to chew, to digest, to empty the belly, than to use the lawful and permitted pleasure of the body? But virtue (ye say) is to be obeyed rather than nature. As though that is to be called virtue which repugneth[52] with nature, from whence, if virtue have that his first beginning, certes it can not be it, which may with exercise and learning be made perfect.

But the apostles' life delighteth you, for they also followed bachelorship, and exhorted other to the same. Letteth apostolical then follow the apostles, which (because their office is to teach and instruct the people) cannot both satisfy their flock and their wives, if they should have any. Howbeit that the apostles also had wives, it is evidently clear. Let us graunt bachelorship to the bishops. [Why][53] do ye follow the apostles' form of living, being so far from the office of an apostle, sith ye be a man both temporal and also without office? It is licensed them to be without wives, to the intent they may the better attend to beget the more children to Christ. Let this be the privilege of priests and religious men which (as it appear) have succeeded the Essenes'[54] form of living, which damned holy matrimony. Your estate requireth otherwise. But Christ himself (ye will say) have pronounced them *blessed which have gelded themselves for the kingdom of God.*[55] I reject not the authority, but I will expound Christ's meaning. First of all, I think this saying of Christ to appertain especially to those times when it was expedient to be most ready and loose from all worldly businesses. Then was the time that they should flee and run hither and thither through all lands; the persecutor was at hand on every side. But now, such is the state of things and times that no where ye may find the pureness and perfection of manners less spotted and contaminate[d] than among wedded persons. Let the swarms of monks, friars, canons, and nuns avaunce[56] their

52. Literally "fights back"; opposes.
53. Illegible—"why" conjectured from the Latin, *quid.*
54. One of the three principal sects of the Jews at the time of Jesus.
55. Matt. 19:12.
56. Boast of. A puzzling translation on Taverner's part of the Latin *miror* 'to admire, revere'.

profession as much as them lust. Let them boast as much as they will their ceremonies and disguised coats (whereby they be chiefly known from the temporal); surely the most holy kind of life is wedlock purely and chastely kept. Furthermore not he only geldeth himself which liveth without a wife, but he which chastely and holily doth the office of wedlock. And would God they were truly chaste, so many as cloak their vices under the glorious title of chastity and castration, which under the shadow of chastity do more fouly rage in filthy and beastly abomination. For I am ashamed, so help me God, here to reckon up into what shameful abominations they ofttimes fall, which do thus repugn against nature. To be short, Christ never commanded bachelorship to none earthly person, but he openly forbiddeth divorcement. Surely me think, he should be not the worst counselor for the commonweal (considering the fashions and manners of men) which would grant also the priests and religious persons license to marry, namely sith there is everywhere so great a multitude of priests, of which (alas) how few live a chaste life? How much better were it to turn their concubines into wives, so that those whom they have now with great infamy and with an unquiet conscience, they might then have openly with an honest fame, and beget children whom they may love as truly legitimate, and bring them godly up, so that neither the father shall be ashamed of them, nor they of their father. And this (I trow) the officials[57] of bishops should have procured long ago, but that greater gains arise by the concubines than should by the wives.

But virginity (ye will say) is a divine thing, an angelical thing. Truth it is, but, on the contrary side, wedlock is an human thing. I now speak to a man, being myself a man. A commendable thing, certes, is virginity, but yet so that this praise be not transferred to over many, which commendation if every man commonly will begin to usurp, what can be said or thought more hurtful and more pynious[58] than virginity? Moreover, though in other men virginity should most of all deserve praise, yet surely in you it can not lack blame, in whom it now standeth to preserve your noble stock, worthy of an immortal continuance. Finally, he is but a very little off from the praise of virginity, which keepth purely the law of wedlock and which hath a wife to the intent to beget children and not to satisfy his wanton lust. If the brother, in the law of Moses, be commanded to raise the seed of his brother which died without issue,[59] will ye suffer the hope of your whole lineage to be utterly extinct, namely sith it is returned to you only? Nor I am not so ignorant but that I know well enough that the praises of

57. Decrees.
58. Pernicious?
59. Deut. 25:5–10.

virginity have been rehearsed and celebrate[d] with great volumes of some of our old fathers.[60] Among whom Jerome so advanceth it, that in manner he despiseth wedlock and was provoked of the bishops that were of the true opinion to recant and sing a new song. But let this heat be granted to those times. Now I would with those that thus everywhere without discretion do exhort the youth (not yet known to themselves) to bachelorship and virginity, to bestow their labor in describing the form of chaste and pure matrimony.

But yet they which are so well pleased with virginity be not displeased with the wars against the Turks which pass us so far in number, whose judgment, if it be right, it shall follow that it be chiefly thought right and holy busily to beget children and supply youth sufficient for the use of the wars. Except, perchance, they think to prepare guns, weapons, ships to the wars, and think little need of men. The same do allow to slay with sword the parents of infidels, to the intent that their children might be baptized, yea unknowing also. If this be true, how gentler a deed were it to bring the same to effect with the office of intermarrying, each with other. No nation is so cruel that abhorreth not the murder of infants. Laws of princes in manner with like rigor punish them that cause that which is conceived in the woman to come forth dead and them that make them barren with medicines.[61] Why so? For there is small diversity betwixt him that murdereth that which begin to be born and him which procureth that nothing can be born. This that in your body either drieth up or with the great danger of your health putrifieth and corrupteth, which in your sleep falleth away, had been a man if ye were a man yourself. The old law of the Jews curseth him which, when he is commanded to lie with his brother's wife that is dead, casteth his seed on the earth that nothing should be engendered,[62] and is judged unworthy life, which envieth life to the fruit that is to be born. But how little from him differ they, which have enjoined themselves perpetual barrenness? Do they not seem to kill so many men as should have been born if they had given their labor to the begetting of children? I pray you, if a man have a piece of ground rank of nature, which untilled, he suffereth to be continually barren, is not this man punishable by the civil law, because it is for the profit of the common weal that every man tendeth well his own? If he be punished which neglecteth his ground which (be it never so well tilled) bring forth nothing else than wheat or beans or peas, what punishment is he worthy which refuseth to till that

60. The church fathers, for instance, Augustine, Jerome, Ambrose, Lactantius.

61. Erasmus is referring to the primitive and often ineffective methods of abortion then current.

62. Deut. 25:5–11.

ground which tilled beareth men? And in tillage of the earth is required a long and painful labor, here the short tillage is also enticed with a pleasure, as it were a reward prepared therefore. Wherefore, if the sense of nature, if honesty, if natural affection, if devotion, if gentleness, if virtue anything move you, why abhor ye from that which God ordaineth, nature enacteth, reason enticeth, the Scriptures both of God and man praise, the laws command, the whole consent of all nations approve, to which the ensample of every good man provoketh? That if the most part of things (yea which be also bitter) are of a good man to be desired for none other purpose but because they be honest, matrimony doubtless is chiefly to be desired, whereof a man may doubt whether it hath more honesty than pleasure.

For what thing is sweeter than with her to live, with whom ye may be most straightly coupled, not only in the benevolence of the mind, but also in the conjunction of the body? If a great delectation of mind be taken of the benevolence of our other kinsmen, sith it is an especial sweetness to have one with whom ye may communicate the secret affections of your mind, with whom ye may speak even as it were with your own self, whom ye may safely trust, which supposeth your chances to be his, what felicity (think ye) have the conjunction of man and wife, than which no thing in the universal world may be found either greater or firmer? For with our other friends we be conjoined only with the benevolence of minds; with our wife we be coupled with most high love, with permixtion of bodies, with the confederate band[63] of the sacrament, and finally with the fellowship of all chances. Furthermore, in other friendships how great simulation is there? How great falsity? Yea they, whom we judge our best friends, like as the swallows flee away when summer is gone, so they forsake us, when fortune turneth her wheel. And sometime the fresher friend cast out the old. We hear of few, whose fidelity endure till their lives' end. The wife's love is with no falsity corrupted, with no simulation obscured, with no chance of things [di]minished, finally with death only (nay, not with death neither) withdrawen. She, the love of her parents, she, the love of her sisters, she, the love of her brethren despiseth for the love of you; her only respect is to you, of you she hangeth,[64] with you she coveteth to die. Have ye riches? There is one that shall save it; there is one that shall increase it. Have ye none? There is one that may seek it. If ye have wealth, your felicity is doubled, if adversity, there shall be one which may comfort you, which may sit by your side, which may serve you, which may covet your grief to be hers. Do ye judge any pleasure to be compared with this so great a conjunction? If ye tarry at home, there is at hand which shall drive

63. Bond.
64. Depends.

away the tediousness of solitary being. If from home, ye have one that shall kiss you when ye depart, long for you when ye be absent, receive you joyously when ye return. A sweet companion of youth, a kind solace of age.

By nature, yea, any fellowship is delectable to man, as whom nature hath created to benevolence and friendship. This fellowship then, how shall it not be most sweet, in which everything is common to them both? And contrarily, if we see the savage beasts also abhor solitary living and delighted in fellowship, in my mind he is not once to be supposed a man, which abhorreth from this fellowship most honest and pleasant of all. For what is more hateful than that man which (as though he were home only to himself) liveth for himself, seeketh for himself, spareth for himself, doth cost to himself, loveth no person, is loved of no person? Shall not such monster be adjudged worthy to be cast out of all men's company into the mid sea with Timon the Athenian, which because he fled all men's company, was called Misanthropus, that is to say hate man? Neither dare I here propound unto you those pleasures which (whereas they be naturally most sweet to man) yet (I can not tell how) of the great wits they be dissembled, rather than despised. Albeit, who can be born with so rigorous a disposition (I will not say dumpish and dastardly) which may not be taken with such kind of pleasures, namely if he may attain them without the offense of God and man, without the loss of his good name? Certes I would call him no man but a plain stone. Albeit that pleasure of bodies is the least part of the goods that wedlock hath, but imagine that ye can contemn[65] this, as unworthy for a man (howbeit without these we deserve not once the name of a man) let it be put (if ye will) among the most base commodities of wedlock, now sir, what can be more amiable then chaste love, nay what more holy and honest? There acreaseth by the means a sweet flock of allies,[66] there is doubled the number of parents, of brethren, of sisters, of nephews. For nature can give one only mother, one only father. By wedlock, another father, another mother is gotten, which (because they have committed their own flesh unto you) cannot but love you most tenderly. Now sir, how highly will ye esteem this thing, when your fair wife shall make you a father with a fair child? When some little young babe shall play in your hall which shall resemble you and your wife? Which with a mild lisping, or amiable stammering shall call you "Dad." Now add unto your wife's love, the bond more strong then any adamant, which not death himself can braste[67] asunder.

65. Be contemptuous of, scorn.
66. From L. *affines* 'in-laws'.
67. Burst.

(Horace.) Oh how blessed (saith Flaccus) be they
Whom the fast knot of wedlock doth tey
Whose steadfast love by no plaint can start
Till only death them twain do part.[68]

Ye have them that may delight your age, that may close your eyes, that may do the office of the burials, in whom ye may seem regenerate[d], whom being alive, ye shall be thought not to have died. Your goods which ye have gotten go not to strange heirs. Thus, when ye are passing out of the world, and have fully executed all together, yet not death himself can seem sharp nor bitter unto you. Age must creep upon us all, whether we will or not. By this policy nature hath provided that in our children and nephews we may be renewed and flourish fresh again. For who can bare age heavily when in his son he beholdeth his own visage that he himself bare when he was young? Death is prepared for all. But by this only way the providence of nature assayeth (as it were) a certain immortality, while she thus maketh one thing to issue out of another (like as a young plant which is cut off from the tree spriggeth freshly by, nor he seemeth not to be utterly quenched, which dieth, leaving issue behind).

But I know well enough what among these, ye murmur against me. A blessed thing is wedlock, if all prove according to the desire. But what if a wayward wife chanceth? What if an unchaste, what if unnatural children? There will run in your mind the examples of those whom wedlock have brought to utter destruction. Heap up as much as ye can, but yet these be the vices of men and not of wedlock. Believe me, an evil wife is not wont to chance, but to evil husbands. Put this unto it, that it lieth in you to choose out a good one. But what if after the marriage she be marred? Of an evil husband (I will well) a good wife may be marred. But of a good, the evil is wont to be reformed and mended. We blame wives falsely. No man (if ye give any credence to me) had ever a shrew to his wife, but through his own default. And of good parents commonly be born like children. Howbeit the children also (howsoever they be born) commonly do prove such as they be formed and fashioned in their bringing up.

Now sir, I see no cause why ye should fear jealousy. This is the sickness of foolish lovers. The chaste and lawful love knoweth no jealousy. What, do the tragedies come to your mind? This adulterous woman stroke in sunder her husband with an ax. This poisoned him. That woman with her hateful manners did drive her husband to death. Why rather do not Cornelia, wife to Tiberius Gracchus, come to your remembrance?[69] Why do

68. Horace, *Carmina* I.13, 17–20. Horace's ode, though it treats of love, does not necessarily treat of conjugal love.

69. Famous as a virtuous wife.

not Alcestis, so good a wife of not so good an husband?[70] Why do not [illegible, "either"?] Julia, wife of Pompey or Portia, the wife[71] of Cato, run in your mind? Why do not Artemisia, worthy eternal memory? Why do not Hypsicratea, wife to Mithridates, king of Pontus? Why come not into your mind the most gentle behavior of Aemilia Tertia, the wife of Scipio Africanus? Why do not the faithfulness of Turia? Why do not Lucretia and Lentula come in mind? Why do not Arria so highly commended of Pliny?[72] Why do not other innumerable, whose honest and chaste living, and faithfulness toward their husbands could not be altered nor corrupted not by death? A rare bird in earth (ye say) is an honest woman. And imagine ye again yourself worthy to have a rare wife? *A good woman* (saith the wise man) *is a great felicity.*[73] Be bold to hope one worthy for your manners. And very much (as touching this matter) lieth in the fashioning of her and in the behaving of your self towards her whom ye choose.

But sweeter (ye will say) is liberty. Whosoever taketh a wife, taketh a pair of fetters which nothing save only death can shake off. What can be sweet to a man alone? If liberty be sweet, it were best (by mine advice) to take a companion with whom ye may part this so pleasant a thing. Howbeit, what is more free than this bondage, where either is so bond to other that neither wolde be enfranchised? Is not every man bound to his friend? Yet no man complaineth that his liberty is take[n] away. But ye fear lest if death should take away your children, ye should fall into sorrow. If ye fear to be childrenless, for this very cause ye ought to marry a wife which only may be the cause they be not childrenless.

But what search ye out so diligently (nay so narrowly and curiously) all the incommodities of matrimony, as who should say the single life had no incommodity at all? As who should say there were any life of man that is not subject to all the chances of fortune. He must get him out of the world which will bear no incommodity. That if ye will have respect to the life in heaven, this life of man is to be said a death and no life. But if ye keep your mind within the bounds of man's estate, nothing is neither safer, neither quieter, neither pleasanter, neither amiabler,[74] neither happier, than the wedded life. Mark the thing by the end. How many see ye, which have once assayed wedlock, that go not greedily to it again. Did not my friend Mauricius[75] (whose excellent prudence is not unknown unto you) after the

---

70. Wife of Admetus, who chose to die in place of her husband.
71. Portia was the daughter of Cato.
72. Famous chaste wives of antiquity.
73. Jesus, son of Sirach; Prov. 12:4; 18:22.
74. More amiable.
75. Fantazzi suggests that Erasmus refers here to Thomas More (*Collected Works,* vol. 26, p. 533).

death of his wife whom he so singularly loved, marry the next month after, a new wife? Not so greatly for the impatience of his lust, but he thought his life no life without a wife, a sweet companion of all things. Doth not Jovius,[76] our friend, now woo his fourth wife? So he loved them when they lived that he seemed comfortless. So, when one died, he hated to be a widower, as though he faintly had loved them.

But what reason we of honesty and pleasantness, when not only profit enticeth but also necessity constraineth to wedlock? Take matrimony away, and within few years mankind shall be utterly gone. Zerxes, king of Persia, when he beheld out of an high tower the great multitude of men, he could not refrain weeping because that of so many thousands of men within three score years none should be left alive.[77] Why the thing that he understood of his army, do not we consider of all mankind? Wedlock taken away, who one, of so many regions, provinces, realms, cities, towns, within an hundred years, shall be left alive? Go we now and avaunce bachelorship, which bringeth mankind to destruction. What pestilence, what plague, can be sent on man either from heaven or from hell more hurtful? What of any flood can be feared more dangerous? What can be looked for, more heavy and grievous, though the fire of Phaethon should come again when all the world was destroyed with fire.[78] And yet (for all that) in such troubleous seasons many are wont to be left alive, but by bachelorship, surely, nothing can be left. We see what a rout of diseases, how many casualties, daily and nightly lie in wait upon the fewness of men. How many do the pestilence take away? How many do the sea swallow up? How many do battle consume. For I will not speak of these quotidian deaths. Death flyeth about everywhere; he runneth, he carrieth, he hasteth to quench mankind, and do we yet avaunce bachelorship and flee wedlock? Unless perchance the life of the Essenes and Dulopolitans[79] (which do damn wedlock) do please us, whose pestilent sects be multiplied and increased with ungracious people never failing. Do we look that God will give us the same virtue that he hath given (as they say) to the bees,[80] so that without the company of

76. Fantazzi follows Telle's suggestion that Erasmus refers here to Mountjoy, "already married to his fourth wife when the *Encomium Matrimonii* was published" (*Collected Works*, vol. 26, p. 533).

77. In 480 b.c. Cf. Herodotus, *Histories* 7.45–46; Nepos, *Themistocles* 2.4.

78. Phaethon, son of Helios (the sun) and Clymene, chose to drive the chariot of the sun. He could not manage the horses and nearly burnt up the earth.

79. The inhabitants of Dulopolis. Cf. Pliny, *Natural History* V.104. Fantazzi suggests a "play upon the meaning of the name, 'city of slaves,' is probably intended" (vol. 26, p. 533).

80. Fantazzi notes a reference to Virgil, *Georgics* 4.197–202 (*Collected Works*, vol. 26, p. 534).

woman we might be great with child, and gather with our mouths seeds of posterity out of the flowers? Do we require that like as the poets fain that Minerva issued out of Jupiter's brains, so in like manner children should leap out of our heads? Or (to be short) that according to the old fables, men should spring out of the earth, out of the stones thrown forth,[81] out of hard trunks of trees? Out of the lap of the earth many things do spring without our labor. Little plants spring up oftentimes under the shadow of their mother. But unto man nature hath given only one way of deriving issue, which is, that by the mutual labor of man and woman, mankind should be preserved, which if men wolde flee as ye do, truly these things which ye so highly avaunce should not be. Ye avaunce bachelorship, ye magnify virginity. But neither bachelors, neither virgins should be if ye take away the use of wedlock. Why then is virginity preferred? Why is it in so high reputation, if it be the destruction of man? It was commended, but for a time, and but in few, for it pleased God to shew to men a certain token, and as it were a representation of the heavenly life *where they neither marry nor be given in marriage.*[82] But, for an example, a few be sufficient; a multitude is not profitable. For like as not all grounds (be they never so rank) be sown to the sustenance of man, but part is let alone, part dight to the pleasure and feeding of the eyes. For the very copy and plenty of the thing in so much arable ground suffereth some part to be left barren and fruitless. But if none at all were sown, who seeth not but that we must return to the fruit of trees wherewith they lived in old time before the invention of tillage. So bachelorship in so great a multitude of men, in a few (I grant) is commendable, in all, a thing greatly to be dispraised.

But admit that in other men virginity had the name of an high virtue, yet in you surely it should be vicious.[83] For other men shall seem to have intended a pureness of living; ye shall be judged a traitorous murderer of your lineage, which, when ye might have maintained by honest wedlock, ye have suffered to perish by foul bachelorship. Admit it lawful, out of a great number of children to offer one virgin to God. The uplandish men which dwell in the country offer to God the first of their fruit, not their whole crop. But ye must remember that ye only be left the last and the leavings of your stock. And I pray you what diversity is there whether ye flee or refuse to save him which may by you only be saved and easily saved? But the example of your sister provoketh you to chastity. Nay, for this very cause only, ye ought most chiefly to eschew bachelorship. For now ye understand that the hope (which before was common to you both) of

---

81. The reference is to Deucalion. Ovid, *Metamorphoses* I. 375–406.
82. Matt. 19:10–12; 1 Cor. 7:39.
83. From L. *vitiosus* 'immoral, wicked'.

preserving your stock is revolved and cast whole upon your back. Let us pardon the frail kind of the woman, let us pardon the undiscreet age. The maid overcome with sorrow did amiss. Through the enticements of foolish women and foolish friars she hath cast herself headlong. Ye being elder must needs remember that ye be a man. She wold needs die with her ancestors, but your labor must be that they die not. Your sister hath withdrawn herself of her duty, remember now that ye ought to fulfill the parts of two. The daughters of Loth sticked not to lie with their father, judging it better to maintain their lineage by unlawful and abominable incest than to suffer it clean to fall away.[84] And will not ye then by matrimony which is honest, holy, chaste, without offense, with high pleasure maintain your stock, which shall else be utterly extinct?

Wherefore let us suffer them to follow the life of Hippolitus,[85] let them (I say) embrace bachelorship, which either can be husbands but fathers can be none, or whose bare living is not able to bring up children, or whose stock may be maintained by other, or surely is such, that better it were for the common weal to be quenched, than maintained. But ye, when (witnessing the physician a man neither unlearned nor no liar) ye seem by your nature very apt to engender much posterity, when ye have great inheritance, coming also of a stock, so good, so noble, that without great sin and the great hurt of the common weal it cannot be quenched. Furthermore, sith your age is lusty and flourishing, nor ye lack not the beauty of the body, and when there is offered you a wife, so lusty a maid, so well born as may be, chaste, sober, demure, godly, having an angel's face, with fair lands, when your friends beseech you, your kindred weep, your affinity call on, your native country requireth, the very dead corses[86] of your ancestors rising out of their graves obtest[87] the same of you, do ye yet tarry, do ye yet think upon bachelorship? If a thing scase[88] honest should be required of you, if an hard thing, yet either the requests of your friends, either the love of your stock ought to overcome your mind. How much then more right and convenient is it that the tears of your friends, the affection of your country, the natural love of your ancestors ought to obtain that of you whereunto God's laws and man's exhort, nature pricketh, reason leadeth, honesty allureth, so many commodities provoke, necessity also constraineth? But now we have brought forth arguments abundantly enough. I

---

84. Gen. 19:30–38.
85. See Euripides, *Hippolytus*. He was pledged to the chaste goddess, Artemis, and so rejected women.
86. Corpses.
87. Call to witness.
88. Scarce.

trust long ago (through mine advertisement) ye have changed your purpose, and applied your mind to wholesomer counsels. Fare ye well.

Telos[89]

Defense of His Declamation in Praise of Marriage

[106 F][1] Since the matter[2] is too well known to ignore, as you might expect from its being treated publicly in a large and mixed gathering, and since suspicion has taken hold of the minds of nearly all men too firmly to be likely to fade away on its own accord—especially as there is no lack of people who in speeches filled with innuendo try to fix this suspicion in men's minds even more than before—I therefore resolved through this Defense to rid everyone of his deep-seated mistrust and at the same time to preserve both my innocence and the dignity of that esteemed theologian Jan Briart of Ath, the Vice-Chancellor of this well-known university.[3] At any rate, in an open meeting held a few days ago [Feb. 21, 1519] for the purpose of granting to a certain Carmelite theologian[4] the licentiate (a term [107 A] more appropriate to current usage than to classical Latin), Briart, in his usual fashion, delivered a speech replete with all sorts of affectations and poeticisms which was obviously directed against me. Since this matter concerning me came to be the subject of much talk and suspicion by many learned men, and since at the same time many other likely conjectures were current (which out of a sense of prudence I here omit), I wished to free myself of this suspicion, in part owing to my feeling that I am undeserving of any such words (for innocence is free of suspicion) and in part because the character and ability of [107 B] Jan Briart have long been familiar to me and I do not judge it worthy of someone of his integrity to cast aspersions in a defamatory speech against an undeserving man, nor, even if there has been some understandable error on this man's part, do I judge it worthy of Briart's humanity for him to traduce publicly with the heinous charge of heresy someone who is wholeheartedly friendly to him; especially since this man was close by, not only willing to be advised but even asking, strenuously and often, for advice. At any rate, it may have been that what I wrote was not understood or that it was taken in another

89. From Gk. 'the end'.
1. Numbers and letters in brackets refer to pages and paragraphs in the 1706 Leyden (Latin) edition of Erasmus's *Opera Omnia*.
2. Erasmus's statements about marriage and the controversy they aroused.
3. The University of Louvain. Briart mounted his attack on February 21, 1519.
4. Jan Robyns.

sense than was intended by the author. In sum, as it must be, just as I can make a human error in writing, so too can others, no less human than I, err in their reprimands. Finally, it does not seem to be a mark of prudence in so great a man to open a window [107 C] that allows entry into this Faculty of Theology a dangerous precedent, which would permit further invectives against almost anybody's reputation. At first, as in the present case, it may be directed against a deserving target, but it would soon be directed against an undeserving party. This is all the more serious for having occurred in such an august assembly. For this same thing might be more properly found in disputations of the sort called *quodlibets*[5] or in the preludes called *vespers,* with which, in a manner more traditional than elegant, someone about to be granted the doctoral degree is attacked in raucous fashion—a pagan custom we derive from classical antiquity, when an initiand to the Mysteries would be harassed with playful jibes of this sort, as is attested by both Plato's *Euthyphro* and the *Ass* of Apuleius.[6] [107 D] But where, as in the present situation, a serious matter was being dealt with, its author equally serious, it was clearly desirable to dissent from an almost universally held opinion. My view is confirmed by Maarten van Dorp,[7] who visited me the next day, affirming in the presence of the venerable Gillis van Delft[8] that nothing in that speech [of Briart] had been directed against me. All that perhaps referred to me was his remark on the heresy of preferring matrimony to celibacy. On this point, Dorp said that it had been falsely conveyed to Briart regarding my declamation *de Laude Matrimonii* that I there seemed to some people to place marriage above celibacy. And here too I recognize the civility of Briart, who, although he had somehow been persuaded that this was the case, yet refrained from mentioning my name, being content to limit himself to the issue. [107 E] Nor is it surprising that one person was persuaded when there are so many urging him on and nobody calling him back with sound advice to another opinion. It remains therefore that I state in a few words that Dorp spoke the absolute truth when he said that Briart had been falsely informed, because, as I have heard, he had not yet read my booklet, occupied as he was with more serious matters. Thus, in my opinion, whoever was my accuser harmed Briart no less than me. Indeed, unless through the most straightforward arguments I demonstrate that I neither said nor intended anything of this

5. Literally, whatever you please. This term came to be used of scholastic or philosophical exercises.

6. *Euthyphro* 277D-E. The entire narrative of *The Golden Ass* may be considered a prelude to the final initiation into the mysteries of Isis and Osiris.

7. Maarten van Dorp (1485–1525) was a conservative professor of philosophy at Louvain.

8. A colleague of Dorp?

sort, I would not want to benefit from any other defense against the charge of heresy. [107 F]

To begin with the weakest of these arguments, I should mention that I wrote this booklet as a young man approximately twenty-five years ago. It was with just such an excuse that St. Jerome excused his earlier commentary on Obadiah,[9] a work of the greatest theological importance. But let it be granted, people will say, that you wrote it when young; you were old when you published it. I published it indeed, but I published it as a juvenile work, and for this reason it deserves to be read with some leniency, especially as I see nothing in it that ought to be repressed. Only because Virgil published his *Culex*[10] when old and Homer likewise his [108 A] *Batrachomyomachia*[11] in order that these early exercises not perish can they as old men be judged from these works too. I wished to furnish the young with an example from my own youth, so that they too, when similar matters are to be treated, could exercise their talents and skills in writing. And I wanted this to be affirmed in both my preface and in that of Frobenius.[12] Does not the very title *Declamation* sufficiently preserve me from all attack, even if thereafter throughout the entire work I should prefer matrimony to celibacy? For who does not know that declamations are customarily written on artificial topics for the sake of exercising one's talents? The Greeks, in fact, give witness of this by calling them *meletai,* i.e., "exercises."

Furthermore, it is in the nature [108 B] of these exercises to treat both sides of the question; for example, in favor of tyrannicide and against tyrannicide, or for and against rapine, for and against war, for and against Alexander the Great. This, when propositions and proofs have been laid out on both sides, is most conducive to judgment and invention, the two most important elements of eloquence. And if I had praised fever or drunkenness, it would have been unfair to brand such a fictitious argument as heretical. And if, furthermore, there exist some people ignorant of Greek *melete* or Latin *declamatio,* I do not think it fair for me to suffer as a result of their unfamiliarity with the genre. In order to make it even clearer that my modest booklet was written with no other idea in mind, I have a copy, as do many others, of a work of mine written long ago, [108 C] *De Con-*

---

9. "Preface to Pammachius," A.D. 403, *Obadiah.* For Jerome's extreme praise of virginity, see especially his "Letter to Eustochium" (Letter 22), A.D. 384, and his "Letter to Demetrius" (Letter 130), A.D. 414, in *Letters and Select Works,* vol. 6 of *A Select Library of Nicene and Post-Nicene Fathers of the Christian Church,* gen. ed. Philip Schaff, 2d series (Grand Rapids, Mich.: Wm. B. Eerdmans Publishing Co., 1954), pp. 22–41, 260–72.

10. *The Gnat,* a satiric poem doubtfully attributed to Virgil.

11. *Battle of the Frogs and Mice,* a parody of an epic poem falsely attributed to Homer in antiquity.

12. Johann Froben, Erasmus's publisher at Basel.

scribendis Epistolis[13] [*The Art of Letter Writing*], in which this same argument
will be found treated as an example of the hortatory letter. But in this
work you will find that the contrary view has been added, an argument
against the taking of a wife.[14] I did not publish this part in my declamation
along with the positive side because at that time I was worn out with work
and only brought together the propositions and their arguments, leaving
it to the reader to figure out at his leisure how the other part of the argument
was to be treated. And since this part is more copious, it would have called
for a thicker volume, especially as I saw that it had several times been the
subject of Greek and Latin declamations. Thus, I neither had the time to
treat the matter when the book was about to be published nor did I feel
like going over ground that had been covered by so many writers before
me. But if someone should maintain that [108 D] nothing opposed to
Christian truth should ever appear in print, how are we to classify nearly
all recent theologians, who first bring together all the arguments showing
why "simple fornication" (to use their own language) is not a sin before
they adduce the opposing arguments to conclude that it is a capital sin.
This one example should suffice, as the argument for fornication is dan-
gerously attractive to too many people. The theologians, furthermore, present these arguments in a serious work, whereas I promise nothing more
than a declamation. What if in a declamation I had censured virginity in
order to spur others on to its praise? This is what Glaucon did in Plato's
Republic,[15] pretending to criticize [108 E] justice and to praise injustice for
the express purpose of provoking Socrates to a defense of justice. This
may be called boldness or ineptitude, but not heresy. Whoever promises
a declamation forswears honesty; his talent may be at stake, but not his
honesty. In praising marriage, I am engaged in a most laudable activity;
and if I prove persuasive, there should be no danger in this for me, for I
also reveal that I yet prefer virginity, since I attribute this to angels, the
Apostles, and to apostolics; but what I prefer in others I do not approve
of for the man I write about.

Let me say, however, that the situation I treat is not a general one, but
one hedged in by circumstances. I depict a noble youth from the best of
families, [108 F] whose entire hope of propagating depends on one thing;
for this man I prefer marriage, not for all. This is obvious from many
passages, in particular in the very first section, where I say that "unless I

13. Erasmus published a version of his *Encomium Matrimonii* as an example of a letter
of persuasion in his *De Conscribendis Epistolis* (Basel, August, 1522).

14. When *De Conscribendis Epistolis* appeared in 1522, it contained only the brief
outline of a dispraise of marriage.

15. *Republic* 2.357–63.

show by clear reasons that this shall be for you most honest, most profitable, and most pleasant, what does it matter that it is also at this time necessary for you?"[16] Nobody, I think, is so religious as to deny that there are those for whom marriage ought to be more important than celibacy. Moreover, the argument for the propagation of the species has so much force that the compiler of *Theologiae Sententiae*[17] [109 A] does not hesitate either to equate the polygamy of the Patriarchs with our marriage or to compare the fornication of those days to our matrimony, and with no other name does he justify either Abraham's lying with his maidservant or the incest of Lot with his daughters, which Origen almost prefers to the marriage of some other.[18] If all this is the case, why should we hesitate to come to a similar conclusion if a similar case for marriage is made? For, as I have said, my argument depends upon the specific circumstances that make marriage necessary, and I thus prefer marriage not to virginity but to celibacy. Perhaps the man who brings this charge (or should I say [109 B] calumny) against me thinks that the Romans called *coelebs*[19] only the man who lived a pure and uncorrupted life, when in fact pimps and playboys (not to use more obscene words) could also be called celibates as long as they did not have a legitimate wife. And, on the other hand, nothing prevents there being a place for virginity within marriage. On the contrary, in the present work, I would hope to obtain dispassionate readers, especially in such a serious charge as this, who would not allow someone's inadequate knowledge of Latin, as I have shown to be the case with Briart, to be used against me, for after his oracular utterance at the University he declared in my presence that he understood celibacy to be a heavenly and pure life, and a declamation to be a sacred discourse. Now, while I readily pardon ordinary human error, I am at a loss to explain those men [109 C] who would force someone into a palinode over a trifle but who would not think to reconcile themselves with their brother with even a single word, or to heal a reputation that had been badly bruised. It is as if they would prefer to see the whole world go up in flames rather than yield an inch of their own authority. I do not think it fraught with danger to praise marriage, especially since I do so in terms very similar to the praise of virginity, and since I say that a wife is to be maintained for the purpose of producing offspring not pleasure.

16. *Encomium Matrimonii*, 386.27–29, ed. J.-C. Margolin, in *Opera Omnia Desiderii Erasmi Roterodami*, Ordinis Primi, Tomus Quintus (Amsterdam: North-Holland Publishing Company, 1975).

17. Bk. 4.33, "Considerations of the Ancients."

18. Gen. 16:1–7, 19:31–38. Origen said that the "polygyny" of the patriarchs figures forth the multiplicity of virtues. See Origène, *Homélies sur la Genèse* (Paris: Éditions du Cerf, 1976), pp. 281–83, 169–81.

19. Unmarried.

But let me not pursue individual details which this man or that, according to his talent or pleasure, gnaws away at piecemeal in my book. For I am concerned with more universal arguments, of the sort that has been said in one passage: "the stimuli for propagation have been established by nature, not by sin" [*Enc. Matr.*, 398.190f.]; the matter, that is, concerns stimuli that are open to rational argument. [109 D] And note also the following: "I call the one untouched by pleasure truly a stone more than a man" [*Enc. Matr.*, 408.294f.], where I clearly show that I am speaking of legal marriage, since I add "especially if this can come about short of giving offense to God" [*Enc. Matr.*, 408.292f.]. Let me now come to the passage that I suspect gives most offense, the one where my fictitious persuader says "the most holy kind of life is wedlock purely and chastely kept" [*Enc. Matr.*, 402.217f.]. For here I seem plainly to prefer marriage to any other state. To this I could reply that "most holy" is admittedly an exaggeration, meaning nothing other than "*among* the most holy." Then too, it was deemed appropriate to add not merely "wedlock," but also "purely and chastely kept," so that it is not so much an institution of life that is at issue [109 E] as the character of those who observe both conditions of marriage. Just as nothing prevents us from calling men who have assembled an "Assembly" or from calling Patricians or Knights the Patrician or Equestrian order, so those engaging in one or another kind of life can be styled a "kind of life." The immediately preceding words will dispel any doubts one may have about this. They are as follows: "But now, such is the state of things and times that nowhere may ye find the pureness and perfection of manners less spotted and contaminated than among wedded persons" [*Enc. Matr.*, 402.213f.]. What, dear reader, can be stated more openly? Also in agreement are the words following soon after: "And would God they were truly castrated, all who cloak their vices under the glorious title of castration, under the shadow of chastity, fouly raging; [109 F] for which I am ashamed here to reckon up into what shameful abominations they often fall, which fight against nature" [*Enc. Matr.*, 402.219]. Does this not sufficiently proclaim that I speak not about a kind of life but about the corruption of character? There are so many among the ranks of Christians who embrace celibacy in this way that they have forever forsworn the enjoyment of marriage, and of these by far the greater part devote themselves to this institution not so much out of any zeal for chastity as for the sake of profit and leisure. All who [110 A] listen to daily confession know the signs and the frequency of the pleasures indulged in by these people. I urgently ask, however, that nobody force me to spell out the details here. I would not wish any people or any order of men to be sullied by my words. Let the prudent reader silently recognize by himself what I mean and what I bewail. Let these hints of mine be sufficient.

As to the matter at hand, if I had been thoroughly experienced in serious argumentation and in my zeal to praise marriage had somewhere demeaned the dignity of virginity, what would have happened to me other than what happened to St. Jerome? He fought with all his might for the glory of virginity, often, it is not unjust to say, being rather unfair to the cause of marriage, with the result that he was led to write a palinode to meet the many criticisms published in opposition. [110 B] Indeed, St. Augustine so praises the benefits of marriage[20] that I think there will be nothing left to say that is not open to niggling criticism; but, without the prerogatives granted him for the authority due his antiquity, he would have as many unfair critics as have shown themselves to me, calumniating him too for things they do not understand. It should not be a matter for concern if one makes distinctions in drawing a comparison, provided that one respects both sides, just as if one man should prefer the Carmelites and another the Dominicans, provided that each man admire each order so that the degree of difference between them is slight. Finally, it must be added that I do not now question (I reserve the entire matter for a later time) whether, if it may be called an error for someone simply to prefer marriage to celibacy, it may also be called heresy. [110 C] Just as if juxtaposed to the dictum of Tychonius[?]—"what we desire is not altogether holy"—one were to add "nor likewise is what displeases us altogether heretical." Nor indeed does Christ call them simply "blessed" who castrate themselves, without adding "for the sake of the kingdom of Heaven."[21] Nor is St. Paul's preference for celibacy absolute, but only under certain conditions, so that if these were removed or altered the order of his preference would perhaps be reversed. But for the present let us neither dispute nor assert this.

I think that these few words should suffice for the present to remove from everyone's minds the altogether false suspicion of many, which neither Briart's prudent seriousness nor my innocence deserves. As for the remaining aspersions cast against me like missiles, [110 D] I have been satisfied by Briart himself as well as by Dorp and even van Delft and Bintius[?],[22] to say nothing of the satisfaction already provided me by my own thoughts. Although it was I who stood charged on the subject of the standing of celibacy, Briart addressed himself to the issue rather than to me, not yet having determined whether I was responsible for the error. I should, therefore, be able to say now what Archelaus said when he had been mistakenly splashed with water: "It was not me he splashed, but the

20. See Augustine, *On the Good of Marriage* (*De Bone Conjugali*), *Nicene and Post-Nicene Fathers*, vol. 3, pp. 399–413.
21. Matt. 19:12.
22. Perhaps Jean Lengherant of Binche.

man he thought I was," although it cannot be denied that it is far more trivial to be hit with water than with a charge of heresy. But now this very thing, I think, will be the cause of indignation, namely that I attribute such carelessness to the leading theologian of this academy that he would in denunciation publicly damn what he had not read. [110 E] And yet, he himself ought to have taken care lest he deserve to be addressed with the line, "This was their doing, who stirred the old man with this tale." And those who did the stirring will be the most indignant—unless perhaps they think it fair for me to err on the side of heresy rather than allow people who openly show their hatred for me to seem too lax in any matter. I think that there is nothing in any of my books with the power to make anybody worse. I confess that I am but a man. I have shown my intention to aid the cause of piety; I am unable, however, to guarantee the result. I always write for the honest and fair reader; if the reader is unfair, there is nothing that cannot be charged with heresy in Cyprian, in Hilarius, in Jerome, in Ambrose, in Augustine, in Scotus, in Thomas Aquinas, in Peter Lombardus, [110 F] in Gerson;[23] in short, in no writer, ancient or modern, is there freedom from the possibility of being charged with heresy. Let me not mention how quiet we are when we read Lactantius, Poggio, and even Pontanus.[24] Furthermore, the person who establishes himself as censor over other people's books should first of all understand the subject thoroughly; then let him display reason, not emotion, in public assembly. Malice cannot judge fairly, and hate and anger have cloudy vision. Finally, let him remember Christian civility, [111 A] lest he in turn someday himself meet up with unfair judges. For who among mortals has attained wisdom in all these things? Who has written so carefully as to please all men in all things?—especially, as I have had cause to realize more than once, since there exists such a wide variety of opinions among even a few men?

But let there now be an end both to my Defense and to false suspicion. For I, you may be sure, would rather have spent my time on my Paraphrase, already begun, of the Letter to the Galatians. Fare well, whoever you are, dear reader.

Louvain, March 1, 1519.

---

23. Church fathers and modern theologians.

24. Lactantius (ca. 260–340) was an unorthodox theologian. Giovanni Francesco Poggio Bracciolini (1380–1459) and Giovanni Pontano (1426–1503) were Italian humanists.

Juan Luis Vives
A Very Fruitful and Pleasant Book Called the Instruction of a Christian Woman
1523, trans. Richard Hyrde,
London [1529?] and
The Office and Duty of an Husband
1529, trans. Thomas Paynell,
London [1555?]

Introduction

Juan Luis Vives was born in Valencia, Spain, in 1492 and learned Latin and Greek at an early age. He went to the University of Paris in 1509, and thereafter lived outside Spain in the Low Countries, France, and England.[1] He was a humanist, a pupil and friend of Erasmus, and like Erasmus he was concerned with classical learning and Christian exegesis. He spent some time in England at the invitation of Cardinal Wolsey, was introduced to Henry VIII and Catherine of Aragon, and became closely acquainted with Thomas More and his circle. During this period, he was asked to draw up a plan of studies for Mary Tudor, the daughter of Henry VIII and Queen Catherine. He was also commissioned by Catherine to write the *De Institutione Feminae Christianae* for Mary, which he finished in April, 1523. It was published in Latin in Antwerp in 1523 and translated from Latin soon after its publication by Richard Hyrde (d. 1528), a tutor in the More household.

The Instruction of a Christian Woman was widely known throughout Europe, in Latin and in translations into English, Castilian, French, German, and Italian. Vives intended it to be used by women as a book of moral instruction, which he emphasized by addressing women directly throughout his text. After its initial publication in English, there followed eight other English editions.

The Instruction of a Christian Woman was not only the first but also the most influential Renaissance treatise on the education of women. It is within the humanist tradition in that it advocates educating women in classical as well as Christian literature, although it prohibits "void verses" and "trifling songs." But it reveals stronger ties to the Middle Ages and to orthodox Catholicism in its insistence upon women's duty to practice chastity, piety, obedience, and silence. Indeed, Vives insists that chastity is woman's primary virtue, with which she can withstand all evils, without which she is lost. Virginity is so valuable a commodity, Vives tells women, that no rapist, however depraved, would knowingly violate its possessor. The loss of virginity is so heinous, he adds (in a scarcely veiled threat which conveniently disregards the commandment against murder), that fathers have been known to cut the throats of their unchaste daughters, and brothers to "thrust swords" into the belly of an unwed sister who has just given birth, "the midwife looking on." (Vives does not appear to believe, however, that men are required to follow the same stringent rules of chastity. Certainly in his long, scarifying story of the marriage of Clara to Bernard Valdaura, he nowhere suggests that a forty-six-year-old man in an advanced stage of syphilis was culpable either in contracting a marriage with an eighteen-year-old girl or in failing to reveal his disease to her until their wedding night.) Vives's blend of humanism and conservatism, or better, perhaps, the dichotomy between them, is sustained in his insistence that only a very few women, Catherine of Aragon, for instance, are worthy of admiration. Most women, he is convinced, are weak in mind and body, inferior in every way to men, and perhaps even threats to their well-being.[2]

Vives wrote *The Office and Duty of an Husband* in Bruges in 1529 at the request of a fellow Spaniard, Alvaro de Castro, who urged Vives to complete the work he began in *The Instruction of a Christian Woman* by writing a companion volume on the duties of a husband. The *De Officio Mariti* was published in Bruges in 1529, reprinted in Latin twice in 1540, and once again in 1546. The English translation, however, was probably not published until 1555, two years after Mary Tudor ascended the throne.

Vives never made any secret of his allegiance to Catherine of Aragon. In 1528, after Henry began divorce proceedings against Catherine, Henry banished Vives from the court and England under orders not to engage in the "royal dispute." Nonetheless, Catherine asked Vives to defend her in the divorce trial.[3] Vives refused on the grounds that "it would be better [for her] to be condemned unheard than to accept the delusive pretense of such a trial,"[4] a position consistent with the premises of his two books on marriage. Although Catherine was angered by his refusal to defend her and withdrew her financial support from him, in his book on the duties of a husband, Vives listed her name among the saints, calling her "a divine thing and a godly, sent down from heaven." Under these circumstances, Henry could not have allowed Vives's book on the duties of a husband to be published in England; Mary may have sanctioned its publication in large part because of its vindication of and praise for her mother.

Unlike *The Instruction of a Christian Woman,* Vives's treatise on the duties of a husband was never reprinted in England, perhaps because its praise of Catherine was no longer politically expedient after Elizabeth's accession. Nor was this work as popular on the Continent as was Vives's *Instruction of a Christian Woman,* perhaps because men were more willing to use Vives's directions to women as textbooks in the education of their wives and daughters than they were prepared to follow him in his instruction of themselves. Some of those instructions may well have been unpalatable to sixteenth-century husbands. Vives said, for instance, that a husband and his wife could copulate without sin only when they did so in order to conceive a child. When men indulge in sexual play for its own sake, Vives added, they become like children, losing their God-given supremacy over their wives: "give not thyself to those unmeet and voluptuous love and lusts by the which men are compelled to say and to do many things which are filthy and childish. . . . thou canst not keep thy majesty in such filthy love." For "a woman cannot suffer nor take him for her master that was sometime her servant." In fact, Vives went so far as to counsel something close to sexual abstinence in marriage—because, he said, "carnal copulation of itself is a beastly thing."

The Office and Duty of an Husband complements Vives's book on the education of a Christian woman, except that in it Vives does not discuss training men for marriage—as he did at great length in the case of women. Instead, he instructs a man of marriageable age how to choose a wife and, once married, how to rule her and his household. He insists throughout on the need for male dominion, even though he advocates the advantages of mutual love, which he understands principally as companionship. Thus he instructs the husband (who is God's surrogate in the family unit) how to teach his wife godliness and the management of his household, how to control her weaknesses, how to castigate her, and how to treat her when she is old. It is clear throughout that Vives sees a wife as the physical, social, and religious extension of her husband, inferior and subject to him in all things.

Hyrde's translation, last published in its entirety in 1592, is still the only complete English translation of *The Instruction of a Christian Woman.* In

Vives and the Renascence Education of Women (1912), George Foster Watson published excerpts from it which deal mainly with women's education. I have tried in my selections to present a more balanced, if less sympathetic, picture of Vives's book, and thus have included selections from his chapters on chastity and virginity as well as excerpts from the second and third books dealing with marriage and widowhood. As far as I know, Paynell's English translation of *The Office and Duty of an Husband* has never been reprinted.

NOTES

1. See Francesco Cordasco's unpaged foreword to *Vives: On Education*, intro. Foster Watson (1912; rpt., Totowa, N.J.: Rowman and Littlefield, 1971).

2. Erasmus thought Vives was far too severe upon women and in one epistle, *Erasmi Epistoles* (1642), said he hoped Vives treated his wife more kindly than he did the women for whom his book was written (col. 835). See *Vives: On Education*, p. lxxxviii. At a workshop on Vives's *Instruction of a Christian Woman*, held at the University of Maryland, College Park, in November of 1990, three presenters argued that the extreme misogyny of the work may in part reflect the author's anxiety over the Inquisition's persecution of his own family of converted Jews, for he wrote the work during his father's trial. This material will be discussed in the introduction to a forthcoming edition of the work by Virginia Walcott Beauchamp et al. A useful analysis of Vives's instructions to women can be found in Valerie Wayne's "Some Sad Sentence: Vives's *Instruction of a Christian Woman*" in *Silent But for the Word: Tudor Women as Patrons, Translators, and Writers of Religious Works,* ed. Margaret Patterson Hannay (Kent, Ohio: Kent State University Press, 1985), pp. 15–29.

3. Henry began divorce proceedings in 1528; they were not concluded until 1532.

4. See *Vives: On Education*, pp. lxxx–lxxxi.

The Instruction of a Christian Woman

The First Book of the Instruction of a Christian Woman

[In Chapters I–IV, Vives instructs parents how to raise their daughters from infancy. Mothers should nurse their own daughters. From about the age of seven, young maids should be given moral and religious instruction. At the same time, daughters should be taught how to "keep" and "order" a house. Children should not be overindulged by their parents. "The cherishing and sufferance of the fathers and mothers hurteth much the children, that giveth them an unbridled liberty unto infinite vices, and [e]specially the maids. But these[1] be refrained and holden under for the most part by fear; which, if it lack, then hath she all the bridle of nature at large, and runneth headlong unto mischief and drowneth herself therein, and cometh not lightly to any goodness.[2] Therefore, let her both learn her book, and beside that, to handle wool and flax, which are two crafts yet left of that old innocent world,[3] both profitable and keepers of temperance, which thing specially women ought to have in price." Sigs. Aii–Dii omitted.]

From Chapter IV. Of the Learning of Maids

Of maids, some be but little meet for learning: likewise as some men be unapt, again some to be even born unto it, or at least not unfit for it. Therefore they that be dull are not to be discouraged, and those that be apt, should be heart[en]ed and encouraged. I perceive that learned women be suspected of many: as who sayth, the subtlety of learning should be nourishment for the maliciousness of their nature. Verily, I do not allow in a subtle and crafty woman such learning as should teach her deceit and teach her no good manners and virtues. Notwithstanding, the precepts of living and the examples of those that have lived well and had knowledge together of holiness be the keepers of chastity and pureness, and the copies of virtues, and pricks to prick and to move folks to continue in them. . . . And she that hath learned in books to cast this[4] and such other things, and hath furnished and fenced her mind with holy counsels shall never [find] to do any villainy. For if she can find in her heart to do naughtily,[5] having so many precepts of virtue to keep her, what should we suppose she should do, having no knowledge of goodness at all? [Vives gives examples of many learned and good women, including the daughters of Isabel, queen of Castile, and the daughters of Sir Thomas More.]

But here, peradventure, a man would ask, what learning a woman should be set unto, and what shall she study? I have told you, the study of wisdom, which doth instruct their manners and inform their living and teacheth them the way of good and holy life. As for eloquence, I have no great care, nor a woman needeth it not, but she needeth goodness and wisdom. Nor it is no shame for a woman to hold her peace, but it is a shame for her and abominable to lack discretion and to live ill. . . . When she shall be taught to read, let those books be taken in hand that may teach good

1. Maids.
2. If a maid is not restrained by fear, she will run into mischief and not easily into goodness.
3. Vives seems to be referring here to the classical Golden Age, not Eden.
4. The vanity of "bodily pleasure."
5. Wickedly.

manners. And when she shall learn to write, let not her example be void verses nor wanton or trifling songs, but some sad sentences prudent and chaste, taken out of holy Scripture, or the sayings of philosophers, which by often writing she may fasten better in her memory. And in learning, as I [ap]point none end to the man, no more I do to the woman: saving it is meet that the man have knowledge of many and diverse things that may both profit himself and the commonwealth, both with the use and increasing of learning. But I would the woman should be altogether in[6] that part of philosophy that taketh upon it to inform and teach, and amend the conditions.

Finally, let her learn for herself alone and her young children or her sisters[7] in our Lord. For it neither becometh a woman to rule a school, nor to live amongst men, [n]or speak abroad, and [thereby] shake off her demureness and honesty, either all together, or else a great part; which if she be good, it were better to be at home within and unknown to other folks, and in company to hold her tongue demurely, and let few see her, and none at all hear her. The apostle Paul, the vessel of election, informing and teaching the Church of the Corinthians with holy precepts, sayth: "Let your women hold their tongues in congregations."[8] For they be not allowed to speak but to be subject as the law biddeth. If they would learn any thing, let them ask their husbands at home. And unto his disciple, Timothy, he writeth on this wise: "Let a woman learn in silence with all subjection."[9] But I give no license to a woman to be a teacher, nor to have authority of the man, but to be in silence. For Adam was the first made, and after, Eve; and Adam was not betrayed; the woman was betrayed into the breach of the commandment.[10] Therefore, because a woman is a frail thing and of weak discretion, and that may lightly be deceived, which thing our first mother Eve sheweth, whom the Devil caught with a light argument; therefore a woman should not teach, lest when she hath taken a false opinion and belief of any thing, she spread it into the hearers by the authority of mastership, and lightly bring other[s] into the same error, for the learners commonly do after the teacher with good will. [Sigs. Eiii–Fii[v] omitted.]

6. Study only.
7. Nuns.
8. 1 Cor. 14:34–35.
9. 1 Tim. 2:10–14.
10. By the serpent to eat the forbidden fruit. But Paul in 1 Tim. 2:15 says of the woman, "yet she shall be saved through childbearing, if she continue in faith and love and sanctification with sobriety." Quotations from Scripture in Vives's works are taken from the Douay version, the English translation of the Latin Vulgate.

Chapter VI. Of Virginity[11]

Now will I talk altogether with the maid herself, which hath within her a treasure without comparison, that is, the pureness both of body and mind. How so many things come unto my remembrance to say, that I wote[12] not where is best to begin: whether it were better to begin where as Saint Augustine doth when he will entreat of holy virginity. All the whole Church is a virgin, married unto one husband, Christ, as Saint Paul writeth unto the Corinthians. Then what honor be they worthy to have that be the members of it, which keep the same office in flesh that the whole Church keepeth in faith, which followeth the mother of her husband and lord: for the church is also a mother and a virgin? Nor there is nothing that our lord delighteth more in than virgins, nor wherein angels more gladly abide, and play with, and talk with, for they be virgins also themselves,[13] and their lord, which wolde have a virgin unto his mother, and a virgin to his most dear disciple, and the church his spouse a virgin. And also he marrieth unto himself other virgins,[14] and goeth unto marriages with virgins. And whithersoever he goeth, that lamb without spot which made us clean with his blood, an hundred and forty thousand virgins follow him. . . .

Be not proud, maid, that thou art holy of body if thou be broken in mind, nor because no man hath touched thy body if many men have pierced[15] thy mind. What availeth it thy body to be clean when thou bearest thy mind and thy thought infected with a foul and an horrible blot? O thou maid, thy mind is withered[16] by burning with man's heat; nor thou frettest not with holy love, but hast dried up all the good fatness of the pleasures of paradise. Therefore art thou the foolish maid, and hast no oil; and while thou runnest to the cellar, art shut forth; and as our lord in the gospel threateneth, when thou comest again, and knockest, thou shalt be answered: Who art thou? I know thee not.[17] Thou shalt say then: knowest thou not this body closed and untouched of men? Our lord shall say again: I see not the body. I see the soul open unto men and unto devils worse than men, and often knocked at. Thou art proud, maid, because thy belly hath no cause to swell, when thy mind is swollen, not with man's seed but with devils. . . .

---

11. Watson omits from his edition chapters VI (Of Virginity) and VII (Of the Keeping of Virginity and Chastity).

12. Know, from O.E. *witan*.

13. The text reads "themself," normalized to "themselves" throughout.

14. Nuns, when they take the veil, marry themselves in spirit to Christ.

15. The text reads "persed." Vives perhaps refers here to thoughts of men's love.

16. The text reads "widdred."

17. Matt. 25:1–13.

I pray thee, understand thine own goodness, maid, thy price cannot be estimated.[18] If thou join a chaste mind unto thy chaste body, if thou shut up both body and mind, and seal them with those seals that none can open but he that hath the key of David, that is thy spouse[19] which resteth so in thee, as in a temple most clean and goodly. . . . Wherefore virgins and all holy folks engender Christ spiritually, howbeit corporally only one virgin[20] did bear god and man, which is spouse and also father unto all other virgins. O thou maid, thinkest thou this but a small thing that thou art both mother, spouse, and daughter to that god, in whom nothing can be but it be thine, and thou mayest with good right challenge for thine? For both thou gettest and art gotten and married unto him. . . .

Now think with what diligence this pearl[21] ought to be kept that maketh thee like unto the church, like unto our lady, sister unto angels, mother unto God, and the spouse of Christ, beside worldly honors, which ought to have no place or a very little place in a Christian body's heart? But yet also they, as it were, feasting[22] their eyes upon a virgin. How pleasant and dear to everybody is a virgin? How reverend a thing even unto them that be ill and vicious themselves. . . . Virginity was ever an holy thing even among thieves, breakers of sanctuary, ungracious livers, murderers, and also among wild beasts. . . . Virginity hath so much marvelous honor in it that wild lions regard it.

From Chapter VII. Of the Keeping of Virginity and Chastity

How much, then, ought that to be set by, that hath ofttimes defended women against great captains, tyrants, and great hosts of men? We have read of women that have been taken and let go again of[23] the most unruly soldiers only for the reverence of the name of virginity, because they said that they were virgins, for they[24] judged it a great wickedness for a short and small image of pleasure to [di]minish so great a treasure. And every of them had leaver[25] that another should be the causer of so wicked a deed[26] than himself. O cursed maid and not worthy to live, the which willingly spoileth herself of so precious a thing[27] which men of war that

18. The text reads "estemedde."
19. Christ? Cf. Song of Sol. 8:6.
20. Mary.
21. Of virginity. Vives reinterprets the biblical reference to the pearl of great price.
22. The text reads "festyne."
23. By.
24. The soldiers.
25. Rather.
26. Rape.
27. Willingly surrenders her virginity.

are accustomed to all mischief yet dread to take away. Also lovers, which be blind in the heat of love, yet they stay and take advisement.[28] For there is none so outrageous a lover if he think thee be a virgin, but he will alway[s] open his eyes and take discretion to him and deliberation, and take counsel to change his mind. Every man is so sore adread to take away that which is of so great price that afterward neither can they themselves keep nor restore again, though they shall have no loss by the means. And the ungracious maid doubteth not[29] to lose that, which once gone, she shall by no means recover again, when she hath once lost the greatest treasure that ever she had. . . .

Let her that hath lost her virginity turn her which way she will, she shall find all things sorrowful and heavy, wailing, and mourning, and angry, and displeasureful. What sorrow will her kinfolks make when everyone shall think themselves dishonested by one shame of that maid? What mourning? What tears? What weepings of the father and mother and bringers up? Dost thou [re]quite them with this pleasure for so much care and labor? Is this the reward of thy bringing up? What cursing will there be of her acquaintance? What talk of neighbors, friends, and companions, cursing that ungracious young woman? What mocking and babbling of those maidens that envied her before. What a loathing and abhoring of those that loved her? What fleeing of her company and demesnes,[30] when every mother will keep not only their daughters but also their sons from the infection of such an unthrifty maid? And worse also, if she had any, all flee away from her. And those that before [dis]sembled love with her, they openly hate her. Yea and now and then with open words will cast the abominable deed in her teeth, that I wonder how a young woman seeing this can either have joy of her life or live at all, and not pine away for sorrow.

Now, whereto should I rehearse the hate and anger of folks?[31] For I know that many fathers have cut the throats of their daughters, brethren of their sisters, and kinsmen of their kinswomen. Hippomenes, a great man of Athens, when he knew his daughter desoiled[32] of one, he shut her up in a stable with a wild horse, kept meatless. For the horse, when he had suffered great hunger long and because he was of nature fierce, he waxed mad and all to-tore[33] the young woman to feed himself with. . . . [Vives goes on to describe the deaths or murders of other unchaste women.]

28. Before they seduce a virgin.
29. The maiden [probably literally] without God's grace does not hesitate to lose that . . . ?
30. Domains. The text reads "desermes."
31. Toward a girl who has lost her virginity.
32. Debauched. Cf. Ovid, *Ibis* 459–60, 335–36; Aeschines, *Against Timarchus* 182.
33. The text reads "to tare."

In Spain by our father's days in Tarraco, two brethren that thought their sister had been a maid, when they saw her great with child, they dissembled their anger so long as she was with child. But as soon as she was delivered of her child, they thrust swords into her belly and slew her, the midwife looking on. In the same part of Spain, when I was a child, three maidens with a long towel strangled a maid that was one of their companions, when they took her in the abominable deed. Histories be full of examples and daily ye see; neither it is marvel that these be done of[34] fathers and friends, and that the affection of love and charity is turned so suddenly into hate when the women, taken with the abominable and cruel love,[35] all love[36] cast quite out of their heart, hate their fathers and mothers, brethren and children, not only their friends and acquaintance. And this I wolde not that only maidens should think spoken unto them, but also married women and widows, and finally all women.

Now let the woman turn to herself and consider her own ungraciousness. She shall fear and abhor herself, nor take rest day nor night; but ever vexed with the scourge of her own conscience and burned as hot fire brands, shall never look steadfastly upon anybody, but she shall be in fear, lest they know somewhat of her lewdness, that then no body shall speak softly, but she shall think they speak of her unthriftiness. She shall never hear talking of naughty women, but she shall think it spoken because of her. Nor she shall never hear name of corruption spoken by any other, but she shall think it meant by her or of herself. Nor nobody shall stoure[37] prively in the house, but she shall fear least her ungraciousness be opened and that she shall be punished straight. What realm wouldst thou buy with such perpetual vexation, which many a man supposeth to be none other pain in hell. The same pain have wicked men, but women far sorer because their offenses be reckoned fouler, and they be more timorous of nature, and doubtless, if it be well considered, women be worthy these punishments and much worse that keep not their honesty[38] diligently.

For as for a man needeth many things, as wisdom, eloquence, knowledge of things, with remembrance, some craft to live by, justice, liberality, lusty stomach,[39] and other things more that were too long to rehearse. And though some of these do lack, it is not to be disliked, so that many of them be had, but in a woman no man will look for eloquence, great wit, or prudence, or craft to live by, or ordering of the commonweal, or justice, or liberality.

34. By.
35. For their lovers.
36. For family and friends.
37. Cause a tumult, fuss.
38. Chastity.
39. Courage.

Finally no man will look for any other thing of a woman, but her honesty, the which only, if it be lacked, is like as in a man, if he lack all that he should have. For in a woman, the honesty is in stead of[40] all.

It is an evil keeper that cannot keep one thing well committed to her keeping and put in trust to her with much commendation of words, and [e]specially which no man will take from her against her will, nor touch it, except she be willing herself.[41] The which thing only if a woman remember, it shall cause her to take better heed and to be a more wary keeper of her goodness. Which alone, though all other things be never so well in safety, so lost, all other things perish together therewith. What can be safe to a woman, sayth Lucretia, when her honesty is gone? And yet had she a chaste mind in a corrupt body.[42] Therefore, as Quintilian sayth, she thrust a sword into her body and avenged the compulsion, that the pure mind might be separated from the defiled body as shortly as could be. But I say not this because other should follow the deed, but the mind.[43] Because[44] she that hath once lost her honesty, should think there is nothing left. Take from a woman her beauty, take from her kindred, riches, comeliness, eloquence, sharpness of wit, cunning in her craft, give her chastity, and thou hast given her all things. And on that other side, give her all these things, and call her a naughty packe,[45] with that one word thou hast taken all from her, and hast left her bare and foul.

Chapter VIII. Of the Ordering of the Body in a Virgin

[Mothers and fathers must] keep[46] their daughters, [e]specially when they begin to grow from child's state, and hold them from men's company. For that time they[47] be given unto most lust of the body. Also the maidens should keep themselves both at all other and at that time [e]specially from either hearing or seeing or yet thinking any foul thing, which thing she shall labor to do. Nevertheless at other times, too, and unto the time they be married, much fasting shall be good, which doth not feeble the body, but bridle it and press it down and quench the heat of youth. . . . I condemn not with these words meats that God hath ordained to use with surrendering of thanks. But I take from young men and maidens the kindling of lust. For neither the burning Etna, nor the country of Vulcan, nor Vesuvius, nor

---

40. In place of.
41. Vives later admits that rape can take place against a married woman's will.
42. Quintilian, *Declamatio* III.11.
43. As a Christian, Vives cannot recommend suicide.
44. Here "by cause." Vives's translator uses both forms.
45. Applied to a person of worthless character—almost always with *naughty*.
46. Control, watch over.
47. Daughters.

yet Olympus boileth with such heat as the bodies of young folks enflamed with wine and delicate meats. . . . When I speak of hot meats, I wolde be understand in such exercises also that heat the body, and of ointments, spices, talking, and also sight of men. For all these be hurtful unto the chastity; for they fire the mind with filthy and jeopardous heat. [Sigs. Hiii– Liv omitted.]

From Chapter XI. Of the Virtues of a Woman and Examples That She Should Follow of Her Life
. . . first let her understand that chastity is the principal virtue of a woman, and counterpeiseth[48] with all the rest. If she have that, no man will look for any other; and if she lack that, no man will regard other. And as the stoic philosophers reckon that all goodness standeth in wisdom, and all ill in folly, insomuch that they said only the wise man to be[49] rich, free, a king, a citizen, fair, bold, and blessed; and a fool poor, a thrall, an outlaw, a stranger, foul, a coward, a wretched [man]. Likewise it is to be judged of chastity in women, that she that is chaste is fair, well-favored, rich, fruitful, noble, and all best things that can be named; and contrary, she that is unchaste is a sea and treasure of all illness. Now shamefastness and soberness be the inseparable companions of chastity, insomuch that she can not be chaste that is not ashamed; for that is as a cover and a veil of her face. For when nature had ordained that our faces should be open and bare of clothes, she gave it the veil of shamefastness wherewith it should be covered, and that for a great commendation, that who so did look upon it should understand some great virtue to be under that cover. . . . Now I suppose it be shewed plainly enough that chastity is as the queen of virtues in a woman, and that inseparable companions ever follow it, and that of shamefastness cometh soberness of which cometh all the other sort of virtues [be]longing unto women, demureness, measure, frugality, scarcity, diligence in house, cure[50] of devotion, meekness. [Vives cites the example of Mary[51] and then recounts stories of maidens who, when ravished, killed themselves for shame.]

From Chapter XII. How the Maid Shall Behave Herself Forth Abroad
Forth she must needs go sometimes, but I wolde it should be as seld[om] as may be, for many causes. Principally because as oft as a maid goeth forth among people, so often she cometh in judgment and extreme peril

48. Counterbalances, counterpoises.
49. Is.
50. Care.
51. Unlike Erasmus, Vives says Mary was always virgin.

of her beauty, honesty, demureness, wit, shamefastness, and virtue. For nothing is more tender than is the fame and estimation[52] of women, nor nothing more in danger of wrong; insomuch that it hath be[en] said and not without a cause to hang by a cobweb, because those things that I have rehearsed be required perfect in a woman, and folk's judgments be dangerous to please and suspicious. . . .

But before she go forth at door, let her prepare her mind and stomach none otherwise than if she went to fight. Let her remember what she shall hear, what she shall see, and what herself shall say. Let her consider with herself that something shall chance on every side that shall move her chastity and her good mind. Against these darts of the devil flying on every side, let her take the buckler of stomach defended with good examples and precepts, and a firm purpose of chastity, and a mind ever bent toward Christ. [Sigs. Niii–Q omitted.]

From Chapter XIIII. Of Loving

Love is bred by reason of company and communication with men; for among pleasures, feasts, laughing, dancing, and volupties[53] is the kingdom of Venus and Cupid. And with these things folk's minds be enticed and snared, and [e]specially the women's, on whom pleasure hath sorest dominion. O miserable young woman, careful[54] mayest thou be if thou depart out of that company entangled all ready; how much better had it been for thee to have bidden at home and rather to have broken a leg of thy body than a leg of thy mind? Howbeit, yet I will go about to find a remedy to save thee from taking if thee be untaken;[55] and if thou be taken, that thou mayest escape out again. . . . St. Jerome sayth of love in this manner, after the opinion of Aristotle and Plutarch: love of the beauty is a forgetting of reason and the next thing unto frenzy, a foul vice, and an unmannerly for an whole mind.[56] It troubleth all the wits, it breaketh and abateth high and noble stomachs, and draweth them down from the study and thinking of high and excellent things unto low and vile, and causeth them to be full of groaning and complaining, to be angry, hasty, foolhardy, strait in ruling, full of vile and servile flattering, unmeet for everything, and at the last unmeet for the love itself. . . . [Vives adduces stories of unwise, disastrous, loves; then he lists precepts on how to avoid love.] Give none ear unto the lover, no more than thou woldest do unto an enchanter or a

---

52. Reputation.
53. Acts of voluptuousness? not listed in the *OED*.
54. Full of care.
55. Untaken with love.
56. Jerome, *Against Jovinianus* I.49, *Nicene and Post-Nicene Fathers*, vol. 6, pp. 385–86.

sorcerer; for he cometh pleasantly and flattering, first praising the maid, shewing her how he is taken with the love of her beauty, and that he must be dead for her love. For these lovers know well enough the vain-glorious minds of many which have a great delight in their own praises wherewith they be caught like as the birder[57] beguileth the birds. He calleth thee fair, proper, witty, well-spoken, and of gentle blood, whereof peradventure thou art nothing at all, and thou, like a fool, art glad to hear those lies and weenest that thou dost seem so indeed when thou art never a whit so. . . .

He sayth he shall die for thee, yea, and that he dieth even straightway. Believest thou that? A fool; let him show thee how many have died for love among so many thousands as have been lovers. Love doth pain sometimes, but it never slayeth. Or though he did die for thee, yet it were better for thee to let him perish than be perished thyself, and that one should perish rather than twain. [The best way for a maid to avoid love is to avoid her would-be lover. Sigs. Qiv–Rii^v omitted.]

From Chapter XV. *How a Maiden Ought to Love*

And yet I wolde not a maid should clearly be without love, for mankind seemeth to be made and shapen unto love, to the intent they may be coupled together in charity and not with this carnal and filthy [love], earthly Cupid and Venus, but the heavenly and spiritual [love] which causeth holy love. Wherefore the maid shall have to love the Father, almighty God, her spouse Christ, and his mother, the holy virgin, and the church of God. . . . She hath also her own father and mother, which brought her into the world, and brought her up and nourished with so great labor and care, whom she ought to have in the stead of God, and love and worship and help with all her power. Therefore let her regard greatly their commandments and meekly obey them; neither shew in mind, countenance, nor gesture any stubbornness, but reckon them to be as it were a very image of almighty God, the father of all thing. She hath also to love her own virtues and soul and mind given unto God; and moreover the eternal pleasure and wealth which never shall have end.[58] Which things, if she love truly, she shall neither love man above God, neither set more by a bawdy fellow than her spouse, Christ, nor regard more an old filthy bawd then the pure virgin, Mary, neither love better the stinking stews than the holy church of God, nor the company of unclean women above the company of holy virgins, nor strangers above father and mother, nor her body above her soul, neither set more by other folk's vices than their virtues, nor minds that serve the

57. A fowler, who takes birds with snares and traps; also a common metaphor for the devil.
58. In paradise.

devil above those that serve God, neither them that wolde have her destroyed above them that wolde have her saved, nor a short pleasure above joy everlasting, nor the misery of damned folks above the perfect wealth of them that be saved. . . .

From Chapter XVI. How the Maid Shall Seek an Husband

[Virgil] signifieth that it becometh not a maid to talk where her father and mother be in communication about her marriage, but to leave all that care and charge wholly unto them which love her as well as her self doth. And let her think that her father and mother will provide no less diligently for her than she wolde for herself, but much better, by the reason they have more experience and wisdom. Moreover, it is not comely for a maid to desire marriage, and much less to shew herself to long therefore. . . . Therefore, when the father and the mother be busy about their daughter's marriage, let her help the matter forward with good prayer and desire of Christ and his mother with pure affection that she may have such a husband which shall not let nor hinder her from virtuous living, but rather provoke, exhort, and help her unto it. . . .

It is a great charge for a man to seek an husband for his daughter; neither it ought not to be gone about negligently. It[59] is a knot that cannot be lightly loosed; only death undoeth it. Wherefore the fathers and mothers procure unto their daughters either perpetual felicity if they marry them to good men or perpetual misery, marrying them unto ill. Here is much to be studied and great deliberation to be taken with good advisement and counsel afore a man determine ought. For there is much weariness in marriage and many pains must be suffered. There is nothing but one that shall cause marriage to be easy unto a woman, that is, if she chance on a good and wise husband. O foolish friends and maids also that set more by them that be fair or rich or of noble birth than them that be good, and cast yourself into perpetual care. For if thou be married to a fair one, he will be proud of his person; and if thou marry to a rich one, his substance maketh him stately; and if thou be married to one of great birth, his kindred exalteth his stomach. . . . And in very deed it were bett[er] to be married unto an image or a picture or to a painted table than to be married to a vicious or a foolish or a brainless man. [Sigs. Si^v–Tii^v omitted.]

But they that would keep the nature of things whole and pure, nor corrupt them with wrong understanding, should reckon that wedlock is a band and coupling of love, benevolence, friendship, and charity; comprehending within it all names of goodness, sweetness, and amity. Therefore let the maid neither catch and deceive by subtlety him that should be her

59. Marriage.

inseparable fellow, nor pull and draw by plain violence, but take and be taken by honest, simple, plain, and good manner, that neither of them complain with both their harms, or say they were deceived or compelle[d].

The Second Book of the Instruction of a Christian Woman

[The second book is concerned with the duties and obligations of married women. Sigs. Tiii–Uiii omitted.]

From Chapter III. Of Two the Greatest Points in a Married Woman

Among all other virtues of a married woman, two there ought to be most special and greatest, the which only if she have them may cause marriage to be sure, stable, durable, easy, light, sweet, and happy; and again, if the one be lacked, it shall be unsure, painful, unpleasant, and intolerable, yea, and full of misery and wretchedness. These two virtues that I mean be chastity and great love toward her husband. The first she must bring with her forth of her father's house. The second she must take after she is once entered in at her husband's door; and both father and mother, kinfolks, and all her friends left, she shall reckon to find all these in only her husband. And in both these virtues she shall represent the image of holy church, which is both most chaste and most faithfully doth keep truth and promise unto her spouse, Christ. . . .

A married woman ought to be of greater chastity than an unmarried. For if that thou then pollute and defile thy chastity, as God forbid thou shouldest, hark, I pray thee, how many thou shalt offend and displease at once with one wicked deed. How many revengers thou shalt provoke against thee. They be so many and so heinous that among some a man can make no difference, but I shall gather them without any order and set them before thine eyes. First thou offendest two, which ought to be unto thee both most in price and most dear and best, that is to say, almighty God, by whose means ye were coupled together and by whose deity thou hast made oath to keep the pureness of body. And next unto God, thou offendest thine husband, unto whom only thou hast given thyself, in whom thou breakest all loves and charities if thou once be defiled. For thou art unto him as Eve was unto Adam, that is to say, his daughter, his sister, his companion, and his wife, and as I might say another himself.

Wherefore, thou desperate woman that hast abused thyself so, thou farest in like manner as though thou haddest strangled, destroyed, or murdered thyself. Thou hast broken the greatest band that can be in the world. Thou hast broken, thou false woman, the most holy band of temporal law, that is to say, thy faith and thy truth, which once given, one enemy in the field will keep to another though he should stand in danger of death, and thou like a false wretch doth not keep it to thine husband, which ought to be more dear unto thee by right than thyself. Thou defilest the most pure church, which holp[60] to couple thee; thou breakest worldly company; thou breakest the laws; thou offendest thy country; thou beatest thy father with a bitter scourge; thou beatest thy sorrowful mother, thy sisters, thy brethren, thy kinfolks, alliances,[61] and all thy friends; thou givest unto the company once an example of mischief and castest an everlasting blot and shame upon thy kin; thou, like a cruel mother, casteth thy children into such a necessity that they can never hear speak of[62] their mother without shame nor of their father without doubting. What greater offense can they do; or what greater wickedness can they infect themselves withal that destroy their country and perish[63] all laws and justice, and murther their fathers and mothers, and finally defile and mar all things both spiritual and temporal? What good saint or God or what man, thinkest thou, can favor thee that dost so? All thy country folks,[64] all rights and laws, thy country itself, thy parents, all thy kinfolk and thine husband himself shall damn and punish thee. Almighty God will avenge most rigorously his majesty so displeased and offended of[65] thee.

And know thou this, woman, that the chastity and honesty which thou hast is not thine, but committed and betaken unto thy keeping by thine husband. Wherefore thou dost the more wrong to give away that thing which is another body's, without the owner's license. And therefore the married woman of Lacedemon, when a young man desired of her that unhonest thing,[66] answered him, I wolde grant thee thine asking, young man, if it were mine own to give that thou askest, but that thing which thou woldest have while I was unmarried was my father's and now is my husband's. She made him a merry and wise answer. But St. Paul speaketh full wisely for the [ad]monition of good women where he teacheth the church of God, saying: "A woman hath no power of[67] her own body, but her husband . . . no not unto the goodness of continence."[68] [Sigs. X–Xii[v] omitted.]

60. Helped.
61. The text reads "alyantes"; relatives by marriage.
62. Speech about? spoken of?
63. Here transitive; cause to perish.
64. Citizens of your country.
65. With? by?
66. The loss of her chastity?
67. Over.
68. 1 Cor. 7:3–6. (Vives says that a woman may not even remain continent without her husband's permission.)

From Chapter IV. How She Shall Behave Herself unto Her Husband

... if it be true that men do say that friendship maketh one heart of two, much more truly and effectually ought wedlock to do the same, which far passeth all manner both friendship and kindred. Therefore, it is not said that wedlock doth make one man, or one mind, or one body of two, but clearly one person. Wherefore the words that the man spake of the woman, saying for her sake a man should leave both father and mother and [a]bide with his wife, the same words the woman ought both to say and think with more reason. For although there be one made of two, yet the woman is as daughter unto her husband, and of nature more weaker. Wherefore she needeth his aid and succor. Wherefore if she be destitute of her husband, desert[ed], and left alone, she may soon take hurt and wrong. Therefore if she be with her husband, where he is, there hath she both her country, her house, her father, her mother, her friends, and all her treasure. [Sigs. Xiii^v–Yii omitted.]

Neither I wolde that she should love her husband as one loveth his friend or his brother, that is to say, I will that she shall give him great worship, reverence, great obedience, and service also; which thing not only the example of the old world teacheth us, but also all laws, both spiritual and temporal, and Nature herself cryeth and commandeth that the woman shall be subject and obedient to the man. And in all kinds of beasts the females obey the males, and waiten upon them, and fawn upon them, and suffer themselves to be corrected of them. Which thing Nature sheweth must be and is convenient to be done. Which, as Aristotle in his book of beasts sheweth, hath given less strength and power unto the females of all kinds of beasts than to the males and more soft flesh and tender hair.[69] Moreover, these parts which nature hath given for weapons of defense unto beasts, as teeth, horns, spurs, and such other, the most part of females lack, which their males have, as harts[70] and boars. And if any females have any of these, yet be they more stronger in the males, as horns of bulls be more stronger than of kine.[71] In all the which things Nature sheweth that the male's duty is to succor and defend, and the female's to follow and to wait upon the male and to creep under his aid and obey him, that she may live the better.

But let us leave the examples of beasts which make us ashamed of ourselves without[72] we pass them in virtue, and let us ascend up unto man's

69. *Historia Animalium* (History of Animals) IX.2, 608^a–608^b.
70. Stags.
71. Cows.
72. Unless.

reason. . . . For in wedlock the man resembleth the reason and the woman the body. Now reason ought to rule and the body to obey if a man will live. Also St. Paul sayth the head of the woman is the man.[73] Here now I enter into the divine commandments, which in stomachs of reasonable people ought of reason to bear more rule and value than laws, more than all man's reasons, and more than the voice of nature herself. God the maker of this whole world in the beginning, when the world was yet but rude[74] and new, giving laws unto mankind, he gave this charge unto the woman. Thou shalt be under thine husband's rule, and he shall have dominion over thee. . . .[75] But foolish women do not see how sore they dishonest themselves that take the sovereignty of[76] their husband, of whom all their honor must come. And so in seeking for honor, they lose it. For if the husband lack honor, the wife must needs go without it. Neither kindred, riches, nor wealth can avail her. For who will give any honor to that man whom he seeth mastered by a woman. And again, if thy husband be honorable, be thou never so low of birth, never so poor, never so uncomely of face, yet canst thou not lack honor. . . .

Nor let them[77] love goodly men for their beauty, nor rich men for their money, nor men of great authority for their honor; for if they do so, then shall they hate the sickly, the poor, and those that bear no rule. If thou have a learned husband, learn good holy lessons of[78] him; if he be virtuous, do after him. . . . if she chance upon an infortunate husband, neither hate nor despise him therefore, but rather contrary. She ought, if he be poor, to comfort him, and advertise[79] him to call into remembrance that virtue is the chief riches. . . . But beware thou fall not into such a wicked mind to will him for lucre of[80] money to occupy any unhonest crafts or to do any unhappy deeds that thou mayst live more delicately, or more wealthily, or go more gaily and gorgeously arrayed, or dwell in more goodly housing; and at few words, compel not him to use any filthy occupation or drudgery for thy welfare, nor to sweat and to toil that thou mayst lie at ease. For it were better for thee to eat brown bread and drink clay and mirey[81] water

73. I Cor. II:3. "But I would have you know that the head of every man is Christ: and the head of the woman is the man: and the head of Christ is God." See also Eph. 5:23; Gen. 1:26.

74. In a natural state?

75. Gen. 3:16.

76. Over.

77. Women.

78. From.

79. Advise.

80. Gain of.

81. As in mire.

than cause thy husband to fall unto any slubbery[82] work or stinking occupation and exceeding labor for to escape thy scolding and chiding at
home. For the husband is his own ruler and his wife's lord, and not her
subject; neither the wife ought to crave any more of her husband than she
seeth she may obtain with his heart and good will, wherein many women
do amiss which with their ungodly crying and unreasonable calling, craving, and bullying upon them,[83] driveth them to seek unlawful means of
living and to do ungracious deeds, to bear out with all their[84] gluttony and
vain pride. . . . but thou, good daughter that wilt do well, shalt not withdraw
thine husband from goodness, but rather exhort him unto virtue though
thou shouldest be sure to lose all thy goods. . . .

Wherefore if thine husband be foul, yet love his heart and mind whereunto thou art married in deed. And if thine husband be sick, then must
thou play the true wife, comfort him, nourish him, and make as much of
him as though he were never so whole and so strong, and so shall he be
the less pained if he see thee as it were take pain with him, and in a
manner translate and shift part of his sickness unto thy self. For she is no
good wife that is merry when her husband is sorry, or whole and lusty
when he is sick and heavy. Bide thou still by his bed's side and lighten
his dolor sometime with comfortable words, sometime with gentle fomentations.[85] Touch thou his wounds thyself; touch thou his sore and painful
body with thine own hands. Do thou both cover and uncover him thine
own self; take and bear away the chamber vessel[86] with his water thyself.
Nor abhor not these services, nor put them not unto thy servant's [hands],
which will go more slowly about them because they love him not so
much. . . .

Though that virtue by itself can not fail to come to light and shineth
well enough in the dark by the brightness of itself, notwithstanding, as
much as lieth in me, I will not suffer but that [I will declare what] I have
seen myself and many more know as well as I. I will declare that both
they that now be and they that shall come hereafter may know it: Clare,
the wife of Bernard Valdaura,[87] a fair and a goodly maid, when she was

82. Slovenly.
83. Their husbands.
84. Their wives'.
85. The application to the body of flannels, etc., soaked in hot water, whether simple
or medicated, or of any other warm, soft, medicinal substance.
86. Urinal.
87. This lady later became Vives's mother-in-law. When she married Bernard Valdaura, he was forty-six and she eighteen. The family was distantly related to Vives
himself before he married Margaret Valdaura, Bernard's daughter, in 1524. Erasmus took
Vives to task for including family stories in his book of instruction. See *Vives: On*

first married at Bruges and brought to bed unto her husband, which was 46 year of age, the first night saw his legs rolled and wrapped with clouts,[88] and found that she had chanced on a sore and sickly husband. Yet for all that she loathed him never the more, nor began not to hate him whom yet she had no space[89] to love. Not long after that, the foresaid Valdaura fell into a great sickness, insomuch that all physicians despaired his life; then she and her mother gave such diligence unto the sick man that of six weeks continually together neither of them once put off their clothes except it were to change their smocks, nor rested in the night past one hour or three at the most, and that but in their clothes. The root of the disease was that we call the French pox,[90] a wondrous sore and contagious sickness. Physicians counselled her not to touch him so, nor come so near him, and the same her friends counselled her. And her companions and gossips said it was sinfully done to vex the man in the world, or keep him longer on live[91] with his sickness, and bade her provide some good thing for the soul, as for the body care no more but how it might be buried. With which saying, she was never a whit abashed, but very diligently procured both such as was for the wealth of his soul and prepared wholesome meats for his body, and gave great intendance[92] about him, often changing his sheets and his clouts because he had an exceeding lax,[93] and matter and filth ran out of diverse parts of his body. Wherewith she was so busied that the most part of the day she never rested but ran up and down all the day long. So at the last, by the good means of his wife, Valdaura escaped the great jeopardy that both the physicians and all other men feared. His wife had plucked him from death by strong hand. And some jested more merrily than becometh Christian folks and said that God had purposed to have slain Valdaura but his wife wolde not let him go out of her hands.

After that, by the reason of an hot humor[94] running from his head, the gristle within his nose began for to canker.[95] Wherefore the physicians had given him a powder which must be blowen in with a pen or a reed into his nose, which service when every man abhorred because of the tedious

---

Education, p. lxxxii. It is worthwhile reprinting this section in its entirety because it provides us with an almost unique portrayal of nursing practices and of the relationship between one man and his wife in early modern Europe.

88. Pieces of cloth, patches.
89. Time.
90. Syphilis.
91. Alive.
92. Attendance.
93. Loose bowels?
94. Moisture; perhaps one of the four chief fluids of the body (blood, phlegm, choler, and melancholy or black choler).
95. Become cancered.

savor,[96] his wife refused not to do it. Also within a while his cheeks and
his chin brake out of[97] scabs, wheals,[98] and of scales, that no barber neither
well could nor gladly wolde shave him; then his wife, with a pair of scissors,
found the means to clip his beard wondrous properly. Straight after, he
fell into another long disease which lasted near seven year[s]. Where she,
never being weary with continual diligence and labor about him, prepared
his meat, and every day did salve and bind his sore and stinking legs and
running of matter so handsomely that thou woldest say, if thou haddest
seen her, that she had handled musk and not such stinking gear. And did
all this her own self with all other business that was for to do about him,
and yet had she in her house three maids and a daughter of her own of
good age. Moreover, when the air of him and breath was such that no man
might abide near by ten passes, she wolde swear that she thought it marvelous sweet. And once she was very angry with me because I said it stank,
for she said it seemed unto her like the savor of ripe and sweet fruit.
Moreover, when there was required great roast[99] daily in the house to help
and nourish the man oppressed with so many sicknesses, nor had neither
rents nor other profits coming in, she spoiled herself of all her rings, chains,
brooches, and clothes lest he should lack ought during his sickness. She
was content as for herself with any fare, so that her husband might have
that should do his painful body good, so he by the means of his wife, with
that doleful body, more like unto a grave than a body, continued ten year
from the beginning of his sickness, in the which space she had two children
by him and six before, for she was married twenty years in the whole; and
yet was she never infected nor once touched with the contagious scab,
neither she nor yet none of her children, but had all their bodies both
whole and clean. Whereby a man may clearly perceive how much their
holiness and virtue is worth that love their husbands with all their hearts
as duty is, which doubtless God will never leave unrewarded. So at the
last this foresaid man died sick and old, and passed out of his continual
pain. For whose departing this same Clara his wife made much sorrow,
that all that ever knew her say they never saw woman make such sorrow
for her husband that were both young, whole, fair, lusty, and rich. . . . [Sigs.
b–pii^v omitted.]

The Third Book of the Instruction of a Christian Woman
[This is the shortest by far of Vives's three books and deals with widows.]

96. Smell.
97. Into.
98. In medicine, a flat, usually circular, elevation of the skin, esp. that characteristic
of urticaria.
99. Roast meats?

From Chapter I. Of the Mourning of Widows

Good woman, when her husband is dead, ought to know that she hath the greatest loss and damage that can bechance her in the world, and that there is taken from her the heart of mutual and tender love toward her, and that she hath lost not only the one half of her own life (as learned men were wont to say when they had lost them whom they loved dearly) but herself also to be taken from herself all together and perished. Of this cause may come honest weeping, sorrow, and mourning with good occasion, and wailing not to blame. It is the greatest token that can be of an hard heart and an unchaste mind, a woman not to weep for the death of her husband. Howbeit there be two kinds of women which in mourning for their husbands in contrary ways do both amiss: that is, both they that mourn too much and those that mourn too little. I have seen some women no more moved with the death of their husbands than it had been but one of light acquaintance that had died, which was an evident sign of but cold love unto their husbands. Which thing is so foul that none can be more abominable nor more cursed. And if a man ask them why they do so or rebuke them, they answer again, the nature of the country so requireth. . . .[100] I have seen some nothing moved with the death of their husbands. [Sigs. piii^v–[q4^v] omitted.]

From Chapter III. Of the Minding of Her Husband

Let a widow remember and have still before her eyes in her mind that our souls do not perish together with the body, but be loosed of the bonds of our corporal grossness, and be lightened from the burden of the body, and that death is nothing but a separation of the soul from the body, and that the soul departeth not so from the body into another life that it clearly giveth over our matters here in this world, and they have been ofttimes heard of them that were on live, and they know much of our acts and fortunes by the shewing of angels that go between.[101] Wherefore a good widow ought to suppose that her husband is not utterly dead, but liveth both with life of his soul, which is the very life, and beside with her remembrance. For our friends live with us though they be absent from us or dead, if the lively image of them be imprinted in our hearts with often

---

100. The deleted passage resembles Edmund's speech in *King Lear* 1.2.118–26, about the planets: "And the same excuses lay them for them that use to put the cause of their vices in some planet or qualities of the air or earth where they dwell. But the nature of the country is cause of no vice. For then the country ought to be punished and not the offensours. We take no vice of the heaven or air, but of our own manners. For under every sky is both good living and ill."

101. This is a controversial and, indeed, an extreme doctrine.

thinking upon them, and daily renewed, and their life ever wax fresh in our minds. And if we forget them, then they die towards us. . . .

Then what should a Christian woman do? Let her keep the remembrance of her husband with reverence and not with weeping, and let her take for a solemn and a great oath to swear by her husband's soul and let her live and do so as she shall think to please her husband, being now no man but a spirit purified and a divine thing. Also let her take him for her keeper and spy, not only of her deeds, but also of her conscience. Let her handle so her house and household and so bring up her children that her husband may be glad, and think that he is happy to leave such a wife behind him. And let her not behave herself so that his soul have cause to be angry with her and take vengeance on her ungraciousness.[102] [Sigs. r^v–[s4^v] omitted.]

From Chapter VII. Of Second Marriages

For to condemn and reprove utterly second marriages, it were a point of heresy. Howbeit that better is to abstain than marry again is not only counselled by Christian pureness, that is to say by divine wisdom, but also by pagans, that is to say, by worldly wisdom. [Vives gives examples of pagan widows who did not marry again.] Notwithstanding, widows lay many causes wherefore they say they must marry again. Of whom Saint Jerome speaketh in this manner, writing unto the holy woman, Furia. "Young widows, of whom there hath many gone backward after the devil after that they have had their pleasure by marrying in Christ be wonted to say, My goods spill daily; the heritage of mine ancestry perisheth; my servants speak stubbornly and presumptuously; my maid will not do my commandment. Who shall go before me forth? Who shall answer for my house rent? Who shall teach my young sons? Who shall bring up my young daughters? And so they lay that for a cause to marry for, which should rather let[103] them from it. For she bringeth upon her children an enemy, and not a nourisher, not a father, but a tyrant. And she, inflamed with vicious lust, forgetteth her own womb, and she that late afore sat mourning among her children, that perceive not their own loss and harms, now is picked up a new wife. Whereto layest thou the cause[104] in thine inheritance and pride of thy servants? Confess thine own viciousness. For none of you take a husband but to the intent that she will lie with him nor except her lust prick her. What a ragiousness[105] is it to set thy chastity common like an harlot, that

102. The idea that the soul of a husband can take vengeance upon his living wife is unorthodox.

103. Prevent.

104. Of the new marriage?

105. Rage, frenzy?

thou mayst gather riches? And for a vile and a thing that shall soon pass away to [de]file thy chastity, that is a thing most precious and everlasting. If thou have children already, what needest thou to marry? If thou have none, why dost thou not fear the barrenness that thou hast proved afore; and adventurest upon an uncertain thing and forgoest thine honesty and chastity that thou wast sure of?

Now thou hast writing of spousage[106] made thee that within short while after thou may be compelled to write a testament.[107] The husband shall feign himself sick and shall do on live and in good health that he wolde have to do when thou shalt die. And if it chance that thou have children by thy second husband, than riseth strife and debate at home within thy house. Thou shalt not be at liberty to love thine own children equally, neither to look indifferently upon them that thou hast borne; thou shalt reach them meat secretly; he will envy him[108] that is dead and except thou hate thine own children, thou shalt seem to love their father yet. And if he have children by another wife, then shall players and jesters rail and jest upon thee as a cruel stepdame.[109] If thy stepson be sick or his head ache, thou shalt be defamed for a witch; and if thou give him not meat, thou shalt be accused of cruelty; and if thou give any, thou shalt be called a poisoner. What, I pray thee, hath second marriages so pleasant that can be able to recompense these evils."[110] Thus saith Saint Jerome. As for the praise of continence and chastity and counselling from second marriages, what can I be able to say after that eloquent fountain of Saint Jerome or the sweet delicates[111] of Saint Ambrose's speech? Therefore, who so desireth to know any thing of those matters, let him look it of them. . . .

Nevertheless, I would counsel a good woman to continue in holy widowhead, namely if she have children, which thing is the intent and fruit of matrimony. But and she doubt lest she can not avoid the pricks of nature with that life, let her give an ear unto St. Paul the apostle writing unto the Corinthinans in this wise: "I say to unmarried women and widows, it were good for them if they kept themselves as I am: but yet if they cannot suffer, let them marry. For it is bett[er] to marry than burn." And the same apostle writeth unto Timothy thus: "Put away young widows, for

---

106. Spousal, marriage.

107. Now you have a contract of marriage; soon you will be compelled to write a will.

108. Her first husband.

109. Stepmother.

110. St. Jerome, "To Furia on the Duty of Remaining a Widow" (Letter 54), A.D. 394, in *Select Letters of St. Jerome*, trans. F. A. Wright (Cambridge, Mass.: Harvard University Press, 1933, rpt. 1963), pp. 228–65.

111. Delicacies.

when they have abused themselves at large, then wolde they marry to Christ, and are condemned because they have refused their first promise, and walk idle from house to house, neither only idle, but trifling and babbling, prating and talking such things as becometh not. Therefore I wolde that the younger should marry and bring forth children and rule their house and give their enemy none occasion to say ill by them. For there be some which straight after their conversion have followed Satan."[112] Yet let them beware that they do it not by and by[113] after their husband's death, for that is a token that they loved not them, for whose departing they have so soon left sorrowing, mourning, and all desire of them. And if they must provide ought for their house or children, let them see to it before the business of marriage and dominion of a new husband. And let them get such husbands as be according for widows to be married unto, nor young men, wanton, hot, and full of play, ignorant, and riotous, that can neither rule their house nor their wife nor themselves neither; but take an husband something past middle age, sober, sad, and of good wit, expert with great use of the world, which with his wisdom may keep all the house in good order, which by his discretion may so temper and govern all thing that there may be alway[s] at home sober mirth and obedience, without frowardness, and the household keep in their labor and duty, without pain, and all thing clear and holy. And let them weet and know that these content him, whose pleasure only they shall all more esteem than the whole country's beside.

The Office and Duty of an Husband
From the "Epistle" of the Translator to
Sir Anthony Brown, Knight

I have translated this excellent and fine piece of work of Master Vives, a philosopher most famous, the which doth teach men how to choose their wives, how to love and to entreat[1] them, how and wherewith to instruct them, how to array and seemly to apparel them, how to chasten and correct them, how in their absence and in their age to use them, and at their departing unto God, how to leave them. And on the other side, it teacheth your wives how to fear and to honor God, how to love, obey, and serve their husbands, how to bring up and nourter[2] their children, how to have

---

112. 1 Tim. 5:11–15.
113. Immediately.
1. Treat.
2. Nurture.

an eye to their husband's honesty and profit, whether they should be learned or no, what authors they should read, what company they should haunt and avoid, how to keep their houses in good report, and themselves clean and undefiled. O how excellent then, and how profitable a book is this, for the wealth[3] both of man and woman, and most worthy to be read of all Christians, and of those which desire and seek to live quietly in matrimony, and joyfully in this transitory vale and dungeon of all misery.

Of the Office and Duty of an Husband

It seemed unto the author of nature,[4] when he laid the foundation of the ages and time that was to come, that all such beasts which were subject unto sickness and death should at one generation and birth bring forth but few younglings, to the end their generation might increase and endure for ever, and that they of a little beginning might multiply and arise unto an infinite multitude, and of mortal things obtain, as it were, an immortality. But all other beasts do indifferently (without any order or law) obey nature and give themselves unto procreation. And this is, as it were, an universal law whereunto we do perceive and see that all manner of beasts do willingly obey, although there be among these that live in society and observe the holiness of matrimony so undefiledly that they may well instruct and teach many thousands of men the chastity, the charity, and faith, the manner and quality of matrimony; and in this number are swans, turtledoves, crows, and doves. But man, being born to live in company and in the communion of life, was bound by the author of nature with more exact and straighter[5] laws of matrimony. Nor he would not that man untemperately should meddle with many women, nor that the woman should submit herself to many men. Therefore he bound them together in lawful marriage, and delivered her unto the man, not only for generation's sake, but also for the society and fellowship of life. And this is it, that Moses doth say in Genesis, that the prudent and wise maker of the world said: It is not good that man should be alone; let us make him a help like unto himself.[6] [Sigs. A[v]–[C-7] omitted.]

Of the Election and Choice of a Wife[7]

Or ever I do speak of the choice of a wife, I must remove from the mind of those which I do instruct and teach that fury, wherewith they choose

3. "Welthe"—perhaps well-being.
4. God.
5. More severe.
6. Gen. 2:18
7. No chapter numbers are indicated in the text.

not their wives but invade them; they marry them not but ravish them and deceive them, and contrary to their wills do take them. If the woman were a certain kind of merchandise, peradventure it should not seem so unseemly[8] by all manner of means and subtlety to obtain her; for howsoever she were obtained, she would serve to that use; but considering that now she shall be his fellow for ever, if she love him not (be she never so fair, nor never so burdened with riches) she shall be continually molestious.[9] And what a madness were it to begin such a mystery of love with hatred? Love is gotten by love, by honesty and fidelity, and not by violence. For a time, peradventure, thou mayst enjoy her goods, her beauty, and her parentage and kindred, but you shalt never enjoy thy wife. Those things are best which are most conformable unto nature. . . . Adam did not ravish Eve but received her, delivered unto him by God, the father, he gave her not unto him perforce, but that they should mutually love one another. He drew the one out of the other, and gave them like nature and fashion, to the intent that they or ever[10] they were married, should seem and appear to be one thing and not two. [Sigs. [C8–D8] omitted.]

But to the intent that every man may know what he should look to have of a woman or ever he choose her, I have determined with few words to describe the nature of a woman,[11] to the end that no man looking to have of her things impossible should be deceived. . . . After that nature hath cast the seed of man into the motherly and natural place,[12] it incorporateth the same, and if it find sufficient heat,[13] it bringeth forth a man child; if not, a woman. So that, when it wanteth the most excellent, active, and lively quality, the woman remaineth feeble and weak, not only in human generation, but also in all other proportion of her kind. And through such filthiness[14] as increaseth in her (the which the feeble heat that is in her is not sufficient nor able to cast forth) she is less of stature, and more sickly than other[15] be, and of this by and by (if she be not great-bellied), she suffreth her menstruation. She is timorous also, for it is heat that encourageth the man and maketh him bold and hardy. And through fear, she is

8. The text reads "unseembly."
9. Troublsome or vexatious? not listed in the *OED*.
10. Before.
11. Later (Sig. [E5]) Vives defines a man: "that is, a feeble beast, impotent, mutable, subject unto infirmities and affections, inclining to evil, the which by learning may be amended, and impaired by evil customs."
12. The place of natural generation, the womb.
13. In humor psychology, heat was a quality pertaining more to men than to women, who were thought to be colder. (All material things—including emotions, which derive from the dispositions of the body—were thought to be variously cold, hot, moist, dry.)
14. Vives seems to be referring to the menses.
15. Men.

covetous,[16] and taught secretly by nature. She knoweth her self to be feeble, and needful of many things, and busy about many trifles, and like unto a ruinous house, that must be underset and upholden with many small props. And through fear she is full of suspicion, complaints, envious, and troubled with many and diverse thoughts. And for lack of experience of things, of wisdom, and of knowing her own debility, she thinketh continually that she shall be despised. And therefore in this feeble and weak nature, anger and a desire to be revenged doth kindle, as it were inflare,[17] continually. She loveth also to be gay and well apparelled, because she wolde not be contemned. And as impotent and subject to all casualties[18] on every side, she doth seek whereunto she may lean and stay herself. And thou shalt easily perceive that certain of them do attribute unto glory things of no estimation, as to have some great man to her neighbor, or that some great and mighty prince did salute her, or call unto her. . . .

Many women are full of words, partly through the variety of thoughts and affections, the which, as they succeed one another, so they come into their minds and from thence unto the mouth, partly by suspicion and fear, lest that by holding their peace, they be not judged capable or that through ignorance they know not what they say. All these foresaid things are of nature[19] and not of the women themselves, and therefore they are not only found in women, but also in such men as other[20] of nature or else by the first constitution and making of the body, the which can not be changed, are woman-like. . . .

Nor yet all women have not these faults in like sort and manner, for there hath been, and are yet not a few, which are of a more strong and constant mind than many men be. [Examples follow.] Nor Christ wolde not that even in our time we should be without an example, the which should flow and descend unto our posterity, left and exhibited unto us by Catherine, the Spaniard Queen of England, and wife unto King Henry the eight of most famous memory, of whom that may be more truly spoken of than that, that Valerius[21] writeth of Lucrece, that there was in her feminine body a man's heart by the error and fault of nature. I am ashamed of myself and of all those that have read so many things when I behold that woman so strongly to support and suffer so many and diverse adversities, that there is not one (although he were well worthy to be remembered and spoken of among our elders) that with such constancy of mind hath suffered cruel

16. The text reads "conetous"—a misprint?
17. The text may read "inflaxe"—inflame?
18. Chances.
19. Innate.
20. Either.
21. Valerius Maximus in *Facta et Dicta Memorabilia* Liber VI.I.I.

fortune or could so have ruled flattering felicity as she did. If such incredible virtue had fortuned then, when honor was the reward of virtue, this woman had dusked[22] the brightness of the Heroes[23] and, as a divine thing and a godly, sent down from heaven, had been prayed unto in temples, although she lack no temples, for there cannot be erected unto her a more ample or a more magnificent temple than that, the which every man among all nations marveling at her virtues, have in their own hearts builded and erected. . . .

But as women are far more weaker than man, so they are far more meek and humble: therefore thou mayst bring them under and rule them other by manly power or by sharpness of wit, by wisdom, or by the long use and experience of things. And it is much more grievous to suffer an evil master then an evil servant. And truly a woman, seeing that she is under the dominion and power of man, ought to be such a one,[24] nor we should not mistrust but that the divine sapience hath touched all things strongly from one end to another, and doth order them most lovingly. . . . [thus] man should not will, nor wish a woman to have any other affections or conditions[25] although they might change them. For if the woman were robust and strong both of mind and body, how could she suffer to be obedient and subject to him that were no stronger then herself? Would she not wax insolent and proud, having in will to rule both house and household, and to strive peradventure with her husband for the mastery? Who could keep such a bold piece at home, but that she would be abroad? If she be prodigal, she will never save that her husband gaineth, the which saving is for a man's household a thing most necessary. If she neglect or little regard small things, how shall she keep the instruments of her house, the which are made of many small pieces? How shall she keep her household stuff, among the which are many vile things, worn, destroyed[26] and broken? Who wolde take upon him the office and charges of a house? Or the office of a cook? Who would nourish and bring up children? What a torment were it for a man to do those things? A man wolde rather leave all and dwell in a desert than to dwell in such misery and bondage.

[Vives goes on to discuss the relative merits of marrying virgins, young widows, old widows, or widows with or without children.] I wolde not counsel thee to marry her with whom thou hast been in amors withal,[27] whom thou flatteredst, whom thou didst serve, whom thou calledst thy

22. Darkened.
23. Vives is referring to the Greek heroes—among whom is, for instance, Hercules.
24. One who is weaker and more humble than man?
25. Than they are born with.
26. The text reads "destrued," from L. *destruere*.
27. In a love affair.

heart, thy life, thy mistress, thy light, thy eyes, with other such words as foolish love doth persuade, using impiety against God, which is the end[28] of all desire and goodness. This submission[29] is and should be the cause that she doth not regard thee, but disdaineth to serve thee, whose lady she was as she esteemed, and whom she found more obedient unto her, even with the peril and danger of life than any other slave that was bought for money. Thus it appeareth that it is not convenient that the servant[30] should rule the mistress, for after that love, hatred, reverence, contempt, and fear hath once occupied the mind of man they leave certain continual marks.[31] [Sigs. Kv^v–Li omitted.]

Of the Access and Going unto Marriage

[Sigs. Li^v–Nv^v omitted.]

... when thou goest a-wooing, thou must beware and take heed that thou (whether the woman be promised thee, or now brought home unto thee) give not thy self to those unmeet and voluptuous love and lusts by the which men are compelled to say and to do many things which are filthy and childish. ... Nor thou canst not keep thy majesty in such filthy love, for Ovid doth say that majesty and love doth not agree, nor remain nor tarry not in one place.[32] But the poet doth speak of this earthly and blind love, for cordial[33] and wise love doth not diminish majesty. Nor a woman cannot suffer nor take him for her master that was some time her servant. And the weaker a woman is in mind, the more she desireth to be in power, and if she had once domination and rule, she taketh it as an injury, if she rule not still. Nor there is no rule more violent or more grievous than theirs, that by all reason ought to be subjects, as the rule of servants, artificers, children, and women.[34] But as we would that the man when he loveth should remember his majesty, so we would that when he ruleth he forget not his love, nor to temper it with majesty. And when he doth think himself to be the head and the soul, and the woman as it were the flesh and the body, he ought in like manner to remember that she is his fellow and companion of his goods and labors, and that their children be common between them, bone of bones, and flesh of the flesh of man. And thus there shall be in wedlock a certain sweet and pleasant conversation, without the which it is no marriage but a prison, a hatred, and a perpetual torment of

28. Purpose.
29. Of the man.
30. The lover.
31. Habitual actions, habits of life.
32. Ovid, *Ars Amatoria* (*Art of Love*) II.195–233.
33. Of the heart.
34. This catalogue derives from Aristotle.

the mind. Let thy wife perceive and know that for the good opinion that thou hast of her, thou dost love her simply and faithfully, and not for any utility or pleasure. For who so doth not perceive that he is beloved for his own sake, will not lightly do the same to another, for the thing that is loved, loveth again. . . . [Sigs. [N7ᵛ]–Ovᵛ omitted.]

Of the Discipline and Instruction of Women

. . . Our flesh, being infected and corrupted with sin and continually and inseparably united unto the mind, doth first of all and principally offer unto itself the perverse and evil opinions of all things, and then as much as it may doth fasten such things unto it as be hurtful as well to the one sect[35] as to the other. And to extirpate and weed out such sinister opinions and judgment, we have need of discipline, the which with the knowledge of good letters may easily be obtained and gotten. But it is now in question whether it be expedient for a woman to be learned or no. [Sigs. Oviᵛ–Piᵛ omitted.]

The woman is, even as man is, a reasonable creature and hath a flexible wit both to good and evil, the which with use and counsel may be altered and turned. And although there be some evil and lewd women, yet that doth no more prove the malice[36] of their nature than of men, and therefore the more ridiculous and foolish are they, that have inveighed[37] against the whole sect for a few evil; and have not with like fury vituperated all mankind because that part of them be thieves and part enchanters. And what a madness were it to judge or to think that the ignorance of good things should cause a man to be the better? Although that in the mind of man were not great and thick darkness letting[38] him to behold and see that good is, for that evil is[39] doth abound and is plentiful and needeth no teacher, nor doth not continue as it entered but groweth by little and little and so buddeth forth that it offendeth all other. . . .

Shall thy wife or thy daughter learn how to comb her hair, adorn and paint herself, perfume her gloves, to go pompously, and with what words she shall use to set forth her wantonness and her pride withal, and shall not hear how she may flee and contemn such trifles, adorn her mind and please Christ? Art thou, O thou Christian, of that mind? Then thou dost affirm that no fond nor foolish gentile would at any time have believed.

---

35. Sex.

36. Vives is probably thinking of inveterate malice.

37. The text reads "invied." Perhaps envied is the correct word here, although inveighed seems to make better sense.

38. Preventing.

39. "For that evil is" seems to function as a noun clause which is the subject of the verb "doth abound."

Shall the woman then be excluded from the knowledge of all that is good, and the more ignorant she is be counted better? Some there be so rude and dull, the which esteem those to be best that are most ignorant. I would counsel all such rather to beget asses than men, or to give their diligence and labor to extinguish the figure and force that God hath given them to know good and worthy things withal, and to make them liker beasts than men, for so they shall be even such as they wolde have them. If erudition and learning be noiful unto honesty and goodness and hurtful to be brought up among those that be learned, then it shall be better and most convenient to nourish and to bring them up in the country than in the city, and much better in a forest, than in a village among men. But experience doth declare the contrary and that children should be brought up among those that be best learned and have best experience.

But to return and to speak of women as I began: I, by experience, have seen and known the contrary, and that all lewd and evil women are unlearned and that they which be learned are most desirous of honesty, nor I cannot remember that ever I saw any woman of learning or of knowledge dishonest. Shall not the subtle and crafty lover sooner persuade that pleaseth him the ignorant, than to her that is fortified with wit and learning? And this is the only cause why all women for the most part are hard to please, studious and most diligent to adorn and deck themselves, marveling at trifles, in prosperity proud and insolent, in adversity abject and feeble, and for lack of good learning, they love and hate that only the which they learned of their unlearned mothers, and examples of the evil, leaning to that part only, that the ponderous and heavy body is inclined and given unto. . . . Socrates, that is an earthly oracle of humane wisdom, in *Symposium* of Xenophon doth say . . . that the woman's wit is no less apt to all things, than the man's is; she wanteth but counsel and strength.[40] Therefore I exhort you husbands to teach your wives those things that ye would they should do. . . .

Such virtuous and holy books as may learn her to be wise, and inflame her to live virtuously must be delivered unto her, wherein yet a certain judgment and prudency must be used, that is, that they deliver her no vain, no childish, no barbarous, nor no superstitious books. Likewise she shall not be meddling with those curious and deep questions of divinity, the which thing beseemeth not a woman. And as concerning moral philosophy, those religious and virtuous books do suffice. For virtue doth teach us all good fashions and manners. But yet if we will or intend privately to teach them any customs, let them be such as shall stir and provoke them to live well and virtuously, and such as be far from all contention and

40. Xenophon, *Symposium* II.9.

altercation, whereunto women are but too much of themselves inclined. Let her read many things to subdue and bring under the affections and to appease and pacify the tempests and unquietnesses of the mind. [Vives lists the authors women should read: Plato, Cicero, Seneca, Plutarch, Valerius Maximus, Aristotle, Xenophon, and others.] And as for the knowledge of grammar, logic, histories, the rule and governance of the commonwealth, and the art mathematical, they shall leave it unto men. Eloquence is not convenient nor fit for women. . . . But thou shalt number silence among other thy wife's virtues, the which is a great ornament of the whole feminine sex. And when she speakth, let her communication be simple, not affectate[41] nor ornate, for that declareth the vanity of the mind. . . .

This holy and sincere institution[42] shall increase through the good example of the husband, the which to inform and fashion the woman's life and his family withal is of no less valure[43] and force than the example of a prince to inform the public manners and customs of a city, for every man is a king in his own house, and therefore as it beseemeth a king to excel the common people in judgment and in example of life, and in the execution and performance of the thing that he commandeth, so he that doth marry, must cast off all childishness. [Sigs. Qiiii^v–Rii omitted.]

Thou shalt not only abstain from unclean sports, but also from plays[44] and filthy touchings, lest thou shew thyself rather to be a lover then a husband. Zistus[45] doth say that the fervent lover of his own wife is an adulterer. For a wife is (as the prince of Rome said) a name of dignity and not of pleasure. Be not thou that desirest to have a chaste wife (for what is he that coveteth not that, although he be foolish) the first that shall inflame her to lechery and to think evil. What a madness were it to defile and corrupt that thing the which if thou shouldest not enjoy it pure and whole, should be unto thee a thing most molestious and grievous. Never kindle thou that fire, the which thou canst not quench again. We are made all of tow,[46] and to what part soever the fire approacheth we burn, and lechery is throughout all the body dispersed. . . . Chastity is kept with shamefastness, nor the one cannot be without the other, for shamefastness is it that keepeth the woman, insomuch that I wolde wish that the young woman after she be deflowered, should be kept close for a certain days. . . .

41. Affected.
42. Of marriage.
43. Valor, but perhaps also value.
44. Foreplay? games?
45. Misprint for Xystus, i.e., Pope Sixtus IV (d. 1484). See *Io. Lodovici Vivis valentini opera* (Basileae, 1555), vol. 2, p. 627.
46. Uncleansed wool or flax, which is easily burned.

They that cast God from them and marry to content and satisfy bodily lust, as doth the horse and mule, which have no understanding,[47] may soon be overthrown by the devil; but after thou hast married thy wife, go thy way into thy chamber, and abstaining three days from her, give thyself to prayer with her, and in the first night thou shalt burn the liver of the fish, and the devil shall be driven away. The second night thou shalt be admitted unto the company of saints. The third night shalt thou obtain the blessing of God, so that whole children shall be born of you. And after the third night be past, take thy wife unto thee in the fear of God and more for the desire of children than bodily lust, that in the seed of Abraham thou mayst obtain the blessing in children. This did Raphael say unto Toby.[48]

Therefore if thou have married a wife to have children, give thy mind to that only and not to luxuriousness, following the steps of those old and holy fathers, the which did marry for that thing only: and therefore when they[49] were great with child, they[50] used them no more. And in this thing beasts do excel men, the which at certain times appointed do give themselves to carnal copulation, and afterwards do abstain. [Sigs. Rvi[v]–Si omitted.]

What should I say of those husbands, the which with unlawful pleasures provoke their wives and cause them in a manner to be mad? [Sigs. Si–Siiii omitted.] Paul's mind is that we, being given to this meditation,[51] should abstain from carnal copulation, lest that the ponderous flesh draw us from it[52] inasmuch as that carnal copulation of itself is a beastly thing, twining the mind from his high contemplation. And that wise man, when it was asked him when that a man should use that carnal and fleshly act, answered that when he wolde be equal with a beast.

. . . And they which are married, must so honestly give themselves to the generation of children, that the faithful man preparing and giving himself to that act, may by the help of God in that be modestious. And in another place he[53] saith: Let those which are married principally remember that they give themselves to alms[54] deeds and to prayer and not continually to continue and stand in the infirmity and weakness of the flesh, but to

47. Ps. 32:9 (Douay Ps. 31:9), although the psalmist is speaking of sin in general, not lust in particular. Again, Vives is following traditional interpretation of the Scriptures.

48. Tob. 6.

49. Their wives.

50. Their husbands.

51. Prayer and the contemplation of God and spiritual things. See 1 Cor. 2:6–14; Matt. 6; Luke 18:18–30.

52. Prayer and contemplation. See esp. Gal. 5:16–25.

53. Fulgentius as identified by Vives, Sig. Sv.

54. The text reads "almose."

study to ascend to a better life, that the mind may come to continency, and that carnal lust may every day more and more be bridled and refrained, that after we have passed over that state and degree wherein the infirmity of man requireth pardon and forgiveness, we may obtain the reward of a better life, for the which we do tarry and look. [Sigs. [S6]–Tiiii omitted.]

Of the House[55]

[Sigs. Tiiii–Ui omitted.]

There are certain things in the house that only do pertain to the authority of the husband, wherewith it were a reproof for the wife without the consent of her husband to meddle withal: as to receive strangers or to marry her daughter. There are other things in the which the husband giveth over his right unto the woman, as to rule and govern her maidens, to see to those things that belong unto the kitchen and to the most part of the household stuff; other mean things, as to buy and sell certain necessary things, may be ordered after the wit and fidelity of the woman. [Sigs. Ui^v–Uiiii^v omitted.]

. . . I would wish that this custom of Flanders were everywhere used, that women when they go forth were so covered that no man might know them, and that they looking right forth, might see all men. Nor it is not expedient that she go forth alone, nor that she be accompanied with many, and that as well to avoid great costs and charges, as to eschew pomp and pride, for being so accompanied, she will covet and desire to be seen. . . .

Of the Exterior and Outward Things

The strangers and guests, the which that thou dost receive into thy house, do oftentimes become thy enemies and through a certain benevolence do cause much wickedness. Thou must therefore consider the company and search what manner of men they be, lest they convey any flagitious person into thy house, they which may bring it into an evil name and fame. . . . Thou shalt not admit nor call no young men unto thy house, for of that come these dances, plays, banquets, and other things that hurt and waste men's substance, nothing profitable for their honor and worship, the enemies of quietness, the very pestilence of chastity, and unto God, the which is principally to be regarded most odious. Thou shalt not bring these things into thy house, nor commend them in none other man's, nor lead thy wife nor thy daughter thither, for that were to put fire and tow together. And therefore we do say, as we have said, that shamefastness of the which proceedeth chastity, must specially be nourished and maintained in women,

---

55. The brevity of the following sections reflects the brevity of these chapters in Vives's text.

and chiefly to be had and shewed there where we fear of those to be reprehended, unto whom we bear most reverence, as of our fathers, our friends, and familiars, and of those whose company we have used of children if they be good and honest. [Sigs. Xi–Xiiii omitted.]

Of Apparel and Raiment

God at the beginning did clothe Adam and Eve to hide and to cover their secret parts withal. The other parts of the body were covered for diverse necessities after the quality and disposition of the air, some where to withstand cold, and other where to repel and withstand heat. And therefore in all cities certain apparel for very necessity to satisfy the eye of man withal was invented and appointed. But the evil and corrupt nature of man hath desired and searched for honor and ornaments in all things, in good, in evil, in sorrow, in shame, turning and winning that to honor and glory, the which at the beginning was given and appointed to shame and necessity. And thus there is no end of superfluous raiment, and [e]specially among those that study to honor their garments more than themselves, as for the most part all women do, and many men also. . . .

The husband must consider that the woman ought to adorn and deck herself for his eyes and pleasure only. . . . [But] he is very simple and foolish whom his wife cannot please except she be pricked up and trimmed. Man should be in love with virtue and not with the apparel, with jewels, nor with the fair native skin, how much less than with that that is painted and filthy? And if thou delight in these things, thou shalt when thou dost behold her natural face and visage both loath it and abhor it. Be thou so affectioned to thy concubine, but not to thy wife: for thou seekest to be provoked to lust and carnal pleasures by the senses, and not by any interior or inward love. If thy wife howsoever she be apparelled do content thee and please thee (for she is one mind and body with thee), to what purpose are these anxious, molestious, perilous, and hurtful ornaments sought for and desired? Such gorgeous and trimly decked wives are greedy and desirous to wander abroad and to be seen, and that is the fruit of all that cost and charge, and they that behold them so gorgeously apparelled are thereby the more enticed and provoked: for such array and ornaments do set them forth, and much commend them. [Sigs. [X7–Y5ᵛ] omitted.]

Oh how great a sign and token of chastity and of a pure and clean heart is that[56] simple and mean apparel, the which do then appear most manifestly when all men do know that she had rather adorn herself with wisdom, gravity, and faith, with governing of her family and household, and in-

---

56. [T]he? The abbreviation is not clearly legible.

structing and teaching of her children, than with gold, silk, or precious stones. [Sigs. [Y6]–Zi[v] omitted.]

Of Reprehension and Castigation

The vice and fault of a man's wife must (as saith Varro) other be suffered and born withal, or else clean taken away,[57] the which thing chanceth but seldom, but if it cannot, it must then needs be born withal. . . . For the master and ruler of the house must know and understand that he is set as it were in an high tower, to behold and see who cometh into the house and to withstand all such things as may hurt the emoluments and commodities of the same or the good name and report of his wife. [But the husband should not be be jealous.] Reprehension and correction must be done for amendment or for the example of others. For otherwise it is vengeance or else a spice of cruelty, the which some do use against those that they do hate, yea and do kill them, and yet do say that they do but chasten them. . . .

There be three kinds of sins and trespasses in wedlock and three ways to amend them. The first and most grievous is adultery, the which doth separate the man and the woman and doth so break the band of matrimonial love and charity that even by the Lord's own words and sentence, he may refuse her, although his will be that she, infected or inflamed with any other vice, be kept and retained. In this thing men do use the castigation by the law permitted. A wise surgeon doth not burn nor cut any man, except very necessity constrain him or that there be none other remedy. And yet or ever he begin, he considereth his instruments, his audacity, and his knowledge, and then if he perceive that he be not able to do it, he will not meddle withal. There are other like faults, and likewise other that are mean between them both, the which by reprehension and correction may soon be amended. . . .

Furthermore thou must consider that women be sickly and feeble of body, troubled with many diseases, and in mind sore vexed with diverse tempests and motions. And what grief doth she suffer monthly in purging of herself? What fastidiousness being with child, and after that she is delivered? And how is she rent and broken at her uprising? And to how many perils and dangers is she subject? Wonder it is that any of them do escape death. And what other thing do they all their lifetime but serve us? The daughter serveth her father, the wife her husband, the mother her children. Of mind they are not so strong as man, their judgment, their erudition, and their experience is far under man's. Who is so cruel then, that will not pity this their miserable estate and condition? And therefore we ought

57. M. Terentius, *Saturarum Menippearum Fragmenta* 83.

to wink at many of their faults and as the stronger, suffer and bear with the weaker. [Sigs. [Z7]–Aaii omitted.]

Thou must not reprehend her furiously, but with judgment, not fervently, but coldly and discreetly, for that reprehension which is annexed with gravity and temperancy of mind is most approved and most effectuous, as when thou shewest thyself to be moved with the greatness of the fault, and not for any disdain, nor to satisfy and content thine affections, but to amend her whom thou rebukest. . . . Furthermore, thou must allege the reason and cause that moveth thee to rebuke her, that both now and in time to come, she may be admonished. . . .

An honest matron hath no need of any greater staff but of one word or one sour countenance of her husband. But where that this cannot help, but that brawling and stavesacre⁵⁸ must needs be used, I give no precepts nor rules, for there they use violence, but yet by mine advice the husband shall never come to that extremity, for if thy wife be often rebuked and will not bow,⁵⁹ but waxeth more stiff and crooked, yet inasmuch as she keepeth herself pure and chaste, she must be supported and borne withal. [Sigs. Aavᵛ–[Bb7ᵛ] omitted.]

What Utilities and Profits the Mutual Love of Those Which Are Married Doth Bring

It cannot be well rehearsed nor told how many utilities and profits this concord doth bring to great things both at home and abroad, nor how many losses and incommodities do grow of the dissension and discord that is between the good man and his wife. The household when their master and their mistress are at debate can no otherwise be in quiet and at rest than a city whose rulers agree not, but when it seeth them in concord and quietness, then it rejoiceth, trusting that they will be even so unto them as it perceiveth them to be among themselves, wherein surely they are not deceived,⁶⁰ for if the man and his wife do benignly and gently support and entreat one another, they learn not to disdain or for every light fault to be angry with their servants, or yet for any household words to be vexed or angry with each other, but to set aside all hasty and cruel words and correction with all other things that proceed of a disdainful and a furious mind. And the servants are not only merry therefore, but also they do their service the more obediently and gladly, shewing reverence unto the majesty that proceedeth and increaseth of quietness and concord. For the husband doth defend his wife's majesty with love and benevolence, and the wife her husband's with honor and obedience. [Sigs. Cci–[Cc7] omitted.]

58. A staff or stick.
59. Bow down.
60. The text reads "deceyned."

Of Her That Is in Age

After that an honest and a well nurtured woman waxeth old, we must do as men use to do to all faithful and diligent servants, we loose and unbind our old horse and ox, and suffer them to wander and to feed where they wil! themselves and put them to less labor; we make our bondmen free, and we assign to old soldiers certain possessions and fields to live upon; we make our free minister and servant after that he hath well and faithfully served us equal as it were unto us and call him to our affinity. How much more oughtest thou then honorifically to entreat thy wife, being aged and old, the which is no brute beast, no bondmaid, nor of no worse condition than thou thyself, nor thy hired servant, but equal with thee and assigned by God to be thy fellow, and with such love coupled unto thee as far passeth and exceedeth all other. And reason it is, that she which hath been so long obedient and subject to her husband be now even like and equal with him, for now those agitations and troubles of the mind (the which by the majesty and as it were by the kingdom of the husband should be refrained) are now through use and time pacified and cooled, so that now it shall not need that he rule his wife or study to observe and retain his majesty any more: for it cannot now diminish, seeing that all such things as required a just and a moderate empire and rule are dispatched and taken away. [Sigs. [Cc8ᵛ]–Ddivᵛ omitted.]

PART III

Puritan Views

PHILIP STUBBES
A Crystal Glass for Christian Women, Containing a Most Excellent Discourse of the Godly Life and Christian Death of Mistress Katherine Stubbes
London, 1591

Introduction

Philip Stubbes was born about 1555 and educated at the University of Cambridge. He also spent time at the University of Oxford, although he did not take a degree from either. He was a Puritan, but perhaps not an extreme one. He was not, however, a minister, even though his works resemble the writings of popular preachers and Puritan moralists. The book he is most remembered for today is his *Anatomy of Abuses* (London, 1583), in which he rails against what he believed were the sins of the times. In his own words, *The Anatomy of Abuses* contains "a discovery or brief summary of such notable vices and imperfections as now reign in many countries of the world, but (especially) in a very famous Island called Ailgna [i.e., Anglia or England]."[1] In 1583 he also published his *Rosary of Christian Prayers and Meditations* and *The Second Part of the Anatomy of Abuses*. In 1592, he published *A Perfect Pathway to Felicity* and in 1593, his *Motive to Good Works, or rather, to True Christianity*.

A Crystal Glass for Christian Women (1591) is a narrative of the last weeks of Stubbes's wife, Katherine, who died in December, 1590, at the age of nineteen, shortly after the birth of her son. (She had married Stubbes when she was fifteen and he about forty.) Stubbes wrote it, he says, to benefit all Christian women and intended it to be read as a mirror or example of true Christian womanhood. Unlike humanist authors, and like most Puritan ones, Stubbes avoids reference to classical and scholastic authorities, finding truth instead in Scripture and personal "witness." *A Crystal Glass for Christian Women* went through thirty-four editions between 1591 and 1700, which suggests that it was indeed read by many as the life and death of a saint. The mirror of womanliness that is the crystal glass reveals a woman who, although she seems to have spent her days reading Scripture rather than attending to housework, was otherwise a model wife—passive, withdrawn, and submissive: "so gentle was she and courteous of nature that she was never heard to give any the lie in all her life, nor so much as to (thou) any in anger . . . so solitary was she given, that she would very seldom or never . . . go abroad with any, either to banquet or feast. . . . If she saw her husband merry, then she was merry; if he were sad, she was sad: if he were heavy or passionate, she would endeavor to make him glad; if he were angry, she would quickly please him, so wisely she demeaned herself towards him." But when questions of Scripture or morality were at issue (contrary to Paul's command that women remain silent), she expounded the Bible and denounced evil to Catholics and unbelievers of all ranks: "if she chanced at any time to be in place where either Papists or Atheists were and heard them talk of religion, of what countenance or credit soever they seemed to be, she would not yield a jot, nor give place unto them at all, but would most mightily justify the truth of God against their blasphemous untruths and convince them, yea and confound them, by the testimonies of the word of God."

Even before she gave birth to her son, she prophesied that his birth would be her death. She seems, in fact, to have seized the occasion of childbirth to renounce the life of the flesh in order to participate exclusively in the life of the spirit. During those few weeks after the birth of her son, she gave him up into her husband's care, divorced herself from her husband (she also repulsed the little dog they both used to delight in), took to her bed, and, convinced that the spirit of God dwelled within her, made a long confession of faith to the many less sanctified who gathered around her bed to hear her.

It is clear from her last testament that Katherine Stubbes not only prophesied her own death; she urgently willed it to come: "And when her husband and others would desire her to pray for health, if it were the will of God, she would answer, 'I beseech you pray not that I should live, for I think it long to be with my God. Christ is to me life, and death is to me advantage.'" She consciously and deliberately forsook a mortal husband in order to gain in Christ an immortal bridegroom. She forsook what she thought was a "miserable world" for the "joys of heaven." Only by dying a holy death, she clearly felt, could she achieve superiority over men and equality with the angels—a state barred all those frail, worldly men and women who lived on.

NOTE

1. Title page, *Anatomy of Abuses* (London, 1583).

A Crystal Glass for Christian Women[1]

Calling to remembrance (most Christian reader) the final end of man's creation, which is to glorify God and edify one another in the way of true godliness, I thought it my duty as well in respect of the one as in regard of the other to publish this rare and wonderful example of the virtuous life and Christian death of Mistress Katherine Stubbes, who whilest she lived was a mirror of womanhood, and now being dead, is a perfect pattern of true Christianity. She was descended of honest and wealthy parents. Her father had borne diverse offices of worship in his company, amongst whom he lived in good account, credit, and estimation all his days. He was zealous in the truth and of a sound religion. Her mother was a Dutch woman, both discreet and wise, of singular good grace and modesty, and which did most of all adorn her, she was both religious and also zealous.

This couple living together in the city of London certain years, it pleased God to bless them with children, of whom this Katherine was youngest save one. But as she was youngest save one by course of nature, so was she not inferior to any of the rest, or rather far excelled them all without comparison by many degrees in the induments[2] and qualities of the mind. At fifteen years of age (her father being dead), her mother bestowed her in marriage to one Master Philip Stubbes, with whom she lived four years and almost a half, very honestly and godly, with rare commendations of all that knew her, as well for her singular wisdom as also for her modesty, courtesy, gentleness, affability, and good government. And above all, for her fervent zeal which she bare[3] to the truth, wherein she seemed to surpass many, in so much, as if she chanced at any time to be in place where either Papists or Atheists were and heard them talk of religion, of what countenance or credit soever they seemed to be, she would not yield a jot, nor give place unto them at all, but would most mightily justify the truth of

1. The title continues: *"Wherein they may see a most wonderful and rare example of a right virtuous life and Christian death, as by the discourse following may appear."*
2. Endowments.
3. Bore.

God against their blasphemous untruths and convince them, yea and confound them, by the testimonies of the word of God. Which thing how could it be otherwise? For her whole heart was bent to seek the Lord, her whole delight was to be conversant in the Scriptures, and to meditate upon them day and night.[4] In so much, that you could seldom or never have come into her house and have found her without a Bible or some other good book in her hands. And when she was not reading, she would spend the time in conferring, talking, and reasoning with her husband of the word of God and of religion, asking him what is the sense of this place, and what is the sense of that? How expound you this place, and how expound you that? What observe you of this place, and what observe you of that? So that she seemed to be as it were ravished with the same spirit that David was when he said: "The zeal of thy house hath eaten me up."[5] She followed the commandment of our Savior Christ who biddeth us to search the Scriptures, for in them ye hope to have eternal life.[6]

She obeyed the commandment of the Apostle who biddeth women to be silent, and to learn of their husbands at home.[7] She would suffer no disorder or abuse in her house to be either unreproved or unreformed. And so gentle was she and courteous of nature that she was never heard to give any the lie in all her life, nor so much as to (thou) any in anger.[8] She was never known to fall out with any of her neighbors, nor with the least child that lived, much less to scold or brawl, as many will now-a-days for every trifle or rather for no cause at all. And so solitary was she given, that she would very seldom or never, and that not without great constraint (and then not neither, except her husband were in company) go abroad with any, either to banquet or feast, to gossip or make merry (as they term it) in so much that she hath been noted to do it in contempt and disdain of others. When her husband was abroad in London or elsewhere, there was not the dearest friend she had in the world that could get her abroad to dinner or supper, or to any disports,[9] plays, interludes, or pastimes whatsoever. Neither was she given to pamper her body with delicate meats, wines, or strong drinks, but rather refrained [from] them altogether, saying, that we should eat to live, and not live to eat. And as she excelled in the gift of sobriety, so she surpassed in the virtue of humility. For it is well

4. Ps. 1:2; though the psalmist refers only to the man who meditates.
5. Ps. 69:9. The preceding lines describe the psalmist's alienation from his brethren.
6. John 5:39.
7. 1 Tim. 2:11.
8. "Thou" was used to intimates, children, and servants. "You" was the polite form of address.
9. Entertainments.

known to divers yet living that she utterly abhorred all kind of pride both in apparel and otherwise.

She could never abide to bear any filthy or unseemly talk of scurrility, bawdry, or uncleanness, neither swearing or blaspheming, cursing, or banning,[10] but would reprove them sharply, shewing them the vengeance of God due for such deserts. And which is more, there was never one filthy, unclean, indecent, or unseemly word heard to come forth of her mouth, nor ever once to curse or ban, to swear, or blaspheme God any manner of way. But always her speeches were such as both might glorify God and minister grace to the hearers, as the Apostle speaketh.[11] And for her conversation, there was never any man or woman that ever opened their mouths against her, or that ever either did or could once accuse her of the least shadow of dishonesty, so continently she lived and so circumspectly she walked, eschewing even the very outward appearance or shew of evil.

Again, for true love and loyalty to her husband and his friends, she was (let me speak it without offense) I think the rarest paragon in the world, for she was so far off from dissuading her husband to be beneficial to his friends that she would rather persuade him to be more beneficial to them. If she saw her husband merry, then she was merry. If he were sad, she was sad. If he were heavy or passionate, she would endeavor to make him glad. If he were angry, she would quickly please him, so wisely she demeaned herself towards him. She would never contrary him in any thing, but by wise counsel and sage advice, with all humility and submission seek to persuade him. And so little given was she to this world, that some of her neighbors marveling why she was no more careful of it, would ask her sometimes, saying, "Mistress Stubbes, why are you no more careful for the things of this life, but sit always pouring upon a book and reading?" To whom she would answer, "If I should be a friend unto this world, I should be an enemy to God,[12] for God and the world are two contraries. *John* biddeth me love not the world, nor anything in the world, affirming that if I love the world, the love of the father is not in me.[13] Again, Christ biddeth me first seek the kingdom of heaven and the righteousness thereof, and then all these worldly things shall be given to me.[14] Godliness is great riches, if a man be content with that that he hath. I have chosen with good *Mary* in the 10. of *Luke,* the better part, which shall never be taken from me."[15] "God's treasure" (she would say) "is never drawn dry. I have enough

---

10. Cursing or chiding.

11. Eph. 4:29.

12. James 4:4.

13. 1 John 2:15.

14. Matt. 6:33.

15. Luke 10:42. Mary sat at the feet of Jesus, refusing to help her sister, Martha, serve in the house.

in this life, God make me thankful, and I know I have but a short time to live here, and it standeth me upon to have regard to my salvation in the life to come."

Thus, the godly young gentlewoman held on her course three or four years after she was married, at which time it pleased God that she conceived with a man child. After which conception, she would say to her husband and many other her good neighbors and friends yet living not once, nor twice, but many times, that she should never bear more children, that that child should be her death and that she should live but to bring that child into the world. Which thing (no doubt) was revealed unto her by the spirit of God, for according to her prophecy so it came to pass.

The time of her account being come, she was delivered of a goodly man-child with as much speed and as safely in all women's judgments as any could be. And after her delivery, she grew so strong that she was able within four or five days to sit up in her bed and to walk up and down her chamber and, within a fortnight, to go abroad in the house, being thoroughly well and past all danger as every one thought. But presently upon this so sudden recovery, it pleased God to visit her again with an extreme hot and burning quotidian ague,[16] in which sickness she languished for the space of six weeks or thereabouts. During all which time, she was never seen nor perceived to sleep one hour together, neither night nor day, and yet the Lord kept her (which was miraculous) in her perfect understanding, sense, and memory to the last breath, praised be his holy name therefore. In all her sickness, which was both long and grievous, she never shewed any sign of discontentment or of impatience. Neither was there ever heard one word come forth of her mouth sounding either of desperation or infidelity, of mistrust, or distrust, or of any doubting or wavering, but [she] always remained faithful and resolute in her God.

And so desirous was she to be with the Lord that these golden sentences were never out of her mouth: "I desire to be dissolved and to be with Christ and, oh miserable wretch that I am, who shall deliver me from this body subject to sin? Come quickly, Lord Jesus, come quickly. Like as the hart desireth the water springs, so doth my soul thirst after thee, O God.[17] I had rather be a doorkeeper in the house of my God than to dwell in the tents of the wicked"[18]—with many other heavenly sentences which (least I should seem tedious) I willingly omit.

She would always pray in her sickness absolutely that God would take her out of this miserable world. And when her husband and others would

16. An intermittent fever or ague, recurring every day.
17. Ps. 42:1.
18. Ps. 84:10.

desire her to pray for health, if it were the will of God, she would answer, "I beseech you pray not that I should live, for I think it long to be with my God. Christ is to me life, and death is to me advantage. I cannot enter into life but by death, and therefore is death the door or entrance into everlasting life to me. I know and am certainly persuaded by the spirit of God that the sentence of my death is given already by the great Judge in the court or parliament of heaven, that I shall now depart out of this life. And therefore pray not for me that I might live here, but pray to God to give me strength and patience to persevere to the end and to close up mine eyes in a justifying faith in the blood of my Christ." Sometimes she would speak very softly to her self and sometimes very audibly these words, doubling them an hundred times together. "Oh my good God, why not now? Why not now, oh my good God? I am ready for thee, I am prepared, oh receive me now for thy Christ's sake. Oh send thy messenger death to fetch me, send thy sergeant to arrest me, thy pursuivant to attach me, thy herald to summon me; oh send thy jailer to deliver my soul out of prison, for my body is nothing else but a stinking prison to my soul. Oh send thy holy angels to conduct my soul unto the everlasting kingdom of heaven." Other sometimes she would lie as it were in a slumber, her eyes closed, and her lips uttering these words very softly to her self: "Oh my sweet Jesus, oh my love Jesus, why not now? sweet Jesus, why not now? Oh sweet Jesus, pray for me, pray for me, sweet Jesus," repeating them many times together. These and infinite the like were her daily speeches and continual meditations, and never worser word was there heard to come forth of her mouth during all the time of her sickness. She was accustomed many times as she lay, very suddenly to fall into a sweet smiling and sometimes into a most hearty laughter, her face appearing right fair, red, amiable, and lovely, and her countenance seemed as though she greatly rejoiced at some glorious sight. And when her husband would ask her why she smiled and laughed so, she would say, "If you saw such glorious visions and heavenly sights as I see, you would rejoice and laugh with me. For I see a vision of the joys of heaven and the glory that I shall go to, and I see infinite millions of angels attendant upon me and watching over me, ready to carry my soul into the kingdom of heaven." In regard whereof, she was willing to forsake her self, her husband, her child, and all the world besides. And so calling for her child which the nurse brought unto her, she took it in her arms, and kissing it, said "God bless thee, my sweet babe, and make thee an heir of the kingdom of heaven." And kissing it again, [she] delivered it to the nurse with these words to her husband standing by, "Beloved husband, I bequeath this, my child, unto you. He is no longer mine. He is the Lord's and yours. I forsake him, you, and all the world, yea, and mine own self, and esteem all things dung, that I may win Jesus Christ. And I pray you, sweet husband, bring up this child in good letters, in learning, and discipline, and above all things, see that he be brought up and instructed in the exercise of true religion."

The child being taken away, she espied a little puppy or bitch (which in her life time she loved well) lying upon her bed. She had no sooner espied her, but she beat her away, and calling her husband to her, said, "Good husband, you and I have offended God grievously in receiving this bitch many a time into our bed. We would have been loth to have received a Christian soul, purchased with the precious blood of Jesus Christ, into our bed, and to have nourished him in our bosoms, and fed him at our table, as we have done this filthy cur many a time. The Lord give us grace to repent for it and all other vanities." And afterward could she never abide to look upon the bitch any more.

Having thus godly disposed of all things, she fell into an ecstasy, or into a trance, or swound[19] for the space almost of a quarter of an hour, so as every one thought she had been dead. But afterward she coming to herself spake to them that were present (as there were many both worshipful and others) saying, "Right worshipful and my good neighbors and friends, I thank you all for the great pains you have taken with me in this bed of my sickness. And whereas I am not able to requite you, I beseech the Lord to reward you in the kingdom of heaven. And for that my hour-glass is run out, and that my time of departure hence is at hand, I am persuaded for three causes to make a confession of my faith before you all. The first cause that moveth me hereto is for that those (if there be any such here) that are not thoroughly resolved in the truth of God, may hear and learn what the spirit of God hath taught me out of his blessed and allsaving word. The second cause that moveth me is for that none of you should judge that I died not a perfect Christian and a lively member of the mystical body of Jesus Christ, and so by your rash judgment might incur the displeasure of God. The third and last cause is for that, as you have been witnesses of part of my life, so you might be witnesses of my faith and belief also. And in this my confession, I would not have you to think that it is I that speak unto you, but the spirit of God which dwelleth in me and in all the elect of God, unless they be reprobates, for Paul saith, Romans 8, 'If anyone have not the spirit of Christ dwelling in him, he is none of his.'[20] This blessed spirit hath knocked at the door of my heart and God hath given me grace to open the door unto him and he dwelleth in me plentifully. And therefore I pray you give me patience a little, and imprint my words in your hearts, for they are not the words of flesh and blood, but of the spirit of God by whom we are sealed to the day of redemption."

19. Swoon.
20. Rom. 8:9.

[What follows is "A most heavenly confession of the Christian faith, made by this blessed servant of God, Mistress Katherine Stubbes, a little before she died." Sigs. B–C2 omitted.]

She had no sooner made an end of this most heavenly confession of her faith, but Sathan was ready to bid her the combat, whom she mightily repulsed, and vanquished by the power of our Lord Jesus, on whom she constantly believed. And whereas before she looked with a sweet, lovely and amiable countenance, red as the rose and most beautiful to behold, now upon the sudden, she bent the brows, she frowned, and looking (as it were) with an angry, stern, and fierce countenance, as though she saw some filthy, ugglesome[21] and displeasant thing, she burst forth into these speeches following, pronouncing her words (as it were) scornfully and disdainfully in contempt of him to whom she spake.

[What follows is "A most wonderful conflict betwixt Sathan and her soul, and of her valiant conquest in the same, by the power of Christ."]

"How now Satan? What makest thou here? Art thou come to tempt the Lord's servant? I tell thee, thou hell-hound, thou hast no part nor portion in me, nor by the grace of God never shalt have. I was, now am, and shall be the Lord's for ever. Yea, Satan, I was chosen and elected in Christ to everlasting salvation before the foundations of the world were laid. And therefore thou maist get thee packing, thou damned dog, and go shake thine ears, for in me thou hast nought. But what doest thou lay to my charge, thou foul fiend? Oh, that I am a sinner, and therefore shall be damned. I confess indeed that I am a sinner, and a grievous sinner, both by original sin, and actual sin, and that I may thank thee for. And therefore, Satan, I bequeath my sin to thee, from whom it first came, and I appeal to the mercy of God in Christ Jesus. Christ came to save sinners (as he saith himself) and not the righteous.[22] Behold the lamb of God (saith John) that taketh away the sins of the world.[23] And in another place he crieth out, the blood of Jesus Christ doth cleanse us from all sin.[24] And therefore Satan, I constantly believe that my sins are washed away in the precious blood of Jesus Christ, and shall never be imputed unto me any more." [Sig. C3 omitted.]

She had scarcely pronounced these last words but she fell suddenly into a sweet smiling laughter, saying, "Now is he gone, now is he gone. Do ye not see him fly like a coward and run away like a beaten cock? He hath lost the field, and I have won the victory, even the garland and crown of

21. Fearful, horrible, gruesome.
22. Cf. 1 Tim. 1:15.
23. John 1:29.
24. 1 John 1:7.

everlasting life, and that not by my own power and strength, but by the power and might of Jesus Christ, who hath sent his holy angels to keep me." And speaking to them that were by, she said, "Oh, would God you saw but what I see. For do you not see infinite millions of most glorious angels stand about me, with fiery chariots ready to defend me, as they did the good prophet *Elijah*.[25] These holy angels, these ministering spirits are appointed by God to carry my soul into the kingdom of heaven, where I shall behold the Lord face to face[26] and shall see him not with other[27] but with these same eyes. Now am I happy and blessed for ever, for I have fought the good fight[28] and by the might of Christ have won the victory. Now from henceforth shall I never taste neither of hunger nor cold, pain nor woe, misery nor affliction, vexation or trouble, fear nor dread, nor of any other calamity or adversity whatsoever. From henceforth is laid up for me a crown of life, which Christ shall give to those that love him. And as I am now in possession thereof by hope, so shall I be anon in full fruition thereof by presence of my soul, and hereafter of my body also, when the Lord shall please."

Then she spake softly to her self as followeth: "Come Lord Jesus, come my love Jesus, oh send thy pursuivant (sweet Jesus) to fetch me. Oh (sweet Jesus) strengthen thy servant and keep thy promise." Then sang she certain psalms most sweetly and with a cheerful voice. Which done, she desired her husband that the 133 psalm might be sung before her to the church.[29] And further, she desired him that he would not mourn for her, alleging the Apostle *Paul* where he saith, "Brethren, I would not have you to mourn as men without hope for them that die in the Lord,"[30] affirming that she was not in case to be mourned for, but rather to be rejoiced of, for that she should pass (she said) from earth to heaven, from men to holy Angels, to Cherubims and Seraphims, to holy saints, patriarchs and fathers, yea to God himself. After which words, very suddenly she seemed as it were greatly to rejoice and look very cheerfully, as though she had seen some glorious sight, and lifting up her whole body and stretching forth both her arms, as though she would embrace some glorious and pleasant thing, said "I thank my God, through Jesus Christ, he is come, he is come, my good Jailer is come to let my soul out of prison. Oh sweet death, thou art welcome. Welcome sweet death. Never was there any guest so welcome to me as thou art. Welcome, the messenger of everlasting life. Welcome

25. 2 Kings 1:9–16.
26. 1 Cor. 13:12.
27. With the eyes of the spirit.
28. 2 Tim. 4:7.
29. At her funeral.
30. 1 Thess. 4:13.

the door and entrance into everlasting glory. Welcome, I say, and thrice welcome, my good Jailer. Do thy office quickly and set my soul at liberty. Strike (sweet death), strike my heart. I fear not thy stroke. Now it is done. Father, into thy blessed hands I commit my spirit. Sweet Jesus, into thy blessed hands I commend my spirit. Blessed spirit of God, I commit my soul into thy hands. Oh most holy, blessed, and glorious Trinity, three persons and one true and everlasting God, into thy blessed hands I commit both my soul and my body." At which words her breath stayed, and so neither moving hand nor foot, she slept sweetly in the Lord. . . .

WILLIAM PERKINS
Christian Economy: or, A Short Survey of the Right Manner of Erecting and Ordering a Family According to the Scriptures
trans. Thomas Pickering
London, 1609

Introduction

In his time, William Perkins (1558–1602) was one of the most famous and respected of Puritan preachers and writers. Indeed, most Puritan readers studied his works even more intently than they did the works of Calvin or Hooker.[1] He was educated at Cambridge—for years a center of Puritan learning—and continued at Christ's College, Cambridge, as a fellow from 1584 to 1594. He vacated his fellowship upon his marriage in 1594.

Perkins was a prolific, popular writer and preacher. He wrote many of his treatises, though not his sermons, in Latin, and they were usually translated by others into English. Many of his treatises were also translated into Dutch, German, Spanish, Welsh, Irish, and Hungarian. Breward counts fifty editions of Perkins's writings printed in Switzerland, fifty in Germany, "almost ninety in the Netherlands," and smaller numbers of editions printed elsewhere in Europe.[2] Several treatises appeared both in single editions and in his collected *Works,* and at least seven editions of a single-volume *Works* were printed between 1597 and 1605. In 1609, his *Works* were enlarged until they comprised three volumes. The handsome three-volume folio *Works* went through approximately ten editions by 1635.[3] Among his most important writings were *Armilla Aurea* (*A Golden Chain*), which went through fourteen editions in the course of thirty years and was also included in his *Works; The Foundation of Christian Religion*, which went through nineteen single editions and was also included in his *Works;* three versions of his treatise on the cases of conscience, which went through a total of fourteen single editions and in its later form (*The Whole Treatise of the Cases of Conscience, distinguished into Three Books*) was also included in his three-volume *Works; An Exposition of the Lord's Prayer, in the Way of Catechising*, which went through seven single editions, one of them unauthorized, and was also included in his *Works; Death's Knell, or The Sick Man's Passing-bell*, which seems to have had sixteen editions; *A Declaration of the true manner of knowing Christ Crucified*, which went through seven single editions; *A Direction for the Government of the Tongue*, which went through thirteen single editions and was also included in his *Works; A Discourse of the Damned Art of Witchcraft*, which went through two single editions and was also included in his *Works;* and many others, such as *A Reformed Catholic, A Salve for a Sick Man, Satan's Sophistry Answered by Our Savior Christ, A Treatise Tending unto a Declaration Whether a Man be in the Estate of Damnation or Salvation, A Treatise of Man's Imaginations*, and *Two Treatises . . . of Repentance*.[4]

Christian Economy, or A Short Survey of the Right Manner of Erecting and Ordering a Family, According to the Scriptures, was written in Latin in the 1590s and translated into English in 1609 by Thomas Pickering.[5] It appears to have been designed to be read against contemporary books on common and canon law as well as other theological treatises. That is, instead of composing hortatory, discursive prose, as did Pickering in his "Epistle," Perkins divided *Christian Economy* into axioms or rules supported by Scripture and explained in terms of hypothetical "cases" and "answers," presumably in order to suggest that his book of rules governing the family had the force of English common law.[6] Perkins probably also wanted to suggest that his rules had the force of canon law, because they were based on what he certainly regarded as the prior and absolute authority of Scripture. Indeed, Perkins may even have intended his rules to supersede what he may have regarded as less authoritative common and canon laws. That *Christian Economy* was so read and practiced whenever possible by godly Puritans is probably confirmed by its secure place in the collected *Works*.

In *Christian Economy*, Perkins insists upon the Puritan position that marriage is a higher state of Christian life than celibacy. But he defies common law and may compromise his requirement that each party in the marriage contract freely consent to it when he insists that Christian marriage also requires the consent of parents. He stresses that sexual union in marriage is not sinful in itself even when it occurs apart from the desire for procreation, a position which did much to foster what became the Puritan emphasis on companionate marriage. In fact, Perkins's language often implies true mutuality in marriage, as, for instance, when he says "the communion of man and wife is that duty whereby they do mutually and willingly communicate both their persons and goods each to other for their mutual help, necessity, and comfort." Perhaps as a corollary, Perkins also insists, contrary to English common law, that husbands may not beat their wives "either with stripes or strokes"—because husband and wife are one flesh, "and no man will hate, much less beat, his own flesh, but nourish and cherish it." At the same time, he insists that "loathsome" diseases like leprosy or syphilis, as well as other incapacities, are impediments to marriage. Finally, while Perkins makes it clear that adultery is the primary grounds for divorce, he also takes the radical position, which is contrary to English common law, that marriages may be "dissolved" for reasons other than adultery, specifically desertion or "malicious and spiteful dealing of married folks one with the other."[7] (Although married persons in England could not obtain a divorce on such grounds, it appears that Puritans in New England, largely on Perkins's authority, could and did do so.)[8] Nonetheless, although Perkins advocates mutuality and communality in marriage, he may seem to modern readers to be lacking in charity when (contrary to English common law but in accordance with Old Testament injunctions) he advocates that adulterers or adulteresses be put to death,[9] and when (contrary to the practice of English magistrates) he would prevent men from marrying women to whom they were not previously betrothed and whom they had "deflowered."

NOTES

1. See, for instance, Thomas F. Merrill, ed., *William Perkins, 1558–1602: English Puritanist* (The Hague: Nieuwkoop & B. De Graaf, 1966), p. ix; Everett H. Emerson, *English Puritanism from John Hooper to John Milton* (Durham, N.C.: Duke University Press, 1968), p. 154; Ian Breward, ed., *The Works of William Perkins* (Appleford, Abingdon, Berks.: Sutton Courtenay Press, 1970), pp. xi-xii. (This abridged text of the *Works,* now out of print, is based on the 1616–18 edition published by John Legate and Cantrell Legg and contains selections from *Christian Economy.* It did not come to my attention until after I had completed my own somewhat different selections from the first English edition of *Christian Economy* [1609].)

2. Breward, *Works of William Perkins,* p. xi.

3. It is difficult to make an exact count of Perkins's *Works* because the three-volume sets are often found composed of volumes from different editions. See *A Short-Title Calalogue of Books Printed in England, Scotland, and Ireland . . . 1475–1640,* first compiled by A. W. Pollard and G. R. Redgrave (2d ed., rev. and enlarged, begun by W. A. Jackson and F. S. Ferguson, completed by Katherine F. Pantzer, vol. 2 [London: Bibliographical Society, 1976]), p. 227 (*STC* 19648). I based my count of the editions of Perkins's works printed in the British Isles on this edition of the *Short-Title Catalogue.*

4. For a brief synopsis of Perkins's religious beliefs, see H. C. Porter, "The Theology of William Perkins," in his *Reformation and Reaction in Tudor Cambridge* (Cambridge: Cambridge University Press, 1958), pp. 288–313.

5. There were two editions of the 1609 translation of *Christian Economy*, thereafter it was included in the *Works.*

6. This organization is sometimes obscured in my selections from *Christian Economy* because I occasionally omit specific "cases" and "answers."

7. This position is ambiguously stated in Perkins. In *A Society Ordained by God: English Puritan Marriage Doctrine in the First Half of the Seventeenth Century,* James Turner Johnson says Perkins really believed that only adultery and desertion were grounds for divorce ([Nashville: Abingdon Press, 1970], pp. 74–87). Chilton L. Powell says that Perkins also allowed divorce in the case of "malicious dealing" between spouses (*English Domestic Relations, 1487–1653* [New York: Columbia University Press, 1917], pp. 79–80). But see also M. M. Knappen, *Tudor Puritanism: A Chapter in the History of Idealism* (Chicago: University of Chicago Press, 1939; rpt. 1965), p. 461, and Breward, p. 414.

8. For the reliance on Perkins as an authority, see Leon Howard, who says that the early settlers of New England "dwelt under the Covenant of Grace as expounded by William Perkins and accepted the five points of Calvinism as determined by the Synod of Dort" (*Essays on Puritans and Puritanism,* ed. James Barbour and Thomas Quirk [Albuquerque, N.M.: University of New Mexico Press, 1986], pp. 89–90). See also Merrill, who says that Perkins's works "were reverently carried by the Pilgrims to the New World, and were considered as authoritative commentary on virtually every phase of the Christian life by Protestants everywhere" (*William Perkins,* p. ix). John Demos, in his chapter on "Husbands and Wives," describes the more independent legal and economic position of wives in Plymouth Colony, the increased equality of spouses, and the liberalized grounds for divorce and separation (desertion and cruelty) (*A Little Commonwealth: Family Life in Plymouth Colony* [New York: Oxford University Press, 1970], pp. 82–99).

9. Lev. 20:10.

Christian Economy

"The Epistle Dedicatory to the Right Honorable
Robert, Lord Rich, . . ." [written by Thomas Pickering]

Right Honorable, among all the societies and states whereof the whole world of mankind from the first calling of Adam in paradise unto this day hath consisted, the first and most ancient is the family. For if we look into the Scriptures, the writings of Moses, which in time go beyond all the histories and records of men, do evidently declare it was the will of God to sanctify that first conjunction of Adam and Eve as the root wherein man's whole posterity was virtually contained, and whence in the ages succeeding both church and commonweal should spring and grow to their perfection.[1] And all those nations and countries before the flood, the heads whereof lineally descended from the two first houses of Seth and Cain,[2] had no outward form of civil government by which they were ruled, nor any visible face of a church whereto they had relation, but the whole frame of their policy both civil and ecclesiastical was confined within the precincts of private families. And from the flood, the house of Noah became the common mother in which the other two states were included and out of whose bowels they issued afterward in the multiplication of posterity, for number equal to the stars of the sky and the sands by the sea shore.

Answerable to the voice of the Scripture hath been the verdict of the heathen in this point. Some[3] of the learned among them have called the family the first society in nature and the ground of all the rest.[4] Some again have compared it to the beehive, which we call the stock, wherein are bred many swarms which thence do fly abroad into the world, to the raising and maintaining of other states. Others do not unfitly resemble[5] the same to a metropolis, or mother city, which first traineth up her native inhabitants and then removeth some of them to other places of abode where they may be framed as members to live in obedience to the laws of their head.[6]

Upon this condition of the family, being the seminary of all other societies, it followeth that the holy and righteous government thereof is a direct mean for the good ordering both of church and commonwealth, yea, that the laws thereof being rightly informed and religiously observed are available to prepare and dispose men to the keeping of order in other governments. Hence it is that the Holy Ghost in the book of the Scriptures hath in great wisdom commended both rules for direction and examples for imitation to husbands and wives, to parents and children, to mothers and servants in every point of Christian carriage touching God and man. For this first society is as it were the school wherein are taught and learned the principles of authority and subjection. And look as the superior that faileth in his private charge will prove uncapable of public employment, so the inferior, who is not framed to a course of economical subjection will hardly undergo the yoke of civil obedience. . . .

I hold it a thing both necessary and behooveful[7] for all estates to be thoroughly informed of the right manner of erecting and ordering the pri-

---

1. Pickering takes it for granted that Scripture (and thus the creation of Adam and Eve) is literally true.
2. The first children of Adam and Eve.
3. Side note to Xenophon and Aristotle.
4. I.e., kinds of social structures.
5. Compare.
6. Cicero, *De Natura Deorum* 3.
7. Proper.

vate condition of the family, whereby they may be furnished with fit grounds for the common good in more public and open courses.[8] For which end this present *Discourse of Christian Economy* was first contrived by the author and now thought fit to be set forth for the instruction and edification of the multitude. . . .[9]

The main scope of the author in the several branches hereof is to make plain this truth in particular, that no family can be interested in the blessing and favor of God which is not founded in his fear and ordered according to his revealed will. For though the heathen in their writings of the like argument do show that Nature by her dim light may afford some good directions to this purpose and that men merely natural have prospered in the practice of economical virtues, yet the true happiness of houses and inhabitants wholly dependeth upon the special grace of God and issueth out of his promise, and that is directed only "to them that fear him and walk in his ways,"[10] it being "godliness alone which hath the promises of this life and the life to come."[11]

Therefore to dream of a blessing in any other state which is not seasoned with godliness and ordered by direction of divine law is but a witless presumption, considering that the family itself from whence they grow hath no further assurance of blessedness than it hath right and title in the promise.

Lastly, it containeth here and there some special grounds of truth tending to the discovery of diverse errors of Popish doctrine in points appertaining to marriage, as namely these: that this estate is free to all men . . . that marriages consummate[d] without the free and advised consent of parents either explicit in terms or implicit by connivance are in the court of conscience[12] mere nullities . . . wherein is challenged the Jesuit's proposition that the sole consent of the parties is sufficient, that matrimony lawfully begun and consummate[d] is made void only by way of divorce in the case of adultery.[13] . . . And this liberty granted by Christ both to dissolve and to marry again cannot be restrained or cut off by any human ordinance. [Sigs. 6-7ᵛ omitted.]

    8. Courses of life.
    9. Pickering suggests that Perkins wrote in Latin for the learned few, and that he has translated it for the benefit of all English people.
    10. Ps. 128:1. In general I have omitted Perkins's long quotations from the Bible. But I have kept his biblical citations.
    11. 1 Tim. 4:8.
    12. As opposed to the courts of England.
    13. Matt. 5:32.

Of Christian Economy or Household Government

Chapter 1. *Of Christian Economy and of the Family*

Christian economy is a doctrine of the right ordering of a family. The only rule of ordering the family is the written word of God. By it David resolved to govern his house when he saith, "I will walk in the uprightness of my heart in the midst of my house."[14] A family is a natural and simple society of certain persons having mutual relation one to another under the private government of one. These persons must be at the least three because two cannot make a society. And, above three under the same head, there may be a thousand in one family as it is in the households of princes and men of state in the world.

Chapter 2. *Of the Household Service of God*

A family, for the good estate of itself, is bound to the performance of two duties, one to God, the other to itself. The duty unto God is the private worship and service of God, which must be established and settled in every family. And the reasons hereof are these. First, because this duty standeth by the express commandment of God, who by his apostle willeth men "to pray everywhere, lifting up pure hands, without wrath or doubting."[15] Again, it is confirmed by the custom and practice of holy men in their times. Thirdly, common reason and equity showeth it[16] to be a necessary duty for the happy and prosperous estate of the family, which consisteth in the mutual love and agreement of the man and wife, in the dutiful obedience of children to their parents, and in the faithful service of servants to their masters, wholly dependeth upon the grace and blessing of God, and this blessing is annexed to his worship, for 1 Timothy 4:8. "Godliness hath the promises of this life, and the life to come."[17] [Pp. 5–9 omitted. Perkins goes on to discuss the appropriate times for family prayer.]

Chapter 3. *Of Married Folks*

A family is distinguished into sundry combinations or couples of persons. A couple is that whereby two persons standing in mutual relation to each other are combined together as it were in one. And of these two, the one is always higher and beareth rule, the other is lower and yieldeth subjection. Couples are of two sorts, principal or less principal.[18] The principal is the

14. Ps. 101:2.
15. 1 Tim. 2:8.
16. Duty to God.
17. Pss. 127, 128; 1 Sam. 1:27.
18. Perkins never clearly defines "less principal," but the context suggests that he means a single person (a single man or a widow) and his or her household.

combination of married folks, and these are so termed in respect of marriage. Marriage is the lawful conjunction of the two married persons, that is, of one man and one woman into one flesh. . . .

Marriage of itself is a thing indifferent, and the kingdom of God stands no more in it than in meats and drinks; and yet it is a state in itself, far more excellent than the condition of single life.[19] For first, it was ordained by God in Paradise above and before all other states of life in Adam's innocency before the fall. Again, it was instituted upon a most serious and solemn consultation among the three persons in the holy trinity.[20] Thirdly, the manner of this conjunction was excellent, for God joined our first parents, Adam and Eve, together immediately. Fourthly, God gave a large blessing unto the estate of marriage, saying, "Increase and multiply and fill the earth." Lastly, marriage was made and appointed by God Himself to be the fountain and seminary of all other sorts and kinds of life in the commonwealth and in the church.

Now, if mankind had continued in that uprightness and integrity which it had by creation, the state of single life had been of no price and estimation amongst men, neither should it have had any place in the world, without great contempt of God's ordinance and blessing. Nevertheless, since the fall, to some men who have the gift of continence, it is in many respects far better than marriage, yet not simply, but only by accident, in regard of sundry calamities which came into the world by sin. For, first it[21] freeth a man from many and great cares of household affairs. Again, it maketh him much more fit and disposed to meditate of heavenly things, without distraction of mind. Besides that, when dangers are either present or imminent, in matters belonging to this life, the single person is in this case happy because he and his are more secure and safe than others be who are in married state. . . .[22]

The end of marriage is fourfold: the first is procreation of children, for the propagation and continuance of the seed and posterity of man upon the earth.[23] The second is the procreation of an holy seed whereby the church of God may be kept holy and chaste, and [whereby] there may always be a holy company of men that may worship and serve God in the church from age to age.[24] The third is that after the fall of mankind, it might be a sovereign means to avoid fornication and consequently to subdue

19. That marriage is better than celibacy is a Protestant tenet.
20. Perkins refers here to Gen. 1:26 and Gen. 2:18, although Genesis does not refer to the triune God, only to "us."
21. Celibacy.
22. 1 Cor. 7:8, 28, 32.
23. Gen. 1:28.
24. Mal. 2:15.

and slake the burning lusts of the flesh.[25] And for this cause, some schoolmen[26] do err, who hold that the secret coming together of man and wife cannot be without sin unless it be done for procreation of children. Lombard,[27] the master of the *Sentences,* saith the contrary, namely "that marriage before the fall was only a duty, but now since the fall it is also a remedy." The fourth end is that the parties married may thereby perform the duties of their callings in better and more comfortable manner.[28]

Marriage is free to all orders and sorts of men without exception, even to those that have the gift of continence; but for them which cannot abstain,[29] it is, by the express commandment of God, necessary.[30] By which it appeareth to be a clear case that the commandment of the Pope of Rome, whereby he forbiddeth marriage of certain persons, as namely of clergymen, is merely diabolical.[31]

Chapter 4. Of the Contract

Marriage hath two distinct parts, the first is the beginning; the second, the accomplishment or consummation thereof. The beginning is the contract or espousals; the end or accomplishment is the solemn manifestation of the contract, by that which properly we call marriage.[32] Between the contract and marriage there ought to be some certain space or distance of time. The reasons whereof may be these: First, a business of so great importance as this is would not be rashly or unadvisedly attempted, but should rather be done by degrees in process of time. . . . Secondly, that during such a space, inquiry may be made whether there be any just cause which may hinder the consummation of marriage, considering that before the parties come and converse[33] together what is amiss may be remedied and amended, which to do afterward will be too late. Thirdly, in these cases, persons espoused must have regard of honesty as well as of necessity, not presently upon the contract seeking to satisfy their own fleshly desires after the manner of brute beasts, but proceeding therein upon mature deliberation.

The contract is a mention or mutual promise of future marriage before fit and competent judges and witnesses. The best manner of giving this

---

25. 1 Cor. 7:2.
26. Scholastics.
27. *Sententiarum* Liber IV, Distinctio XXVI, "De duplici institutione conjugii." Peter Lombard (ca. 1100–1160) was archdeacon and then bishop of Paris, 1156–60.
28. Prov. 31:11.
29. From sexual contact.
30. Heb. 13:4; 1 Cor. 7:9.
31. 1 Tim. 4:1; 1 Cor. 7:5, 32.
32. Deut. 20:7; Matt. 1:18.
33. To consort, keep company. Perkins may also mean sexual converse.

promise is to make it "in words touching the present time,"[34] and simply without any exception or condition expressed or conceived. For by this means it comes to pass that the bond is made the surer, and the ground or foundation of future marriage the better laid. And hence alone it is that the persons betrothed in Scripture are termed man and wife. Jacob speaking of Rachel, who was only betrothed unto him, saith to Laban, "Give me my wife."[35]

Now, if the promise be uttered in words *for time to come*,[36] it doth not precisely bind the parties to performance. For example, if one of them saith to the other: "I will take thee, etc.," and not, "I do take thee, etc.," by this form of speech the match is not made but only promised to be made afterward. But if, on the other side, it be said, "I do take thee," and not "I will take thee," by these terms, the marriage at that very instant is begun, though not in regard of fact, yet in regard of right and interest which the parties have each in another in deed and in truth. And this is the common opinion of the learned. Yet notwithstanding, if the parties contracting shall say each to other, "I will take thee to, etc.," with intention to bind themselves at the present, the bond is in conscience precisely made before God and so the contract is indeed made "for the present" time before God. True it is that he which standeth to his promise made as much as in him lieth doth well; yet if the promise hath or conceiveth some just cause why he should afterward change his purpose, the contract expressed in terms for time to come, though it were formerly made and confirmed by oath, must notwithstanding give place to the contract made for time present. . . .

Furthermore, if the parties betrothed do lie together before the condition (though honest and appertaining to marriage) be performed, then the contract for time to come is without further controversy sure and certain. For where there hath been a carnal use of each other's body, it is always presupposed that a mutual consent as touching marriage hath gone before.

Chapter 5. Of the Choice of Persons Fit for Marriage

For the making of a contract, two things are requisite: first, the choice, and then the consent of the parties. Choice is an inquiry after persons marriageable. Persons marriageable are such as be fit and able for the

---

34. The Latin formula is given in a sidenote: "In verbis de praesenti et [illegible]" ("In words of the present [tense] and . . ."). In *The Works . . . of William Perkins,* vol. 3 (Cambridge, 1618), p. 672, the sidenote reads "et purè" (adv., "and simply").

35. Gen. 29:21. Perkins also cites Deut. 22:23 and Matt. 1:20.

36. This is a direct translation from the Latin legal formula, part of which is cited in a sidenote: "In futurum."

married state. This fitness or ability is known and discerned by certain signs which are either essential to the contract or accidental.

An essential sign is that without which the contract in hand becomes a mere nullity. And of this sort there are principally five. The first is the distinction of the sex, which is either male or female. The female is woman of an inferior sex, fit to conceive and bear children.[37] By this distinction is condemned that unnatural and monstrous sin of uncleanness between parties of the same sex commonly termed sodomy, as also the confusion of the kinds of creatures, when one kind commits filthiness and abomination with another.[38] The second sign is the just and lawful distance of blood. Distance of blood is then just and lawful when neither of the persons that are to be married do come near to the kindred of their flesh or to the flesh of their flesh, for so the Scripture speaketh.[39] [Pp. 25–53 omitted. Perkins goes into details of "kindred in consanguinity."]

The third essential sign of a person marriageable is ability and fitness for procreation. And this in an holy and modest sort is always supposed to be in the party contracted, unless the contrary be manifestly known and discerned by some apparent infirmity in the body. Hence I gather that it is unlawful to make a contract with such a person as is unfit for the use of marriage, either by natural constitution of body or by accident. For example, in regard of sickness, or of frigidity, or of the palsy uncurable, or lastly of the deprivation of the parts belonging to generation.

These and such like impediments are of force, though a contract should already be made, yet to make it a mere nullity, considering that God maketh known his will in them that he approveth not of such espousals, but would have them to be dissolved.[40] Again, that which is made between two persons that are under age is to be holden[41] and accounted as unlawful. And though it should be done by consent or commandment of parents, yet it is of no moment. This always remembered, except it be ratified by a new consent of the parties after they be come to age,[42] or that they in the mean time have had private and carnal copulation one with another. . . .

The fourth essential sign is a sound and healthful constitution of body, free from diseases incurably contagious.[43] Whereupon it followeth that a promise of marriage made between those whereof the one hath a disease

---

37. 1 Cor. 11:7; 1 Tim. 2:12.
38. Perkins is speaking of intercourse between humans and animals.
39. Lev. 18:6.
40. Perkins's point is that the inability to perform the "duties of marriage" in any particular instance is an indication that God does not sanction the marriage.
41. Held.
42. Of age.
43. Deut. 23:2, 27:20.

so loathsome as that the other upon good ground cannot possibly endure familiar society and company with him, though it do not wholly hinder the use of the body, is utterly unlawful. Of this sort is the leprosy, the French pox,[44] and such like. For seeing there cannot be any matrimonial use of them that are tainted with such contagious diseases without apparent danger of infecting each other and those also which have society with them and others, yea, and by this means the issue of their bodies growing of a corrupted seed are even born to perpetual misery and to the great hurt and hindrance of the commonwealth, the case is plain, that such marriages cannot be undertaken with good conscience. . . .

The fifth essential sign of a person marriageable is freedom from marriage, whereby both the parties which enter contract are so at liberty that neither the man hath in present another wife or is promised to another, nor the woman hath another husband or is promised to another. The reason is because God himself esteemeth that marriage only lawful wherein one man is joined to one woman and they both into one flesh, and consequently judgeth it unlawful as for one man to have more wives, so for one woman at the same time to have more husbands. Hence it followeth that it is against the law of God and the first institution of marriage that a contract should be made between such persons whereof the one is formerly betrothed to another. For so long as the first promise stands in force, the man can no more be betrothed to two women than he may be the husband of two wives, because the spouse by the bond of her promise to the man becomes a wife and the man by the bond of his promise to the woman becomes an husband.[45]

Hitherto I have treated of essential marks which belong to the being of marriage. Now I come to those that are accidental. An accidental mark of a person fit for marriage is that which belongeth not to the being but to the well-being, that is, to the holiness and purity of that estate. And of this sort there be three that are the principal. The first is parity or equality in regard of Christian religion. For in marriage there is special care to be had that believers be matched with believers and Christians with Christians, not believers with infidels, or Christians with pagans. . . . [Pp. 60–62 omitted.]

If it be here alleged that the sin of adultery dissolves the bond both of contract and marriage, and therefore much more doth idolatry or infidelity,[46] which is a sin far more detestable than adultery, I answer, that the question is not whether of these is the greater sin or more heinous in the sight of

---

44. Syphilis.
45. Deut. 22:23–24.
46. Lack of faith in God.

God, for infidelity in both respects far exceedeth the other, but whether of them is more repugnant to the nature and condition of wedlock. Now the sin of adultery is that alone which breaks the bond and renounceth the troth plighted in marriage, and is the proper cause of a divorce, and not idolatry or infidelity.

The second note is parity or equality in regard of age and condition. First of age, because though the marriage of persons whose years are far unequal is not expressly forbidden in the word,[47] yet is it agreeable to the rules of expediency and decency that the aged should match with the aged, the younger with the younger. Reasons are these: first, because the comforts of this society in likelihood will by this means always be equal and consequently bring the more contentment to either party. Secondly, these unequal marriages are oftentimes offensive to others. Thirdly, they cannot but in some cases prove offensive even to themselves. For when a man of great years matcheth with a woman very young, or a young stripling marrieth an aged woman, the elder party growing weak and impotent may the sooner come to be unfit for marriage duties, and the younger, being of greater strength and ability, the more in danger of being exposed to incontinence and that in the highest degree unless he be restrained by God's special grace. . . .

Secondly of condition and estate: for this also is answerable unto the apostle's rule, who exhorteth men to think of and to do those things which are "true, just, commendable, and of good report," Philippians 4:8. Thus it is a seemly and commendable practice that the prince, the nobleman, the free-man, the gentleman, the yeoman, etc., should be joined in society with them that are of the same or like condition with themselves and not otherwise. . . .

The third note is public honesty and credit, whereby the contract made becomes a matter of good report, well thought and spoken of abroad. "Whatsoever things are of good report, think on them," Philippians 4:8. From hence I gather: I. That it is an unseemly thing for a man to make promise of marriage to such a woman as hath been formerly deflowered or hath and is or may be convinced[48] of adultery and uncleanness. Nay, I add further that a contract made with such a one as himself hath before deflowered is by the law of God unlawful. For the adulterer and adulteress by divine law should be put to death and be cut off from human society.[49] II. It is altogether inexpedient that a woman should be married to such a man as hath a concubine, unless he formerly renounce her and testify the

47. The word of God, Scripture.
48. Convicted.
49. Lev. 20:10.

same by true and unfeigned repentance. III. That no man professing Christian religion, much less a minister of the word, ought to take to himself in marriage a harlot, a defamed woman, or one that comes of infamous parents, though she be repentant.[50] [Pp. 66–68 omitted.]

Chapter 6. Of Consent in the Contract

The second thing required to the making of a contract is the free and full consent of the parties, which is indeed the very soul and life of the contract. And this consent standeth in the approbation, or (as we commonly call it) the *sure-making* of the parties contracted. Consent in this case is twofold, either of the man and the woman or of their parents. Touching the first, that the man and the woman may yield free consent each to other, it is necessary that in respect of understanding, their judgment should be sound, and in regard of will, their choice should be free. [Pp. 69–75 omitted.]

Consent of the parents is that act whereby they give their word and promise to bestow their children in marriage and in regard of right do indeed presently bestow them. Therefore private contracts that are made without free and lawful consent of parents are not only unprofitable and unlawful but even by the law of God mere nullities. Reasons: I. They are contrary to the express will and commandment of God.[51] II. They are flat repugnant to natural equity, which teacheth that he who hath not power nor right over himself cannot bind himself by promise to another. Now, children have not power over themselves, but are under the government,[52] and at the disposition of their parents, therefore the covenants which they make are not made and appointed of God, and those which God maketh not, are indeed and truth none at all.

Chapter 7. Of Rejection, or Refusal of the Contract

Contrary to a complete and lawful contract is rejection, whereby the contract is dissolved or broken off. A lawful contract is then dissolved when some great and heinous fault followeth immediately upon it, in either of the parties espoused. And from hence arise diverse and sundry cases to be set down and resolved.

The first is this: what is to be done when some disease befalls one of the parties immediately after the contract made. Answer: Those diseases which take away the use of the body and altogether disable the party from the performance of the promise made in respect of marriage duties are

---

50. Lev. 21:7.
51. Exod. 20: "Honor thy father and thy mother."
52. Gal. 4:1.

very just impediments of marriage and consequently do break off the contract. Of which sort are uncurable palsies, frigidity, and such like, whereof I have spoken before. . . . Now, if the disease do not for the present take away the use of the body and yet in time proves incurably contagious and so loathsome that the one may justly fear to keep and converse with the other, as it falleth out when one is tainted with leprosy, then the contract is utterly to be dissolved as if God himself should have commanded it, though the promise was formerly made and the parties themselves should be unwilling. God hath ordained matrimony to help, not to hurt either the persons themselves or others. Where therefore these diseases be which may infect, hurt, or destroy others, there God hath, as it were, testified from heaven that the act done is not pleasing unto him and that presently it ought to be frustrate[d].

The contract being thus once dissolved, the sounder party shall be at his or her liberty to marry again. But the diseased is by the magistrate's authority to be forbidden society with any other in way of marriage and commanded to lead his life where he may conveniently from[53] company, for fear of infection. And withal he is for his own part to sue unto God by prayer in faith for the gift of continence. For certain it is that he to whom God hath denied the power of using marriage with good conscience is thereby even called to continence and single life. [Pp. 80–83 omitted.]

Chapter 8. Of Marriage

Marriage is that whereby the conjunction formerly begun in the contract is solemnly manifested and brought to perfection. Marriage is consummate[d] by three sorts of actions, one of the parents of the bride and bridegroom, the other of the minister in public, the third of the persons coupled together. The action of the parents is upon the marriage day, to bring the bride and deliver her to the bridegroom, that they two may become actually man and wife, and perform each to other all matrimonial duties. And where the marriage is complete in any other manner, so as the parents upon sound judgment and deliberation shall deny their full and free consent, either in express words or by connivance and silence and that upon just and lawful cause, there, though in the civil courts of men it may stand and the children born therein be legitimate before men, yet the truth is before God it is of no force, but a mere nullity. And because this doctrine touching consent of parents in these cases is of great use and availeth much to the supporting and maintaining of families, I will first open the truth thereof and then prove it by reasons.

53. Away from.

Under the name of parents are comprehended first the father and mother, secondly all tutors and guardians who have the proper and sole charge of wards or others under years of discretion, thirdly all such as are kindred of blood who are in stead[54] of parents to children, as the uncle by the father's side, the uncle by the mother's side, and such like. Now, touching the consent of parents, that is, of father and mother, I hold it requisite of necessity to marriage. For the authority of parents must not be resisted or violated. As for tutors and such as have the place of parents, their consent is not required of necessity but of honesty, at least, because the power and authority of the parent, though it be not taken away, yet it is lessened when it is either transferred to another person or in part resteth in the child already bestowed. Secondly, by parent's consent, I understand that which they give not rashly, unadvisedly, or foolishly, but out of good and wise consideration and upon true and sound judgment of the business in hand. For otherwise as much as in them lieth, they make the marriage void and of none effect. . . .

Children are either subject to the authority of their parents in the family or at their own liberty and out of their parents' subjection.[55] Those that are at liberty are tied necessarily to subjection in respect of marriage but the other being still of[56] the family and under jurisdiction are bound to be ordered by their parents in the bestowing of themselves.

This is briefly the meaning of the question in hand. Now, for the proof of this point, I will propound three sorts of arguments whereof some are drawn from the law of God, some from the light of nature, and some from the judgment of the ancient church. For the first sort: according to the law of God, marriage is not only a civil and politic, but also a divine and spiritual conjunction, the author and ordainer whereof, upon special cause, was God himself. This our saviour Christ witnesseth when he saith, "Those whom God hath joined together, let no man separate."[57]

The second argument is taken from the light of nature and it is gathered by proportion on this manner: A son privily alienateth and selleth away his father's lands either in whole or in part. The question is whether this alienation be good in law, yea or no? Answer is No. And why? Because the land did not belong to the son, but was part of his father's substance. In like manner a son alienates himself and is betrothed to a woman, to marry her without his parents' knowledge. Is this act of the son warrantable and sound? By no means; for the son in respect of his body is part of the

---

54. In place of.
55. Presumably Perkins is speaking of children that are of age.
56. A part of, dependent upon?
57. Matt. 19:6. Perkins goes on to cite Deut. 7:3, Jer. 29:6, 1 Cor. 7:36.

father's goods and may not be alienated from him without consent. . . . Again, for the accomplishment of marriage, there must needs be a mutual donation[58] between the spouse and the espoused. And what is that which is mutually given? Surely their persons or rather their bodies each to other, for so Paul saith, 1 Corinthians 7:2, "Let every man have his wife, and let every woman have her own husband." But by whom is this donation to be made? By sons and daughters that are in the family, under the jurisdiction of their parents? It may not be, for nature herself taketh it for granted that he which is not at his own liberty cannot yield to the giving of himself. The donation therefore remains in the right of the parent, inasmuch as the will and consent of the child ought to depend upon his will and consent to whom God hath given power and authority in this behalf.

In the third place, let the judgment of the ancient church be observed. Ambrose[59] in his first book of the patriarch Abraham, chapter 9, requires this consent in marriages which he saith is so equal and agreeable to nature that even the poets acknowledged the same. For which purpose he reciteth two verses out of the Grecian poet, Euripides, in his tragedy called *Andromache,* wherein when Orestes desired to marry Hermione, she frames him this answer, that the matter of her marriage wholly depended upon the pleasure and authority of her father, and was not in her own power or liberty.[60]

The second action touching the consummation of marriage is the action of the minister. And that is the blessing of sanctification thereof, which is a solemn work, whereby the minister pronouncing the parties contracted to be man and wife before the whole congregation, commendeth them and their estate unto God by solemn prayer. . . .

The third and last action belonging to the accomplishment of this estate is that of the parties themselves, whereby the bride is in decent and modest manner brought unto the house and home of the bridegroom. It is the law of this estate published by God himself in paradise that the man, even in respect of habitation, "should leave father and mother and cleave to his wife," Genesis 2:24. [Perkins says that marriage may be celebrated with "mirth and feasting" if it be done modestly and in the "fear of God."]

Chapter 9. Of the Duties of Married Persons

Thus far have we proceeded in the doctrine of marriage; and now we come to the duties which they who be married are to perform each to

---

58. Gift.

59. *De Patriarchis.* Saint Ambrose (ca. 339–97) was bishop of Milan (374–97). With Augustine, Jerome, and Gregory, he was one of the four early "doctors" of the western church. (Later doctors of the church include Catherine of Siena.)

60. *Andromache* 987–88.

other. These are principally two: cohabitation and communion. Cohabitation is their quiet and comfortable dwelling together in one place for the better performance of mutual duties.[61] And the ground of this commandment no doubt is that they might learn to know one another's conditions and that they might work a settled affection one towards another, which afterward upon no occasion might be changed.

Yet they may be absent each from other in two cases: first, upon mutual consent for a time, for the performing of some business that is requisite for the family.[62] Secondly, the like absence is allowed when some great and weighty affairs either in the church or commonwealth are in hand.[63]

The contrary to cohabitation is desertion. . . . Touching this point, there be sundry cases expounded: I. Case. Suppose that an husband which is an unbeliever or an heretic in the foundation of his own accord upon detestation of true religion quite forsakes the believing wife and denies any more to dwell with her. What is to be done? Answer: All good means must be first used to bring the infected party to repentance, and when none will succeed, but the case remaineth desperate, then marriage is dissolved on his part and the believing wife is free to marry another. So saith the Apostle, 1 Corinthians 7:15. II. Case. What if there fall out a desertion between two married folks which are both believers? Answer: The faulty person who is the cause of this desertion is to be forced by course of civil and ecclesiastical censure to perform his or her duty. Upon which proceeding, if he remain obstinate and perverse in will, the other must in patience and earnest prayer unto God wait the time until his mind may be changed and he made to relent by the order of the magistrate. . . . Again, be it that the one is resolutely unwilling to dwell with the other and thereupon flies away without any fault of the other, if the thing after a long space be sufficiently known before hand and all possible means have been used to reclaim the guilty person, yea being called, he doth not personally appear before the judge to yield a reason of the fact, after public and solemn declaration made, the minister upon such desertion may pronounce the marriage to be dissolved. For he that upon malice flieth away from his mate is to be holden[64] in the same terms with an unbeliever, who departs upon detestation of religion and the service of God. . . .[65]

Like unto desertion is malicious and spiteful dealing of married folks one with the other. Malicious dealing is when dwelling together they re-

---

61. 1 Cor. 7:10–13; 1 Pet. 3:7; Deut. 24:5.
62. Prov. 7:19.
63. 2 Sam. 11:9–10.
64. Held.
65. 1. Tim. 5:8.

quire each of other intolerable conditions, and when the one doth not regard nor relieve the other, being in danger or extremity, as is meet. For this is as much as to betray one another's estate and life to their utter enemies. Here it may be demanded what a believer should do, who is in certain and imminent danger either of loss of life or breach of conscience if they both abide together. Answer: . . . If the husband threateneth hurt, the believing wife may fly in this case, and it is all one, as if the unbelieving man should depart. For to depart from one and drive one away by threats are equipollent.[66] Neither may this seem strange unto any, that the believer in such case is allowed to depart. For a husband that is a Christian is married two ways: first with Christ and secondly with his wife. The former marriage is made in baptism and is a more holy conjunction than is the latter. Therefore when these two cannot stand together but one of them must needs be dissolved; the latter must rather be left than the former. . . .

III. Case. When the husband is perpetually absent from the wife, what is to be done? Answer: If he be absent either because he is in captivity or upon malice or fear or any such like cause, the wife must rest in expectation of his return till she hath notice of his death. . . .

Chapter 10. Of the Communion of Married Folks, and of Due Benevolence
The communion of man and wife is that duty whereby they do mutually and willingly communicate both their persons and goods each to other for their mutual help, necessity, and comfort.[67] Due benevolence must be shewed with a singular and entire affection one towards another, and that three ways principally. First by the right and lawful use of their bodies or of the marriage bed, which is indeed an essential duty of marriage. The marriage-bed signifieth that solitary and secret society that is between man and wife alone. And it is a thing of it[s] own nature indifferent, neither good nor bad.[68] Wherefore the church of Rome erreth two contrary ways. First in that it maketh marriage to be a sacrament and so every action of it to be of the[69] own nature good. Secondly in that they prohibit marriage of certain parties[70] and the reason of the prohibition may seem to be this, that they think this secret coming together of man and wife to be filthiness. . . .

This coming together of man and wife, although it be indifferent, yet by the holy usage thereof, it is made a holy and undefiled action.[71] The

66. Equal.
67. Eph. 5:28; 1 Cor. 7:3.
68. Perkins refers here to sexual intercourse. He cites 1 Cor. 7:27.
69. Its.
70. Men and women in religious orders, as priests or nuns.
71. Heb. 13:4; 1 Tim. 4:3.

word of God giveth direction to married folks two ways. First by giving them warrant that they may lawfully do this action, because whatsoever is not done of faith (which faith must be grounded on God's word) is a sin. Secondly, by prescribing the right and holy manner of doing the same. The holy manner stands in these particulars. First, that it be done in moderation. For even in wedlock excess in lusts is no better than plain adultery before God. . . . Secondly, that it be used in an holy abstinence . . . while the woman is in her flowers;[72] secondly, in the time of a solemn fast, when some grievous calamity is imminent. . . . Next unto the word, this action may be sanctified by prayer, for a blessing upon it.

Children are the gift of God, and therefore married folks are not only to use the means but also to pray for the obtaining of them.[73] Now the fruits, which are reaped and enjoyed by this holy usage of the marriage bed are three: I. The having of a blessed seed.[74] II. The preservation of the body in cleanness, that it may be a fit temple for the Holy Ghost to dwell in.[75] III. The holy estate of marriage is a lively type of Christ and his church, and this communion of married persons is also a figure of the conjunction that is between him and the faithful.[76]

Here some questions are to be resolved. Case I. Whether may marriage be dissolved in the case of barrenness? Answer: No. For barrenness is an hidden infirmity for the most part and which God hath many times cured, even when it seemed to be desperate, as in Sarah. Again, the fruit of the womb is God's blessing, and wholly dependeth upon him. He therefore that in want of children rejecteth his wife whom he hath received at the hands of God, offereth wrong even to God himself.

Case II. What if either of the married folks commit fornication or any sin of the same kind greater than fornication, as incest, sodomy, lying with beasts or such like.[77] Answer: Adultery and fornication are most grievous and open crimes which do break the very bond and covenant of marriage[78] and therefore when they are certainly known by such persons, they are at no hand to be winked at, but the magistrate is presently to be informed of them. Howbeit, if the innocent party be willing to receive the adulterer again in regard of his repentance, lest he should seem to favor and maintain sin, and to be himself a practicer of uncleanness, he is to repair to the

---

72. Menses (Lev. 18:19; Ezek. 18:6).
73. Pss. 113:9, 127:3; Gen. 25:21; 1 Sam. 1:26–27.
74. Deut. 28:1. (Perkins refers to Deut. 28:1 but quotes Deut. 28:4.)
75. 1 Thess. 4:3–4.
76. Hos. 2:19; Eph. 5:23.
77. Perkins takes up only cases of adultery and fornication, not cases of incest, sodomy, or animal intercourse.
78. Prov. 2:17.

congregation and declare the whole matter to the minister, that he may understand the party's repentance and desire of forgiveness. And if the adulteress hath conceived and is in travail,[79] the husband to avoid the imputation of having an heir in bastardy, is to make relation to the church of the repentance of the adulteress or to acquaint some certain persons therewith not to the end that she should be punished for the fact, but that they may take notice of a child conceived in adultery, whom afterward he may lawfully put off, as none of his. The matter being known, the innocent party may require a divorcement. For adultery is such a sin as doth quite break off not only the use but the bond and covenant of marriage.[80] And yet the same bond may be continued and grow up again by the good will and consent of the party innocent and consequently they may be reconciled and dwell together still.[81]

Now in requiring of a divorce, there is an equal right and power in both parties, so as the woman may require it as well as the man; and he as well as she. The reason is because they are equally bound each to other and have also the same interest in one another's body, provided always that the man is to maintain his superiority and the woman to observe that modesty which beseemeth her towards the man. . . .

So much of the first way of performance of due benevolence. The second way is by cherishing one another.[82] This cherishing is the performing of any duties that tend to the preserving of the lives one of another. Wherefore they are freely to communicate their goods, their counsel, their labors each to other, for the good of themselves and theirs.

The third way is by an holy kind of rejoicing and solacing themselves each with other in a mutual declaration of the signs and tokens of love and kindness.[83] This rejoicing and delight is more permitted to the man than to the woman; and to them both, more in their young years than in their old age.

Chapter 11. Of the Husband

. . . The husband is he which hath authority over the wife; hereupon in Scripture he is called the guide of her youth,[84] and they twain being but one flesh, he is also the head over his wife. The duties of the husband

---

79. Pregnant and in labor[?].
80. Matt. 19:9.
81. 1 Sam. 25:45; 2 Sam. 3:14.
82. Eph. 5:29.
83. Prov. 5:18–19; Gen. 26:8. The biblical citations make it clear that Perkins is referring to sexual pleasure.
84. Prov. 2:17.

towards the wife are these: I. To love her as himself.[85] He is to show this love in two things: first in protecting her from danger,[86] secondly, in regarding her estate as his own, and providing maintenance for her both for his life time and as much as he may for time to come after his death.[87] II. To honor his wife.[88] This honor stands in three things: first, in making account of her as his companion or yoke-fellow. For this cause, the woman, when she was created, was not taken out of the man's head, because she was not made to rule over him, nor out of his feet, because God did not make her subject to him as a servant, but out of his side, to the end that man should take her as his mate. Secondly, in a wise and patient bearing or covering of her infirmities, as anger, waywardness, and such like, in respect of the weakness of her sex. Thirdly, by suffering himself sometimes to be admonished or advised by her. . . .

Here question is moved, whether the husband may correct the wife?[89] Answer: Though the husband be the wife's head, yet it seemeth he hath no power nor liberty granted him in this regard. For we read not in the Scriptures any precept or example to warrant such practice of his authority. He may reprove and admonish her in word only, if he seeth her in fault. For, thus we read that Jacob censured his wife, being impatient, even in anger.[90] But he may not chastise her either with stripes[91] or strokes. The reason is plain. Wives are their husbands' mates, and they two be one flesh. And no man will hate, much less beat, his own flesh, but nourish and cherish it. [Pp. 128–129 omitted.]

Chapter 12. Of the Wife

The wife is the other married person who, being subject to her husband, yieldeth obedience unto him. . . . Now the duties of the wife are principally two. The first is to submit herself to her husband and to acknowledge and reverence him as her head in all things. The reason hereof is good. For the wife enjoyeth the privileges of her husband, and is graced by his honor and estimation amongst men. His nobility maketh her noble, though otherwise she is base and mean;[92] as contrariwise, his baseness and low degree causeth her, though she be by birth noble and honorable, to be by estate base and mean.

85. Eph. 5:33; Gen. 24:67.
86. Gen. 20:16; 1 Sam. 30:5–8.
87. Exod. 21:10; Ruth 3:9.
88. 1 Pet. 3:7.
89. By beating or striking.
90. Gen. 30:2.
91. Blows or strokes with a staff, sword, or other weapon.
92. Of low estate or social position.

The second duty is to be obedient unto her husband in all things, that is, wholly to depend upon him both in judgment and will. For look as the church yields obedience to Christ her head and yields herself to be commanded, governed, and directed by him, so ought the woman to the man. . . . Hence it followeth that the woman is not to take liberty of wandering and straying abroad from her own house without the man's knowledge and consent. . . . Again, that she is to follow her husband when he flitteth or departeth from place to place, unless he forsake either her or Christ. . . .

Contrary to these duties are the sins of wives: to be proud, to be unwilling to bear the authority of their husbands, to chide and brawl with bitterness, to forsake their houses. . . . Lastly, to be a cause of grief to their kindred.

[The remaining chapters deal with the duties and estate of parents, sons and daughters, servants, "the master of the family or goodman of the house," "the mistress of the family or goodwife of the house." Pp. 134–75 omitted.]

PART IV

Women at Home

EUCHARIUS ROESLIN
The Birth of Mankind, otherwise named The Woman's Book
"newly set forth, corrected, and augmented" by Thomas Raynalde
London, 1545

Introduction

The Birth of Mankind is the earliest English printed textbook on obstetrics for midwives and married women. It was first translated into English by Richard Jonas (1540) from the Latin version (*De partu hominis*) by Christian Egenolph (1532), who had translated it from the original German *Der swangern Frauwen und Hebammen Rosegarten* (*The Rosegarden of Pregnant Women and Midwives*), published in 1513 by Eucharius Roeslin. Our text of *The Birth of Mankind* was considerably revised and enlarged in 1545 by Thomas Raynalde, who was styled a "physitian" in one of his extant books and a "Doc[tor] of Phisik" in another. It was the most popular textbook on childbirth in our period, going through at least fourteen editions from 1545 to 1654, and was intended to be read mainly by women. For this reason, the preface to editions after that of 1552[1] said this text is "so plainly set forth, that the simplest midwife which can read may both understand for her better instruction, and also other women that have need of her help, the more commodity."[2] Its directions, together with the observations added by Raynalde, considerably influenced ideas in our period about conception, birthing practices, and the care of the newborn.

Raynalde does women some services in his book. He suggests that there is nothing "lewd" or "loathsome" about women's genitals, as many believed. They were, he said, made good by God and thus honorable for the purposes of conception and birth. He also insists that women's menstrual periods are not "purgations" or "cleansing" of woman's blood, as Jonas, following his authors, had suggested in the 1540 edition of this text:[3] "for undoubtedly this blood is even as pure and wholesome as all the rest of the blood in any part of the body else." Raynalde's reasons for his position are simple and obvious, however much they contradicted long-held biblical injunctions.[4] Would, he asked, nature "feed the tender and delicate infant in the mother's womb with the refuse of the blood, or not rather with the purest of it?" He also said that women have a more important role in conception and birth than men do, even though men initiate the process, for women nourish the unborn child, bear it in pain, and nurse it after birth. But Raynalde sidesteps the prevalent theory of male superiority by saying only that "the woman in her kind . . . is even as absolute and perfect as man in his kind."

One important idea reaffirmed in Raynalde's book—wrong though it was—may have positively affected sexual relationships between men and women in our period. Raynalde said that when a woman begins to desire a man, "thin clear matter" moves from her "stones"[5] into her uterus (the "mother" or matrix) and her vagina. This "matter" lubricates both the uterus and the vagina and prepares them for the reception of man's seed. But it is a man's seed which, when it is drawn or attracted by the uterus into itself, produces conception. Raynalde believed, consequently, that a woman, like a man, must also be aroused in order to draw out from her "stones" the "seed" and other "matter" which prepare the womb for conception. Thus husbands were urged to caress their wives so that the sexual pleasure they experienced might initiate the process in a woman by which conception was achieved. (By the late seventeenth century, it was known that the female ovum must be impregnated by male sperm for conception to take place. This understanding, however right, meant that husbands no longer had a duty to arouse their wives. Indeed, this knowledge was often taken later to imply that wives, if they were to remain "innocent" and avoid lust, should be kept the passive instruments of conception.)

On the other hand, Raynalde did women a grave disservice when he urged midwives to enlarge the vagina manually during labor so that the fetus could more easily impel itself out of the uterus. (No one understood that the contracting muscles of the uterus move the fetus forward.) Raynalde also placed women in jeopardy when he urged midwives either to pull the placenta out by the tube (a practice which could cause the uterus to prolapse) or to scrape the placenta out of the uterus with their fingers (a practice which often caused infection and puerperal fever). Because Raynalde did not know that the uterus in time would expel a still birth, he also placed women at risk when he directed midwives to withdraw the dead fetus manually, often in horrifying ways (by hooks put through the eyes of the dead child, or by cutting off its arms and legs to facilitate delivery). It is painful as well to read about the way in which caesarean sections were performed—only on a dead mother, her body butchered to release the child.[6] One must remember, however, that surgery was the profession of the dentist, not the medical doctor, and that Raynalde always stresses the need to save the lives of the mother and the child. And that, despite the occasional barbarism, is the aim of the book—to preserve the mother and the child and, when the child is born, to keep it alive and well.

Because *The Birth of Mankind* was translated from the Latin, which in turn was translated from the German, certain problems arose in modernizing it. Latin words, for instance, often influenced by the original German, were sometimes literally translated into English. In this text I have occasionally modernized the Latinate forms (i.e., participate[d] for participate). But I have otherwise tried to stay as close as possible to the actual syntax of the original English translation and Raynalde's additions. As far as I know, *The Birth of Mankind* has not been reprinted since 1654.

NOTES

1. The preface to the 1545 and 1552 editions is in Latin.

2. 1560 edition, Sig. Aᵛ, and thereafter.

3. See *The Birth of Mankind* (1540), trans. Richard Jonas, fol. xii. Roeslin or Egenolph had claimed that the placenta and the chorion are needed to protect the fetus from the bad effects of its mother's menstrual blood. They (the cauls) "defendeth the birth from noisome and ill humors encreasing in the matrice after conception by retention of the flowers otherwise wont to pass and issue forth ones [once] in the month, the which ill humors, if they sholde touch or come near to the birth, wolde greatly perish and hurt the same."

4. See Lev. 15:19–20.

5. By stones Raynalde probably means her ovaries. Raynalde's diction suggests that he is following in part the old theory that the reproductive organs in women inversely mirror those of men. See Audrey Eccles, *Obstetrics and Gynaecology in Tudor and Stuart England* (Kent, Ohio: Kent State University Press, 1982), pp. 26–27.

6. Eccles notes that "no successful caesarean section on a living woman was recorded in England until 1793" (p. 115).

The Birth of Mankind

A Prologue to the Women Readers

Here in the beginning of this present prologue I will follow the example of them which, when they bid any guests to dinner or supper, are wont[1] first to declare what shall be their cheer, what fare,[2] and how many dishes they shall have, praying them to take it in good worth and to look for neither better nor[3] worse than hath been mentioned of. And even so here will I do. Before that ye enter into the reading of this little treatise, I shall succinctly and in few words recite the sum and chief contents of the same, with the utility and profit which may ensue to the diligent and attentive over-reader thereof, to the end that ye of these things being first well advertised, may have the more or less courage to employ your labor in over-looking and perusing of the same. . . .

Wherefore now to come to our purpose: ye shall understand that about three or four years passed, a certain studious and diligent clerk,[4] at the request and desire of diverse honest and sad[5] matrons being of his acquaintance, did translate out of Latin into English a great part of this book, entitling it, according to the Latin inscription, *De Partu Hominis,* that is to say, *Of the Birth of Mankind,* which we now do name *The Woman's Book,* for so much as the most part, or well-near all therein entreated of, doth concern and touch only women. In which his translation he varied or declined nothing at all from the steps of his Latin author, observing more fidelity in translating than choice or discretion (at that time) in admitting and allowing many things in the same book greatly needing admonition and wary advice or counsel to the readers, which otherwise might sometimes use that for a help, the which should turn to a hindrance.[6] Wherefore I, resolving and earnestly revising from top to toe the said book, and herewithal considering the manifold utility and profit which thereby might ensue to all women (as touching that purpose) if it were more narrowly looked over, and with a straiter judgment more exactly everything therein pondered and tried, thought my labor and pains should not be evil employed, nor unthankfully accepted and received of all honest, discreet, and sage

1. Accustomed.
2. Food.
3. "Ne" has been replaced by "nor" throughout the text.
4. A learned man.
5. Sober.
6. Thomas Raynalde suggests that the original English translation by Richard Jonas in 1540 contained directions which, if followed, could hurt mother or child or both, and his caution about his predecessors must remind us of the practical reasons for which this book in particular was designed and used.

women if I, after good and diligent perusing thereof, did correct and amend such faults in it as seemed worthy of the same, and to advise the readers what things were good or tolerable to be used, which were dangerous, and which were utterly to be eschewed. The which thing I have not only so done, but over this, have thereunto adjoined and annexed diverse other more experimented[7] and more familiar medicines. And farther, [I] have in the first book set forth and evidently[8] declared all the inward parts of women (such as were necessary to be known to our purpose) and that not only in words but also in lively and express figures, by the which every part before in the book described may in manner be as exactly and clearly perceived, as though ye were present at the cutting open or anatomy of a dead woman.[9]

And think not the utility and profit of this first book and knowledge thereof to be little or of small value, but take it as the foundation and ground, by the perceiverance[10] whereof, your wits and understanding shall be illuminated and lightened, the better to understand how every thing cometh to pass within your bodies in [the] time of conception, of bearing, and of birth. And further, by the perfect knowledge of this book, ye shall clearly perceive the reason of many diseases which happen peculiarly to women and the causes thereof. By which perceiverance, again ye shall have the readier understanding how to withstand and remedy the said infirmities or diseases. For note ye well, that as there is no man, whatsoever he be, that shall become an absolute and perfect physician unless he have an absolute and perfect knowledge of all the inwards and outwards of man's and woman's body, even so shall ye never groundly[11] understand the matters contained in the second book, or any other communication or writing touching the same intent, except ye first have true and just cognizance in the first book. . . .

In the second book we shall declare the diverse sorts and manners of the deliverance or birth of mankind, and all the dangers, perils, and other cases happening to the laboring woman in that season, with remedies and manifold medicines concerning the same. . . .

In the third book shall be entreated of the election and choice by certain signs and tokens of a good nurse, which may foster and bring up the child

7. Proven by experiment.

8. According to the evidence.

9. I have not included these figures in this anthology. Anatomy was a much-admired discipline at the time and encompassed the study of organs as well as bone structure. Witness Rembrandt's "The Anatomy Lesson." Cadavers, however, were still hard to come by, which may explain the unscientific nature of some of Raynalde's drawings at the end of his book.

10. Perception.

11. Fundamentally.

being born. Item, medicines increasing, diminishing, attenuating, engrossing, and amending the milk in the nurse's breasts. Also remedies for many and sundry diseases, which ofttimes chance unto infants after their birth.

In the fourth and last book we will somewhat commune of conception, with the causes hindering or farthering the same, showing certain counsel and remedies whereby (and by the grace of God) the unfruitful may be made more fruitful, and impediments of conception, by virtue of medicines, removed and overcome, the woman being made more apt to conceive. And farther, in this last book shall be uttered and set forth certain embellishing[12] receipts concerning only honest and healthsome decoration and cleanliness, always most allowable and commendable in a woman. . . .

[Some might say that this book] dishonors woman by telling them too much. . . . Yet another sort is there which would that neither honest nor unhonest men should see this book, for because (as they say) be a man never so honest, yet by reading here of things to them before unknown, they shall conceive a certain loathsomeness and abhorring towards a woman. To these I answer, that I know nothing in woman so privy nor so secret that they should need to care who know of it, neither is there any part in woman more to be abhorred than in man. And if the knowledge of such things which commonly be called the woman's privities should diminish the hearty love and estimation of a woman in the mind of man, then by this reason, physicians' and surgeons' wives should greatly be abhorred and misbeloved of their husbands, and I myself likewise. . . .

Let no woman be grieved who shall see or behold this book, for if the party be lewd, unhappy, and knavish that shall read it, here I am sure he shall learn neither lewdness, unhappiness, nor knavery. . . . [Furthermore] it shall be no displeasure to any honest and loving woman that her husband should read such things, for many men there be of so gentle and loving nature towards their wives that they will be more diligent and careful to read or seek out any thing that should do their wives good, being in that case,[13] than the women themselves. Briefly, I require all readers hereof to interpret and construe everything herein contained according to the best and to use everything herein entreated of to the purpose wherefore it was written. [Sigs. [C7ᵛ]–Dii omitted.]

The First Book

. . . In this first book then shall be declared the form, manner, and situation of the inward parts of a woman, such as are in them by nature dedicated and assigned to the propagation, conception, and bearing of mankind. In

12. Beautifying.
13. Pregnant.

whom truly is the receptacle, and as ye would say, the camp or field[14] of mankind to be engendered therein. And although that man be as principal mover and cause of the generation, yet (no displeasure to men) the woman doth confer and contribute much more, what to the increasement of the child in her womb and what to the nourishment thereof after the birth, than doth the man. And doubtless, if a man would demand to whom the child oweth most his generation, ye may worthily make answer that to the mother, whether ye regard the pains in bearing, other else[15] the conference[16] of most matter[17] in begetting. [Sigs. Dii^v–Eiii omitted.]

Here ye shall understand that these three words, the matrix, the mother, and the womb, do signify but one thing, that is to say, the place wherein the seed of man is conceived, fetified,[18] conserved, nourished, and augmented unto the time of deliverance, in Latin named *Uterus et Matrix*. The neck of this womb otherwise called the woman's privity, we will call the womb passage or the privy passage, in Latin, *Cervix uteri, et pudendum muliebre.* . . . To make especial mention of the length of this womb passage were but folly, for the diversities thereof. Notwithstanding, in women it is esteemed of the length of 5, 6, 7, or 8 fingers' breadth, some more, some less. And this we may say, that nature hath so provided that it is of sufficient length to receive the privy part of man in the generation, directing the same towards the womb port, through the which the seed is naturally sent from the man into the womb or mother, thereto helping an attractive power, which is inset and given to the womb to attract and draw towards itself the seed parted from the man (so that there be no other let).[19]

Chapter VI. Of the Womb and His Parts

At the head or upper end of this womb passage is situated the womb itself, which in women (being not with child) is very little, contract[ed] and drawn together, so that the amplitude or largeness thereof passeth not the amplitude and largeness of the privy passage, the which thing to some may seem incredible, yet by anatomy ye may see it to be true. . . . This contraction of the matrix, no doubt, was made by nature for these causes, partly that at such time that the woman is not with child it should occupy the less room in the belly, but chiefly that in time of conception of the

14. Ground to be sown.
15. Or else.
16. Coming together, from the Latin *conferro*.
17. Material substance.
18. Fortified?
19. Hindrance. It was commonly believed not that the sperm propelled itself into the womb, but rather that the "attractive" power of the womb pulled the sperm into it.

seed, the little bulk or quantity of the said seed, at his first conceiving into the woman's mother, may be touched round about everywhere of the mother, and as ye would say, amplexed or embraced, and contained (as the nutshell containeth immediately the nut) of[20] the inner walls or face of the matrix. And as the seed is vivified, shaped, and doth increase, so doth the amplitude of the matrix enlarge and wax bigger, so that at the last when the infant cometh to his full growth, or when the woman is great with child, then this coat or kell[21] of the matrix is as thin as a bladder, where that in time of his contraction, or when the woman is not with child, the coat or wall of the matrix is as good as half an inch thick.

Now ye shall understand, that the sound or bottom of the matrix is not perfectly round bowlwise, but rather like the form of a man's heart as it is painted, saving that the partition or cleft in the matrix between both corners, the right and the left, is not so profoundly dented inwards as the cleft in the heart. . . . This seam then is as it were a little separation, mark, or limit dividing the womb in two equal parts or sides, the right and the left. . . . Other distinctions or separations in the matrix is there none, albeit that in times past, diverse clerks have written and many other[s] have believed that there should be seven cells or seven distinct places in the matrix, in three of the which on the right side should only men children be conceived, and in the other three on the left side women children. And if it chanced that the seed were conceived in the seventh cell, which was the middlemost, then that should become a monster, half a man, and half a woman, the which all is but lies, dreams, and fond fantasies. For the woman's matrix, as I have said, is even as a strong bladder, having in it but one universal holeness,[22] and the child when it lieth in it, lieth ever on the one side more than on the other, the head being towards one of the corners or angles, and not upright toward the middle bridge.

Chapter VII. Of the Mother Port

The entrance of the matrix or womb is named the womb port, or mother port. . . . Whereas at such time that the man [ac]companieth with the woman, the privy passage is dilated and opened to the quantity of man's privy part; yet, notwithstanding, the mouth or the cleft of the womb port is not moved thereby nor dilated except that it be at such time that the matrix, being apt and disposed thereto, and other conditions requisite, this womb port do naturally open itself, attracting, drawing, and sucking into the womb the seed by a vehement and natural desire. . . . If the seed be

20. By.
21. Caul, the amnion or inner membrane enclosing the fetus before birth.
22. Wholeness, as well as hollowness?

retained still in the matrix, then doth the womb port close itself so fast and so firmly that the point of a needle cannot enter in thereat without violence, and so doth remain until the time of deliverance. At what time again it dilateth and openeth itself in such amplitude and largeness that it is wonderful to speak of.

Chapter VIII. Of the Vessels of Seed Called the Stones with Other Thereto Appertaining

On each side of the matrix lieth a stone which both be called the women's stones,[23] wherein is engendered the seed and sperm that cometh from the woman, not so strong, firm, and mighty in operation as the seed of man, but rather weak, fluy,[24] cold, and moist, and of no great firmity, howbeit as convenient and proper for the purpose for the which it was ordained, as the seed of man for his purpose. These stones be nothing so big as the stones of the man, but less, flatter, much fashioned after the shape of a great and broad almond. The substance and body of these stones is not made massive or compact and soft as men's stones be, but as it were many little kernels set together, between the which is much hollowness and therein contained a certain thin watery substance. . . .

Chapter IX. Of the Seed Bringers

The seed bringers called in Latin *vasa semen adferentia* be two veins and two arteries which come to these two stones: to each one a vein and one artery. [Sigs. Fv–Gv omitted.]

Chapter X. Of the Office and Use of These Seed Bringers

. . . This foresaid seed, as we have said before, is nothing so firm, perfect, absolute, and mighty in woman as in man, and yet can you not call this any imperfection or lack in woman. For the woman in her kind and for the office and purpose wherefore she was made is even as absolute and perfect as man in his kind. Neither is woman to be called (as some do) unperfecter than man (for because that man is more mightier and strong, the woman weaker and more feeble). For by this reason, the horse, the lion, the elephant, camel, and many other beasts should be called more perfect than man, to the which man is not able to compare in natural might and strength.

But truly, comparing one man to another such as be gelded and want the genetories,[25] be much feebler, weak, and effeminate than other: in

23. Ovaries.
24. Fluid.
25. As, for instance, a eunuch.

voice womanlike, in gesture and condition nice, in softness of skin and plumpness of the body fatter and rounder, in strength and force impotent, nothing manly nor bold, the which imbecility[26] in them may well be named imperfection. For imperfection is when that any particular creature doth lack any property, instrument, or quality which commonly by nature is in all other or the more part of that kind. . . .

Chapter XI. Of the Way by the Which the Seed Is Sent from the Stones to the Angles or Corners of the Matrix

[Sigs. Giii–Giiii^v omitted.]

This seed carriers receiveth the seed conficted,[27] concocted, and digested in the stones and foresaid seed bringers, conveying and directing the same from the stones to the inside of the corners of the matrix, so that they which do open dead women, shall always perceive in the hollowness of the matrix these two angles or corners specially bedewed or imbrued with a white slimy and thin clear matter, which no doubt is the woman's seed. And in women having great and fervent desire to any man, this seed doth issue from this foresaid place down along to the woman's privy passage, moistening all that part as it were with a dew. Aristotle and other[s] more do suppose that this seed in woman serveth for no other purpose but only to excite, move, and stir the woman to pleasure.[28] But some peradventure would think that this were but a simple and an idle or slender[29] purpose, which if they did more nearly consider the matter, should perceive it to be a just, great, and necessary cause. For if that the God of nature had not instincted[30] and inset in the body of man and woman such a vehement and ardent appetite and lust the one lawfully to company with the other, neither man nor woman would never have been so attentive to the works of generation and increasement of posterity, to the utter decay in short time of all mankind.

For ye shall hear some women in time of their travail, moved through great pain and intolerable anguish, forswear and vow themselves never to company with a man again. Yet, after that the pangs passed within short while, for entire love to their husbands and singular natural delight between man and woman, they forget both the sorrow past and that that is to come. Such be the privy works of God and such be the pricks of nature, which never createth no special pleasure unaccompanied with some sorrow, nei-

26. Bodily weakness.
27. L. *confectus*, made up into.
28. Aristotle, *Generation of Animals* I.xx.
29. Insignificant.
30. Made instinctive.

ther is there for the most part any sorrow, but that it hath annexed some joy or comfort, less or more, to alleviate and lighten the burden and weight of displeasure. [Sigs. Gv^v–[H7] omitted.]

Chapter XIV. Of the Three Cauls or Wrappers Wherein the Infant Is Lapped

The seed conceived into the womb or matrix of the mother, anon[31] it is amplected, clipped, and embraced of the inner face of the matrix, the mouth or port thereof in the mean while [is] closed and shut exquisitely. The seed then, when it hath been a certain little space in the womb, by the natural heat or rather by the inset and ingenite[32] virtue of that place is environed and enclosed round with three diverse coats, cauls, or wrappers, which in Latin they call *involucra*. [Sigs. [H8]–Iv^v omitted.]

The terms,[33] then, which were wont at other times to stir themselves in the matrix veins and at certain circuits to issue forth, now when there is a feature,[34] or child in the same matrix conceived, they proceed no more forth (as superfluous) but remain and be reserved to the necessary nutriment of the feature and some part thereof reflueth and is reverted to the woman's breasts, there to become milk. And now hath nature her purpose wherefore she made and created this course of blood. . . .

But here ye shall note that they be greatly deceived and abused which call the terms the woman's purgation or the cleansing of their blood, as who should say that it were the refuse, dross, and viler part of the other blood remaining in the body, naturally every month sequestrated and separated from the purer, for the vility and evil quality therein comprehended. For undoubtedly this blood is even as pure and wholesome as all the rest of the blood in any part of the body else.[35]

Is it to be thought that nature would feed the tender and delicate infant in the mother's womb with the refuse of the blood, or not rather with the purest of it? Yes and therefore because that she would that the pure blood

31. At once (but, by misuse, soon).
32. From L. *ingenerare*, innate.
33. Menstrual periods.
34. Fetus?
35. Raynalde seems here to be taking issue with Leviticus 15:19–20, wherein God spoke to Moses, saying that "also when woman shall have an issue, and her issue in her flesh shall be blood, she shall be put apart seven days; And whosoever toucheth her, shall be unclean unto the even. And whatsoever she lieth upon in her separation, shall be unclean, and every thing that she sitteth upon shall be unclean." Calvin glosses this passage thusly: "That is, when she hath her flowers, whereby she is separate from her household, from the tabernacle and from touching of any holy thing." See also Lev. 12:1–8.

coming from the matrix veins should be made yet purer, she suffereth not the same to enter immediately into the infant, but first useth another mean, and sendeth it into *chorion*,[36] or the hoop caul (as I have said before), where truly it hath a certain circulation and another digestion, whereby it is defecated and cleansed very exquisitely by the diligence of nature attenuated and [re]fined, and so at the last sent forth into the infant, leaving all the grosser part in the spongy body of the hoop caul.

Yet much more are to be detested and abhorred the shameful lies and slander that Pliny, Albertus Magnus [in] *De Secretis Mulierum* [*Of the Secrets of Women*] and diverse others more have written of the venomous and dangerous infective nature of the woman's flowers or terms,[37] the which all be but dreams and plain dotage. To rehearse their fond words here were but loss of ink and paper; wherefore let them pass with their authors. [Sigs. [I8ᵛ] – [Hhh6ᵛ] omitted.]

The Second Book

Chapter I. Of the Time of Birth and Which Is
Called Natural, or Unnatural

... And now here in this second book we will declare the manner of the quitting and deliverance of the infant out of the mother's womb, with other things thereto appertaining. . . . Ye shall note that there is two manner of births, the one called natural, the other not natural. Natural birth is when the child is born both in due season and also in due fashion. The

36. Gk., the outermost membrane enveloping the fetus before birth. But perhaps the placenta, because the passage seems to describe placental circulation.

37. "Venomous": poisonous. Pliny, *Natural History* VII.xv.64–65: "But nothing could easily be found that is more remarkable than the monthly flux of women. Contact with it turns new wine sour, crops touched by it become barren, grafts die, seeds in gardens are dried up, the fruit of trees falls off, the bright surface of mirrors in which it is merely reflected is dimmed, the edge of steel and the gleam of ivory are dulled, hives of bees die, even bronze and iron are at once seized by rust, and a horrible smell fills the air; to taste it drives dogs mad and infects their bites with an incurable poison." See Pliny, *Natural History, with an English Translation in Ten Volumes*, vol. II, Libri III–VII, trans. H. Rackham (London: William Heinemann, 1942), pp. 548–49. Albertus Magnus (probably a spurious attribution), *De Secretis Mulierum Libellus* (*A Little Book of the Secrets of Women*) (Lyon, 1584), Sigs. A3–A3ᵛ (collated with the editions of Lyon [?], 1498, and Strasbourg, 1607): "Et hoc ideo quia mulieres sunt tempore menstrui venenosa [*sic*], ita quod intoxicant animalia per visum, inficiunt pueros in cunis, maculant speculum bene tersum, & quandoque faciunt coeuntem cum ipsis leprosum fieri quandoque cancrosum." ("And because women at the time of their menstrual periods are poisonous, they corrupt living things by sight, kill [or infect] young male babies in cradles, spot a well-polished mirror, and cause those who copulate with them sometimes to become leprous and at other times cancerous.")

due season is most commonly after the ninth month or about forty weeks after the conception, although some be delivered sometimes in the seventh month, and the child proveth very well. But such as are born in the eighth month, other[38] they be dead before the birth, or else live not long after.

The due fashion of birth is this: first the head cometh forward, then followeth the neck and shoulders, the arms with the hands lying close to the body toward the feet, the face and forepart of the child being towards the face and forepart of the mother. . . . The birth not natural is when the mother is delivered before her time, or out of due season, or after any other fashion than is here specified before, as when both the legs proceed first, or one alone, with both the hands up, or both down, other else[39] the one up and the other down, and diverse otherwise, as shall be hereafter more clearly declared.

Chapter II. Of Easy and Uneasy, Difficult, or Dolorous Deliverance, and the Causes of It: With the Signs How to Know and Forsee the Same

Very many be the perils, dangers, and throngs[40] which chance to women in their labor, which also ensue and come in diverse ways and for diverse causes, such as I shall here declare. First when the woman that laboreth is conceived over young, as before twelve or fifteen years of age (which chanceth sometimes, though not very often) and that the passage be over angst,[41] strait, or narrow, other naturally or else for some disease and infirmity which may happen about that part, as apostumes,[42] pushes,[43] piles, or blisters, and such other. Through the which causes, nature cannot (but with great dolor and pain) open and dilate itself to the expelling and deliverance of the child. . . .

Furthermore, if the party be weak and of feeble complexion, or of nature very cold, or too young, or very aged, or exceeding gross and fat, or contrariwise too spare and lean, or that she never had child before, or that she be over timorous and fearful, diverse, wayward, or such one that will not be ruled, removing her self from one place to another, all such things causeth the labor to be much more painful, cruel, and dolorous then it otherwise be. Also ye must understand that generally the birth of the man is easier then the birth of the female.

Item, if the child be of a fuller and greater growth than that it may easily pass that narrow passage or, contrariwise, if it be so faint, weak, and

38. Either.
39. Or else.
40. Troubles.
41. Narrow.
42. Abscesses.
43. Pimples or boils.

tender that it cannot turn it self, or doth it very slowly, or if the woman have two children at once, other else that it with the which she laboreth be a monster, as for example, if it hath but one body and two heads. . . .

Also, if the child be dead in the mother's belly, it is a very perilous thing, forsomuch as it can not be easily turned, neither can it weld[44] or help it self to come forth. Or if the child be sick or weakened, so that it can not for feebleness help it self.[45] The which thing may be foreseen and known by these tokens: if the woman with child have been long sick before her labor, if she have been sore tasked, if after her conception she have had daily and unwontly her flowers, if straight after one month upon the conception her breasts yield any milk, if the child stir not, nor move at such time as is convenient for it, these be arguments and tokens that it should be very weak. . . . And further, if the woman have used to eat commonly such meat or fruits which do exicate or dry and constrain or bind,[46] as medlers, chestnuts, and all sour fruits, as crabs, chokepears, quinces, and such other, with overmuch use of verjuice,[47] and such like sour sauces with rice, mill,[48] and many other things; all this shall greatly hinder the birth. Also the use of cold baths after the fifth month following the conception, or to bathe in such water where alome[49] is, iron, or salt, or any such things which do coarct[50] and constrain, or if she have been oftentimes heavy[51] and mourning, or ill at ease, or if she have been kept over hungry and thirsty, or have used overmuch watch and walking, other if she used a little before her labor things of great odor, smell, or savor, for such things in many men's opinions attract and draw upward the mother or matrix, the which is great hindrance to the birth. [Sigs. [K8]–Li[v] omitted.]

Chapter III. How a Woman with Child Shall Use Herself and What Remedies Be for Them That Have Hard Labor

. . . And if it chance that (the labor drawing near) she wax faint or sickly, then must ye comfort her with good comfortable meat, drink, wholesome

44. Wield?

45. It was generally believed that the child pushed itself out of the womb when it was ready to be born. The function of the contractions of the uterine muscles in childbirth were not understood.

46. Constipate.

47. The acid juice of green or unripe grapes, crab apples, or other sour fruit, expressed and formed into a liquor.

48. Milled flour?

49. Alum? (Mineral salts?)

50. Confine.

51. Sad, mournful.

and noble electuaries,[52] and in this time must she do all such things the which can make her apt and sufficient to her labor, and to use such things the which may [re]lax, open, and mollify[53] the nature and passage, so that the birth may the more freely proceed, and that chiefly in the younger women. The elder women, for because that those parts in them be somewhat drier and harder, therefore they must be hot and moist things which have property to lenify[54] and supple,[55] and that both in meat and drink, and also in outward fomentations, bathings, suppositories, and anointments. Anointments wherewith ye may supple the privy place be these: hen's grease, duck's grease, goose grease, also oil olive, linseed oil, the oil of the fenugreek, or the viscosity of holioke,[56] and such other; and for drink let her use good ripe wine, mixed with water. . . .

Also, as I said before, she must take good heed to her diet, that she take things the which may comfort and strengthen the body, feeding not overmuch of anything, and to drink pleasant and well-savoring wine or other drink, also moderately to exercise the body in doing some thing, stirring, moving, going, or standing, more than otherwise she was wont to do. These things further the birth and make it the easier. [Sigs. Lii–Liiii^v omitted.]

Now when the woman perceiveth the matrix or mother to wax lax or loose, and to be dissolved, and that the humors issue forth in great plenty, then shall it be meet for her to sit down, leaning backward in manner upright. For the which purpose in some regions (as in France and Germany) the midwives have stools for the nonce,[57] which being but low and not high from the ground be made so compasswise and cave,[58] or hollow in the middest, that that may be received from underneath which is looked for,[59] and the back of the stool, leaning backward, receiveth the back of the woman. . . .

And when the time of labor is come, in the same stool ought to be put many clothes or cloutes in the back of it, the which the midwife may remove from one side to another according as necessity shall require. The midwife herself shall sit before the laboring woman and shall diligently observe and wait, how much and after what means the child steereth itself. [She] also

52. A medicine, consisting of a powder or other ingredient mixed with honey, jam, or syrup.
53. Make smooth.
54. Relax.
55. Make supple.
56. Hollyhock.
57. For the particular purpose, expressly.
58. Cavitylike, concave.
59. The baby.

shall with her hands, first anointed with the oil of almonds or the oil of white lilies, rule and direct every thing as shall seem best. Also the midwife must instruct and comfort the party, not only refreshing her with good meat and drink, but also with sweet words, giving her good hope of a speedfull deliverance, encouraging and enstomaching[60] her to patience and tolerance, bidding her to hold in her breath so much as she may, also striking gently with her hands her belly above the navel, for that helpeth to depress the birth downward.

But if the woman be any thing gross, fat, or fleshy, it shall be best for her to lie groveling,[61] for by that means the matrix is thrust and depressed downward, anointing also the privy parts with the oil of white lilies. . . . And if it so be that the birth be of a great growth, and the head stick in the coming forth, then must the midwife help all that she may, with her hands first anointed with some oil, opening and enlarging the way that the issue may be the freer. Likewise [this] must be done if she bear two children at once. And all this is spoken of the natural birth, when first proceedeth the head and then the rest of the body ordinately.[62] . . . But when the birth cometh not naturally, then must the midwife do all her diligence and pain (if it may be possible) to turn the birth tenderly with her anointed hands, so that it may be reduced again to a natural birth. [Sigs. [L8]–Miiii^v omitted.]

Chapter IV [misnumbered V]. Remedies and Medicines by the Which the Labor May Be Made More Tolerable, Easy, and without Great Pain

The things which help the birth and make it more easy are these: first the woman that laboreth must other sit groveling or else upright, leaning backward, according as it shall seem commodious and necessary to the party, or as she is accustomed. And in winter or cold weather, the chamber wherein she laboreth must be warmed; and in summer or hot weather let in the air to refresh her withal, lest between extreme heat and labor the woman faint and sound.[63] And furthermore, she must be provoked to sneezing, and that either with the powder of hellebore or else of pepper. Also the sides of the woman must be stroken downward with the hands, which helpeth greatly and furthereth [the birth]. And let the midwife always be very diligent, providing and seeing what shall be necessary for the woman. . . . [Recipes follow. Sigs. Mv–[M8] omitted.]

60. Literally, giving her a good stomach; figuratively, encouraging her.
61. On her elbows and knees?
62. In order.
63. Swoon.

Chapter V. How the Secundine or Second Birth[64]
Shall Be Forced to Issue Forth, If It Come
Not Freely of His Own Kind

Here also sometime it cometh to pass, that the secundine,[65] which is wont to come together with the birth, remain and tarry behind, and follow not, and that for diverse causes. One is because peradventure the woman hath been so sore weakened and feeblished[66] with travail, dolor, and pain of that first birth that she hath no strength remaining to help herself to the expelling of this second birth. Another may be that it be entangled, tied, or let[67] within the matrix (which chanceth many times) or that it be destitute of humors,[68] so that the water be flown from it sooner then time is, which should make the places[69] more slippery and more easy to pass through. Or else that the places, overwearied with long and sore labor, for pain contract or gather together and enclose themselves again, so that the places be swollen for anguish and pain, and so let[70] the coming forth of the second birth.

But, to be short, of whatsoever it be thus stopped, the midwife in any wise must find such means that it may be unloosed and expulsed. For otherwise, great inconvenience should chance to the party, and specially suffocation and choking of the matrix, which also must so much the more be taken heed to for because the second birth retained and kept within will soon putrefy and rot, whereof will ensue ill, noisome, and pestiferous vapors ascending to the heart, the brains, and the midriff, through the which means the woman shall be short-winded, faint-hearted, often sounding,[71] and lying without any manner of moving or stirring in the pulses, yea, and many times is plainly suffocated, strangled, and dead of it. . . .

And if it be so that any part of the secundine do appear, let the midwife receive it tenderly, loosing it out fair and softly lest it break, and if ye doubt[72] that it will break, then let the midwife tie that part of the which she hath handfast to the woman's leg or foot, not very strait,[73] lest it break, neither very lax, lest it slip in again and then cause her to sneeze. Now if

64. Afterbirth, placenta.
65. The afterbirth.
66. Enfeebled.
67. Kept.
68. Fluids.
69. Uterus and birth canal?
70. Prevent.
71. Fainting.
72. Fear.
73. Tight.

the secundine tarry or stick, so that it come not quickly forward, then loose it a little and a little very tenderly, wreathing it from one side to another, till such time as it be gotten out, but ever beware of violent and hasty moving of it, least with the second birth ye remove the matrix also. . . .

Chapter VI. How That Many Things Chance to Women
after Their Labor, and How to Avoid, Defend,[74]
or to Remedy the Same

It is also to be understood that many times after the deliverance happeneth to women other[75] the fever, or ague, or swelling, or inflation of the body, other tumbling in the belly, or else commotion or settling out of order of the mother or matrix. Cause of the which things is sometimes lack of due and sufficient purgation and cleansing of the flowers after the birth, or else contrariwise overmuch flowing of the same, which sore doth weaken the woman. Also the great labor and stirring of the matrix in the birth. . . . [There follow more recipes and a discussion of excessive bleeding. Sigs. Nv^v–Ov omitted.]

Many times also it chanceth that the fundament gut cometh forth both in man and woman,[76] and especially in women in this business by reason of their great labor and striving with themselves. Wherefore in this case it is the midwife's part, with her hand warmed and wet in white wine, to reduce it back into his place again, the which if she cannot by this means for because peradventure it be swollen, then let her dissolve butter into white wine warmed, and therein dip wool, with the which wrap the same gut a while, so doing oftentimes till it be [a]swaged, that it may be returned in again. And ye may use (in stead of white wine) luke warm milk. . . . Again, sometime it cometh to pass that after the woman's labor, the matrix is removed out of his place and appeareth forth.[77] Then let it be washed and soaked with the water in which be sodden these things following. Take of Cypress nuts, Spikenard,[78] Balaustine,[79] acorn cups, of each an ounce, of Mespilles and unripe wild pears, and unripe apples, plums, and damsons, or bullace,[80] of each an handful. And such of those as be to be powdered, beat them to powder and the rest divide and cut them small. Then seeth[81]

74. To avert, keep off.
75. Either.
76. Hernia?
77. Prolapsed uterus?
78. An aromatic substance obtained from an eastern plant, identified as *Nardostachys Jatamansi* of northern India.
79. The flower of the wild pomegranate, used when dried as an astringent.
80. Wild plums.
81. Boil.

them altogether in rainwater, or else in water in the which steel being red hot hath been often times quenched. And in the same water let the party bathe her up to the navel, or else dip a sponge or lock of wool in it, and therewith wash and soak the same matrix oftentimes. . . .

Chapter VII. Of Abortments or Untimely Births and the Causes of It, and by What Remedies It May Be Defended, Holpen, and Eased

Abortment or untimely birth is when the woman is delivered before due season and before the fruit be ripe (as in the third, forth, or fifth month) before the birth have life, and sometimes after it hath life, it is delivered before it stir, being by some chance dead in the mother's womb. Of the which things there be many and diverse causes.

First, sometimes the mouth of the matrix is so large and ample that it cannot conveniently close itself together, neither contain the feature or conception. Or else it may be so corrupted and infected with vicious,[82] slimy, phlegmatic, and other waterish humors, that the cavity or hollowness thereof is thereby made so slippery that the feature conceived cannot there remain, but slippeth and slideth forth again. Also sometimes the matrix is apostumated and sore, so that for pain it cannot contain the conception. [Sigs. [O8ᵛ]–Qiᵛ omitted.]

Chapter IX. Of Dead Births, and by What Signs or Tokens It May Be Known, and by What Means It May Also Be Expelled

. . . Signs then that the birth is dead in the mother's womb be these: First, if the mother's breasts do suddenly slake, as I touched before. 2. If it move itself no more, being wont before to stir. 3. If when the mother turneth her from the one side to the other, she feel it falling from the one side to the other like a stone or a dead weight. 4. If her belly and navel begin to wax cold, which before was wont to be temperately hot. 5. If any stinking and filthy humors flow from the matrix, and chiefly after some fell[83] disease. 6. If the woman's eyes wax hollow, and that her color change from white to swart[84] and dun color, and that her eyes and nose wax astonied and have not their right use, and her lips wax wan. 7. If beneath the navel and about the secret parts she feel great throng and pain, the color of her face changing into worse and worse, otherwise than it was wont to do. 8. If she have appetite to eat such things which be against nature, and not wont to be eaten or drunken. 9. If she be in her sleep vexed with vain

82. Diseased.
83. Deadly.
84. Dark in color; black or blackish.

and terrible dreams. 10. If she be pained continually with the strangury,[85] or that she enforce herself much to the stool and with all her power, and yet cannot do anything. 11. If her breath begin to stink, the which thing lightly happeneth two or three days after the birth be dead. 12. If the hands put into very warm water and then laid on the woman's belly, and the child stir not, is a sign that it is dead. Of all these signs now, the more that come together of them at one time and in one person, the surer may ye be that the birth is dead, the which being once dead, all diligence must be had that it may be expelled out of the woman's body.

But here must ye see again whether it may be expelled, the mother's life saved or no. For sometime it chanceth that the mother dieth withal, and sometimes the mother doth well and prospereth. Whether the mother shall be in peril withal or no, by these things shall ye know: If the woman being in the labor sowne or fear, as though she were in a trance. If her remembrance fail her and she wax feeble and scant able to move or steer[86] herself. If she ([being] called with a loud voice) can answer nothing at all or else very little and that very softly, as though her voice began to fail her. If she be invaded or taken among in the laboring with convulsion or shrinking together. If she refuse or cannot brook meat. If her pulses beat very fast, the which signs when ye see in the woman laboring, it is an evident token that she shall not live long after her deliverance. Wherefore commit the cure of her to the hands of almighty God. But if none of these signs do appear, then have good hope, for the woman shall do well, the birth being once departed. Wherefore give all diligence to the expulsion of it that the woman may be delivered of this dead burden, the which thing may be done by two ways, either by medicines expulsive or else by certain instruments made for the nonce.

First, without instruments with this fumigation: take other the hoof or dong of an ass and put it on coals, and let the woman receive the fume underneath. Another, take the skin of an adder, myrrh, castrium,[87] brimstone,[88] galbanum,[89] oppoponacum,[90] madder[91] that the dyers occupy, pigeon's dung, or hawk's dung; beat all these to powder and temper them with ox gall, and make pills of it, each the quantity of a filbert nut, and

85. A disease of the urinary organs characterized by slow and painful emission of urine.
86. Steare in original—stir?
87. Castor? strongly smelling substance from two sacs in the inguinal region of the beaver.
88. Sulphur.
89. Galbanum, a gum resin obtained from certain Persian species of *Ferula*.
90. Opopanax? A fetid gum-resin obtained from the root of *Opopanax Chironium*.
91. A herbaceous climbing plant cultivated for the dye obtained from it.

then put one after another on the coals, and receive the fume through a pipe or conduit made for that purpose into the privities. [Other recipes follow.]

But if all these medicines profit not, then must be used more severe and hard remedies with instruments, as hooks, tongues, and such other things made for the nonce. And first the woman must be laid along upright, the middle part of her body lying higher than all the rest, accompanied of women assisting her about to comfort her and to keep her down, that when the birth is plucked out she rise not withal. Then let the midwife anoint her left hand with oil of white lilies, or other that may make it supple and smooth, and holding out her fingers, shutting together her hand, let her put it into the matrix to feel and perceive after what fashion the dead birth lieth in the mother's womb so that she may the better put in hooks and such other instruments to pluck it out withal.

If it be so that it lie the head forward, then fasten a hook either upon one of the eyes of it, or the roof of the mouth, or under the chin, or on one of the shoulders, which of these parts shall seem most commodious and handsome to take it out by, and the hook fastened, to draw it out very tenderly for[92] hurting of the woman. But if it lie the feet forward, then fasten the hook on the bone above the privy parts, or by some rib, or some of the back bones, or of the breast bones; and when this hook is thus fastened, the midwife may not by and by draw and pluck at it, but holding it in her left hand, let her with her right hand fasten another in some other part of the birth right against the first and then tenderly let her draw both together, so that the birth may proceed and come forth on both sides equally. . . . Again, if it chance that one of the hands only of the birth do appear, and that it cannot conveniently be reduced and returned upward again by reason of the narrownesss of the place, then bind it with a linen cloth that it slip not up again, and then to pluck it outward until such time that the whole arm be out, and then with a sharp knife cut it off from the body; and even so do if both hands appear first at once, or one leg, or both, if they cannot be returned back to be otherwise taken out conveniently. . . .

But contrary to all this, if it chance that the woman in her labor die and the child having life in it, then shall it be meet to keep open the woman's mouth and also the nether places, so that the child may by that means both receive and also expel air and breath which otherwise might be stopped, to the destruction of the child. And then to turn her on the left side and there to cut her open and so to take out the child. They that be born after this fashion are called *Caesarians* for because they be cut out of their mother's belly. Whereupon also the noble Roman Caesar the first took his name. [Sigs. Ri–[R8ᵛ] omitted.]

92. To prevent.

The Third Book

*Chapter I. In This First Chapter of the Third Book Is First
Declared the Matters Therein Contained, and
Then How the Infant Newly Born Must Be Handled,
Nourished, and Looked to*

... When that the navel is cut off and the rest knit up, anoint all the
child's body with the oil of acorns, for that is singularly good to confirm,
steadfast, and to defend the body from noisome[93] things which may chance
from without, as smoke, cold, and such other things which, if the infant
be grieved withal straight after the birth, being yet very tender, it should
hurt it greatly.

After this anointing, wash the infant with warm water, and with your
finger (the nail being pared) open the child's nostrils and purge them of
the filthiness. And also that the nurse handle so the child's sitting place
that it may be provoked to purge the belly. And chiefly it must be defended
from overmuch cold or overmuch heat. ...

Furthermore, when the infant is swaddled and laid in cradle, the nurse
must give all diligence and heed that she bind every part right, and in his
due place and order, and that with all tenderness and gentle entreating,
and not crookedly and confusedly, the which also must be done oftentimes
in the day, for in this is it, as it is in young and tender imps,[94] plants, and
twigs, the which even as ye bow them in their youth, so will they evermore
remain unto age. And even so the infant, if it be bound and swaddled, the
members lying right and straight, then shall it grow straight and upright.
If it be crookedly handled, it will grow likewise. And to the ill negligence
of many nurses may be imputed the crookedness and deformity of many
a man and woman which otherwise might seem as well-favored as any
other.

Item, let the child's eyes be oftentimes wiped and cleansed with a fine
and clean linen cloth or with silk. And let the arms of the infant be very
straight laid down by the sides, that they may grow right, and sometimes
stroking the belly of the child before the vesicle[95] or bladder to help to
ease and to provoke the child to making of water.[96] And when ye lay it in
the cradle to sleep, set the cradle in such a place that neither the beams
of the sun by day, neither the moon by night come on the infant, but rather
set it in a dark and shadowy place, laying also the head ever somewhat
higher then the rest of the body.

93. Annoying.
94. Young shoots, saplings.
95. The text reads "vesike," a misprint?
96. Urine.

And farther, let it be washed two or three times in the day and that anon[97] after sleep, in the winter with hot water, in the summer with luke warm water. Neither let it tarry long in the water but unto such time as the body begin to wax red for heat. But take heed that none of the water come into the infant's ears, for that should greatly hurt his hearing another day. Then, to be short, when it is taken out of the bath let it be wiped and dried with gentle and soft linen cloths warmed, and then to lay it on her lap the back upward, the which with her hands let her tenderly stroke and rub, and then to lap it up, and to swaddle it, and when it is swaddled, to put a drop or two of water into the nostrils of it is very good for the eye sight. And so to lay it to rest.

Chapter II. Of the Nurse and Her Milk, and
How Long the Child Should Suck

So concerning the bringing up, nourishment, and giving of suck to the child, it shall be best that the mother give her child suck herself, for the mother's milk is more convenient and agreeable to the infant than any other woman's, and more doth it nourish it, for because that in the mother's belly it was wont to the same,[98] and fed with it, and therefore also it doth more desirously covet the same, as that with the which it is best acquainted. And to be short, the mother's milk is most wholesome for the child.

. . . It shall be sufficient to give it suck twice or thrice in a day. And always beware ye give not the child too much suck at once in this tender age of it, for cloying of it, and lest also it loath [the milk] but rather let it have often of it and little at once then few times and overmuch at once. For such as be overcloyed with the mother's milk causeth their body to swell and inflate, and in their urine shall it appear that it is not overcome nor concocted or digested in the child. Which thing yet if it chance, let the infant be kept fasting until such time as that the which it hath received already be completely digested.

Item, if the mother's milk be somewhat sharp or choleric, let her never give the child her breast fasting. If it be so that the mother cannot give the infant suck herself, either for because of sickness, or that her breasts be sore and her milk corrupted, then let her choose a wholesome nurse,[99] with these conditions following.

First, that she be of a good color and complexion and that her bulk and breast be of good largeness. Secondly, that it be not too soon nor too long

97. At once, immediately.
98. Was used to the same. It was believed that mother's milk nourished the fetus before birth.
99. A wetnurse.

after her labor, so that it be two months after her labor at the least and that (if it may be) such one which had a man child. Thirdly, that she be of mean and measurable liking, neither too fat nor too lean. Fourthly, that she be good and honest of conversation, neither over hasty or ireful,[100] nor too sad or solemn, neither too fearful or timorous. For these affections and qualities be pernicious and hurtful to the milk, corrupting it, and pass forth through the milk into the child, making the child of like condition and manners. Also that they[101] be not over light and wanton of behavior. Fifthly, that her breasts be full and have sufficient plenty of milk, and that they be neither too great, soft, hanging, and flagging, nor too little, hard, or contract[ed], but of a measurable quantity. Also look upon her milk, that it be not blackish, blueish, gray, or reddish, neither sour, sharp, saltish, or brackish, neither thin and fluy, neither over gross and thick, but temperately white and pleasant in taste. And to be short, that milk is best and most to be chosen of the which a drop being milked softly upon the nail of the thumb holding your finger still, it rolleth not off, neither flitteth abroad, but if ye move your hand a little it will slide off by and by.[102] But if, when it is milked on the nail, it spread abroad and flit by and by, then is it too thin, but if it cleave still when that ye move a little your hand, then is it too stiff[103] and thick. The mean between both is best. [Recipes follow.]

Avicenna adviseth to give the child suck two years.[104] Howbeit, among us most commonly they suck but one year. And when ye will wean them, then do it not suddenly but a little and a little, and to make for it little pills of bread and sugar to eat, and accustom it so till it be able to eat all manner of meat. . . .

Chapter III. Of Divers Diseases and Infirmities Which Chance to Children Lately Born, and the Remedies Therefore
[Descriptions of various diseases, as "unsleepiness," with recipes follow. Sigs. [S7ᵛ]–Xiiii omitted.]

The Fourth Book

Chapter I. Here in this Fourth Book
(by the leave of God) shall briefly be declared such things which may farther or hinder the conception of man, which as it may be by diverse

100. Prone to anger.
101. The nurses.
102. Straightway, at once.
103. The text reads "spiffe," a misprint?
104. Avicenna was a Moslem physician and philosopher, A.D. 980–1037. See *The First Book of the Canon of Medicine of Avicenna* 710, "Duration of Lactation," in O. Cameron Gruner, *A Treatise on The Canon of Medicine of Avicenna Incorporating a Translation of the First Book* (New York: Augustus M. Kelley, 1970), pp. 370–71.

means letted and hindered, so also by many other ways it may be furthered and amended. Also to know by certain signs and tokens, whether the woman be conceived or no, and whether the conception be male or female, and finally certain remedies and medicines to further and help conception. . . .

Chapter II. Of Conception, and How Many Ways It
May Be Hindered and Letted[105]

There is nothing under heaven which so manifest and plainly doth declare and show the magnificent mightiness of the omnipotent living God as doth the perpetual and continual generation and conception of living things here in earth, by the which is saved, prorogued, and augmented the kind[106] of all things. And where that this almighty Lord and creator hath so institute[d] and ordained that no singular thing in itself (here upon earth) should continually remain and abide, yet hath he given from the beginning and instincted such a power and virtue unto these mortal creatures that they may ingender and produce other like things unto themselves and unto their own similitude, in the which always is saved the seed of posterity. Were not this provision had by almighty God, the nature and kind of all manner of things would soon perish and come to an end, the which virtue and power of generation many times doth halt and miss, by defect and the contrary disposition in the parts generant, as ye may evidently see in the sowing of corn and all other manner of seed. So that there be in all manner of generation three principal parts concurrent to the same, the sower, the seed sown, and the receptacle or the place receiving and containing the seed. If there be fault in any of these three, then shall there never be due generation, unto such time as the fault be removed or amended.[107]

The earth unto all seeds is as a mother and nurse, containing, clipping, and embracing them in her womb, feeding and fostering them as the mother doth the child in her belly or matrix until such time as they come unto the growth, quantity, and perfection due unto their nature and kind. But if this seed conceived in the bowels of the earth do not prove or fructify, then be thou sure that other there is let in the sower, in the seed, or else in the earth. . . .

Chapter III. How Many Ways Conception May Be
Letted, and How the Causes May Be Known

Everything then the which doth increase in this kind must first be conceived in the womb and matrix of the mother, which is apt and convenient

105. What follows may have been read as covert instructions on birth control.
106. Genus or species.
107. This seems to contradict the prevailing notion that if a woman does not conceive a child, it is due to the will of God.

for the receipt of such seed. And (as I said before) as there may be defect and lack in the mother receiving the seed, so may there be fault and defect in the sower, and in the seed itself also.

And in women three or four general causes by the which the conception may be impedite[108] and let: over much calidity or heat of the matrix, overmuch coldness, overmuch humidity or moistness, and overmuch dryness.[109] Any of these four qualities exceeding temperance may be sufficient causes to let due conception. . . .

Chapter IV. How to Know Whether Lack of Conception
Be of the Woman or of the Man, and How It May Be
Perceived Whether She Be Conceived or No

If ye be desirous to know whether the man or the woman be hindrance in conception, let each of them take of wheat and barley corns, and of beans, of each seven, the which they shall suffer to be steeped in their several urine the space of twenty and four hours; then take two pots, such as they set gilliflowers[110] in, fill them with good earth, and in the one let be set the wheat, barley, and beans steeped in the man's water, and in the other the wheat, barley, and beans steeped in the woman's water, and every morning the space of eight or ten days, let each of them, with their proper urine, water the said seeds sown in the forenamed pots, and mark whose pot doth prove, and the seeds therein contained doth grow, in that party is not the lack of conception, and see that there come no other water or rain on the pots. But trust not much this far fet[111] experiment. . . .

Whether she be conceived already or no, ye shall know by these signs. First the flowers issue not in so great quantity as they are wont, but wax less and less and in manner nothing at all cometh from them. Also the breasts begin to wax rounder, harder, and stiffer than they were wont to be. The woman shall long after certain things otherwise than she was used to do before that time, also her urine waxeth spish[112] and thickish by retention of the superfluities. Also the woman feeleth her matrix very fastly and closely shut insomuch that, as Hippocrates saith, the point of a needle may scarce enter.

Item, to know whether she be conceived or no, according to Hippocrates' mind:[113] Give unto a woman when she is going to bed a quantity of mil-

---

108. Impeded.
109. Raynalde refers to the four humors.
110. Clove pinks.
111. Fetched.
112. A misprint for stiff?
113. Hippocrates, *Aphorisms* (probably spurious) V.41.

licratum to drink and if after that drink she feel great pain, gnawing and tumbling in her belly, then be ye sure that she is conceived. This millicratum is a drink made of one part wine, another part water, sodden together with a quantity of honey.

But if ye be desirous to know whether the conception be man or woman, then let a drop of her milk or twaine be milked on a smooth glass, or a bright knife, other else on the nail of one of her fingers, and if the milk spread abroad upon it by and by, then is it a woman child. But if the drop of milk continue and stand still upon that the which it is milked on, then is it the sign of a man child.

Item, if it be a male, then shall the woman with child be well-colored and light[114] in going, her belly round, bigger toward the right side than the left (for commonly the man child lieth in the right side, the woman in the left side), and in the time of her bearing she shall better digest and like her meat, her stomach nothing too queasy nor feeble.

Chapter V. Of Certain Remedies and Medicines
Which May Further the Woman to Conceive

All sterility then for the most part ensueth and cometh of the distemperancy of one of these four named qualities,[115] wherefore the remedy and cure of the same when it chanceth must be done by such things the which have contrary power and operation to the excessive quality, for by that shall it be reduced to his temperancy again. As if that coldness and moistness exceeding temperancy in the matrix be occasion of sterility, then must she apply such things to that place the which be of nature hot and dry, the which may calify and warm the place and also dry up the ill moistness and humors contained in the same, hindering conception. [Sigs. Yii^v–[ ]2^v omitted.]

114. Moving readily; active, nimble, quick.
115. Humors (that which is hot, cold, moist, or dry).

Thomas Tusser
The Points of Housewifery, United to the Comfort of Husbandry
London, 1580
(collated with 1573 and 1577)

Introduction

Thomas Tusser was born about 1525 in Rivenhall, Essex.[1] He must have had a fine singing voice because he was placed as a child of seven in the collegiate chapel choir of the castle of Wallingford, Berkshire—where he was perpetually cold and hungry. He was then transferred to the choir of St. Paul's Cathedral, London, where he fared considerably better. In 1540 or 1541 he entered Eton, and in 1543, King's College, Cambridge, although he soon moved to Trinity Hall, Cambridge. He lived at court, probably as a musician under the patronage of William, Lord Paget, and retired to the countryside to farm his small estates after Paget's death.

It was presumably while Tusser was engaged in farming that he began to write his points of husbandry. Tusser published *A hundreth good points of husbandry* in 1557, and then, in 1562, he enlarged it, or to use his own words, "married it unto" his *Hundreth good points of housewifery*. (In fact, the last piece in Tusser's points of husbandry deals with the kind of wife a husbandman should choose in order to "thrive.") A pirated edition was printed in 1561–62, and two more authorized editions were printed before 1573, when Tusser enlarged both his *Hundreth good points of husbandry* and his *Good points of housewifery* into *Five hundreth points of good husbandry united to as many of good housewifery now lately augmented*. (Contrary to the title page, however, the points of good housewifery were never as numerous as those of good husbandry.) This book, to which were added various smaller pieces, went through nineteen editions by 1638. Most of the editions published after 1638 were reprints of *Five hundreth points of good husbandry,* although *One hundreth points* was reprinted in 1810, 1834, and 1931.[2] Editions of *Five hundreth points of good husbandry* were published in 1663, 1672, 1692, 1710, 1744, 1774, 1812, 1848, 1878, 1883, and 1931. The English Dialect Society edited the *Five hundreth points of good husbandry* in 1878, and this edition was reprinted in 1965 by Kraus Reprint Ltd., Vaduz.

Such a printing history suggests that Tusser's work, in one form or another, was continuously in print from 1557 to the present day. Furthermore, until the English Dialect Society published its edition in 1878, every edition of Tusser's work seems to have been printed for its practical use, not its antiquarian value. Daniel Hilman's important edition of 1710, for instance, which he called *Tusser Redivivus,* carefully compared Tusser's agricultural practices with contemporary eighteenth-century practices. That few of Tusser's counsels needed radical modification over the centuries suggests that country life, particularly life on self-sustaining farms, was far less subject to change than we might have expected, at least until the advent of mechanized farming. Certainly it was not until the English Dialect Society published its edition in 1878 that Tusser was read for other than agricultural reasons, in this case for his use of dialect words. It is even possible to suppose that Tusser's treatise on husbandry and housewifery was read, memorized, and consulted more than any other comparable work for at least two centuries, and that its importance as an authority did not cease until a century later. Indeed, it is hard to find another work in English (apart from the Bible, *The Book of Common Prayer,* and the *Homilies*) that has had a more distinguished publishing history (of at least thirty-eight recorded editions) and that takes a more modest, unassuming stance.

Tusser always wrote for publication in verse, usually in iambic (sometimes anapestic) four-stress couplets. Although his verse was probably meant to be memorized, and it is certainly memorable, Tusser took extraordinary care to ensure that his lines ended in eye rhymes as well as ear rhymes. Indeed, he often fractured spelling and sense in order to achieve both.[3] He was also elliptical in the extreme. He strove for a pithiness close to that of proverbs and, in the process, omitted articles, conjunctions, adverbs, adjectives, and auxiliary verbs. If his verse cannot be said to be "literary," it has the considerable merit of direct, economical statement.

Tusser organized his *Five hundreth points of good husbandry* according to the different tasks that needed to be done on a farm each month, beginning with September. It is thus a kind of farmer's almanac, composed mainly of directions for planting and harvesting crops. But Tusser's treatise on husbandry also deals with other than purely agricultural matters. He tells a farmer, for instance, to lock his doors, to beware of thieves, to treat good servants fairly, and to watch for lazy ones.

Tusser's shorter treatise on housewifery, unlike his treatise on husbandry, is organized according to the household tasks that need to be done on a typical day. As he proceeds from morning to evening tasks, he avoids the assertions of women's inferiority that dominate conduct books written for women. Nor does he ever suggest that wives, because they are women, are therefore physically or morally frail. On the contrary, he makes it plain that a good wife is a necessary and welcome adjunct to her husband. Tusser also takes it for granted that a good housewife will work as hard and as continually as does a husbandman. "The housewife is she that to labor doth fall, / the labor of her I do housewifery call." For this reason his points of housewifery are as practical as his points of husbandry. But they are far less specific, and deal mainly with the ways in which a housewife should manage her servants. For it is the housewife who has charge of the house: "When husband is absent, let housewife be chief, / and look to their labor that eateth her beef." (Vives believed that a wife should stay at home to preserve her chastity. Tusser keeps his housewife at home to run her household.)

> Dame practice is she that to housewife doth tell,
>   which way for to govern her family well.
> Use laborers gently, keep this as a law,
>   make child to be civil, keep servant in awe.

The day begins for the family at four in the morning in summer and at five in winter. The housewife dispenses breakfast and orders women-servants to work in the house or outbuildings: "Set some to peel hemp or else rushes to twine, / to spin and to card, or to seething of brine." She also orders men-servants and boys to work on the farm: "Set some about cattle, some pasture to view, / some malt to be grinding against ye do brew." She beats the maids: "Make maid to be cleanly, or make her cry creak, / and teach her to stir, when her mistress doth speak." She practices economy: "Three dishes well dressed, and welcome withal, / both pleaseth thy friend and becometh thine hall." She uses everything:

> Put chippings in dippings, use parings to save,
> fat capons or chickens that lookest to have.
> Save droppings and skimmings, how ever ye do,
> for medicine for cattle, for cart and for shoe.

She encourages honest mirth at supper, then sends her servants to bed and locks up: "Such keys lay up safe, ere ye take ye to rest, / of dairy, of buttery, of cupboard, and chest."

Tusser's housewife is obviously an impressive, efficient, busy but charitable woman who runs a substantial household, one that contains a dairy, a buttery, a spinning room, a brewhouse, a hen house, pig pens, and a kitchen garden. She is preeminently a manager, and has under her charge men, women, and boys. Tusser does not often mention his housewife's husband when he counsels her, but when he does, he makes it clear that her husband is as thankful for his wife's labor and her saving ways as he is for the good cheer she provides him.

> Good usage with knowledge, and quiet withal,
> > make housewife to shine, as the sun on the wall.
> What husband refuseth all comely to have,
> > that hath a good housewife, all willing to save.

Tusser's *Book of Housewifery*, with the exception of a few introductory passages, is reprinted in its entirety. It is based on the edition of W. Payne and Sidney Herrtage for the English Dialect Society, which in turn is based on Tusser's edition of 1580 collated with the editions of 1573 and 1577. Although I have used Payne and Herrtage's text of Tusser as a basis for my own, I have revised and sometimes silently corrected their annotations. With some exceptions, I have normalized spelling.

NOTES

1. Much of the biographical information in this introduction derives from *Five Hundred Points of Good Husbandry*, ed. W. Payne and Sidney J. Herrtage, (London: Trubner & Co., 1878) and from Tusser's own verse autobiography, "The Author's Life" (pp. 205–15). I also consulted Sir Walter Scott's "Introduction" to *Somers Tracts*, 1809–15, rpt. in Tusser, *Five Hundred Points of Good Husbandry*, foreword by E. V. Lucas (London: James Tregaskis & Son, 1931), pp. vii–xii.

2. Dorothy Hartby's edition of the *Good Points of Husbandry* was based on the 1571 edition of *One Hundreth Points of Good Husbandry* (London: Country Life, Ltd., 1931).

3. I have not kept all Tusser's eye rhymes in my text because they often interfere with the sense of the passage. Nor have I distinguished between ear rhymes where Tusser adjusted the spelling to create eye rhymes and eye rhymes that may not have been ear rhymes in Tusser's day (because Tusser uses many dialect words and phrases whose pronunciation is now lost).

The Points of Housewifery

To the right honorable and my especial good lady
and mistress, the Lady Paget.[1]

Though danger be mickle,
　　and favor so fickle,
Yet duty doth tickle
　　　my fancy to write:[2]
Concerning how pretty,
how fine and how netty,[3]
Good housewife should jetty,
　　　from morning to night.

Not minding by writing,
to kindle a spiting,
But shew by enditing,
　　　as afterward told:
How husbandry easeth,
to housewifery pleaseth,
And many purse greaseth
　　　with silver and gold.

For husbandry weepeth,
where housewifery sleepeth,
And hardly he creepeth,
　　　up ladder to thrift:
That wanteth to bold him,
thrift's ladder to hold him,
Before it be hold him,
　　　he falls without shift.

Least many should fear me,
and others forswear me,
Of troth I do bear me
　　　upright as ye see:
Full minded to love all,
and not to reprove all,
But only to move all,
　　　good housewives to bee.

1. Probably Anne, wife of William, Lord Paget.
2. The text reads "wright," in order to rhyme with "night," but perhaps Tusser also means "craft."
3. Natty, nice. Unless otherwise noted, definitions are taken from the English Dialect Society Edition.

For if I should mind some,
or descant behind some,
          displease so I mought:⁴
Or if I should blend them,
and so to offend them,
What stir I should send them
          I stand in a doubt.

Though harmless ye make it
and some do well take it,
If others forsake it,
          what pleasure were that?
Naught else but to pain me
and nothing to gain me,
But make them disdain me
          I wot neer for what.

Least some make a trial,
as clock by the dial,
Some stand to denial,
          some murmur and grudge:
Give judgment I pray you,
for justly so may you,
So fancy, so say you,
          I make you my judge.

In time, ye shall try me,
by troth, ye shall spy me,
So find, so set by me,
          according to skill:
How ever tree groweth,
the fruit the tree showeth,
Your Ladyship knoweth,
          my heart and good will.

Though fortune doth measure,
and I do lack treasure,
Yet if I may pleasure
          your Honor with this:
Then will me to mend it,
or mend ere ye send it,

---

4. Past tense of may (*OED*).

Or any where lend it,
    if ought be amiss.

Your Ladyship's servant,

Thomas Tusser

To the Reader

Now listen, good housewives, what doings are here
    set forth for a day, as it should for a year.
Both easy to follow, and soon to achieve,
    for such as by housewifery looketh to thrive.

The forenoon affairs, till dinner (with some),
    then after noon doings, till supper time come.
With breakfast and dinner time, sup, and to bed,
    stands orderly placed, to quiet thine head.

The meaning is this, for a day what ye see,
    that monthly and yearly continued must be.
And hereby to gather (as prove I intend),
    that housewifely matters have never an end.

I have not, by hearsay, nor reading in book,
    set out (peradventure) that some cannot brook,
Nor yet of a spite, to be doing with any,
    but such as have skared[5] me many a penny.

If widow, both housewife and husband may be,
    what cause hath a widower lesser than she?
Tis needful that both of them look well about:
    too careless within, and too lazy without.

Now, therefore, if well ye consider of this,
    what losses and crosses comes daily amiss,
Then bear with a widower's pen as ye may:
    though husband of housewifery somewhat doth say.

The Preface to the *Book of Housewifery*

Take weapon away, of what force is a man?
Take housewife from husband, and what is he then?

As lovers desireth together to dwell,
So husbandry loveth good housewifery well.

5. Cheated.

Though husbandry seemeth to bring in the gains,
Yet housewifery labors seem equal in pains.

Some respite to husbands the weather may send,
But housewives' affairs have never an end. [P. 162 omitted.]

A Description of Housewife and Housewifery

Of housewife doth housewifery challenge that name,
    of housewifery housewife doth likewise the same,
Where husband and husbandry joineth with these,
    there wealthiness gotten is holden with ease.

The name of a housewife what is it to say?
    the wife of the house, to the husband a stay.
If housewife doth that, as belongeth to her,
    if husband be godly, there needeth no stir.

The housewife is she that to labor doth fall,
    the labor of her I do housewifery call.
If thrift by that labor be honestly got,
    then is it good housewifery, else is it not.

The woman the name of a housewife doth win,
    by keeping her house and of doings therein.
And she that with husband will quietly dwell,
    must think on this lesson, and follow it well.

Instructions to Housewifery
Serve God is the first.
True love is not worst.

A daily good lesson, of housewife in deed,
    is God to remember, the better to speed.
Another good lesson, of housewifery thought,
    is housewife with husband to live as she ought.

Wife comely no grief,
Man out, housewife chief.
Though trickly to see to, be gallant to wive,
    yet comely and wise is the housewife to thrive.
When husband is absent, let housewife be chief,
    and look to their labor that eateth her beef.

> *Both out not allow,*
> *Keep house housewife thou.*

Where husband and housewife be both out of place,
    there servants do loiter, and reason their case.
The housewife so named (of keeping the house,)
    must tend on her profit, as cat on the mouse.

> *Seek home for rest,*
> *For home is best.*

As housewives keep home, and be stirrers about,
    so speedeth their winnings, the year thorough[6] out.
Though home be but homely, yet housewife is taught,
    that home hath no fellow to such as have aught.

> *Use all with skill,*
> *Ask what ye will.*

Good usage with knowledge, and quiet withal,
    make housewife to shine, as the sun on the wall.
What husband refuseth all comely to have,
    that hath a good housewife, all willing to save.

> *Be ready at need,*
> *All thine to feed.*

The case of good housewives, thus daily doth stand,
    whatever shall chance, to be ready at hand.
This care hath a housewife all day in her head,
    that all thing in season be housewifely fed.

> *By practice go muse,*
> *How household to use.*

Dame practice is she that to housewife doth tell,
    which way for to govern her family well.
Use laborers gently, keep this as a law,
    make child to be civil, keep servant in awe.

> *Who careless do live,*
> *Occasion do give.*

Have every where a respect to thy ways,
    that none of thy life any slander may raise.
What many do know, though a time it be hid,
    at length will abroad, when a mischief shall bid.

6. The text reads "thorow."

No neighbor reprove,
Do so to have love.
Thy love of thy neighbor shall stand thee in stead,
 the poorer, the gladder, to help at a need.
Use friendly thy neighbor, else trust him in this,
 as he hath thy friendship, so trust unto his.

Strike nothing unknown,
Take heed to thine own.
Revenge not thy wrath upon any man's beast,
 least thine by like malice be bid to like feast.
What husband provideth with money his drudge,
 the housewife must look to, which way it doth trudge. [Pp.
165–66 omitted.]

Housewifery

Morning works

 No sooner some up
 But nose is in cup.
Get up in the morning as soon as thou wilt,
with overlong slugging good servant is spilt.
Some slovens from sleeping no sooner get up,
but hand is in aumbry,[7] and nose in the cup.

 That early is done,
 Count housewifely won.
Some work in the morning may trimly be done,
that all the day after can hardly be won.
Good husband without, it is needful there be,
good housewife within, as needful as he.

 Cast dust into yard,
 And spin and go card.
Sluts' corners[8] avoided shall further thy health,
much time about trifles shall hinder thy wealth.
Set some to peel hemp or else rushes to twine,
to spin and to card, or to seething of brine.

 Grind malt for drink,
 See meat do not stink.
Set some about cattle, some pasture to view,
some malt to be grinding against ye do brew.

7. Ambry: cupboard, pantry.
8. Places where sluts reside?

Some corneth, some brineth, some will not be taught,
where meat is attainted, there cookery is naught.

Breakfast Doings

To breakfast that come,
Give every one some.
Call servants to breakfast by day star appear,
a snatch and to work, fellows tarry not here.
Let housewife be carver, let pottage be heat,
a mess to each one, with a morsel of meat.

No more tittle tattle,
Go serve your cattle.
What tack[9] in a pudding, saith greedy gut wringer,
give such ye wot what, ere a pudding he finger.
Let servants once served, thy cattle go serve,
least often ill serving make cattle to sterve.

Housewifely Admonitions

Learn you that will thee,[10]
This lesson of me
No breakfast of custom provide for to save,
but only for such as deserveth to have.
No shewing of servant what vittles in store,
shew servant his labor, and shew him no more.

Of havoc beware,
Cat nothing will spare.
Where all thing is common, what needeth a hutch?
where wanteth a saver, there havoc is much.
Where window is open, cat maketh a fray,
yet wild cat with two legs is worse by my fay.

Look well unto thine,
Slut slothful must whine.
An eye in a corner who useth to have,
revealeth a drab, and preventeth a knave.
Make maid to be cleanly, or make her cry creak,[11]
and teach her to stir, when her mistress doth speak.

9. Holding quality, solidity (*OED*).
10. Thrive.
11. A harsh cry, caused by a blow?

Let holly wand threat
Let fisgig[12] be beat.
A wand in thy hand, though ye fight not at all,
makes youth to their business better to fall.
For fear of fool had I wist cause thee to wail,
let fisgig be taught to shut door after tail.

Too easy the wicket,[13]
Will still appease clicket.[14]
With her that will clicket make danger to cope,
lest quickly her wicket seem easy to ope.
As rod little mendeth where manners be spilt,
so naught will be naught say and do what thou wilt.

Fight seldom ye shall
But use not to brawl
Much brawling with servant, what man can abide?
pay home when thou fightest, but love not to chide.
As order is heavenly where quiet is had,
so error is hell, or a mischief as bad.

What better a law.
Than subjects in awe?
Such awe as a warning will cause to beware,
doth make the whole household the better to fare.
The less of thy counsel thy servants do know,
Their duty the better such servants shall show.

Good music regard,
Good servants reward.
Such servants are oftenest painful and good,
that sing in their labor, as birds in the wood.
Good servants hope justly some friendship to feel,
and look to have favor what time they do well.[15]

By once or twice
Tis time to be wise.
Take runagate Robin, to pity his need,
and look to be filched, as sure as thy creed.
Take warning by once, that a worse do not hap,
foresight is the stopper of many a gap.

---

12. A worthless fellow.
13. A small door or gate (*OED*).
14. The latch of a gate or door, by extension, chatter (*OED*).
15. The texts reads "weele."

> Some change for a shift,
> Oft change, small thrift.

Make few of thy counsel to change for the best,
lest one that is trudging infecteth the rest.
The stone that is rolling can gather no moss,
for master and servant, oft changing is loss.

> Both liberal sticketh,
> Some provender pricketh.

One dog for a hog, and one cat for a mouse,
one ready to give is enough in a house:
One gift ill accepted, keep next in thy purse,
whom provender pricketh are often the worse.

Brewing

> Brew somewhat for thine,
> Else bring up no swine.

Where brewing is needful, be brewer thy self,
what filleth the roof will help furnish the shelf:
In buying of drink, by the firkin[16] or pot,
the tally ariseth, but hog amends not.

> Well brewed, worth cost,
> Ill used, half lost.

One bushel well brewed, outlasted some twaine,
and saveth both malt, and expenses in vain.
Too new is no profit, too stale is as bad,
drink dead or else sour makes laborer sad.

> Remember good Gill,
> Take pain with thy swill.

Seeth[17] grains in more water, while grains be yet hot,
and stir them in copper, as porridge in pot.
Such heating with straw, to have offal good store,
both pleaseth and easeth, what would ye have more?

Baking

> New bread is a drivel[18]
> Much crust is as evil.

New bread is a waster, but moldy is worse,
what that way dog catcheth, that loseth the purse.

16. A small cask, a quarter of a barrel (*OED*).
17. Boil.
18. A drudge, a menial servant (*OED*).

Much doughbake I praise not, much crust is as ill,
the mean is the housewife, say nay if ye will.

Cookery

Good cookery craveth,
Good turnbroach[19] saveth.
Good cook to dress dinner, to bake and to brew,
deserves a reward, being honest and true.
Good diligent turnbroach and trusty withal,
is sometime as needfull as some in the hall.

Dairy

Good dairy doth pleasure,
Ill dairy spends treasure.
Good housewife in dairy, that needs not be told,
deserveth her fee to be paid her in gold.
Ill servant neglecting what housewifery says,
deserveth her fee to be paid her with bays.[20]

Good droie[21] worth much.
Mark sluts and such.
Good droie to serve hog, to help wash, and to milk,
more needful is truly than some in their silk.
Though homely be milker, let cleanly be cook,
for a slut and a sloven be known by their look.

In dairy no cat,
Lay bane for a rat.
Though cat (a good mouser) doth dwell in a house,
yet ever in dairy have trap for a mouse.
Take heed how thou layest the bane for the rats,
for poisoning servant, thyself, and thy brats.

Scouring

No scouring for pride,
Spare kettle whole side.
Though scouring be needful, yet scouring too much,
is pride without profit, and robbeth thine hutch.

19. Turnspit (*OED*).
20. The text reads "baies"—chidings, reproofs? (Halliwell, *Dictionary*).
21. Payne and Herrtage in the English Dialect Society edition suggest that droie is
a corruption of droile, a scullion or kitchen boy (p. 306).

Keep kettles from knocks, set tubs out of sun,
for mending is costly, and crackt is soon done.

Washing

Take heed when ye wash,
Else run in the lash.
Maids, wash well and wring well, but beat ye wot how,
if any lack beating, I fear it be you.[22]
In washing by hand, have an eye to thy boll,[23]
for launder[er]s and millers, be quick of their toll.

Dry sun, dry wind,
Safe bind, safe find.
Go wash well, saith Summer, with sun I shall dry,
go wring well, saith Winter, with wind so shall I.
To trust without heed is to venture a joint,
Give tale[24] and take count, is a housewifely point.

Where many be packing,
Are many things lacking.
Where hens fall a cackling, take heed to their nest,
where drabs fall a whisp[e]ring, take heed to the rest.
Through negligent housewives, are many things lacking,
and Gillet suspected will quickly be packing.

Malting

Ill malting is theft,
Wood dried hath a weft.
House may be so handsome, and skillfulness such,
to make thy own malt, it shall profit thee much.
Some drieth with straw, and some drieth with wood,
wood asketh more charge, and nothing so good.

Take heed to the kell,[25]
Sing out as a bell.
Be sure[26] no chances to fire can draw,
the wood, or the furzen, the brake or the straw.

22. The text reads "yow."
23. Washing bowl or tub.
24. A reckoning, an enumeration (*OED*).
25. Hop-kiln.
26. The text reads "suer."

Let Gillet be singing, it doth very well,
to keep her from sleeping and burning the kell.

Best dried, best speeds,
Ill kept, bowd[27] breeds.
Malt being well speered,[28] the more it will cast,[29]
malt being well dried, the longer will last.
Long kept in ill soller,[30] (undoubted thou shalt,)
through bowds without number lose quickly thy malt.

Dinner Matters

For hunger or thirst,
Serve cattle well first.
By noon see your dinner, be ready and neat,
let meat tarry servant, not servant his meat.
Plough cattle a baiting, call servant to dinner,
the thicker together, the charges the thinner.

Together is best,
For hosts and guest.
Due season is best, altogether is gay,
dispatch hath no fellow, make short and away.
Beware of Gill laggose,[31] disordring thy house,
mo dainties who catcheth, than crafty fed mouse!

Let such have enough,
That follow the plough.
Give servant no dainties, but give him enough,
too many chaps walking, do beggar the plough.
Poor seggons[32] half starved work faintly and dull,
And lubbers[33] do loiter, their bellies too full.

Give never too much,
To lazy and such.
Feed lazy that thresheth a flap and a tap,
like slothful, that all day be stopping a gap.

27. Weevil.
28. Sprouted.
29. Reckon.
30. Loft, garret.
31. Laggard.
32. Poor laborers.
33. Louts.

Some litherly lubber more eateth than two,
yet leaveth undone that another will do.

> Where nothing will last,
> Spare such as thou hast.

Some cutteth thy linen, some spoileth[34] their broth,
bare table to some doth as well as a cloth.
Treen[35] dishes be homely, and yet not to lack,
where stone is no laster, take tankard and jack.[36]

> Knap[37] boy on the thumbs,
> And save him his crumbs.

That pewter is never for mannerly feasts,
that daily doth serve so unmannerly beasts.
Some gnaweth and leaveth some crusts and some crumbs.
eat such their own leavings, or gnaw their own thumbs.

> Serve God ever first
> Take nothing at worst.

At dinner, at supper, at morning, at night,
give thanks unto God, for his gifts so in sight.
Good husband and housewife, will sometime alone,
make shift with a morsel and pick of a bone.

> Enough thou art told,
> Too much will not hold.

Three dishes well dressed, and welcome withal,
both pleaseth thy friend and becometh thine hall.
Enough is a plenty, too much is a pride,
the plough with ill holding, goes quickly aside.

Afternoon works

> Make company break
> Go cherish the weak.

When dinner is ended, set servants to work,
and follow such fellows as loveth to lurk.
To servant in sickness see nothing ye grutch,[38]
a thing of a trifle shall comfort him much.

---

34. Spilleth, 1577.
35. Made of "tree," wooden (*OED*).
36. A drinking vessel containing half or a quarter pint (Payne and Herrtage, p. 332).
37. Rap.
38. Grudge (*OED*).

Who many do feed,
Save much they had need.
Put chippings[39] in dippings, use parings to save,
fat capons or chickens that lookest to have.
Save droppings and skimmings, how ever ye do,
for medicine for cattle, for cart and for shoe.

Lean capon unmeet
Deer fed is unsweet.
Such offcorn[40] as cometh give wife to her fee,
feed willingly such as do help to feed thee.
Though fat fed is dainty, yet this I thee warn,
be cunning in fatting for robbing thy barn.

Piece hole to defend.
Things timely amend.
Good seamsters be sowing of fine pretty knacks,
good housewives be mending and piecing their sacks.
Though making and mending be housewifely ways,
yet mending in time is the housewife to praise.

Buy new as is meet,
Mark blanket and sheet.
Though ladies may rend and buy new ery[41] day
good housewives must mend and buy new as they may.
Call quarterly servants to court and to leete,[42]
write every coverlet, blanket, and sheet.

Shift slovenly elf[43]
Be jailer thyself.
Though shifting too oft be a thief in the house,
yet shift slut and sloven for fear of a louse.
Grant doubtful no key of his chamber in purse,
least chamber door lockt be to thievery a nurse.

Save feathers for guest
These other rob chest.
Save wing for a thresher, when gander doth die,
save feather of all thing, the softer to lie,

39. Small pieces of bread.
40. Offal or waste corn (wheat).
41. Every.
42. Manor court.
43. Here, a servant.

Much spice is a thief, so is candle and fire,
sweet sauce is as crafty as ever was friar.

> Wife make thine own candle,
> Spare penny to handle.

Provide for thy tallow, ere frost cometh in,
and make thine own candle, ere winter begin.
If penny for all thing be suffered to trudge,
trust long, not to penny, to have him thy drudge.

Evening works

> Time drawing to night,
> See all things go right.

When hens go to roost go in hand to dress meat.
serve hogs and to milking and some to serve neat.[44]
Where twain be ynow, be not served with three,
more knaves in a company worser they be.

> Make lackey to trudge,
> Make servant thy drudge.

For every trifle leave janting[45] thy nag,
but rather make lackey of Jack boy thy wag.
Make servant at night lug in wood or a log,
let none come in empty but slut and thy dog.

> False knave ready prest,
> All safe is the best.

Where pullen use nightly to perch in the yard,
there two legged foxes keep watches and ward.
See cattle well served, without and within,
and all thing at quiet ere supper begin.

> Take heed it is needful,
> True pity is meedful.

No clothes in garden, no trinkets without,
no door leave unbolted, for fear of a doubt[46]
Thou woman whom pity becometh the best,
grant all that hath labored time to take rest.

44. Cattle.
45. Driving.
46. Danger.

Supper matters

Use mirth and good word
At bed and at board.
Provide for thy husband, to make him good cheer,
make merry together, while time ye be here.
At bed and at board, howsoever befall,
whatever God sendeth be merry withal.

No brawling make,
No jealousy take.
No taunts before servants, for hindering of fame,
no jarring too loud for avoiding of shame.
As fransy[47] and heresy roveth together,
so jealousy leadeth a fool ye wot wither.

Tend such as ye have,
Stop talkative knave.
Young children and chickens would ever be eating,
good servants look duly for gentle entreating.
No servant at table use saucely[48] to talk,
least tongue set at large out of measure do walk.

No snatching at all,
Sirs, hearken now all.
No lurching,[49] no snatching, no striving at all,
least one go without and another have all.
Declare after supper, take heed thereunto,
what work in the morning each servant shall do.

After supper matters

Thy soul hath a clog,[50]
Forget not thy dog.
Remember those children whose parents be poor,
which hunger, yet dare not crave at thy door.
Thy bandog that serveth for diverse mishaps,
forget not to give him thy bones and thy scraps.

47. Frenzy, madness.
48. Saucily.
49. Snatching at food before others (*OED*).
50. An impediment, encumbrance, hindrance (*OED*). The English Dialect Society
defines clog here as "charge, duty," but that is not its usual sixteenth-century conno-
tation.

Make keys to be keepers,
To bed ye sleepers.
Where mouths be many, to spend that thou hast,
set keys to be keepers, for spending too fast.
To bed after supper let drowsy go sleep,
lest knave in the dark to his marrow[51] do creep.

Keep keys as thy life,
Fear candle good wife.
Such keys lay up safe, ere ye take ye to rest,
of dairy, of buttery,[52] of cupboard, and chest.
Fear candle in hayloft, in barn, and in shed,
fear flea smock and mendbreech, for burning their bed.

See door lockt fast.
Two keys make waste.
A door without lock is a bait for a knave,
a lock without key is a fool that will have.
One key to two locks, if it break is a grief,
two keys to one lock in the end is a thief.

Night works troubles head,
Lock doors and to bed.
The day willeth done whatsoever ye bid,
the night is a thief, if ye take not good hid.[53]
Wash dishes, lay leavens,[54] save fire and away,
lock doors and to bed, a good housewife will say.

To bed know thy guise,
To rise do likewise.
In winter at nine, and in summer at ten,
to bed after supper both maidens and men.
In winter at five a clock, servant arise,
in summer at four is very good guise.

Love so as ye may
Love many a day.
Be lowly not sullen, if ought go amiss,
what wresting[55] may loose thee, that win with a kiss.

51. Mate, companion.
52. A store room for liquor; also, for provisions generally (*OED*).
53. Heed, care.
54. Lay the the barm and meal together for fermentation.
55. Struggling for.

Both bear and forebear now and then as ye may,
    then wench God a mercy, thy husband will say.

The plowman's feasting days
                        This would not be slept,
                        Old guise must be kept.
    Good housewives, whom God hath enriched enough,
        forget not the feasts that belong to the plow.
    The meaning is only to joy and be glad,
        for comfort with labor is fit to be had.

Plow Monday[56]
    Plow Monday, next after that Twelftide is past,
        bids out with the plow, the worst husband is last.
    If plowman get hatchet or whit to the skreen,[57]
        maids loseth their cock if no water be seen.

Shrovetide
    At Shrovetide to shroving, go thresh the fat hen,
        if blindfild can kill her, then give it thy men.
    Maids, fritters and pancakes ynow see ye make:
        let slut have one pancake, for company sake.[58]

Sheep shearing
    Wife, make us a dinner, spare flesh neither corn,
        make wafers and cakes, for our sheep must be shorn.
    At sheep shearing neighbors none other thing crave,
        but good cheer and welcome like neighbors to have.

56. The English Dialect Society edition quotes *Coles Dictionary,* 1708: "The Monday next after Twelfth-day, when our Northern plow-men beg plow-money to drink; and in some places if the plowman (after that day's work) come with his whip to the kitchen hatch, and cry 'cock in pot' before the maid says 'cock on the dung-hill,' he gains a cock on Shrove-Tuesday."

57. Probably a a fire screen, perhaps a wooden seat or settle with a high back to keep away draughts (cf. *OED*).

58. The English Dialect Society edition quotes Hillman, *Tusser Redivivus,* 1710: "The hen is hung at a fellow's back who has also some horse bells about him. The rest of the fellows are blinded, and have boughs in their hands, with which they chase this fellow and his hen about some large court or small enclosure. The fellow with his hen and bells shifting as well as he can, they follow the sound and sometimes hit him and his hen, other times, if he can get behind one of them, they thresh one another well favor'dly; but the jest is, the maids are to blind the fellows, which they do with their aprons, and the cunning baggages will endear their sweet-hearts with a peeping hole, while the others look out as sharp to hinder it. After this the hen is boil'd with bacon, and store of pancakes and fritters are made."

The wake day[59]

> Fill oven full of flawnes,[60] Ginnie,[61] pass not for sleep
>> tomorrow thy father his wake day will keep.
> Then every wanton may dance at her will,
>> both Tomkin with Tomlin, and Jankin with Gill.

Harvest home

> For all this good feasting, yet art thou not loose,
>> till plowman thou givest his harvest home goose.[62]
> Though goose go in stubble, I pass not for that,
>> let goose have a goose, be she lean, be she fat.

Seed cake

> Wife, some time this week, if the weather hold clear,
>> an end of the wheat sowing we make for this year.
> Remember you therefore, though I do it not:
>> the seed cake, the pasties, and furmenty pot.[63]

Twice-a-week roast

> Good plowmen look weekly, of custom and right
>> for roast meat on Sundays and Thursdays at night.
> This doing and keeping such custom and guise,
>> they call thee good housewife, they love thee likewise.

The Good Housewifely *Physic*

> Good housewives provide, ere an sickness do come,
>> of sundry good things in her house to have some.
> Good aqua composita,[64] vinegar tart,
>> Rose water and treacle, to comfort the heart.

---

59. *Tusser Redivivus,* 1710: "The Wake-day is the day on which the parish church was dedicated, called so, because the night before it, they were used to watch till morning in the church and feasted all the next. Waking in the church was left off because of some abuses, and we see here it was converted to waking at the oven."

60. Flans, custard pies.

61. Jenny.

62. The English Dialect Society edition quotes Mavor's edition of 1812: "A goose used formerly to be given at harvest-home, to those who had not overturned a load of corn in carrying during harvest."

63. A sweet porridge made of wheat, milk, eggs, sugar, and spices.

64. A liquor made of herbs and spices steeped in ale or wine and then distilled.

Cold herbs in her garden to agues that burn,
    that over strong heat to good temper may turn.
While endive and suckery[65] and spinach enough
    all such with good pot herbs should follow the plough.

Get water of fumentory,[66] liver to cool,
    and others the like, or else lie like a fool.
Conserve of the barberry, quinces and such,
    with syrups that easeth the sickly so much.

Ask *Medicus* counsel, ere medicine ye make,
    and honor that man, for necessities' sake.
Though thousands hate physic, because of the cost,
    yet thousands it helpeth, that else should be lost.

Good broth and good keeping do much now and then,
    good diet with wisdom best comforteth man.
In health to be stirring shall profit thee best,
    in sickness hate trouble, seek quiet and rest.

Remember thy soul, let no fancy prevail,
    make ready to Godward, let faith never quail.
The sooner thy self thou submittest to God,
    the sooner he ceaseth to scourge with his rod.

The good motherly *Nursery*

Good housewives take pain, and do count it good luck
    to make their own breast their own child to give suck.
Though wrauling[67] and rocking be noisome so near,
    yet lost by ill nursing is worser to hear.

But one thing I warn thee, let housewife be nurse,
    least husband do find thee too frank with his purse.
What hillback[68] and fillbelly maketh away,
    that help to make good, or else look for a fray.

Give child that is fitly, give baby the big,[69]
    give hardness to youth and to roperipe[70] a twig.
We find it not spoken so often for naught,
    that children were better unborn than untaught.

65. Wild endive, chicory.
66. *Fumaria officinalis*, so called from its rank disagreeable smell: formerly used as an antiscorbutic.
67. Quarreling.
68. Cover back, i.e., extravagance in dress.
69. Teat.
70. One old enough to be flogged.

Some cockneies[71] with cocking[72] are made very fools,
    fit neither for prentice, for plow, nor for schools.
Teach child to ask blessing, serve God, and to church,
    then bless as a mother, else bless him with birch.
Thou housewife thus doing, what further shall need?
    but all men to call thee good mother in deed.

Think on the poor.
Remember the poor, that for God's sake do call,
    for God both rewardeth and blesseth withal.
Take this in good part, whatsoever thou be:
    and wish me no worse than I wish unto thee.

A Comparison between Good Housewifery and Evil
Ill housewifery lieth till nine of the clock.
Good housewifery trieth to rise with the cock.

Ill housewifery tooteth, to make herself brave,
Good housewifery looketh what household must have.

Ill housewifery trusteth to him and to her.
Good housewifery lusteth herself for to stir.

Ill housewifery careth for this nor for that.
Good housewifery spareth for fear ye wot what.

Ill housewifery pricketh herself up in pride.
Good housewifery tricketh her house as a bride.

Ill housewifery othing or other must crave.
Good housewifery nothing, but needful will have.

Ill housewifery moveth with gossip to spend.
Good housewifery loveth her household to tend.

Ill housewifery wanteth with spending too fast,
Good housewifery canteth[73] the lenger to last.

Ill housewifery easeth herself with unknown.
Good housewifery pleaseth herself with her own.

Ill housewifery brooketh mad toys in her head.
Good housewifery looketh that all things be fed.

71. Spoilt boys.
72. Spoiling.
73. Scanteth, 1577.

Ill housewifery bringeth a shilling to naught.
Good housewifery singeth her coffers full fraught.

Ill housewifery rendeth, and casteth aside.
Good housewifery mendeth, else would it go wide.

Ill housewifery sweepeth her linen to gage.[74]
Good housewifery keepeth to serve her in age.

Ill housewifery craveth in secret to borrow.
Good housewifery saveth today for tomorrow.

Ill housewifery pineth not having to eat.
Good housewifery dineth with plenty of meat.

Ill housewifery letteth the Devil take all.
Good housewifery setteth good brag of a small.

Good housewife good fame hath of best in the town,
Ill housewife ill name hath of every clown.

Thus endeth the book of Housewifery.

74. To place in pawn.

PART V

The Cavalier Lady

RICHARD BRATHWAITE
The English Gentlewoman
London, 1631

Introduction

Richard Brathwaite was the second son of a substantial English country gentleman. He was educated at Oxford and at Cambridge (his tutor was the Royalist Anglo-Catholic divine Lancelot Andrews). He spent some time at the Inns of Court in London and, after his father's death, returned to the country to live out his life on estates his father bequeathed to him. He married twice, and had nine children by his first wife and one by his second. He was a Royalist, and probably fought on the Royalist side during the civil war. He was at all times an easy, voluble, prolific writer. He wrote *Drunken Barnaby's Four Journeys,* a satiric travel book in rhymed Latin and English doggerel verse which went through eleven editions; a prose description of *The Laws of Drinking* (1617); a short description of *The Smoking Age . . . with the life and death of Tobacco* (1617); a poem, *A Good Wife: or a Rare One amongst Women* (1618); several pastorals, including *The Arcadian Princess* (1635); *The English Gentleman* (1630); many religious works in verse and prose such as *A Spiritual Spicerie* (1638); and *Ar't asleep Husband?* (1640), a collection of "bolster lectures" in prose on moral themes, in addition to several romances, elegies, satires, and works in other genres.

The English Gentlewoman was written a year after *The English Gentleman* and was intended to be a companion volume to it. As the title suggests and its text bears out, *The English Gentlewoman* was not written for all women. (That it went through only two editions may have been in part a result of its Royalist, coterie nature.) It is addressed to women of "gentle" birth, in other words, to leisured women who were the daughters and wives of gentlemen and whose fathers or husbands had landed wealth. For this reason, perhaps, Brathwaite writes in a conversational rather than a prescriptive mode, and spends more time describing the life of ladies in society than he does their duties at home. He says of his model gentlewoman, for instance, that "her education hath so enabled her as she can converse with you of all places, deliver her judgment conceivingly of most persons, and discourse most delightfully of all fashions." In fact, Brathwaite would have his gentlewoman live mainly in company. "Society is the solace of the living, for to live without it were a kind of dying." Thus Brathwaite discourses on the benefits a woman's social "grace" will confer not only on her family but also on society at large: "in my judgment . . . a modest and well behaved woman may by her frequent or resort to public places, confer not less benefit to such as observe her behavior then occasion of profit to her private family, where she is overseer." It is civility, furthermore, not obedience, which is a principal ornament of women: "civility is never out of fashion; it ever retains such a seemly garb as it confers a grace on the wearer, and enforceth admiration in the beholder." Brathwaite hopes that his gentlewoman will be virtuous, but he believes that her virtue should be softened by gentility and polished by courtesy: "what is good and amiable in the eye of virtue, she embraceth with an affectionate tender, making it her highest honor to promote the glory of her maker. But lest by being too serious, she might become tedious, she will not stick to walk abroad with you into more pleasing groves or pastures of delight, where she will converse with you of love, and intermix her discourse with such time beguiling tales, as variety shall no less sharpen your attention, than the modesty of her method beget admiration."

Perhaps because Brathwaite is concerned with the social life of a gentlewoman, he focuses his attention on her love, should she fall in love, for a gentleman. But, even though he worries that her passion might degenerate into anger or envy, he does not condemn it outright as do moralists like Vives. He is content to hope that his gentlewoman will temper the excesses of her passion with reason and restraint: "what a furious and inconsiderate thing is woman when passion distempers her? . . . to allay or abate these passionate furies, there is no better means than to enter parley with reason, to chastise all such innovating motions as disquiet the inward repose of the mind, to use the help of such wholesome instructions as may attemper the heat of those indisposed and inordinate passions."

It is consequently in character that Brathwaite does not begin his book with a description of Eve's fall, as do so many other authors who addressed themselves to women in this anthology. He begins instead with a chapter on modest and pleasing attire. When Brathwaite does mention the Fall, he ignores its most unhappy consequences for women and concentrates on Eve's need after the Fall to "put on what before she needed not, a veil to cover her nakedness." Brathwaite moves from the subject of clothes to that of behavior and exchanges of "civil complement," wherein he hopes women will always speak and act so as to preserve their reputations (which he calls "estimation"). When he speaks of honor, he defines honor not only as moral worth, but also as high estate, or "gentility." Thus Brathwaite places nearly as much emphasis upon the outward behavior of his gentlewoman as he does upon her inward virtues. In the process he liberates her from many of the social (and perhaps even religious) restrictions moralists like Vives and Perkins would impose upon her. At the very least he has softened their rigidities and introduced a few privileged women to the pleasures of courtesy and company.

The English Gentlewoman

To her whose true love to virtue hath highly ennobled herself, renowned her sex, honored her house: The Right Honorable, the Lady Arabella Wentworth:[1]

Madam: Some months are past since I made bold to recommend to my Right Honorable Lord, your husband, an *English Gentleman,* whom he was pleased, forth[2] of his noble disposition, to receive into his protection. Into whose most honorable service he was no sooner entertained and upon due observance of his integrity approved, than upon approvement of his more piercive[3] judgment, he became generally received. Out of these respects, my most honorable Lady, I became so encouraged as I have presumed to prefer unto your service an *English Gentlewoman,* one of the same country and family, a deserving sister of so generous a brother, or (if you will) a pleasing spouse to so gracious a lover whom, if your honor shall be but pleased to entertain (and your noble candor is such, as she can expect nothing less) you shall find excellently graced with sundry singular qualities, beautified with many choice endowments, and so richly adorned with diverse exquisite ornaments, as her attendance shall be no derogation to your honor, nor no touch to your unblemish'd self, to retain her in your favor. Sure I am the sweetness of her temper sorts and suits well with the quality or disposition of your honor, for she loves without any painted

1. Lady Arabella Wentworth was the second wife of Thomas Wentworth, first earl of Strafford (1593–1641). When she died in October, 1631, the *Dictionary of National Biography* reports that the whole city had "a face of mourning; never any woman so magnified and lamented even of those who never saw her face," s.v. Wentworth, Thomas.
2. Out of.
3. Ability to pierce? piercing?

pretenses to be really virtuous, without popular applause to be affably gracious, without any glorious gloss to be sincerely zealous. Her education hath so enabled her as she can converse with you of all places, deliver her judgment conceivingly of most persons, and discourse most delightfully of all fashions. She hath been so well schooled in the discipline of this age as she only desires to retain in memory that form which is least affected but most comely, to consort[4] with such as may improve her knowledge and practice of goodness by their company, to entertain those for real and individuate[5] friends who make actions of piety expressivest characters of their amity. Diligent you shall ever find her in her employments, serious in her advice, temperate in her discourse, discreet in her answers. She bestows far more time in eying the glass of her life to rectify her errors, if there be any, then the glass of her face in wiping of such outward stains as might blemish her beauty. Neither in preserving that is she altogether so remiss as not to retain that seemly grace in her feature as may put her in remembrance of the unexpressive beauty and bounty of her maker. Neat she goes usually in her attire, which she puts on with more care than cost. And to these she adds such a well-seeming grace as she bestows more beauty on them than she receives from them. Fantastic habits or foreign fashions are so far from taking her, as with a slight but sweet contempt they are disvalued by her. She wonders how a wise state should employ so much time in inventing variety of disguises to disfigure their shape. This makes her desire rather to be out of request with time than with a civil and well-composed mind, whose honor it is to be prized more by her own internal worth than any outward wear. Constant she is in her behavior, wherein she affects little but observes much. With a bashful admiration she smiles at these civilized simpering dames whose only glory it is to affect a kind of reserved state which, as they hold, consists principally in a minc'd speech, set look, or ginger[6] pace.

She loves always to be herself, nor to entertain ought which may estrange her from herself. So as there is nothing in the whole posture of her behavior but with a native graceful propriety doth infinitely become her. Take upon her to instruct others she will not, such is her humility, albeit every moving posture which comes from her may be a line of direction unto others to follow her. Complement[7] she affects not, as the world takes it. The word in his own nature and unborrowed signification is good and in that sense she admits it; but to be restrained to an enforced formality, she cannot

4. To accompany, to associate oneself with.
5. To be rendered individual, to be distinguished from others of the same species.
6. Hesitant.
7. Ceremony, formality.

relish it. Whence it is that she prefers the incomparable liberty of her mind before the mutable formality of a deluded age. She desires to be complete in the exercise of goodness, to improve her honor not by titles but a lovely and lively proficiency, graced with a continuate practice in all virtues. She cannot endure this later introduc'd kind of complement, which consists in cringies,[8] congies,[9] or supple salutes.[10] A cheerful modesty is her best complement, which she ever wears about her as her cherish't ornament. Decency she affects in her clothes, affability in her discourse. She hath made a covenant with her eyes never to wander nor intentively to bestow themselves on any other object than the glory of her maker. A proper personage is no such attractive motive to her eye to make her loose herself. Whatsoever she undertakes beseems[11] her because she affects naught but what naturally becomes her. Her beauty is her own and whatsoever else may better accomplish her. Her paths are evenly virtuous; her desires truly religious; piety is her practice, which she expresseth so fully in every action as the whole course of her well-disposed life is not so much as justly conscious of the least aspersion. So highly she values her estimation[12] as she will not engage it to suspicion. Promises cannot tempt her nor hope of advancement taint her. She wonders one should prefer a conceit of being great before a desire of appearing good. Protesting lovers she holds for no better than deceiving lures. Be their vows of service never so incessant, their assaults never so violent, her resolves have vow'd her constant. Hope of profit cannot surprise her, nor thought of pleasure vainly delude her. Estimation she holds her highest grace, with which untainted she purposeth to go to her grave.

She knows how to fancy, and in her she retains what she fancies most: a chaste soul, this is that she loves and with which she cheerfully lives. She was never yet acquainted with a passionate *ah me,* nor a careless folding of her arms, as if the thought of a prevailing lover had wrought in her thoughts some violent distemper. So seriously doth she task her self to employment as she never refuses so much time as to treat of so light a subject. Yet she unfainedly vows that if it be ever her fortune to make her choice, her constant affection must never admit any change. To be generous in every action hath been ever the height of her ambition. Howsoever she might boast of descent,[13] her desire is to raise it by desert. She holds no family can be truly generous unless it be nobly virtuous. Her life must

8. Base or servile obeisances, often applied to bows.
9. Congees, ceremonious leave-takings.
10. Greetings.
11. Becomes, fits.
12. The esteem in which others hold her.
13. Lineage.

express the line from whence she came. She scorns to entertain one thought below herself or to detract from the glory of that house from whence she came. As the blood that streams through her veins was nobly derived, so must it not by any action or affection drawn from the rule of her direction become corrupted. For honor, she admits it, but seldom or never admires it; the stairs by which she means to climb to it must be fair and firm or she will never mount them. She rather admires the age's folly while she observes how many hazard their high-priz'd liberty for a vading[14] glimpse of popular glory. Her desires are higher seated, where they are only to be sated. A secure state consists not in styles but virtues, which are honor's surest stays. Therefore her highest honor reflects on her creator, wherein she is so far from fearing as she is ever wishing more co-rivals.

This is the *Gentlewoman* whom I have presumed here to present unto your Ladyship's service, whose sweet converse will at retired hours afford you choicest solace. Neither, should you rank her amongst the lowest of your many,[15] will it displease her, such is her humility, for she hath learned as well to obey as command. Nor will she spare for any pains, so her diligence may please. Only (Madam) be pleased to shine upon her with the gracious rays of your favor, to shroud her bashful endeavors under the wings of your honor, and entertain her blushing approach with your benign censure. So shall you find a constant desire of requital in her, and engage him, whose intimate zeal to your honor recommended her. [Sigs. ¶¶ 3–*3ᵛ omitted.]

Apparel

Had Adam never committed sin, he had never needed fig leaves to cover his shame. Sin made him fly to the grove for shelter, and shame compelled him to play the artless tailor and through mere necessity to make him a cover. Well enough was he before that time attired, albeit naked, and so happily stated[16] as we are to imagine that ignorance kept him not from the knowledge of his nakedness, but that his original purity freed him from these necessities. But no sooner was the forbidden fruit tasted than poor Adam became tainted, his nakedness discovered, so as now for honor of modesty he must of necessity betake himself to that science whereto (being free till that time) he was never bound apprentice. His inhibited taste made him sensible (and therein more miserable) of what before he felt not. No distemperature of cold or heat could before that time annoy him. Now his

14. Alternate form of fading.

15. The text reads meny. Meinie, a family, a household. Often confused with many, servants.

16. That state in which he found himself because he was innocent and in Eden?

failing in performing what he ought brings him to a feeling of that he never knew. Now tender Eve, whose temperate repose ministered her all content in a sweet and cheerful arbor, with all the varieties and delicacies of nature, feels a shaking and shivering in her joints. Such a strange distemper hath the taste of an apple wrought in her. She must fit herself then to endure that with patience which she procur'd to herself and second self[17] through disobedience, and put on what before she needed not, a veil to cover her nakedness, and subject herself to these necessities.

It is true that clothing keeps the body warm two ways: by keeping in the natural heat of the body and by keeping out the accidental cold of the air. All creatures enter the world shielded and shrouded save only poor man, who enters lists[18] naked. Tender and delicate he is by nature, more subject to prejudice by distemper than any other creature. Now to fence himself against all occurrences, and the better to endure all intemperate violence, the divine providence hath accommodated itself to his necessity from the very first entrance of his infancy; yet were it fit, when he reflects upon himself thus decked and attired, to recall to mind the prime occasion of these necessities. So equally tempered was the air where he first breathed,[19] so far from the distemper of heat or cold freed, with such variety of all delights stored, as then in all happiness he seem'd to be stated, but presently after his fall began these to fail. That soil, which before was naturally fruitful, became wild without manuring. Those rivers, which before were purely relishing and delighting, became muddy, brackish, and distasting.[20] Yea, that air, which before was ever sweetly and temperately breathing, became unseasonably scorching or freezing. Necessity then hath provided for Adam and his collapsed posterity a coat to shroud them from the inclemency of all seasons. And whence came this necessity but from sin? To glory then in these necessities is to glory in sin. Which were, as if some grave capital offender, having committed high treason against his sovereign, should notwithstanding out of a princely clemency be pardoned, yet with this condition, that he should wear a cord or halter about his neck during his life to put him in remembrance of his disloyalty and treason. In which badge, this frontless traitor should pride himself more than if it were some ancient crest of honor. Reflect then upon the original source of your sorrow, Eve, ye daughters of Eve. Ambition prompt her to sin, sin brought her to shame, shame to her shroud. Mere necessity compelled her

17. Adam.

18. The barriers of a tilting field; by extension, the field where tournaments are held; by extension a place of combat; here, life.

19. In Eden.

20. Bad tasting.

to wear what before she knew not and to provide herself of that which before she needed not. How is it then that these rags of sin, these robes of shame, should make you idolize yourselves? How is it that ye convert that which was ordained for necessity to feed the light-flaming fuel of licentious liberty? Was apparel first intended for keeping in natural heat and keeping out accidental cold? How comes it then that you wear these thin cobweb attires which can neither preserve heat nor repel cold? [Pp. 4–26 omitted.]

Behavior

Behavior, being an apt composure of the body in arguments of discourse and action, expresseth every person in so fair a character that if his breast were transparent he could not be displayed fuller. Albeit some love to become so estranged or retired rather from the eye of the world as they have made it their highest art and absolute aim to shroud themselves from the conceit or discussion of man by ent'ring covenant or contract with dissimulation to appear least to the eye what they are most in heart. . . . [Brathwaite goes on to say that because behavior is reflected in action, affection, and passion, he will discuss how "what deserves approvement in each" may be "by our nobly disposed gentlewomen cheerfully entertained, carefully retained, and to the improvement of their fame, the choicest odor, chiefest honor of true nobility, employed."]

Virtue is the life of action, action the life of man, without the former all actions are fruitless; without the latter, all our days are useless. Now in this one subject it is strange to observe what diversity of active dispositions we shall find. Some are employed to the purpose, but they are so remiss in their employment as they lose the benefit of it. Others are employed to no purpose, making a passing of time a mere pastime, coming as far short of one useful action at their death as they were incapable of it at their birth. Others sleep out their time in careless security, saluting the morning with a sacrifice to their glass, the noon with a luscious repast, the afternoon with a play or a pallet repose,[21] the evening with a wanton consort, accoutred with a rear-banket,[22] to belull the abused soul with the sleep of an incessant surfeit. Others have crept into such an apish formality as they cannot for a world discourse of ought without some mimic gesture or other which, seem it never so complete to them, appears ridiculous to the beholder. . . .

A woman's honor is of higher esteem than to be thus disvalued. Light[23] occasions are many times grounds of deep aspersions. Actions are to be

21. A nap on a pallet or couch?
22. A late banquet?
23. Frivolous.

seasoned with discretion, seconded by direction, strengthened with instruction, lest too much rashness bring the undertaker to destruction. In the maze or labyrinth of this life, many be our cares, mighty be our fears, strong our assailants, weak our assistants, unless we have that brazen wall within us to fortify us against all occurrences. O then let not the least action betray you to your enemy, for you have many: within you, for they are dangerous because domestical; without you, for they are strangers and therefore doubtful! Let your actions be your applausivest actors; the scene of your life is short, so live that your noble actions may preserve your memory long. . . . Set always before your eyes as an imit[at]able mirror some good woman or other, before whom you may live as if she ey'd you, she view'd you. You may find women, though weak in sex and condition, yet parallels to men for charity, chastity, piety, purity, and virtuous conversation. . . .

In a word, conform yourselves to such patterns as are imi[ta]table; imitate them in all such actions as are laudable. So live that none may have occasion to speak evilly of you if they speak truly. . . . Waste not prodigally the precious lamp of your life without some virtuous action that may purchase love. Your time is less than a minute in respect of eternity; employ that minute so as it may eternize your memory. Let this be your highest task, to promote the honor of your maker, esteeming all things else a slavish and servile labor.

There is nothing which requires more discretion than how to behave or carry ourselves while we are enthralled to affection. The lover is ever blinded (saith wise Plato) with affection towards his beloved. Reason is laid asleep, while sense becomes the master wooer.[24] Whence came that usual saying, "one cannot love and be wise." But I wholly oppose myself to their assertion who seem thus far transported with the sensual opinion of affection. My tenet is "one cannot truly love and not be wise." It is a Beldam frenzy[25] and no fancy which gives way to fury and admits not reason to have sovereignty. Yet in this subject, gentlewomen, is your temper best tried, your discretion most required, and your patience oft-times most exercised. Look therefore how you plant it, lest you bootlessly repent it when it is misplaced.

It is most certain, there is nothing more impatient of delay than love, nor no wound more incurable while we live. There is no exemption, all have a taste of this potion, though it have several degrees of operation.

> Look all about you; who so young that loves not?
> Or who so old, a comely feature moves not?

24. Plato, *Phaedrus* 238, 240D-241D?
25. The frenzy of an aged woman or hag.

Yet what different passions arise from one and the self-same subject?
Here, gentlewomen, you shall see some of your sex so surprised with
affection as it bursts out into violent extremes; their discourse is semi-
brew'd with sighs, their talk with tears; they walk desperately forlorn,
making launds[26] and desolate groves their disconsolate consorts. Their eyes
are estrang'd from sleep, their weakened appetite from repast, their wearied
limbs from repose. Melancholy is their sole melody; they have made a
contract with grief till grief bring them to their grave. And these poor
wenches are much to be pitied because their own tender hearts brought
them to this exigent:[27] having either set their affections where they thought
verily they might be requited and were not, or else where they received
like seeming tender of affection but afterwards rejected, what they wished
to effect they could not. So as in time if continuance of absence reduce
them not to a better temper, they fall into a poor Maudlin's[28] distemper
by giving rains[29] to passion till it estrange them from the sovereignty of
reason.

Whereas others you shall see, though not such kind souls, nor half so
passionate, yet more discreet in their choice, and in the passages of love
more temperate. These will not deign to cast a loose look upon their
beloved, but stand so punctually upon their terms as if they stood indifferent
for their choice, albeit constantly resolved never to admit of any change.
These scorn to paint out their passions in plaints, or utter their thoughts
in sighs, or shed one dispassionate tear for an incompassionate lover. Their
experience hath taught them better notions; they will seemingly fly to make
them follow, and so take them by whom they are most taken. They can
play with the flame and never singe their wings, look love in the face and
preserve their eyes, converse where they take delight, and color their affection with a seeming disdain. These are they who can walk in the clouds
to their intimatest friends, make their eyes strangers to their hearts, and
conclude, nothing more foolish than love if discovered, nothing more wise
if artfully shadowed.

But I neither approve the violence of the former nor indifference of the
latter. The one interlayeth affection with too much passion, the other with
too much dissimulation. These were well to be so allayed or attempered
as neither too much eagerness tax the discretion, nor too much remissness
argue coolness of affection. For the former, I must tell them, they give
great advantage to an insulting lover to entertain love with such vehement

---

26. Open space among woods.
27. State of pressing need.
28. Mary Magdalen's; cf. John 20:10–15.
29. Rains of tears?

ardor; it fares with these as with hot duelists, who fight themselves out of breath and so subject their relenting force to the command of a better tempered enemy. For the latter, they hold constantly that position in arguments of love as well as in other actions of their life. She knows not how to live nor how to love that knows not how to dissemble. I must tell these, dissimulation sorts not well with affection: lovers seldom read love's politics. Let them appear what they are with that discreet temper as they may deserve the embraces of a noble lover. In brief, let such as are too hot in the quest of their desires attemperate that heat with intermissions; such violence is best rebated by absence. Contrariwise, such as are too cool, let them quicken that easiness with their more frequent conference and assiduate presence.

What a furious and inconsiderate thing is woman when passion distempers her? How much is her behavior altered, as if Jocasta[30] were now to be personated? True it is, some with a bite of their lip can suppress an intended revenge, and like dangerous politicians pleasingly entertain time with one they mortally hate till opportunity usher revenge, which they can act with as much hostility as if that very moment were the actor of their injury. But this passion never works more tragic or fearful effects than when it streams from jealousy or competition in the subject where they love. Whereof we have variety of instances even in our own island, to omit Italy, which is a very theater of tragic conclusions in this kind.

It is not long since we had one matchless precedent of this stamp. It sometimes pleased a young gentlewoman, whose fortunes had swell'd her high, to settle her affection on a gentleman of deserving parts, which he entertained with a generous requital. Nothing was omitted that might anyway increase this respect or second the height of their joys. Continual resort and frequent made them inseparably one. No day so pleasing as when they were together. No hour so tedious as when they were asunder. But how short is that moment of vading happiness which hath in it a relish of lightness and is not grounded on essential goodness! Long had they not thus lived and sociably loved but the gentlewoman conceived some private suspicion that herself was not sole sovereigness of his heart, but that another was become sharer in his love. Neither was this competitrice whom she suspected any other than her own attendant, whose caskets she secretly opened, where she found a ring of especial note which she had formerly bestowed on him. This confirmed her conceit, changed her real love into mortal hate, which she seconded with this tragic act. Inviting him one day to a summer arbor where in former times they were usually wont to repose

---

30. Who unknowingly married her son, Oedipus. She killed herself when she discovered the truth.

amidst of an amorous discourse, she casually fixt her eye upon three lennets, one whereof picking some privet leaves purposely to build her nest flew away, while the two which remained lovingly billed one with another, which she intentively observing, used these words, "How tenderly and intimately do those poor fools mate it? Were it not pity they should ever be divided?" Which words she had no sooner uttered then the she-lennet flew away and left the male alone till another returned, with whom the he-lennet billed and amorously wooed as he had done before. Which she more seriously eying, "Oh," quoth she, "How light these males are in their affection. This may seem to you an easy error but were I judge of birds, it should receive due censure." "Why, Lady," replied he, "These poor birds do but according to their kind." "Yea, but what do ye kind men, then, who engage your loves, interest yourselves, empawn your souls to be constant where you profess love, and perform nothing less than what you profess most." Nor would her long intended revenge admit more liberty to her tongue, for with a passionate enterbreath[31] she closed this speech with a fatal stab, leaving so much time to her unfortunate and disastrous lover as to discover to one of that sorrowful family the ground of her hate, the occasion of his fall, which hastned on the doleful scene of her tragedy.

Now to allay or abate these passionate furies, there is no better means than to enter parley with reason, to chastise all such innovating motions as disquiet the inward repose of the mind, to use the help of such wholesome instructions as may attemper the heat of those indisposed and inordinate passions. Anger, being an inflammation of blood about the heart, is such a fury as to give way to it is to disclaim reason. Much wisdom is then required, mature advice to be used, all assistants of art and nature to be employed before this adder can be charmed. For we shall hardly see any one more forget themselves than when they are surprised with this passion. Some you shall observe so amazed or entranced as they become wholly silenced. They cannot utter an articulate word to gain a kingdom. Gladly would they express their distaste and menace revenge, if their tongues would give them leave, but wrath hath tied them to good behavior. Others are so voluble of tongue as nothing can pass them untouch'd to asperse disgrace on such by whom they hold themselves wrong'd. . . .

To remedy which enormities, take along with you these instructions; they will benefit you much in the height and heat of your anger and allay your passion when it rageth and riseth into hugest distemper. Forthwith, so soon as you shall perceive yourselves moved, restrain your passion, but if you cannot appease nor compose your inward commotion, at least restrain your tongue and enjoin it silence, that if it speak no good, it may speak

31. Interbreath; meaning unknown.

no evil, lest being loose and set at liberty it utter what wrath and not reason dictates. More sovereign and peaceful it will be for you to retire from society [and] make recourse to your oratory, by recommending to your best physician the cure of this infirmity. Use likewise this cordial salve to your corroding sore; the receipt is divine, if seasonably applied, and will minister you comfort when you are most distempered. So soon as your disquieted minds begin to expostulate with the quality of your wrongs, which your enemy is apt to aggravate and exasperate purposely to hasten your precipitate revenge, propose and set before you all the disgraces which possibly you can suffer and confer them with those that were aspersed on your savior; this will prepare you to suffer, teach you to conquer, for arrows foreseen menace less danger. . . .

Thus you see what benefits may be procured by attempering, what discommodities incurred by fostring this passion. Whereon I have the rather insisted because I am not ignorant how the strongest and constantest tempers have been and may be distempered and disparaged by it, much more you, whose mainest strength consists in the expression of that passion. At all times, therefore, use a moderate restraint; in the prime of your years when youth sends forth her first promising blossoms, behave youselves mildly without bitterness, humbly without haughtiness, modestly without lightness, soberly without childishness. The cask will retain her first taste, the wool her first dye. If you shew too much waywardness in your youth, small good is to be expected in your age. As you tender your preferment, seem mild while you are maids lest you prove scarecrows to a young man's bed. Conform yourselves likewise to a nuptial state and preserve your honor without stain. Contest not with your head for preeminence; you came from him, not he from you.[32] Honor him then as he cherisheth the love he conceives in you. A domestic fury makes ill harmony in any family. The discord which was hatched and increased towards Mark Anthony by Fulvia[33] was ever allayed and attempered by the moderation of Octavia.[34] Be you all Octavias; the rougher your cross, the richer your crown. The more that injuries press you, the more shall your patience praise you. The conflict is but short and momentary; the triumph glorious and impaled[35] with eternity. And thus much touching those three particulars whereon your behavior principally reflects. We are now to descend to the next branch, which shall shew how a gentlewoman of rank and quality (for to such only is my discourse directed) is to behave herself in company.

32. Brathwaite is referring to Eve's creation from Adam's rib (Gen. 2:21–22).
33. Wife of Mark Antony.
34. Sister of Augustus and second wife of Mark Antony.
35. The text reads "impall'd."

Society is the solace of the living, for to live without it were a kind of dying. Companions and friendly associates are the thieves of time. No hour can be so tedious which two loving consorts cannot pass over with delight and spend without distaste. Be the night never so dark and the place never so mean, the cheerful beams of conceiving consorts will enlighten the one and their affections mutually planted enliven the other. What a desert then were the world without friends? and how poseless[36] those friends without conceiving minds, and how weak those minds unless united in equal bonds? So then, love is the cement of our life, life a load without love. Now, gentlewomen, you are to put on your veils and go into company. Which (I am persuaded) you cannot enter without a maiden blush, a modest tincture. Herein you are to be most cautelous,[37] seeing no place can be more mortally dangerous. Beware, therefore, with whom you consort as you tender your repute, for report will brute what you are by the company which you bear. . . . Would you preserve those precious odors of your good names? Consort with such whose names were never branded, converse with such whose tongues for immodesty were never taxed. As by good words evil manners are corrected, so by evil words are good ones corrupted. Make no reside there where the least occasion of lightness is ministered; avert your ear when you hear it, but your heart especially lest you harbor it. To enter into much discourse or familiarity with strangers argues lightness or indiscretion; what is spoken of maids may be properly applied by an useful consequence to all women: "They should be seen and not heard." A traveller sets himself best out by discourse, whereas their best setting out is silence. You shall have many trifling questions asked, as much to purpose as if they said nothing, but a frivolous question deserves to be resolved by silence. For your carriage,[38] it should neither be too precise nor too loose. These simpering made faces partake more of chambermaid than gentlewoman. Modesty and mildness hold sweetest correspondence. You may possibly be wooed to interchange favors: rings or ribbons are but trifles. Yet trust me, they are no trifles that are aimed at in those exchanges. Let nothing pass from you that may any way impeach you or give others advantage over you. Your innocent credulity (I am resolved) is as free from conceit of ill as theirs, perhaps, from intendment of good. But these intercourses of courtesies are not to be admitted lest by this familiarity an entry to affection be opened which before was closed. It is dangerous to enter parley with a beleaguering enemy. It implies want or weakness in the besieged. Chastity is an inclosed garden; it should not be so much as

36. A misprint?
37. From cautel, a crafty device. Hence cautelous, crafty, cautious.
38. Bearing.

assaulted lest the report of her spotless beauty become soiled. Such forts hold out best which hold themselves least secure when they are securest. . . .

How subject poor women be to lapses and recidivations, being left their own guardians, daily experience can sufficiently discover. Of which number those always proved weakest who were confidentest of their own strength. Presumption is a daring sin, and ever brings out some untimely birth, which viper-like deprives her unhappy parent of life. I have known divers so resolute in their undertakings, so presuming of their womanish strength, so constantly devoted to a single life as in public consorts they held it their choicest merriment to give love the affront, to discourse of affection with an imperious contempt, gear their amorous suitors out of count'nance, and make a very whirligig of love. But mark the conclusion of these insulting spirits. They sport so long with love till they fall to love in earnest. A moment makes them of sovereigns captives,[39] by slaving them to that deservedly which at first they entertained so disdainfully. The way then to prevent this malady is to wean you from consorting with folly. What an excellent impregnable fortress were woman did not her windows betray her to her enemy? But principally when she leaves her chamber to walk on the public theater, when she throws off her veil and gives attention to a merry tale, when she consorts with youthful blood and either enters parley or admits of an interview with love. It is most true what the sententious moral sometimes observed. We may be in security so long as we are sequestered from society. Then and never till then begins the infection to be dispersed, when the sound and sick begin to be promiscuously mixed. Tempt not chastity; hazard not your Christian liberty. You shall encounter with many forward youths who will most punctually tender their useless service to your shadows at the very first sight: do not admit them, lest you prostitute yourselves to their prostrate service. Apelles[40] found fault with Protogenes[41] in that he could not hold his hands from his table, whereas our damsels may more justly find fault with their youthful amorists for that they cannot hold their hands from under the table. It is impossible to come off fair with these light-fingered fools. Your only way is to rampire[42] your chaste intentions with divine and moral instructions, to stop the source, divert the occasion, subject affection to reason so may you become empresses of that which hath sometimes tyrannized over emperors. By this means shall every place where you publicly resort minister to you some

---

39. Makes those who were once sovereign, captive.
40. Painter, ca. 332 B.C.
41. Painter and sculptor, late 4th c. B.C.
42. To strengthen (a bulwark, gate, etc.) against attack.

object of inward comfort. By this means shall company furnish you with precepts of chastity, enable you in the serious practice of piety, and sweetly conduct you to the port of glory. [Pp. 44–58 omitted.]

Complement

Complement hath been anciently defined and so successively retained, a no less real than formal accomplishment. Such as were more nobly and freely educated and had improved their breeding by foreign observations (so sweetly tempered was the equal union and communion of their affections) instructed others in what they had seen and observ'd either at home or abroad, worthy imitation or approvement. Nothing was admitted in those times publicly, but what was by the graver censors first discussed privately. Jealous were the pagans of foreign fashions, for with such constancy they retained their own as they seldom or never itched after others. The Tirian and Sidonian were so suspected of pride through their effeminacy in attire and other light fashions which they used as they were held dangerous to commerce with. So purely did those poor beamlings[43] of nature reflect on her people that formality was held palpable hypocrisy, fair semblances and cool performances mere golden shadows to delude others but gull themselves most. Princes'[44] courts were princely seminaries. Delicacy was there no tutress,[45] nor effeminacy governess. If Alcibiades,[46] albeit in Athens the beautifull'st, for native endowments the pregnan'st and for descent one of the noblest, introduce ought irregularly or express any complement which relisheth not of civility, the author must suffer the censure of the city. It was very usual in former times when any embassy was addressed from one state unto another for the senate or council from whence any such legate was sent to school them in sundry particulars before they took their journey or received their commission, but in no caution were they more strict than in express command that they should use no other garb, complement, nor salute upon their approach in foreign courts than what they have seen used and observed at home. Thus their own native fashion became a note of distinction to every nation.

Neither am I ignorant how even in one and the selfsame province there may be generally introduced a different or distinct garb, which proceedeth either from the commerce and confluence of people there resorting and consequently improving their behavior and elocution by their mutual con-

43. Little beams (of light).
44. It is unclear whether the singular or the plural is intended here because there is no punctuation.
45. Tutoress.
46. Athenian statesman, ca. 450–404 B.C.

ference, or from the prince's[47] court, where all state and majesty hath residence, or from the temperature of the air, to which some have attributed an especial preeminence. Whereas in desert and remote places, on which the beams of civil society seldom reflect, we shall find nothing but barbarism and unsociable wildness. Education is the improver of the one and producer of the other. We shall ever see complement shine most in places eminent. There are objects fit for such subjects, such as expect it and bestow their whole day's practice in exercise of it. These aspire to the nature or definition of no art more eagerly than complement, which they hold the absolute ornament of gentility. Howsoever mainly repugnant be their terms touching the subsistence of complement.

Some have held it consisted in congies, cringes, and salutes, of which error I would this age wherein we live did not too much labor; others, merely in a painted and superficial discourse, wherein they so miserably tied themselves to words as they tired the impatient hearers with foolish repetitions, frivolous extravagances being, in a word, so affianced to the shadow as they forgot the substance. The last, which were only real and complete courtiers, held a seemly graceful presence, beautified with a native comeliness, the deservingst complement that could attend us.

Certainly, if we should exactly weigh the derivation of the word, we could not imagine so meanly of it as to consist merely of words or antic works. It was first intended to distinguish betwixt persons of civil and savage carriage; yea, to appropriate a title of preeminence to such, who exceeded others in grounds or precepts[48] of morality, whose lives appeared as lamps to enlighten others and consequently perpetuate the memory of themselves. Many noble and eminent ladies are recorded both in divine and human writ to have excelled in this complement of honor. These knew the definition of it and molded their conversation to it: They knew what belonged to a posture of state; they could court it without apish curiosity; embrace love with a reserved modesty; express themselves complete without singularity. Foreign fashions they distasted; painted rhetoric they disrelished; real complement was all they affected. Love they could without dissembling; discourse without affecting; shew curt'sy without congying, still retaining what was best beseeming. In the court they resided to better it; not a strayed look could promise a loose lover least hope of a purchase nor coyness dishearten a faithful servant from his affectionate purpose. They knew not what it was to protest in jest, to walk in the clouds, to domineer over their captives or entertain many suitors. They freed complement of dissimulation, made virtue their loadstone to affection, their

47. See the previous footnote.
48. The text reads "pecepts."

actions were dedicated to good ends, by which means they made God and good men their friends. Nor do I fear it but that our flourishing Albion hath many such noble and complete ladies who so highly esteem the true and native definition of complement as they prefer the substance before the shadow. Honor is their dearest tender, goodness their line by which they daily draw nearer to perfection, their proper center. Thus far for the definition, wherein we have the rather enlarged our discourse that the subject whereof we treat may be discovered in her own nature and such as owe attendance to her become better proficient in their instructions derived from her. Neither can we observe what may really deserve your imitation but by discerning the excellence of that whereof we treat by a true and proper definition. [Brathwaite goes on in the next section to discuss the ways in which complement "may be corrupted." Pp. 63–79 omitted. Brathwaite then discusses "Decency," pp. 81–99.]

Estimation[49]

Estimation is a good opinion drawn from some probable grounds, an un-valuable gem which every wise merchant who tenders his honor, prefers before life. The loss of this makes him an irreparable bankrupt. All persons ought to rate it high because it is the value of themselves, though none more dearly than those in whom modesty and a more impressive fear of disgrace usually lodge. These, so cautelous are they of suspicion as they will not engage their good names to purchase affection. Public resorts because they may corrupt, they avoid; privacy they consort with and in it converse with their own thoughts, whether they have in them ought that may betray them. They observe what in others deserves approvement and this they imitate; with an uncorrupt eye they note others' defects, which they make use of as a caveat. Pure is their mold, but far purer the temper of their minds. Fame they hold the sweetest flower that ever grew near the border of time. Which, lest either it should wither for want of moisture or wanting warmth should lose its vigor, they bedew it with gracious affects and renew it with zealous resolves. Descent, as they draw it from others, so would they improve it in themselves. Ancient houses now and then stand in need of props and pillars; these would they have supplied with the cardinal virtues. . . .

Now (gentlewomen) if you make estimation your highest prize, if you prefer honor before pleasure or what else is dear or tender, your fame will find wings to fly with. This will gain you deserving suitors. Portion may woo a worldling, proportion a youthful wanton, but it is virtue that wins the heart of discretion.

49. Sidenote: "Estimation, a gentlewoman's highest prize."

Surely I have seldom known any make this esteem of honor and die a contemptible beggar. Such as have been prodigal of it have felt the misery of it, whereas a chaste mind hath ever had something to succor and support it. Thus you see what this inward beauty is which if you enjoy, you sit far above the reach of calumny; age cannot taint it, nor youth tempt it. It is the estimation within you that so confines you, as you hate that place which gives opportunity, that person which makes importunity his agent to lay siege to your chastity.

Now we are to descend to the second branch wherein we are to shew you how this estimation which is your highest prize may be discerned to be real, which is not gathered by the first appearance but [by] a serious and constant trial. In philosophy a man begins with experience and then with belief; but in divinity, we must first begin in faith and then proceed to knowledge. True it is that the sun, moon, and stars become subject to vanity; yet charity bids me believe that there are many beauteous and resplendent stars in this our firmament, many fresh, fragrant roses in this our inclosed garden of Albion who have preserv'd their beauty without touch, their honor without taint. Where, if vanity did touch them, yet did it not so seize on them as to disfigure or transform them. You (noble gentlewomen) are those stars whose glory can never be eclipsed so long as your estimation lives unstained; you are those fragrant roses whose beauty cannot be tainted so long as your stalk of honor grows untouched. Now, to the end that your luster may not be like to that of the glowworm nor rotten wood, which is merely imaginary compared with that is real, you are not to make fair and glorious pretenses purposely to gull the world and cast a mist before the eyes of bleared judgments. No, you are to be really what you appear outwardly. These that walk in the clouds, though they deceive others much, yet they deceive themselves most. Observe then this rule of direction; it will accomplish you more than any outward ornament that art can bestow on you. Be indeed what you desire to be thought.

Are you virgins? dedicate those inward temples of yours to chastity; abstain from all corrupt society; inure your hands to works of piety, your tongues to words of modesty. Let not a strayed look tax you of lightness, nor a desire of gadding impeach you of wantonness. The way to win an husband is not to woo him but to be woo'd by him. Let him come to you, not you to him. Proffered ware is not worth the buying. Your states are too pure to be set at sale, too happy to be weary of them. So long as you live as you are, so your minds be pure, you cannot possibly be poor. You have that within you will enrich you, so you conform your minds to your means. In the discourse of virtues and true estimate of them, none was ever held more excellent than that which is found in chaste youth. You are conquerors in that wherein the greatest conquerors have fail'd. Your chaste paths are not trac'd with wandring desires; your private chambers arras'd with amorous passions; you spin not out the tedious night in "ah me's." Your repast finds no hindrance in digestion; your harmless repose no lovesick distraction. Others you may command, by none commanded. Others will vow their service unto you, while you are from all servitude freed. Live then worthy the freedom of so noble a condition, for your virgin state wants nothing that may enlarge her freedom.

Again, are you wives? You have attained an honorable state and by it made partakers of that individuate union where one soul ruleth two hearts and one heart dwelleth in two bodies. You cannot suffer in that wherein you have not one share. Grief by your consort is allayed; joy by partaking with him is augmented. You have now taken upon you to become secretaries to others as well as your selves, but being one and the same with yourselves do not betray their trust, to whose trust you have recommended yourselves. Imagine now (to recall to memory an ancient custom) that you have broken the axletree of your coach at your door; you must be no more stragglers. These walking burses[50] and movable exchanges sort not with the constancy of your condition. You must now intend the growth and proficience of those olive branches[51] about your table. Like a curious and continuate builder, you must ever address yourselves to one work or other. From their infancy to their youth, from their youth to their maturer growth. . . . [Brathwaite goes on to give examples of mothers who raised famous men. Pp. 108–10 omitted.]

Again, are you widows? You deserve much honor if you be so indeed. This name both from the Greek and Latin hath received one consonant etymology: deprived or destitute. Great difference then is there betwixt those widows who live alone and retire themselves from public concourse, and those which frequent the company of men. For a widow to love society, albeit her intentions relish nothing but sobriety, gives speedy wings to spreading infamy. . . . for in popular concourse and in court-resorts there is no place for widows. For in such meetings she exposeth her honor to danger, which above all others she ought incomparably to tender. Yea, but will you object: admit our inheritance, family, fortunes, and all lie a-bleeding? May we not make recourse to public courts for redress of our public wrongs? What of all this? Do not complain that you are desolate or alone. Modesty affecteth silence and secrecy; a chaste woman solitariness and privacy. If you have business with the judge of any court and you much

50. Purses, and by extension, meeting places of merchants for the transaction of business.
51. Children (Ps. 128:3).

fear the power of your adversary, employ all your care to this end, that your faith may be grounded in those promises of Christ, "Your Lord maketh intercession for you, rendring right judgment to the orphan and righteousness unto the widow."[52]

This inestimable inheritance of chastity is incomparably more to be esteemed and with greater care preserved by widows than wives, albeit by these neither to be neglected but highly valued. Out of that ancient experience which time hath taught them, their own observations inform'd them, and the reverence of their condition put upon them, they are to instruct others in the practice of piety, reclaim others from the paths of folly, and with a virtuous convoy guide them to glory. It would less become them to trick and trim themselves gaudily or gorgeously than young girls, whose beauty and outward ornament is the hope and anchor-hold of their preferment, for by these do the husbands seek and hope in time to get what they seek. Whereas it were much more commendable for widows neither to seek them nor being offred to accept them; lest enforced by necessity or won by importunacy, or giving way to their frailty, they make exchange of their happy estate for a continuate scene of misery. A widow ought to pray fervently, to exercise works of devotion frequently, that the benefit of her prayer may redound to her effectually and fruitfully, and not return back from the throne of God drily or emptily. For I would (according to Menander's opinion) have a widow not only to demean herself chastely and honestly, but likewise to give examples of her blameless life to such as hear her instruction attentively. For she ought to be as a glass to young maids wherein they may discern their crimes. . . .

Many desire to appear most to the eye what they are least in heart. They have learned artfully to gull the world with appearances and deceive the time wherein they are maskers with vizards and semblances. These can enforce a smile to persuade you of their affability, counterfeit a blush to paint out their modesty, walk alone to express their love to privacy, keep their houses to publish them provident purveyors for their family, receive strangers to demonstrate their love to hospitality. Their speech is minced, their pace measured, their whole posture so cunningly composed as one would imagine them terrestrial saints at least, whereas they are nothing less than what they most appear. Some you observe so demure as in their salutes they forbear to express that freedom of courtesy which civil custom exacts of them. Those true Trojan dames, to pacify their incensed husbands, could find a lip to procure them love and supple their contracted look. Whereas these civilized dames, either out of a reservancy of state or desire to be observ'd, scorn to be so familiarly demeaned, as if they re-

52. Ps. 146:9, although David refers to God.

nounced antiquity and sought by all means that such customs as plead prescription might be reversed. Their lip must be their cheek, which as it retains a better tincture, so many times a sweeter savor. . . .[53]

Would you then be courtiers grac'd in the highest court? Throw away whatsoever is superficial and entertain what will make you divinely real. It is not seeming goodness that will bring you to the fountain of all goodness. The fig tree brought forth leaves, yet because it yielded no fruit it was cursed. Do ye blossom? So doth every hypocrite. Do ye bring forth fruits? So doth a Christian. What is it to purchase estimation on earth and lose it in heaven? This will sleep in dust, but that never. Your highest task should be how to promote God's honor and to esteem all things else a slavish and servile labor. Thus by seeming what you are and really expressing what you seem, you shall purchase that esteem with God and good men which is real, by shunning ostentation, which would set such a vading gloss on all your actions as they will seem merely superficial. [Pp. 117–28 omitted. Brathwaite goes on to discuss "Fancy," pp. 129–55.]

Gentility

Gentility consists not so much in a lineal deblazon[54] of arms, as [a] personal expression of virtues. Yea, there is no ornament like virtue to give true beauty to descent. What is it to be descended great? to retain the privilege of our blood? to be ranked highest in an herald's book[55] when our lives cannot add one line to the memorable records of our ancestors? There should be no day without a line if we desire to preserve in us the honor of our line. Those odors then deserve highest honors that beautify us living and preserve our memory dying. Should we call to mind all those our ancestors who for so many preceding ages have gone before us and whose memory now sleeps in the dust; we should, perchance, find in every one of them some eminent quality or other, if a true survey of their deserving actions could be made known unto us. Yea, we should understand that many of them held it their highest grace to imitate their predecessors in some excellent virtue, the practice whereof they esteemed more praiseworthy than the bare title of gentility. . . .

Let me now reflect upon you, gentlewomen, whose generous birth should be adorned with virtuous worth and so make you moving objects of imitation, both in life and death. Are you nobly descended? Ennoble that descent with true desert. Do not think that the privilege of greatness

---

53. Brathwaite complains that the old custom of kissing on the lips when greeting is being replaced with the newer custom of kissing on the cheek.

54. Blazon? a coat of arms.

55. A book of heraldry.

can be any subterfuge to guiltiness. Your more ascending honor requires more than a common luster. In places of public resort you challenge precedence and it is granted you. Shall the highest place have the least inward grace? No, let not a word fall from you that may unbeseem you. Others are silent when you discourse; let it be worth their attention, lest a presumption of your own worth draw you into some frivolous excursion. There is not an accent which you utter, a sentence you deliver, any motion in your carriage or gesture which others eye not, and eying assume not. Your retinue is great, your family gracious, your actions should be the life of the one and line of direction to the other. To see a light lady descending from a noble family is a spectacle of more spreading infamy than any subject of inferior quality. . . .

It is not the nobility of descent but of virtues that makes any one a graceful and acceptable servitor in the court of heaven. Houses are distinguished by coats[56] and crests, but these are dignified by something else. In heraldry, those are ever held to be the best coats that are deblazoned with least charge.[57] Consequently then must virtue needs be the best coat. She requires the least charge in her attire; she is not sumptuous, in her fare delicious, nor in her retinue (the more is the pity) numerous. She confines her desires upon earth within a strait circumference; a very small portion of that metal will content her. . . . Pleasure may cast out her lure, but virtue is so high a flyer as she scorns to stoop to ought unworthy of her; it pleaseth her to contemplate that on earth which she is to enjoy in heaven. Profit may seek to undermine her, but all her policy cannot work on virtue's constancy. Content is her crown; contempt of the world her care; what worldlings seek, she shuns; whence it is that her beauty in the darkest night of adversity shines. In a word, she is an absolute commandress of her self and easy is it to have that command where no turbulent passions labor to contend. . . .

Let it be your highest scorn to stoop to any base thought. It is not priority nor precedence of place, but propriety and proficiency in grace that makes an honorable soul. That cloth is of most worth that wears best, and that fashion of most esteem that holds longest in request. Virtue is right sempiternum for wear and of that complete fashion as with Christian women it grows never out of date. Make choice of this stuff then to suit you, of this coat to gentilize you. All others are but counterfeits in comparison of her, whose property it is to honor those that serve her, harbor those that fly for refuge to her, and to reward those who constantly stand in defense of her honor. There is nothing can wound you, being thus armed;

56. Coats of arms.
57. The simplest.

nothing ill-beseem you, being thus adorned, nothing disparage you, being thus honored. Heraldry finds a coat for your house, but virtue finds honor to grace your person. Retain those divine impressions of goodness in you that may truly ennoble you; display your gentility by such a coat as may best distinguish your family. So shall you live and die with honor and survive their fame, whose only glory it was to enjoy fortune's favor. [Pp. 167–90 omitted. Brathwaite goes on to discuss "Honor," pp. 191–221.]

Jacques Du Bosc
The Complete Woman
1632, trans. N. N.,
London, 1639

Introduction

Jacques Du Bosc was a French priest and a "bachelier de Sorbonne" who lived and wrote in the first half of the seventeenth century. Although his primary reputation in France was achieved through his anti–Jansenist writings, English readers knew him best through *The Secretary of Ladies* and *The Complete Woman*. *The Secretary of Ladies,* translated into English in 1638, belongs to the tradition of European letter writing which was designed to be morally enlightening, rhetorically pleasing, and public. Du Bosc said that the letters in his *Secretary of Ladies* were written by ladies of fashion for other ladies of fashion, and some of them may well have been. But they are unlike model letters written for men in that they are almost purely complimentary, that is, they show ladies how to compose rhetorically pleasing, graceful compliments—not how to inform or instruct. Du Bosc also composed a book on heroic women, which was not translated into English: *La femme héroïque, ou les héroïnes comparées avec les héros en toute sorte de vertus* (1645).

The first part of Du Bosc's *L'Honneste Femme* (1632) went through several French editions and was translated into English in 1639 as *The Complete Woman*. It was, however, never thereafter reprinted in England, in part perhaps because of the uncertainties of civil war, in part perhaps because of the controversy it generated over its elevation of women to a position of equality with men. Although conservative readers criticized it, its several editions indicate that it probably appealed to the female audience for whom it was written. It certainly appeals more to twentieth-century sensibilities than does any other conduct book in this anthology.

The Complete Woman is even more secular than Brathwaite's *English Gentlewoman*. In his "Epistle," Du Bosc desires women to "know without other lessons that to be virtuous, they have no need to be rigid and that devotion and civility are no ways contrary." Du Bosc is committed, moreover, to the position that reason and experience (together with Scripture) provide the bases of morality: "we acknowledge every day by experience that the light of reason is as a natural virtue which disposeth us to do well." Reason and experience suggest to Du Bosc that men and women are equal; that, consequently, "obedience" and "sovereignty" between husbands and wives "are reciprocal"; that women can and should advise men; and that women should participate in government: "it is also a tyranny and a custom which is no less unjust than old, to reject them from the public government, as if their spirits were not as capable of affairs of importance as well as that of men."

It is not surprising, therefore, to find that Du Bosc urges the education of women: "the helps of learning fortifies the best inclinations, and they who are persuaded that reading of books is a school to learn to do ill with the more dexterity, might do better to believe that women find therein more means to correct than corrupt themselves." Learning helps all women: "Reading shews many things which reason by itself can never discover; it makes us have more solidity in our thoughts and more sweetness in our discourse; it finisheth that which nature but begins." One reason why Du Bosc advocates the education of women may be implicit in his diction. When he speaks of the benefits of education, for instance, he uses the pronoun, "we," and thereby assumes the equality of well-born men and women. Du Bosc makes this assumption explicit when he advises gentlewomen to study not only art but science: "say what they will, they [women] are capable thereof as well as men." He asks, furthermore, "Have we not women as well in country as in court who can write upon the hardest and most serious subjects, who can speak to the purpose of the highest mysteries of our religion? . . . Have we not those [women] who skill[1] the foreign languages as well as ours, and are so universal in the knowledge of good things as it is an extreme loss and mischief to us that the tyranny of custom hath hindered many of them to publish their works and to leave their writings to posterity." It is knowledge, says Du Bosc, not ignorance, that leads women to virtue, and knowledge is the product of learning and experience.

Du Bosc may also have been committed to a belief in the equality of men and women because he wrote for and about women of intellect, position, and wealth. It is just such a woman, Madame De Combalet, upon whom he models his book and to whom, as her humble and obedient servant, he commends it. He says plainly that he is not concerned about ordinary women or matters of housewifery and motherhood; he is interested instead in women's intellectual and social attainments. His readers should not imagine that "we intend to paint you a mother of a family who can command her servants and who hath the care to comb and dress her children. Though we blame it not, yet we must confess that music, history, philosophy, and other such like exercises are more accommodate to our purpose than those of housewifery."

Du Bosc's insistence that women and men are equal, however, and that women are as capable as men of mastering the arts and sciences did not escape criticism. Du Bosc was criticized in France because he did not insist more forcefully upon the supremacy of Christian morality and doctrine. In fact, Du Bosc may have been coerced into promising to write for *L'Honneste Femme* a third part in which he will reconcile Christian doctrine with worldly enjoyments.[2] Certainly an anonymous advocate (apparently Nicolas Perrot d'Ablancourt) went to great lengths in his long "Preface" to Du Bosc's text to defend him from critics who claimed that he flatters women rather than instructs them, that "he is a great deal readier to corrupt their mind than to teach them how to live, and makes them rather good gossips than good women" (sig. B3ᵛ). But d'Ablancourt did not try to defend Du Bosc by accepting the importance of reason and experience. Rather, he attempted, tortuously, to demonstrate that Du Bosc subscribes to the traditional values of patriarchal Christianity. Despite an obvious retreat on the part of d'Ablancourt, however, and later, perhaps, even on the part of Du Bosc himself, the publication of *The Complete Woman* is at least one indication that women in French salons and English drawing rooms may have finally begun to draw nearer to positions of equality with men. Despite the restrictions it still imposes on women, *The Complete Woman* looks to a future for women freer from subordination than any other in this anthology.

NOTES

1. Understand, have knowledge of.

2. N. N., who translated Du Bosc's *L'Honneste Femme*, translated only the first of the book's three parts, probably because only the first part printed in 1632 was available to him. In the last edition of the second part of *L'Honneste Femme* (Rouen, 1643), Du Bosc continues to discuss relatively secular topics such as "De l'humeur Complaisante et de l'humeur Rude," "De la Noblesse du sang et de celle de la Vertu," " De l'ambition comparée à l'amour" (Sig. [Q6ᵛ]). In the "Advertissement" to the second part, Du Bosc promises his readers that he will show in a third part "qu'une Dame peut tout ensemble

estre en la grace de Dieu et dans l'approbation du Monde: que les vertus
Chrestiennes n'empeschent point de plaire dans la conversation"(Sig. [Q5ᵛ]).
In that third part, however, Du Bosc engages in discourses whose subjects are
rather more secular than religious (e.g., "De la vraye science d'une honneste
femme," "La Coquette," "La Superstitieuse," "La Scandaleuse"), and waits
until his very last discourse to write directly "De la Vertu Chrestienne: qu'elle
est absolument necessaire à l'Honneste Femme" (Sigs. [a8]–[a8ᵛ] and Zzᵛ–
Aaaiiii).

The Complete Woman

The Epistle of the Author to Madam De Combalet

If I declare myself the author of this book after the testimony you have
given, it is not only to enjoy the glory you have gained it, and which of
myself I could not hope for without your protection, but also to yield you
thanks for so great a favor vouchsafed me. For verily as I should be insensible not to testify joy for so extraordinary an honor, I should be ungrateful if I published not the feeling I have thereof, and with reason my
acknowledgment should be public, where your approbation was so solemn.
I cannot dissemble how this is it which hath engaged me to labor now anew
in this work, to present it to you with less blemishes and more ornaments
than when one of my friends in my absence offered it to you on my behalf.
I hope, Madam, it shall not be unprofitable for the public good and shall
breed a desire in as many as shall read it to resemble[1] you, therein beholding
the beauty of the virtues you practice and the enormity of the vices whose
enemy you are. I confess, if all women could eye your actions, this same[2]
here would not be necessary for them. They might know without other
lessons that to be virtuous, they have no need to be rigid, and that devotion
and civility are no ways contrary. But being a favor reserved to few to
become witness of a virtue so extraordinary as yours, and that God, shewing
in the same race the wonder of women as well as men, would have the
one and other in court to make them appear in the same time and theater
as the greatest ornaments of our age. Suffer, Madam, this book to do
everywhere where you are not that which you do everywhere where you
are. Suffer it to afford your portrait or image to those who have not the
honor to see you, and that your picture herein may supply the miss of your
native feature. It is fit that where the sun shines not, we light torches; and
that such as cannot approach to you in the *Complete Woman* should be

1. Imitate.
2. Same book.

taught that which the happier learn from your actions and the wonders of your life. Surely it had been enough for the instruction of posterity instead of this book to have framed your history, since in truth it was no ways fitting so good a life should be the example of one age only, and decipher what is excellent in you and not tell withal all the qualities necessary for a woman to make her accomplished. But they had need for that end of a happier quill than mine. This enterprise is as hard for me as it is contrary to your humor. I should have found as much difficulty to express so many rare qualities as you to suffer it. It had been necessary for me to come off well with this enterprise to have had more eloquence and you less modesty. The world knows you strive as much to fly glory as to make yourself worthy of it. And as for praises, that there is none who merits them, and flights them more. Whence it is, Madam, I find the means to justify my impotence in satisfying your humility, since that which would be hard for me to perform would be likewise ungrateful to you. I had rather in this hold my peace than any ways offend you, and perform an action of complacence than of justice. Besides, it is enough for me to have testified to you the purpose I have, to be all my life,

Madam, Your most humble and obedient servant,

DuBoscq

[Preface omitted. Sigs. B–G^v]

Book I

Of Reading

1. It is certain that reading, conversation, and musing are three the best and most excellent things of the world. By reading we treat with[3] the dead, by conversation with the living, and by musing, with ourselves. Reading enricheth the memory, conversation polisheth the mind, and musing frames the judgment.

2. But of these noble occupations of the soul, to say here which is the most important, we must confess that reading setteth the other two awork; and without it, musing is fruitless and conversation unpleasant. It is even necessary for all women, what kind of spirit soever they be of, while it affords a certain luster to such as have it in eminent degree, and lessens much their imperfection who have it not so great; it makes the one tolerable and the other admirable. And truly reading shews many things which reason by itself can never discover; it makes us have more solidity in our thoughts and more sweetness in our discourse; it finisheth that which nature but begins. . . .

3. Deal with, consider.

4. And to say that good wits can shew well without reading as good faces without ornament, not to dissemble, I cannot approve it. On the contrary . . . the spirits of more light have also need of reading to get politeness and fecundity, and especially to moderate this vigor which cannot well come off without hazard, being alone. It is then in this comparable school where they learn what is excellent for the entertainment of good companies and for remedy of the evil, and where women being tired with many importunate visitors who talk but of hunting and hawking, and wars of the Netherlands, find a counterpoison for that which persecutes them. It is reading which makes conversation more sweet and solitude less irksome.

5. There are some notwithstanding who are of another mind and think the conversation of good wits to be enough to learn what is best in the world without the pain of reading books. I grant that society with good persons is very necessary and is a living school which powerfully heartens us, beholding there in example concurring with the rule. Nevertheless, methinks that those who content themselves to communicate with the learned might become yet more perfect in reading their works. I should think that if conversation afford facility, reading gives abundance; that the other distributes only what this purchaseth, and is not liberal but of the riches which the other heaps. . . .

6. Moreover, there needs but a pleasing voice, a magnificent tone, a sweet accent, or a certain good grace to charm those who harken; but there is nothing that delude such as read. It is a great deal more easy to surprise the ear than the eye. Discourses pass very lightly away, and they have hardly any leisure to note their faults, but writing remains always exposed to the censure of judges who never pardon them. This seems to me a pregnant reason to oblige us to the reading of good books, since therein the greatest wits have left us what they had more excellent, and that in writing rather than in speaking they have employed all their watches and studies.

7. Nevertheless, if to prove this we must needs join experience with reason, what can be desired or ornament of the mind which is not in books? Where they find instructions of all sorts, where they see virtue under all kinds of visages, where they discover truth in what manner soever they desire it. They behold it with all its force in philosophers, with all its purity in historians, with all its beauty, dresses, and artificiousness[4] in orators and poets. It is in this pleasing variety that all sorts of humors and conditions find wherewith to content themselves and wherewith to be instructed. Where it is, that verity is not altered through passions, that she[5] speaks

4. Affectedness, artfulness.
5. Verity.

without fear as without interest, and trembles not at the entry of palaces or in the presence of monarchs.

8. For this it is that reading is very requisite for women, for since they have no less need of dumb teachers than princes, and that beauty as well as royalty finds not so easily masters as flatterers, it is necessary to acknowledge their faults; they learn sometimes of the dead what the living dare not tell them. It is only in books where they may note the imperfections of their mind as those of their face in glasses, where they find judges who cannot be corrupted through love or hate, where the fair and foul are treated alike, having to do with arbiters who have no eyes but to put a difference between vice and virtue. [Pp. 4–16 omitted.]

Of Conversation

1. As there is nothing more important for women than to know how to choose good spirits[6] for conversation and good books for reading, so there is nothing more difficult. Because there are so many vicious things which resemble the good, that if one have not sound judgment or a great happiness,[7] he rarely makes any good elections, and we must confess that it is very hard to pass away the time with innocence and pleasure in company or alone.

2. Verily, if we lived yet in the time of that first simplicity, where it was enough but to have a tongue to give content, and where as then was no other sin in society than lying, a genuine plainness (I confess) were enough and prudence were superfluous. But since we are in a cunning age where it seems that words, invented to express thoughts, serve no more than to hide them handsomely, we must acknowledge that even innocence itself hath need of a mask or veil as well as faces, and that it is no less a folly to shew one's heart openly to those who stand always in ambush than to walk naked among armed enemies whom we cannot offend and from whom we cannot defend ourselves.

4. What perfections are necessary to become grateful in conversation, what qualities are required to please many; since even the best men have diverse inclinations, that good judgments are as different in themselves as the good and evil are contrary. If plainness beget a contempt in some, subtlety breeds suspicion in others; if they mock those women that are free, they distrust those who are not so. This here wants a good garb, the other reading; one of the senses is presented while the other is content; and it were a hard adventure to open the eyes and ears at once. . . .

6. Persons of good spirits.
7. Good luck. The French reads "un grand bonheur."

6. To say, then, what seems to me at first most necessary, I should content myself to wish in women the three perfections which Socrates desired in his disciples: discretion, silence, and modesty. These are so fair and necessary qualities in society that to judge the importance of them we need but only represent the vices opposite: imprudence, babble, and impudence. I would not have them think I purpose to take away the use of speech instead of ruling it. I should not do well to go about to frame a conversation of dumb persons; but to make a powerful war against vice, the most importunate and dangerous enemy in society. I only entreat those women who have not the inclination to speak little, to consider that if there be a time to speak something and also to say nothing, there is never any to speak all. That there is not only danger to speak what is false in speaking much, but even to speak what is true, for so they may offend prudence or verity and often both together. That those who speak so much with others do never as it were speak with themselves, that they see not their thought, but when it is escaped from them, that they learn too late by repentance what sooner they might have learned through foresight, and that sorrow and shame always follow very close the discourses when prudence ushers not. That finally the greatest part of those of their sex have less trouble to speak well than to say little, and that discretion is more difficult and necessary for them than eloquence. [Pp. 19–22 omitted.]

15. Since then there is such difficulty to come off well in company of others, that there is such pain to use speech with discretion and to restrain the liberty of the tongue, methinks it were a great remedy for it, for fear of being always in alarm or always in straits, to make good choice of those they mean to converse with more familiarly and not to have a general acquaintance with persons of all sorts. And to tell my opinion in what concerns the election they should make of spirits and humors fit for conversation, I find there are two sorts of people they are absolutely to shun, the vicious and the ignorant, because the conscience is not secure with the first nor the spirit well contented with the other. The society with those who want religion or wit should be wholly avoided, and we may very well think they have very good reason to eschew two so gross errors as impiety and ignorance. [Pp. 23–24 omitted.]

19. Say what they will, we cannot remain in the midst of vices without infection. . . . The soul insensibly is stained when a man converseth with the vicious as the face is tanned unawares when he walks in the sun. It is a misery that we are more susceptible of evil than of good, that malady communicates itself more easily than health, and that the conversation of the wicked hath more power to corrupt the good than that of the virtuous to correct the lewd. [Pp. 25–28 omitted.]

30. Such as speak little as well as they who speak much should consider that modesty is necessary for silence and discourse; because it makes the one without contempt and the other without guile or affection. And of what humor soever they be, to the end they may avoid the danger of being persecuted or debauched, it were good to seek ever the conversation of the best spirits, because they more easily pardon faults and better acknowledge the merit; and that of the most virtuous, because if libertines wrong not the conscience, they wound reputation; if they make them not vicious, they are made infamous.

The Pleasant and Melancholy Humor[8]

1. There is nothing more necessary for women in conversation then to know well their own humor, to reform it if ill, or to polish it if good. It is the ground of all, what is of most importance. But seeing there are two sorts of them that may be good, each in his kind, I think good in the entry of this discourse to compare them together, to note the better what is good or ill in either. And first, to point forth that which is most esteemed of in society, since the noblest scope we can propose therein is to have the gifts of the spirit which make us grateful. We must confess the pleasant humor therein hath a much greater advantage than the melancholy, which in truth is not amiss for sciences, but is too lumpish for discourse and too gross for witty conceits and apt replies. Pleasant humors have a great deal more grace with them and more liberty in all they do, and so are much better received in companies, as more kind in their affection, less forced in their carriages,[9] and more innocent in their designs.

2. Whatsoever they say on the behalf of the melancholy, if their musing be laudable in something, it hath as many ill effects as good, and they who call it the mother of wisdom must needs acknowledge it to be often of extravagance. They will persuade us how their spirits espy many things and travail far in their imaginations, but their voyage is so far sometimes as they return no more, or if they do, it is as travelers who leave their own country, to run unprofitably through foreign, without other fruit than to bring home weariness and poverty thence. This musing is a maze where one easily looseth[10] himself, and whence without great difficulty he gets not forth. [Pp. 30–43 omitted.]

Of Reputation

1. Although reputation be a great treasure and serve no less to virtue than the daylight unto pictures to shew their beauty, nevertheless, to con-

---

8. The sanguine and the melancholic complexion. The other two humors were the choleric and phlegmatic.

9. Deportments, behaviors.

10. The text reads "loose" for "lose" throughout.

sider well how they loose or keep it nowadays, we might well place it
among the goods of fortune, where fools sometimes have a better share
than persons of merit. If there were good judges to distribute it, it would
be enough to be virtuous to purchase it, but it often depends upon so ill
arbiters, that were we not always obliged to avoid scandal, honest men
might well content themselves with the testimony of their conscience,
without troubling themselves for the estimation of the prudent, which
chance may render good or ill. It depends too little of us to make us happy,
and were a very uncertain felicity, whereof the ignorant or malice of an
enemy might despoil us.

2. Renown sometimes is an effect which seems to have no cause, and
which is formed as those alarms which put a whole army into disorder, not
knowing the reason of it. Wherefore I allow well of their opinion who
compared it to the winds, because it grows and lightly passeth away as
they, and especially because we know not certainly their origin. And since
it is so uncertain, why toil we the spirit with so much unquietness to know
the estate wherein we live in the opinion of others, and afflict ourselves
for the error of the vulgar, as if it were but now only the ignorant began
to lie, or to deceive. [Pp. 45-46 omitted.]

5. We live in an age of pomp and ostentation, where the moral is quite
put down and where the virtues of the times consist but in excess and
extravagance. To purchase the opinion of devout, they must become superstitious or hypocrites. And these politicians make of Christianism what
the Stoics made of philosophy, to abuse the vulgar, framing to themselves
imaginary virtues whereto our humanity cannot arrive.[11] It is a great misery
that sincerity is not found in commerce, nor purity in religion. And that
as well as in court they must require often more than they look for or merit
for reputation and credit.

6. But to tell my opinion as well as a philosopher as a casuist, we may
not yield reputation should be quite neglected, because ill distributed.
This disorder acquits us not of our duty, and we should do as ill to grow
infamous for this reason as to commit murders and felonies because thieves
have been absolved and innocents condemned of these crimes. Since all
women are not prudent, and many of them work [more] by example than
by reason, the wiser at least should consider that reputation is a public
good, and that when it is ill, we should seek the remedies for it as to quench
a fire or purge a popular contagion.

7. Verily, it would make one laugh to behold some of these women to
give themselves to all sorts of liberty because that slander puts the most

---

11. Members of a Greek school of philosophy founded by Zeno about 308 B.C., which
taught that all happenings were the result of divine will and should therefore be accepted
with calm and without passion.

virtuous in the same rank with the most dissolute for an ill name, and the most vicious for the most virtuous for a good, which is even to prefer imposture before truth, opinion before a conscience. As if kings should cause torches to be lighted at noonday because the sun shines on swains as well as them, or would be sick and lose their health because their subjects are hale and sound. We may not become vicious for the ill opinion they have of us, but we should always live better, to purchase us a better. Though we have not the happiness to possess it, yet we should not fail to have always virtue to merit it. The testimony of a good conscience is more valuable than all this noise. . . .

10. Verily we are obliged to do all we can to take away the subject of ill tongues and to avoid scandal. But the wisest, yea, and the most virtuous labor herein sometimes to no purpose. For do they what they can or cannot do, there is no infallible rule or means to save one's reputation, and since it depends so upon the opinion of others, there is more fortune than prudence. We may not think that innocence alone is sufficient for it, with a good carriage, if God himself who is the fountain of goodness and wisdom, had his renounce[12] questioned for a time through the impostures of his enemies, and who made him pass for a man addicted unto vice and licentiousness. This only example shews sufficiently that we must have somewhat else than a good comportment and virtue to conserve it.

11. Moreover, there is I know not what unhappiness in some persons, exposing them to tongues not knowing wherefore, and this more often happens to the virtuous than others, because their refusals[13] breed them enemies, and thereby often put themselves in danger as Susanna[14] to be accused of some crime they never would commit. There are also some countenances which incite ill tongues to judge amiss, and this proceeds sometimes for that fools imagine one cannot laugh and not be vicious, and that there is no innocency but where they see a sadness and melancholy. This is the judgment of the ignorant, who imagine that virtue should always weep, and understand not how they are to beware of a sullen humor as a cloudy weather, and that of all spirits there is none better than the most pleasant. Otherwise he had need be very gross to think one cannot have a pleasant humor without an ill conscience. . . .

14. Howsoever they rob or diminish our good name, at least it returns no less than the hair after it is cut, so the root thereof be left behind and that innocence remain with patience. In any case, if they blame us unjustly,

---

12. Obs., renunciation.

13. Refusals of amorous suits?

14. Susanna was falsely accused of adultery by two elders because she would not submit to their lust. See Susanna, Apocrypha.

we should have the more consolation in the truth than disgust for the imposture. The innocent should afflict themselves no more when they are called or accounted guilty than if they should say they were sick when they are well. Hence it is, we may learn why the virtuous are less vindictive being blamed by the vicious, because as the foulest would sometimes seem to be the fairest with their paintings, so the dishonest women endeavor through their craft and subtleties to purchase to themselves the opinion of the most wise. . . .

16. I hold it is better to be good in effect than in shew only and that an honest woman should esteem virtue more than reputation. But if they could well weigh the importance of a good fame, I suppose they would eschew the dangers of losing it, since those women who have the true feeling of honor should hold themselves unfortunate when they are put to justify themselves and are reduced to that point to shew they are not guilty. They should have always before their eyes that which Julius Caesar said when he repudiated his wife Pompeia even after she had shewed her innocence: "It is not enough," said this emperor, "the wife of Caesar to be innocent, who ought not even to be suspected."

Of Inclination to Virtue and Devotion

1. They who imagine that the piety of women is but a tenderness of complexion or a weakness of spirit are not of our opinion. And they offer them no less affront in despoiling them of this divine quality than if they plucked out their eyes. I should think how those who desire a wife without devotion desire her also without pudicity. And that after they have robbed her of the feeling of piety, they purpose likewise to rob her of somewhat else. This is an[15] old wily trick which took beginning with the world, and these libertines herein do no more with the women of this age than the devil practiced with the first, when at the beginning he took away the fear of God from her to persuade her afterwards more easily to all other liberty. . . .

3. It is necessary then that women who would testify they have an inclination to virtue gratify more those spirits which make profession thereof than others, lest we believe that if they favor the libertines or the grosser spirits, that resemblance had wrought this cabal. Those women who shew a hatred or aversion from good persons declare by the repugnance they have to good things that they are not born but for the evil. These weak spirits have not credit enough to publish their virtues nor yet discretion enough to silence their faults.

---

15. The text reads "and."

4. And yet we see often how those women who are vainly given or have some design in hand seek among fools their admirers and confidants, as if it were a blind choice to take so ill judges of their merit and so ill secretaries of their pastimes. Ignorance and simplicity are two uncertain friends; interest and persuasion will make them blab what they list. And even imprudence, though she were not solicited, would often speak when she should hold her peace. . . .

5. And as touching piety, if any imagine it to mar a good humor and hold it makes one too melancholy for company, surely I like not those women who put their devotion on the rack to make them ill faces, as if one could not be saved without being a scare[16] to others. When the grace of God is in a soul, the visage savors of sweetness, and hath not the looks and hew of the damned or of the devils. The weather is cloudy when it is disposed to rain, and those untoward looks prognosticate something sad in their ecstasies.

6. Those women who have no will or purpose to do ill have not this lowring humor with them, which we hold to be as contrary to devotion as decency. By this we entrench not any whit on penance. The summer hath its rains as well as winter, and love sheds tears no less than fear. Joy weeps as well as sadness, and the remembrance of sins makes us not so heavy but the return of grace makes us as glad. As it rains sometimes while the sun shines, so repentance often makes tears to trickle down from smiling faces.

Whatsoever these libertines say, devotion is not contrary to civility. If bees suck out honey from flowers without doing them any hurt in touching them, it[17] doth yet more in every profession where it is found, embellishing it and making it more grateful. As jewels cast into honey take thence a flash of luster according to their natural color, so there is no condition in the world which becomes not the fairer and more valuable when it is accompanied with piety. It makes religious[18] more cheerful and seculars less insolent, moderating pleasures and sweetening austerities. Marriage thereby is more honest, war more just, commerce more faithful, and the court more honorable. Is it not a great ignorance and tyranny to think it cannot be found but in cloisters, and that we cannot enjoy it in the world without dealing with Carthusians and Capuchins?[19] [Pp. 56–58 omitted.]

Of Chastity and Courtesy

1. It is fit to join these two goodly qualities together to reduce them into a perfect temper, since there are some who become curst for being

16. The text reads "scar," which is an obsolete form of scare.
17. Devotion.
18. The clergy.
19. French religious orders.

chaste, and others refuse nothing for being courteous, which is truly to be
of too good or of too peevish an humor and this would be to change one
vice into another, instead of flying it. If virtue have two extremes which
equally offend it, we should not use the one to defend us from the other,
as if we should be covetous for fear of being prodigal, or cast ourselves
into the fire to save us from the water. . . . Those women who imagine
they cannot be honest and courteous at once skill not well the nature of
virtues, since they are not contrary but diverse only, and their correspon-
dency is too natural not to be able to subsist in one and the same subject.
When they are in a just degree, they have the better grace in company
than when alone. . . .

4. But to tell some praises of chastity, it must needs be a divine quality
since even its very enemies make reckoning of it, and the most dissolute
bear least respect to those who yield than who resist. We learn of poets
that Daphne resisting the wooings of Apollo was turned into a laurel,
whereof he ever after wore his garlands; on the contrary that Io consenting
to the ends of Jupiter, was changed into a heifer.[20] How these two metamorphoses are different and how the refusal hath far more glorious marks
than the consent. Respect accompanieth desire; contempt always attends
possession. And it seems they[21] are no longer amiable when they become
amorous. . . .

11. They who like so well to be in the middest of their enemies have
some kind of desire to be vanquished, and truly how good soever the
company be, distrust is always better than confidence and boldness; and
since she,[22] who ought to be the example of her sex, was abashed at first
at the sight of an angel who appeared to her under the shape and visage
of a man, women are always to testify some shamefastness in the company
of men, though they were in the form of angels, unless not having her
purpose, they have no need also of her fear.

12. It is ill reasoning to say that a kind of timorousness withholds women
more than virtue. If their inclination were ill, do they want solicitors?
Experience shews that if they have any fear, it is to be vicious rather than
to be blamed. Though men, who have written books and proverbs, have
done all things for their own advantage, yet they confess that chastity
particularly appertains to women, since they who have it not are held for
monsters. They[23] would not so much wonder at it if this quality were not
natural to them.[24] There are men truly who have enjoyed this virtue, but

20. Ovid, *Metamorphoses* I.452–67, 588–667.
21. Women.
22. Mary.
23. Men.
24. Women.

in occasions where consideration and constraint have taken away all their merit. . . .

13. . . . What praise merits Xenocrates[25] for not enjoying the woman they brought to him? His coldness proceeded from his old age; he was drunk; he sought but his ease. And though he had not been feeble or drowsy, she was a strumpet of whom the most debauched had been ashamed as well as a philosopher. We need no longer discourses to prove that chastity belongs not so to men; they freely acquit themselves of their part thereof, and believe they should entrench somewhat upon the profession of women if they should practice the precepts they give them.

14. Is it not a custom worthy of blame to see that men take to themselves all manner of license without giving the least? One would say to see their tyranny that marriage was instituted but to put jailers upon wives, wherein there is a great deal of ingratitude as well as injustice to pretend a fidelity which they will not tender, especially being no less obliged to keep it. Women have wit enough and conscience to believe it would cost them too dear to revenge themselves by losing their virtue to take satisfaction of the vice of their husbands. Octavia left not to love Mark Anthony dearly while he made love to Cleopatra, and abandoned a great beauty at Rome to possess a lesser in Egypt. Those women of this constancy are worthy of admiration, but they who have it not find[26] pretexts of their feebleness. Example with them stands for reason, and they imagine there is no likelihood that a crystal should resist blows which were able to break diamonds or marbles.

15. If we may be suffered to give some advice after praises, since God himself loved more tenderly one of his disciples than the others, we may have particular inclinations without the offense of chastity, who banisheth not affections but moderates and rules them. Notwithstanding, we must take heed that if friendship[27] within its nature be a virtue, it be not a vice in the practice. Wherein not to deceive ourselves, we should examine the end and scope thereof, as soon as it begins, and assure ourselves that it is dangerous if we pretend somewhat else than affection.

16. And especially to conserve more securely this virtue, it is good to give oneself always to some laudable exercise. Evil thoughts have no less power upon an idle spirit than enemies have on a man asleep, and I am fully of his opinion who calls this languishing repose the sepulcher of a living person; since if worms breed in a body without a soul, desires and

---

25. Disciple of Plato and head of the Academy from 339 to 314 B.C. (Laïs, a celebrated Athenian courtesan, attempted without success to seduce him.)
26. The text reads "finds."
27. Here, the friendship between men and women.

passions are formed in a soul without employment. And if dishonest love be the trade of those women who spend not their time in any laudable thing, we may believe that chastity is conserved in employments as it is corrupted in ease. So likewise she whom our ancients took for the goddess of love, they also took for the mother of idleness. *Diana hunts, Minerva studies, but Venus is idle and doth nothing.*

Book II

Of Courage

1. It seems to men that courage is a quality particularly tied to their sex, not bringing for it other titles than their own presumption. But he who hardly imagined there should be but one courageous and valiant woman in the world made them an honorable amends for so great an injury. . . .

2. But to see now, whether our praises herein given be true or false, it is necessary to examine the opinion of the wise and vulgar touching the true nature of courage. There is nothing truer than that the strength of the brain appears in walking on high places without dizziness or fear of falling, and that of the spirit is testified in beholding dangers and not to be troubled. And yet the simple have no preeminence herein while they wait the occasions nor the rash in hunting after them. They are the wise only who come off from hard adventures without being precipitous or insensible. Since true courage, then, should be always with a free deliberation, and is not a forced virtue or purely natural, I can hardly hold them generous whose complexion makes so light as to carry them on without cause, nor those whom nature hath made so dull and heavy as they cannot be stirred though ill entreated and misused. [Pp. 2–7 omitted.]

11. And to touch the principal vices which are contrary to this virtue: those women who kill themselves are not courageous but desperate. It[28] is to give ground instead of defending one's self; it is to yield to an enemy without his pains to vanquish us. There is no great resolution in it to take death for a remedy of itself; there is no great spirit in it to play our own hangmen. It is a great deal better to seek the end of a malady in medicines than in poison, otherwise it were no resistance but a flight; it were not to seek remedy, but to make our loss more infallible. As we esteem a body feeble when it sinks under a burden, so should we believe a soul is base when it yields to affliction.

12. This is it whereof many accuse women, but men have no reason to twit them for a vice whereof they are more often guilty. If Lucrece slew

---

28. To kill oneself.

herself for the loss of her honor, Cato did no less for that of his liberty. And why should we blame in a young lady what many praise so much in so famous a philosopher? And to say true, whatsoever slanderers invent in disparagement of women, we must confess they are more firm in their purposes than men. At least we learn by the holy Scripture that in the occasion where we own more affection and courage to the service of God were seen three Marys under the cross for one disciple.

Of Constancy and Loyalty

1. They who think that lightness[29] is natural to women, reading this discourse which proves the contrary, will imagine we seek to find a stability in the winds, assurance in the waves, and strength in reeds. But laying aside their opinion, since it is not our purpose or commission to set all the opinions in their right way, we will make it appear that for inconstance, women are more endangered to be prejudiced by it than culpable of it. And that their diffidence is but just in such an age where the most ceremonious amities are without truth or durance. Constancy is but for good things, pertinacity for the bad; otherwise sin should be eternal and repentance, for fear of change, prohibited. When the change is just, it is election; when it is not, it is a levity. As it is unreasonable to have the sick always remain in the same estate for fear to be inconstant, so do I think it as little worthy of blame to leave an ill opinion as to loose a fever, and that to repent is as necessary for spirits as medicines for the body. What danger is it to prefer a greater merit before a less, and to confess the sun hath more light in it than the stars? Otherwise, the first thing we had seen in the world would put our liberty in chains, even to the taking away our right to choose or to make us love what is worthy of hatred. [Pp. 10–12 omitted.]

4. . . . The truth is they [women] have more cause to complain of men than to fear their reproaches. How credulous spirits nowadays are ill paid for their simplicity! What assurances soever men give, we may call them rather foul deceivers than inconstant, for that even while they promise fidelity, they have a purpose to break it. There is no change in their resolution; there is none but in their words. [Pp. 12–15 omitted.]

8. There is no need of proofs to shew that women are a great deal less and more seldom perfidious[30] than men. We have but too many examples thereof, and the only experience shews us sufficiently that they have more need to defend themselves from them than to be blamed for it. See we not among the pagan women how that generous Pompeia Paulina made

---

29. Wantonness or unchastity.
30. Du Bosc says that perfidy is a vice opposed to constancy and loyalty.

her veins to be opened when she saw her husband, Seneca, condemned by Nero, refusing to live after his death who had taught her to love as a philosopher, to wit, with constancy. They stopt her veins against her will, but she testified ever afterwards through the paleness of her countenance that this cure to her was very ungrateful, and that she remained in the world most unwillingly, not seeing him longer therein, from whom she had learned to contemn life and death to testify a constancy in love. . . .

Of Prudence and Discretion

1. Through beauty women are but human, but by prudence they are as it were divine. If beauty win them love, prudence makes them worthy of admiration and respect. It is the virtue which is more necessary for them and which gives them more authority, since without it, all the other goodly qualities are without ornament, or at least without order, as scattered flowers which the winds carry confusedly away. With it, the most vicious sometimes conserve a good renown; without it, very often the most virtuous lose theirs. For this cause, prudence is very requisite for all women whatsoever they do or do not. And as architects have always a compass in hand to measure all their works, so the wise should have every moment the rules of prudence set before their eyes to make all their actions reasonable. . . .

2. Slanderers accuse women for want of manage[31] but where they have passion, that they have no subtlety but for petty or naughty enterprises, that as spiders all their art is poisoned and never spin their webs but to catch flies. But it is a falsehood more worthy of punishment than of an answer; it is also a tyranny and a custom which is no less unjust than old, to reject them from the public government, as if their spirits were not as capable of affairs of importance as well as that of men. At least the examples following will testify that the praises we afford them are not without ground, and we have reason to maintain that they have sometimes brought good remedies to the most desperate maladies of states and provinces. [Examples of stateswomen follow.]

5. Whatsoever they say of the imprudence of women, if men would take sometimes advice of those whom God hath given them for helps in the government of their affairs,[32] happily it had succeeded better with them; they would acknowledge they had done themselves no little wrong to flight[33] and neglect them in occasions where prudence and direction was requisite. . . .

7. Women are not only capable to understand that which is important in affairs and in commerce, but even that also which is subtle and solid in

---

31. Management, self-government.
32. The text reads "affayes."
33. Fly from.

the highest wisdom. If the oracle of Apollo declared Socrates for the wisest of men, Socrates freely confessed after that his Diotima[34] had taught him his prudence, which the gods themselves judged incomparable. It is no small prerogative to this woman to have instructed a philosopher whose life was so full of virtues and whose moral[35] hath more relation to the Christian than all the others. [Pp. 20–22 omitted.]

13. But to examine one of the principal effects of this virtue: ordinarily these women who would seem prudent are not so. . . . it is a treasure which continues while it is hid. . . . Wherefore the holy Scripture had reason to join the prudence of serpents and the simplicity of doves together for fear the one have malice, the other lightness, lest the one deceive, the other be deceived. Verily, they are two companions which should be inseparable, since they give a luster to each other, and prudence takes the charms of simplicity to be more lovely, and simplicity the direction of prudence to be more secure. And to speak with judgment, if dexterity without sincerity be but a malice, simplicity without prudence is but a folly.

Of Learned Women

2. . . . They that distrust a woman of letters are truly weak spirits who deserve what they fear so much, and who ground their suspicions on the reasons which ought to afford them the most security.

3. Besides, women who have some knowledge or reading afford great pleasure in conversation and receive no less in solitude when they are alone. Their idea hath somewhat to content them, while the ignorant are subject much to evil thoughts because not knowing any laudable thing to busy their mind with. As their entertainment is fastidious, their imagination must needs be extravagant. . . .

4. . . . if I would maintain, as reason obliges me, that a woman should be intelligent to appear in conversations, it may be this opinion at first would offend the ignorant and simple, who imagining all like themselves, think a woman cannot study or read without proving vicious, or at least without being suspected. But they who judge so rashly, contemn what they were to desire, as if they ought to hate the perfection they want or were to make no reckoning but of weak spirits instead of judging with themselves that they who have not wit enough to know vice have as little to make choice of virtue or to prefer according to occasions truth before appearance. They, moreover, who understand but somewhat of the moral, are not of this opinion, since we acknowledge every day by experience that the light

34. Legendary priestess at Mantinea and teacher of Socrates. See Plato, *Symposium* 201D. See also *Apology* 21A.
35. Moral teachings.

of reason is as a natural virtue which disposeth us to do well almost without study, and that we see rarely a good spirit without a good conscience. The helps of learning fortifies the best inclinations, and they who are persuaded that reading of books is a school to learn to do ill with the more dexterity, might do better to believe that women find therein more means to correct than corrupt themselves.

5. Reading and conversation are absolutely necessary to make the spirit and humor grateful and, as the one in reading gathers matter of our discourses, the other in speaking gives us the method to deliver them with ornament, to join plenty and facility together. Without which, conversation is an intolerable tyranny, and it is impossible without torment to continue long with those women who cannot entertain you but with the number of their ducks and geese, if they be of the country, and if they be of the city, speak but of gorgets[36] and attires of the fashion. They may not then imagine that speaking of this complete woman, whose image we set forth, we intend to paint you a mother of a family who can command her servants and who hath the care to comb and dress her children. Though we blame it not, yet we must confess that music, history, philosophy, and other such like exercises are more accommodate to our purpose than those of housewifery. And there is none so void of common sense that will not confess with me that without those good parts, though women have an excellent spirit, yet they shall have it full of naughty and fastidious things. Their good nature and good inclination remaining without effect for want of reading or conversation, when the tyranny of their mothers or husbands or else some other bar hinders them to purchase those fair qualities whereof they are born capable.

For, to say that sciences are too obscure for women, and that they cannot comprehend the arts in their principles and grounds by reason the terms which are too hard for them to understand, in truth is a strange error. It is a very extravagant opinion to think that reason speaks not all languages, and that sciences cannot as well be expressed in English as in Greek and Latin. These broking literists,[37] who out of ignorance or malice obscure the arts under rude terms, as coarser rags, who of purpose leave things in confusion for us to have recourse to them as to interpreters of an oracle, do them no less wrong to set them forth to view in so shameful a dress, than libertines do injure virtue in depainting it sullen, austere, and inaccessible, for fear they make profession of it. But the better sort of them can tell how to take away the mask. It is an imposture which troubles but the vulgar spirits. I confess indeed, as for philosophy and theology, there

---

36. Collars, neck, and breast pieces.
37. The original reads "Ces brouillons."

may be found some words sometimes which purely seem not English. I confess that if other arts have their particular terms which they ply not to accommodate themselves to such as make no profession of them, there is no reason the two nobler sciences of the world should make themselves more familiar than others. I confess that in a strong dispute sometimes there are mysterious words which better express the verity than the more polite. But yet saving this necessity, what need is there to affect obscurity in our discourses and writings? As if clarity made sciences less venerable, as if darkness served them for ornament and luster, as if the force of auguring were tied to a rudeness of terms. On the contrary, they diminish no more of their price in renting the veil which hides them than they wrong the gold in fetching it out of the bowels of the earth to refine it and to serve in commerce. I hold that they who clearly explicate sciences discover to us the true treasures and merit some part of the glory of Socrates, who made wisdom to descend from heaven to the earth, that is to say, who make it very intelligible to spirits which seem more capable thereof. There is nothing so true as that when sciences are well conceived, they may express them in any language, and that women are able enough to understand them.

6. On the other side, to say that all the impediment rests in their wit which is not strong enough for it, methinks, is to judge but ill of their complexion which, according to physicians, as being more delicate than ours is also better disposed for study of the arts and sciences. Say what they will, they are capable thereof as well as men. . . .

7. [Du Bosc gives examples of learned women authors in ancient Rome and early Christian times.] But what need is there to seek examples in the ages past? Have not women in these our days virtues extraordinary enough to oppose to those of antiquity? Have we not women as well in country as in court who can write upon the hardest and most serious subjects, who can speak to the purpose of the highest mysteries of our religion, who know well the holy and profane history, and whose entertainment is no less solid than pleasing? Have we not those who skill the foreign languages as well as ours, and are so universal in the knowledge of good things as it is an extreme loss and mischief to us that the tyranny of custom hath hindered many of them to publish their works and to leave their writings to posterity. Verily I know many of them so well versed in the sciences of arguing and disputes and in the subtlest philosophy that the learnedst men disputing with them remain confounded. I know many of them who excel in prose and poetry, and who do so well in each kind that men themselves who have some light in the arts cannot read their pieces without admiring them as master works. I know many of them who can judge so well of things of this nature and are so eminent in them as their conversation

serves as a school to the best wits, so as many excellent authors consult with them as with oracles, holding themselves happy in their approbation and praises.

8. But what need is there to prosecute this matter? Verily it is too ample to pursue, and though men be very sparing and backward to write the praises of women, they cannot choose but testify this verity, and fill their books with such examples, so as if for this I might call the fable to our succor, we shall learn that as men have an Apollo for the author of sciences, women have their Minerva, who invented the best learnings, and who affords them a just right to pretend unto it. If I feared to uphold a verity so known with fictions, I might content myself to send them who doubt thereof to the nine muses[38] of the poets to whom all the ancients attribute the invention of the arts.

Of Habits and Ornaments

1. It is certain that in what fashion soever we be apparelled, we hardly please all sorts of persons; either the young or old will find somewhat to carp at, and it is almost impossible to avoid either the laughter of the one or the censure of the others. There are such sour spirits that will not let men follow the fashion, holding it intolerable if they prove it not to be invented a thousand years ago. It is even to contemn the present times to adore the past, not considering that we must suffer what we cannot hinder and that oftentimes it is a less vanity to follow the fashions received than to keep oneself unto the old. [Pp. 32–34 omitted.]

6. Surely . . . we must confess if they [women] dress and attire themselves but to their husbands, there would be no excess therein; nor should we hear of so many complaints, for that which their riotousness breeds in families so much poverty and jealousies. They carry oftentimes some three or four houses hanging at their ears, and for this goodly pretext, spare not for pearls and diamonds; but truly they are not suspected of many without cause, nor do these attires so maintain their conjugal affection, but that there is some likelihood these gaudy dresses are rather meant for their paramours than their husbands.

Of Beauty

1. They who adore or contemn beauty ascribe too much or too little to the image of God. It is one of the rarest presents which heaven hath afforded to the earth. But we are to attribute the whole merit thereof to the power and goodness of him who pleasures us therewith. By the opinion of Plato,

38. Who are all female.

it is a human splendor, lovely of its nature, which hath the force to ravish the spirit with the eyes.[39]

2. And surely it must needs be a sign of the inclination we have to the good. Since without it the ministers misshapen have been rejected from temples, nor should we have an ill opinion of beauty which God himself hath thought necessary for such as approach to his altars. The judgments we frame of the beauty of the spirit by that of the body are not often much amiss. Souls by the example of great queens cause their dwelling to be well[40] dressed up, or they will take pains to deck it when they are received therein. And verily, if virtue be necessary for the establishment of sovereign authorities, at least beauty seems very decent for it. If we find sometimes good spirits in bodies ill-composed, they are as relics ill-accommodated, whereto many do not give that respect they would if they were set in gold and pearl. [Pp. 36–38 omitted.]

8. There are they who make it a scruple to praise beauty because it passeth soon away, for that it last no more than lightening and very often promiseth no less than it, a storm and tempest. It is a flower, say they, which fades as soon as blown, which the winds shake, which the sun withers, which the rain washeth, and which is so delicate that without touching or having any enemies in a moment it finds its ruin in its feebleness. But what say they therein which they say not of all other things of the world that cannot always endure. If they complain of beauty, it is because it hath not the durance of the stars as it hath the price and luster. And yet we must confess that the fairest of them might find an excellent remedy against vanity, if they could sometimes being of the age of sixteen or twenty years, represent to themselves the defects and incommodities of old age. How fair soever were the plumage which nature or art had lent them, they would be ashamed as well as the peacocks in beholding their feet so foul, could they foresee so great a change and such ruins. I make no profession here to preach the four last things of man. But methinks they should not so much excruciate themselves for a thing which years insensibly steals away from them and which also diminisheth every moment in despite of their art. [Pp. 39–43 omitted.]

Of Curiosity and Slander

6. It is easy to know a chaste woman from her that is not so. For the vicious examines things to the least circumstance, her malice serves her as a pattern to judge evil; her experience and her purpose cause her to make ill interpretations of the best things. . . . These old vicious women are

39. Plato, *Symposium* 206C–D?
40. The text reads "will."

always jealous of others; they are afraid lest they[41] come to abuse the liberty they took, and cannot imagine that a simple walking only or such like conversation should be innocent. They fear lest they[42] do the feats they have done themselves or would commit perhaps, had they but as much power as malice. And yet they have no better means to cloak their sin than to make a shew of wonder and displeasure when they hear others blamed, for so denying their belief of others' slanders, they are easily judged to be far from being culpable in a vice whose very name is odious to them, for they think if they but slightly testify their repugnance to the ill, and that their countenance allow what the mouth forbids it, would give encouragement to the vicious, who would have nothing to do with the stricter sort. [Pp. 44–46 omitted.]

Of Cruel and Pitiful Women

1. Whatsoever most men think of the fury of women, pity is so natural to them, and their inclination is so powerfully carried to mercy, that even the Furies themselves could not choose but weep and lament the disaster of Orpheus when he went to hell to demand his Euridice. [Pp. 47–49 omitted.]

5. Women should always suppose that cruelty proceeds of a feebleness of the spirit and that those women who want compassion want also knowledge and courage. Surely the most generous are the most pitiful. They know it to be more glorious to vanquish their passions than their enemies, and that to give life when they may take it away is as it were to raise the dead without working a miracle. [Pp. 50–51 omitted.]

Of a Good Grace

2. Verily it seems this pleasing quality is natural to women, and that they enjoy it even without pain or study. Yet, though birth contribute much, . . . we must confess yet how the beauty of the body in some things depends on that of the mind, and that the laws of a good grace are tied to those of the moral. Malice hath a remorse with it, which dissimulation cannot long conceal; choler, cruelty, love, and unquietness appear on the brow; the visage shews passions to be troubled or serene, as a dial disposeth the motions of the clock to mark the hours. So as to conserve a good grace, they should know how to rule the motions of the soul as well as those of the body.

3. And to begin with that which is most important, there is nothing they are so much to eschew as this too much strained artificiousness. They must

41. Others?
42. Others?

not aspire to an excellence impossible. Nature cannot employ too much endeavor without producing monsters. It happens often through an extreme desire they have to please that they breed a loathing instead of love. When they use too much care in their discourses, in lieu of expressing their thoughts natively, they are troubled and confounded. . . . As a forcedness displeaseth in the fairest actions, a certain nativeness takes and pleaseth in the least. It hath such sweet charms with it as none can avoid them, because they come from an innocence, and that this affectation is never without some imperfections or too great a love of oneself. [Pp. 53–56 omitted.]

The Dissolute Woman

2. I speak confidently to all, for if they be strumpets, I will not be friends with them; if honest, I have no fear to offend them by it. . . .

3. It is true, then, that this passion of these strumpets should not properly be called love, but is some other malady, which but through a miracle cannot be cured. . . . It is a fire of hell, which hath for smoke, blindness; for light, scandal; for cinders, infamy and shame. [Pp. 58–62 omitted.]

Of Jealousy

1. We lose always with grief what we enjoy with love and conserve with unquietness. Hence it is that jealousy is not so unjust as many imagine, since it makes us fear only least another rob us of what we think to be ours only. Is it such a matter to set a watch on that we prize, especially in a time when fidelity is so rare, as there are not more than such as are certainly deceived, that fear it not? . . . And to say true, to philosophize aright, love seems to be an empire or a kingdom only of two persons, which cannot extend further without destroying itself, and where obedience and sovereignty are reciprocal. . . .

2. Verily it is no less folly to believe that there is no love in a spirit when he becomes jealous than to think a man hath no life when he is sick. On the contrary, as sorrow and grief are not in the deed, so jealousy never is where hatred and indifferency are. [Pp. 64–72 omitted.]

Of Amity, and the Love of Inclination, and Election

1. Since there is no sweetness in life without amity, and that without it, the greatest prosperity is but irksome, as its least affliction is intolerable to us. There is no reason I should forget this divine quality, wherein women have made themselves so recommendable at all times. . . .

2. And to begin by love of inclination. . . . It is violent, and yet constant; though it work in a moment, yet it lasts a long time. It finds sometimes in the same instant its birth and perfection. It is that which made Dido in

love with Aeneas from the first time that ever she saw him, beginning to
love him so soon as she knew him, not regarding that he was a stranger,
whom a tempest and not love had cast on the coasts of Carthage.[43] . . . It
is even as pleasing as strong; it hath no less sweetness than permanence.
. . . They have good reason to say that the love of consideration[44] resembles
the fire here beneath, which hath always need of nourishment and which
extinguisheth, if not always applied to some matter, whereas that of inclination is like to the fire which is in the upper region of the air, which
always equally endures and maintains itself. It is the more natural as it is
more noble; it is not mercenary; it is not fed with infamous pretensions
nor proposeth other end than love itself. . . . So as if there be no better
amity than that which lasts long, we may well judge that, that inclination
is the more excellent, and as it is purer, it is more constant. [Pp. 77–83
omitted.]

7. . . . There are [those] who teach on Plato's grounds that inclination
comes from a certain reminiscence,[45] and that our souls have seen each
other in some other world. It seems to be no commencement of a new
love, but only a continuance of some old. That it is not properly the birth
of an affection, but an awaking of it. . . . There are others who attribute
the inclination to the stars, and who hold that the same causes which
produce flowers in the bosom of the earth breed likewise the sympathy in
our souls. There are some also who attribute it to the four qualities,[46] and
others to a destiny. But not to deliver the opinions of all who are deceived
and who seek the origin of the inclination where it is not, meseems to
philosophize aright that it proceeds merely from a self love. We love all
which resemble us, even our pictures; we affect our image wheresoever
we see it. We esteem all that come from us; for this, fathers love their
children; painters their pictures, and artisans their works. Hence it is we
may learn the great danger wherein love of inclination engageth us, for
since most commonly we love ourselves, even where we are most imperfect,
and that we embrace our very shadow, as Narcissus[47] did, it follows we are
in great danger to love others' imperfections if they chance to resemble
ours. If self love be blind, the love of inclination is no less; it is an effect
very like its cause. . . .

10. . . . It were needful to join these two sorts of love together[48] to make
a perfect one, lest amity without inclination be not too forced, or without

43. Virgil, *Aeneid* I.748–56, IV.1–89, 160–73.
44. Material or social "consideration."
45. See Plato, *Phaedrus* 248–49.
46. Du Bosc is referring to humoral medicine.
47. Ovid, *Metamorphoses* III.402–73.
48. Du Bosc is speaking of love attained by "inclination" and "election," i.e., by
attraction and deliberate choice.

election be too imprudent. If love have no consideration with it, it is without manage or direction; if it have not a sympathy, it is without sweetness. Verily, it seems that these two loves are in one soul. . . . They are two brothers, whereof the one is the first by order of nature, but yet so as not to have the preeminence; the one is more violent and impetuous, the other more sweet and prudent. . . . So reason is to shew us the way to rule the amity of inclination, that that of election may be the mistress.

11. Lastly, if they ask me the most necessary rules of amity as well for satisfaction of their conscience as for that of the mind, I hold there is none better than to believe our affection to be then unjust when it is contrary to that we owe to God. As the ark was between the two cherubim, so is God between two hearts which love each other. He should be the knot of our amities, to make them strong and reasonable. And to speak thereof with that great bishop, who hath written so divinely of this matter, love is the more laudable in earth as it resembles that in heaven.[49]

49. Augustine? Perhaps *Confessions* IV.12.

PART VI

One Woman's Voice

DOROTHY LEIGH
The Mother's Blessing: or, The Godly Counsel of a Gentlewoman not long since deceased, left behind her for her children....
Proverbs 1:8. "My son, hear the instruction of thy father, and forsake not the law of thy mother"
London, 1616

Introduction

From its first publication in 1616 to its last noted edition in 1674, Dorothy Leigh's *The Mother's Blessing* went through at least twenty editions and an untold number of reprints. But few copies of any edition survive, perhaps because *The Mother's Blessing* was read into pieces, perhaps because it was a rather small book, one which could easily be carried in a pocket. (It was never printed in anything other than a 12mo format, even though it was over two hundred pages long.) Copies of *The Mother's Blessing* may also be scarce because it was considered by its printers and perhaps even by its readers as ephemeral and thus, like chapbooks for instance, not worth preserving—unlike the elegant folio editions of the Bible or Perkin's *Works,* both of which were treasured household possessions. The large number of editions and reprints of *The Mother's Blessing* prove nonetheless that Dorothy Leigh's book reached a wider audience over a longer period of time than nearly any other book of moral exhortation written for women in the period.

Despite the book's evident popularity, we know less than nothing about Dorothy Leigh herself. Indeed, futile attempts to discover her identity underline the dependent status of ordinary women in her time and later. In answer to a query "Who was Mrs. Dorothy Leigh?" addressed to *Notes and Queries*,[1] the editors of that journal say that Dorothy Leigh might have been the daughter of William Kemp of Finchingfield and the wife of Ralph Leigh, a soldier under the earl of Essex at Cadiz. (*The Dictionary of National Biography*, however, says that William Kemp died without issue.) On the other hand, the response in *Notes and Queries* also suggests that Dorothy Leigh might have had a quite different father and husband, namely, a Robert Kempe and a Ralph Lee. The attempt to identify her son as the Rev. Lea, a curate at Denston in Suffolk, is equally inconclusive. Thus, not only do we not know who she was, even late in the nineteenth century attempts to identify her did so by trying to discover her father, husband, and son.

Dorothy Leigh herself addresses her book to her sons. She writes to her sons, she says, because children are a mother's proper audience, and she apologizes with that excuse for indulging in the unwomanly occupation of authorship. Why she did "not according to the usual custom of women, exhort you by words and admonitions rather than by writing: a thing so unusual among us . . . was the motherly affection that I bare unto you all, which made me now (as it often hath done heretofore) forget my self in regard of you." She further excuses herself for instructing her sons in print by invoking the authority of her dead husband (and their dead father) who, she says, told her "in his will" to bring them up in knowledge. Another justification for writing rather than speaking is that she believes she may not live long enough to instruct them in person: "Nature telleth me, that I cannot long be here to speak unto you." But we do not know when she died. Although the title page refers to her as "not long since deceased," there is no preface which describes either the circumstances of her death or its date, and she clearly wrote the dedication herself. Her final justification for writing, she says, is the mandate imposed on all Christians to teach the truths of Scripture. "I seek to put you in mind of the words of our Savior Christ." (In a poignant passage, she thanks God for having made her children men, so that they, if not she, may learn "the seven liberal sciences" and "may write and speak the word of God without offending any.")[2] Thus Dorothy Leigh does quite consciously what Vives and others said women must not do—she meddles in the male domain of religion and theology. In fact, her book is a series of sermons, and she instructs her sons in "the right and ready way to heaven." But the ready way to heaven she counsels her sons to follow is based upon her own interpretation of Scripture, and she so exceeds the usual role of women that she assumes the role of minister, that is, a spiritual leader of men.

Although she addresses herself to her sons, the very fact that she caused her book to be published reveals a conscious intention to reach a wider audience, and she clearly intended that audience to be women. She says as much when she insists that yet another reason why she wrote was "to move women to be careful of their children," and she speaks throughout her book of "we women."[3] When she counsels her sons, she often counsels them about matters which involve women and children. Sometimes she even seems to be speaking through her sons to women, as, for instance, when she urges her sons to cherish the women they marry (and urges women to understand that if they cannot be first in the life of the family, they should try to be a close second). She tells her sons that they have the option of choosing a wife from almost "a world of women." Once having chosen her, however, Leigh insists that they are obligated to love her "to the end." If a man has not the "wit, discretion, and policy" to choose a woman he can love throughout his life, "he is unfit to marry any woman." If he loves her truly, she continues, he will take her as a "companion and fellow," not make of her both "a servant and drudge. If she be thy wife, she is always too good to be thy servant, and worthy to be thy fellow." Leigh promises her sons that the love which results from such a union is so "excellent" a love that she "cannot by any means set down the excellency of that love. But this I assure you, that if you get wives that be godly and you love them, you shall not need to forsake me; whereas if you have wives that you love not, I am sure I will forsake you." (Leigh's diction, notwithstanding her assertion, evokes what must have been among the deepest concerns of married women in the period. For the promise of "excellent" wedded love in return for male constancy also points to the desperation and loss that wives experienced when their husbands ceased to regard them with affection and care.)

More often Dorothy Leigh addresses women directly, and when she does, she is obviously intent on establishing as positively as she can the position of women in a dominantly male world. She finds a way to do so through women's relation to Mary, the virgin mother of God. It was Mary, says Leigh, who freed women from their part in the shame of Eve's fall:

I presumed that there was no woman so senseless as not to look what a blessing God hath sent to us women through that gracious Virgin, by whom it pleased God to take away the shame which Eve, our grandmother, had brought to us. For before, men might say, "The woman beguiled me, and I did eat the poisoned fruit of disobedience, and I die." But now man may say, if he say truly, "The woman brought me a Savior, and I feed on him by faith, and live." Here is this great and woeful shame taken from women by God working in a woman: man can claim no part in it; the shame is taken from us and from our posterity for ever.[4]

Dorothy Leigh goes on to counter that other accusation leveled against women, that they are seductresses. For now it is men who seduce women: "we women now may say that men lie in wait everywhere to deceive us, as the Elders did deceive *Susanna.*" But if women are to fulfill the heritage Mary endowed them with, they must espouse the virtue of chastity. Women must be "chaste with Susanna, and being women, to embrace that virtue which being placed in a woman is most commendable." It follows, then, that seduction and rape irreparably harm women. Some women, says Leigh, have even "made away themselves, or at least have separated themselves from company" in order to preserve "the name of a modest maid or a chaste matron" after they have been raped, "though against their wills." By emphasizing rape over licentiousness, Leigh places the burden on men to avoid that damage to women which cannot be undone. However needful it is for women to possess other virtues, she suggests, without "chastity . . . we are mere beasts and no women." Unlike male moralists, however, she insists that the virtue of chastity has the power to free women from the penalties of the Fall, as Mary triumphed over Eve, and thus the power to raise women to something close to equality with men. It is easy to understand why such a promise might have brought comfort to all those women whose male relatives claimed dominion over them.

Although Leigh's stated object is to teach her sons the way to heaven—a task she can hardly be said to neglect—she also argues for the dignity and capability of women in a way that almost refutes the notion of their weakness and for the place of wives in their husband's hearts in a way that almost denies the idea of their subordination. She does this, furthermore, in a book whose popularity over a century was far greater than any other English book addressed to women except possibly the life of Katherine Stubbes and the Anglican homily on marriage. Because her treatise seems to have been ignored by the male writers who dominated the market, however, its obvious and important influence was probably underground. That underground must have included women in thousands of English homes.

NOTES

1. *Notes and Queries,* 4th series, 2 (Oct 10, 1868), 347.

2. In yet another passage, she suggests that women's primary duties are not concerned with housework, but rather with "reading, meditating, or practicing some good thing which she hath learned in the Scripture."

3. It is interesting in this regard that the 1667 copy of *The Mother's Blessing* in the University of Illinois library has the name of its female owner, "Elizabeth Brill," written in a contemporary seventeenth-century hand on the margin of page 193.

4. This statement can be found in earlier sources, among them Agrippa's *Treatise of the nobility . . . of womenkind*, Sig. [C7]: "of a woman only he [Christ] took flesh and blood. For only for the woman Christ was called the son of man." What seems to be new is the use to which Leigh puts the argument. On this point, cf.: Elaine V. Beilin, *Redeeming Eve: Women Writers of the English Renaissance* (Princeton: Princeton University Press, 1987), p. 279. In 1617, a year after the publication of *The Mother's Blessing*, Esther Sowernam (a pseudonym?) repeated Leigh's arguments in order to refute Swetnam's misogynist *Arraignment of Women:* "What more gracious a gift could the Almighty promise to woman than to bring forth the fruit in which all nations shall be blessed? So that as woman was a means to lose Paradise, she is by this made a means to recover Heaven." See *Half Humankind: Contexts and Texts of the Controversy about Women in England, 1540–1640*, ed. Katherine Usher Henderson and Barbara F. McManus (Urbana: University of Illinois Press, 1985), p. 225.

The Mother's Blessing

[To the high and excellent Princess, the Lady Elizabeth, her grace, daughter to the high and mighty king of Great Britain and wife to the illustrious Prince, the Count Palatine of the Rhine. Sigs. A2–A5 omitted.]
To my beloved Sons, George, John, and William Leigh, all things pertaining to life and godliness.

My Children, God having taken your father out of this vale of tears to his everlasting mercy in Christ, myself not only knowing what a care he had in his life time that you should be brought up godlily, but also at his death being charged in his will by the love and duty which I bare him to see you well instructed and brought up in knowledge, I could not choose but seek (according as I was duty bound) to fulfill his will in all things, desiring no greater comfort in the world then to see you grow in godliness, that so you might meet your father in heaven, where I am sure he is, myself being a witness of his faith in Christ. And seeing myself going out of the world, and you but coming in, I know not how to perform this duty so well as to leave you these few lines, which will show you as well the great desire your father had both of your spiritual and temporal good, as the care I had to fulfill his will in this, knowing it was the last duty I should perform unto him. But when I had written these things unto you, and had (as I thought) something fulfilled your father's request, yet I could not see to what purpose it should tend, unless it were sent abroad to you. For should it be left with the eldest, it is likely the youngest should have but little part in it. Wherefore setting aside all fear, I have adventured to shew my imperfections to the view of the world, not regarding what censure shall for this be laid

upon me, so that herein I may shew my self a loving mother and a dutiful
wife; and thus I leave you to the protection of him that made you, and
rest till death,

Your fearful, faithful, and careful mother, D. L. [Sigs. [A8]–[A9] omitted.]

Chapter 1

*The occasion of writing this book was the consideration of the care of
parents for their children*

My children, when I did truly weigh, rightly consider, and perfectly see
the great care, labor, travail, and continual study which parents take to
enrich their children, some wearing their bodies with labor, some breaking
their sleeps with care, some sparing from their own bellies, and many
hazarding their souls, some by bribery, some by simony, others by perjury,
and a multitude by usury, some stealing on the sea, others begging by land
portions from every poor man, not caring if the whole commonwealth be
impoverished, so their children be enriched, for themselves they can be
contented with meat, drink, and cloth, so that their children by their means
may be made rich, always abusing this portion of Scripture: *He that provideth
not for his own family, is worse then an infidel, 1 Tim. 5:8,* ever seeking for
the temporal things of this world and forgetting things which be eternal;
when I considered these things, I say, I thought good (being not desirous
to enrich you with transitory goods) to exhort and desire you to follow the
counsel of Christ: *First seek the kingdom of God and his righteousness, and
then all these things shall be administered unto you. Matt. 6:33.*

Chapter 2

The first cause of writing is a motherly affection

But lest you should marvel, my children, why I do not according to the
usual custom of women exhort you by words and admonitions rather than
by writing, a thing so unusual among us, and especially in such a time
when there be so many godly books in the world that they mold in some
men's studies while their masters are marred because they will not meditate
upon them, as many men's garments moth eat in their chest, while their
Christian brethren quake with cold in the street for want of covering. Know
therefore that it was the motherly affection that I bare unto you all which
made me now (as it often hath done heretofore) forget myself in regard
of you; neither care I what you or any shall think of me, if among many
words I may write but one sentence which may make you labor for the
spiritual food of the soul which must be gathered every day out of the word
as the children of Israel gathered manna in the wilderness. By the which

you may see it is a labor. But what labor? A pleasant labor, a profitable labor, a labor without the which the soul cannot live. For as the children of Israel must needs starve, except they gathered every day in the wilderness and fed of it, so must your souls, except you gather the spiritual manna out of the word every day and feed of it continually; for as they by this manna comforted their hearts, strengthened their bodies, and preserved their lives, so by this heavenly word of God, you shall comfort your souls, make them strong in faith, and grow in true godliness, and finally preserve them with great joy to everlasting life through faith in Christ. Whereas if you desire any food for your souls that is not in the written word of God, your souls die with it even in your hearts and mouths, even as they that desired other food died with it in their mouths, were it never so dainty,[1] so shall you, and there is no recovery for you.

Chapter 3

The best labor is for the food of the soul [Pp. 7–9 omitted.]

My dear children, have I not cause to fear? the Holy Ghost saith by the prophet, *Can a mother forget the child of her womb?* Esther 49:15. As if he should say, is it possible, that she which hath carried her child within her so near her heart and brought it forth into this world with so much bitter pain, so many groans and cries can forget it? Nay rather, will she not labor now till Christ be formed in it? Will she not bless it every time it sucks on her breasts, when she feeleth the blood come from her heart to nourish it? Will she not instruct it in the youth, and admonish it in the age, and pray for it continually? Will she not be afraid that the child which she endured such pain for should endure endless pain in hell? Could Saint *Paul* say unto the *Galatians,* that were but strangers to him concerning the flesh, only he had spent some time amongst them to bring them to the profession of the truth, from which he feared they would fall, and could he, I say, write unto them, *My little children, of whom I do travail again in birth, until Christ be formed in you?* Gal. 4:19. And can any man blame a mother (who indeed brought forth her child with much pain) though she labor again till Christ be formed in them? Could *St. Paul* wish himself separated from God for his brethren's sake, and will not a mother venture to offend the world for her children's sake?

Therefore let no man blame a mother, though she something exceed in writing to her children, since every man knows that the love of a mother to her children is hardly contained within the bounds of reason. Neither must you, my sons, when you come to be of judgment, blame me for

1. Num. 11:3.

writing to you, since nature telleth me that I cannot long be here to speak unto you, and this my mind will continue long after me in writing; and yet not my mind, but I seek to put you in mind of the words of our Savior Christ which saith, *abhor not for the meat that perisheth, etc.*,[2] where you see that the food of the soul is to be gotten by labor. *Why stand you here?* (saith Christ).[3] Here is no time to be idle.[4] They that will rest with Christ in heaven must labor to follow him here on earth. *Blessed are the dead, which die in the Lord: for they rest from their labor.*[5] Thus you see, if you will go to the place which Christ hath bought for you, you must labor to follow Christ. He labored to get it for you, or else all your labor would have been as nothing, and now you must labor to lay hold on him, or else all your labor will be worth nothing. Many there be that labor the clean contrary way, for they leave Christ and take hold of traditions, and a number loiter, and by that means never get hold on Christ. And this is the cause why I write unto you, that you might never fly from him with the one, nor yet loiter with the other, but that you might learn to follow him and to take hold of him in the written Word of God, where you shall find him (as Christ himself witnesseth) and no where else. *Search the Scriptures,* saith he, *for they testify of me.*[6] Labor therefore, that you may come unto Christ.

Chapter 4

The second cause is to stir them up to write

The second cause, my sons, why I write unto you (for you may think that had I had but one cause, I would not have changed the usual order of women) is needful to be known and may do much good. For where I saw the great mercy of God toward you in making you men and placing you amongst the wise, where you may learn the true written word of God, which is the pathway to all happiness and which will bring you to the chief city, New Jerusalem, and the seven liberal sciences, whereby you shall have at least a superficial sight in all things, I thought it fit to give you good example, and by writing to entreat you, that when it shall please God to give both virtue and grace with your learning, he having made you men that you may write and speak the word of God without offending any, that then you would remember to write a book unto your children of the right and true way to happiness, which may remain with them and theirs for ever.

2. John 6:27.

3. The question mark was misplaced and the biblical phrase was not italicized in the first edition. These errors were corrected in later editions.

4. Matt. 20:6.

5. Rev. 14:13.

6. John 5:35.

Chapter 5

The third cause is to move women to be careful of their children

The third is to encourage women (who, I fear, will blush at my boldness) not to be ashamed to show their infirmities, but to give men the first and chief place, yet let us labor to come in the second, and because we must needs confess that sin entered by us into our posterity, let us show how careful we are to seek to Christ to cast it out of us and our posterity, and how fearful we are that our sin should sink any of them to the lowest part of the earth; wherefore let us call upon them to follow Christ, who will carry them to the height of heaven. [Pp. 18–24 omitted.]

Chapter 8

The sixth cause is to persuade them to teach their children[7]

The sixth reason is to entreat and desire you and in some sort to command you that all your children, be they males or females, may in their youth learn to read the Bible in their own mother tongue, for I know it is a great help to true godliness. And let none of you plead poverty against this, for I know that if you be neither covetous, prodigal, nor idle, either of which sins will let no virtue grow where they come, that you need not fail in this. But if you will follow the commandment of the Lord, and labor six days and keep the seventh holy to the Lord and love Him with all your heart, soul, and strength, you will not only be willing but also able to see them all brought up to read the Bible. *Solomon*[8] that was wise by the spirit of God said, *Remember thy Creator in the days of thy youth.*[9] And ye are also commanded to *write it upon the walls of your houses and to teach it your children. I know* (saith God) *that Abraham will teach his children and his children's children to walk in my*[10] *commandments.*[11] Also I further desire you, because I wish all well, and would be glad you should do as much good as could be in the wilderness of this world, that if any shall at any time desire you to be a witness to the baptizing of their child that then you shall desire the person so desiring to give you his faithful word that the child shall be taught to read, so soon as it can conveniently learn, and that it shall so continue till it can read the Bible. If this will not be granted, you shall refuse to answer for the child; otherwise do not refuse to be a witness to any, for it is a good Christian duty. Moreover, forget not, whether

7. Chapter 6 was written to persuade her sons never to fear poverty. Chapter 7 was written to persuade her sons not to fear death.
8. Not italicized in the first edition. Corrected in later editions.
9. Eccles. 12:1.
10. The text reads "thy." Corrected in later editions.
11. Deut. 4:9 (?), although the speaker is Moses, not Abraham.

you answer for the child or no, to pray that the child baptized may receive the Holy Ghost with all other children of the faithful, especially when you are where a child is baptized; for it is your duty to pray for the increase of the Church of God. *Pray for the peace of Jerusalem* (saith the Psalmist) *let them prosper that love thee.*[12]

Chapter 9

The seventh cause is that they should give their children good names

The seventh cause is to entreat you that though I do not live to be a witness to the baptizing of any of your children, yet you would give me leave to give names to them all. For though I do not think any holiness to be in the name, but know that God hath his in every place and of every name, yet I see in the Bible it was observed by God himself to give choice names to his children which had some good signification. I think it good, therefore, to name your children after the names of the saints of God, which may be a means to put them in mind of some virtues which those saints used, especially when they shall read of them in the Bible; and seeing many are desirous to name both their own children and others after their own names, this will be a means to increase the names of the saints in the church, and so none shall have occasion to mislike his name, since he beareth the name of such a saint as hath left a witness to the world that he lived and died in the true faith of Jesus Christ. The names I have chosen you are these: *Philip, Elizabeth, James, Anna, John* and *Susanna*. The virtues of them that bore those names and the causes why I chose them, I let pass, and only mean to write of the last name, *Susanna*,[13] famous through the world for chastity, a virtue which always hath been and is of great account, not only amongst the Christians and people of God, but even among the heathen and infidels, insomuch that some of them have written that a woman that is truly chaste is a great partaker of all other virtues and, contrariwise, that the woman that is not truly chaste hath no virtue in her. The which saying may well be warranted by the Scripture, for who so is truly chaste is free from idleness and from all vain delights, full of humility and all good Christian virtues; who so is chaste is not given to pride in apparel nor any vanity, but is always either reading, meditating, or practicing some good thing which she hath learned in the Scripture.

But she which is unchaste is given to be idle; or if she do anything, it is for a vain glory and for the praise of men more then for any humble,

12. Ps. 122:6.

13. The text reads "Susan." Corrected in later editions. Leigh's sidenote emphasizes that the author of this book was a woman: "The story of Susanna, though it be not canonical, nor to be equaled to those books that are, yet it may be true and of good use, as many other histories written by men are."

loving, and obedient heart that she beareth unto God and his Word, who said, *Six days thou shalt labor;*[14] and so left no time for idleness, pride, or vanity, for in none of these is there any holiness. The unchaste woman is proud, and always decking herself with vanity, and delights to hear the vain words of men in which there is not only vanity but also so much wickedness that the vain words of men and women's vainness in hearing them hath brought many women to much sorrow and vexation, as woeful experience hath and will make many of them confess. But some will say, had they only lent an ear to their words they had done well enough. To answer which, I would have every one know that one sin begetteth another. The vain words of the man and the idle ears of the woman beget unchaste thoughts oftentimes in the one, which may bring forth much wickedness in them both.

Man said once: *The woman which thou gavest me beguiled me and I did eat.*[15] But we women now may say that men lie in wait every where to deceive us, as the Elders did deceive *Susanna*. Therefore let us be as she was, chaste, watchful, and wary, keeping company with maids. Once *Judas* betrayed his master with a kiss, and repented it; but now men like *Judas* betray their mistresses with a kiss and repent it not, but laugh and rejoice that they have brought sin and shame to her that trusted them. The only way to avoid all which is to be chaste with Susanna, and being women, to embrace that virtue which being placed in a woman is most commendable.

An unchaste woman destroyeth both the body and the soul of him she seemeth most to love, and it is almost impossible to set down the mischiefs which have come through unchaste women. *Solomon* saith that *her steps lead to Hell.*[16] Wherefore bring up your daughters as *Susanna's* parents brought up her; teach them the law of the Lord continually and always persuade them to embrace this virtue of chastity.

It may be that some of you will marvel, since I set down names for the imitation of their virtues that bore them, why I placed not Mary in the first place, a woman virtuous above all other women. My reason was this, because I presumed that there was no woman so senseless as not to look what a blessing God hath sent to us women through that gracious Virgin, by whom it pleased God to take away the shame which Eve, our grandmother, had brought to us. For before, men might say, "The woman beguiled me, and I did eat the poisoned fruit of disobedience, and I die." But now man may say, if he say truly, "The woman brought me a Savior, and I feed on him by faith, and live." Here is this great and woeful shame

14. Deut. 5:13.
15. Cf. Gen. 3:12.
16. Prov. 5:5.

taken from women by God working in a woman: man can claim no part in it; the shame is taken from us and from our posterity for ever. *The seed of the woman hath taken down the Serpent's head*,[17] and now whosoever can take hold of the seed of the woman by faith shall surely live for ever. And therefore all generations shall say that she was blessed who brought us a Savior, the fruit of obedience, that whosoever feedeth of shall live for ever. And except they feed of the seed of the woman, they have no life. Will not therefore all women seek out this great grace of God, that Mary hath taken away the shame which before was due unto us ever since the fall of man?

Mary was filled with the Holy Ghost and with all goodness and yet is called the blessed Virgin, as if our God should (as he doth indeed) in brief comprehend all other virtues under this one virtue of chastity. Wherefore I desire that all women, what name soever they bear, would learn of this blessed virgin to be chaste, for though she were more replenished with grace than any other, and more freely beloved of the Lord, yet the greatest title that she had was that she was a blessed and pure virgin; which is a great cause to move all women, whether they be maids or wives, (both which estates she honored) to live chastely; to whom for this cause God hath given a cold and temperate disposition and bound them with these words, *Thy desire shall be subject to thy husband*;[18] as if God in mercy to women should say, "You of your selves shall have no desires, only they shall be subject to your husbands," which hath been verified in heathen women, so as it is almost incredible to be believed, for many of them before they would be defiled have been careless of their lives, and so have endured all those torments that men could devise to inflict upon them, rather than they would lose the name of a modest maid or a chaste matron. Yea, and so far they have been from consenting to any immodesty, that if at any time they have been ravished, they have either made away themselves, or at least have separated themselves from company, not thinking themselves worthy of any society, after they have once been deflowered, though against their wills. Therefore the woman that is infected with the sin of uncleaness is worse than a beast, because it desireth but for nature, and she to satisfy her corrupt lusts.[19]

Some of the Fathers have written that it is not enough for a woman to be chaste, but even so to behave her self that no man may think or deem her to be unchaste. We read that in the primitive church, when there were wars between the Christians and the pagans, if at any time the pagans had

17. Cf. Gen. 3:15.
18. Gen. 3:16.
19. A beast copulates naturally; wicked women do so through lust.

gotten the victory, that then they would seek to deflower the virgins, to the which sin, before the Christians would yield, they would continually lay violent hands upon themselves, in so much that the doctors of the church were oftentimes constrained to make diverse sermons and orations to them to dissuade them from that cruelty which they inflicted upon themselves, rather than they would suffer themselves to be deflowered. Such a disgrace did they think it, to have but one spot of uncleaness, and yet none of these were so holy as this Mary, this pure and undefiled virgin.

Some godly and reverend men of the church have gathered this, that there were five women of great virtue in the time of the law,[20] the first letters of whose names do make her whole name to show that she had all their virtues wholly combined in her: as namely, *Michael, Abigail, Rachel, Judith and Anna.*[21]

She was as faithful to her husband as Michael, who saved her husband, David, from the fury of Saul, although he were her father and her king, not preferring her own life before the safety of her husband's. She was as wise as Abigail, who is highly commended for her wisdom; amiable in the sight of her husband as Rachel; stout and magnanimous in the time of trouble as Judith; patient and zealous in prayer as Anna. Seeing then that by this one name so many virtues are called to remembrance, I think it meet that good names be given to all women that they might call to mind the virtues of those women whose names they bear. But especially above all other moral virtues, let women be persuaded by this discourse to embrace chastity, without which we are mere beasts and no women.

Chapter 10

Reasons of giving good names to Children

If ye shall think me too tedious about the naming your children, I tell you that I have some reason for it, and the first is this, to make them read in the Bible the things which are written of those saints and learn to imitate their virtues. Secondly because many have made a god of the virgin Mary, the Scripture warranting no such thing, and have prayed to her (though there they shall find that she was a woman, yea, and a comfort to all women, for she hath taken away the reproach which of right belonged unto us, and by the seed of the woman we are all saved), it was therefore fit I should speak largely of that name. Thirdly, seeing many have heretofore and now do make images of saints to put them in mind of the saints, and so by little and little have at last worshiped the works of their own hands, and

20. The law of the Old Testament.
21. Maria.

for fear of forgetting the saints, have forgotten the second commandment, I thought it better to have you remember them by bearing their names and by reading what they taught us in the Scripture. . . .

Chapter 11

Children to be taught betimes, and brought up gently

I am further also to entreat you that all your children may be taught to read, beginning at four years old or before. And let them learn till ten, in which time they are not able to do any good in the commonwealth but to learn how to serve God, their king, and country by reading. And I desire, entreat, and earnestly beseech you, and every one of you, that you will have your children brought up with much gentleness and patience. What disposition soever they be of, gentleness will soonest bring them to virtue. For frowardness[22] and curstness doth harden the heart of a child and maketh him weary of virtue. Among the froward thou shalt learn frowardness; let them therefore be gently used and always kept from idleness. And bring them up in the schools of learning if you be able and they fit for it. If they will not be scholars, yet I hope they will be able by God's grace to read the Bible, the law of God, and to be brought to some good vocation or calling of life. Solomon saith, *Teach a child in his youth the trade of his life, and he will not forget it nor depart from it when he is old.*[23]

Chapter 12

Choice of wives

Now for your wives, the Lord direct you, for I cannot tell you what is best to be done. Our Lord saith, *First seek the kingdom of God and his righteousness, and all things else shall be ministered unto you.*[24] First, you must seek a godly wife, that she may be a help to you in godliness. For God said, *It is not good for man to be alone. Let him have a helper meet for him.*[25] And she cannot be meet for him except she be truly godly. For God counteth that the man is alone still if his wife be not godly. If I should write unto you how many the Scripture maketh mention of that have been drawn to sin because they married ungodly wives, it would be tedious for you to read.

The world was drowned because men married ungodly wives.[26] Solomon, who was not only the wisest man that ever was but was also mightily endued

22. Perversity, contrariness.
23. Prov. 22:6.
24. Matt. 6:33.
25. Gen. 2:18.
26. Gen. 6:2–3; 1 Kings 11:4.

with the spirit of God, by marrying idolatrous women fell for the time to idolatry. Never think to stand, where Solomon fell. I pray God that neither you nor any of yours may at any time marry with any of those which hold such superstitions as they did, or as some do now, as namely to pray to saints, to pray in Latin, to pray to go to purgatory, etc. Let no riches or money bring your posterity to this kind of tradition. The beloved apostle of Christ saith, *Love not the world, nor the things that are in the world,*[27] for he knew well that a little that a man loveth not would suffice him; a little with a godly woman is better then great riches with the wicked. Rebecca saith, *I shall be weary of my life, if Jacob take a wife of the daughters of Heth,*[28] as if she should say, If my son marry an ungodly wife, then all my comfort of him and his is gone, and it will be a continual grief to me to see him in league and friendship amongst the wicked. If such a shame and sin cometh upon my son, as can by no means be helped, nor I by no means comforted, what availeth me then to live?"

Be not unequally yoked,[29] (saith the Holy Ghost). It is indeed very unequal for the godly and ungodly to be united together, that their hearts must be both as one which can never be joined in the fear of God and faith of Christ. Love not the ungodly; marry with none except you love her; and be not changeable in your love. Let nothing, after you have made your choice, remove your love from her. For it is an ungodly and very foolish thing of a man to mislike his own choice, especially since God hath given a man much choice among the godly. And it was a great cause that moved God to command his to marry with the godly, that there might be continual agreement between them.

Chapter 13

It is great folly for a man to mislike his own choice

Methinks I never saw a man shew a more senseless simplicity than in misliking his own choice, when God hath given a man almost a world of women to choose him a wife in. If a man hath not wit enough to choose him one whom he can love to the end, yet methinks he should have discretion to cover his own folly. But if he want discretion, methinks he should have policy, which never fails a man to dissemble his own simplicity in this case. If he want wit, discretion, and policy, he is unfit to marry any woman. Do not a woman that wrong as to take her from her friends that love her, and after a while to begin to hate her. If she have no friends, yet thou knowest not but that she may have a husband that may love her. If

27. I John 2:15.
28. Gen. 27:46.
29. 2 Cor. 6:14?

thou canst not love her to the end, leave her to him that can. Methinks my son could not offend me in anything if he served God except he chose a wife that he could not love to the end. I need not say if he served God, for if he served God, he would obey God and then he would choose a godly wife and live lovingly and godlily with her, and not do as some man, who taketh a woman to make her a companion and fellow, and after he hath her, he makes her a servant and drudge. If she be thy wife, she is always too good to be thy servant and worthy to be thy fellow. If thou wilt have a good wife, thou must go before her in all goodness and shew her a pattern of all good virtues by thy godly and discreet life, and especially in patience, according to the counsel of the Holy Ghost: *Bear with the woman, as with the weaker vessel.*[30] Here God sheweth that it is her imperfection that honoreth thee and that it is thy perfection that maketh thee to bear with her. Follow the counsel of God therefore and bear with her. God willed a man *to leave father and mother for his wife.*[31] This sheweth what an excellent love God did appoint to be between man and wife. In truth I cannot by any means set down the excellency of that love. But this I assure you, that if you get wives that be godly and you love them, you shall not need to forsake me. Whereas if you have wives that you love not, I am sure I will forsake you. Do not yourselves that wrong as to marry a woman that you cannot love. Shew not so much childishness in your sex as to say, you loved her once and now your mind is changed. If thou canst not love her for the goodness that is in her, yet let the grace that is in thyself move thee to do it; and so I leave thee to the Lord, whom I pray to guide both thee and her with his grace, and grant that you may choose godlily and live happily and die comfortably, through faith in Jesus Christ. [The following chapters deal mainly with the efficacy of faith and private prayer. Pp. 58–270 omitted.]

30. 1 Pet. 3:7.
31. Matt. 19:5.

Selected Bibliography of Works Related to Women and Marriage in Early Modern England

Agrippa, H. C. *The Commendation of Matrimony.* Trans. David Clapham. London, 1540.

Amussen, S. D. "Gender, Family and the Social Order, 1560–1725." In *Order and Disorder in Early Modern England,* edited by Anthony Fletcher and John Stevenson, 196–207. Cambridge: Cambridge University Press, 1985.

Archer, Ian W. *The Pursuit of Stability: Social Relations in Elizabethan London.* Cambridge: Cambridge University Press, 1991.

Ashley, Maurice. "Love and Marriage in Seventeenth-Century England." *History Today* 8 (1958): 667–75.

Bainton, Roland. *Women of the Reformation.* Minneapolis: Augsburg Publishing House, 1973.

Bayne, Diane Valeri. "*The Instruction of a Christian Woman:* Richard Hyrde and the Thomas More Circle." *Moreana* 45 (Feb., 1975): 5–15.

Beilin, Elaine V. *Redeeming Eve: Women Writers of the English Renaissance.* Princeton: Princeton University Press, 1987.

Belsey, Catherine. *The Subject of Tragedy: Identity and Difference in Renaissance Drama.* London: Methuen, 1985.

Benedek, Thomas G. "The Changing Relationship between Midwives and Physicians during the Renaissance." *Bulletin of the History of Medicine* 51 (Winter, 1977): 550–64.

Blumenfeld-Kosinski, Renate, ed. *Not of Woman Born: Representations of Caesarean Birth in Medieval and Renaissance Culture.* Ithaca: Cornell University Press, 1991.

Bornstein, Diane, ed. *Distaves and Dames: Renaissance Treatises for and about Women.* Delmar, N.Y.: Scholars' Facsimiles and Reprints, 1978.

———. Introduction to *The Feminist Controversy of the Renaissance,* edited by Diane Bornstein. Delmar, N.Y.: Scholars' Facsimiles and Reprints, 1980.

Boxer, Marilyn J., and Jean H. Quataert, eds. *Connecting Spheres: Women in the Western World, 1500 to the Present.* New York: Oxford University Press, 1987.

Bradford, Gamaliel. *Elizabethan Women,* edited by Harold Odgen White. Boston: Houghton Mifflin, 1936.

Bridenthal, Renate, and Claudia Koonz, eds. *Becoming Visible: Women in European History.* Boston: Houghton Mifflin, 1977.

Brink, Jean R. *Female Scholars: A Tradition of Learned Women before 1800.* Montreal: Eden Press Women's Publications, 1980.

Brink, Jean R., Maryanne C. Horowitz, and Alison P. Coudert, eds. *Playing with Gender: A Renaissance Pursuit.* Urbana: University of Illinois Press, 1991.

Brown, Roger Lee. "The Rise and Fall of the Fleet Marriages." In *Marriage and Society: Studies in the Social History of Marriage,* edited by R. B. Outhwaite, 117–36.

Bruyn, Jan de. "The Ideal Lady and the Rise of Feminism in Seventeenth-Century England." *Mosaic* 17 (1984): 19–28.

Bullinger, Henry. *The Christian State of Matrimony.* Trans. M. Coverdale. London, 1541.

Bullough, Vern L. *The Subordinate Sex: A History of Attitudes toward Women.* Baltimore: Penguin Books, 1974.

Bunny, Edmund. *Of Divorce for Adultery and Marrying Again.* Oxford, 1610.

Burton, Elizabeth. *The Early Tudors at Home, 1485–1558.* London: Allen Lane, 1976.

———. *The Elizabethans at Home.* London: Secker and Warburg, 1958.

Cahn, Susan. *Industry of Devotion: The Transformation of Women's Work in England, 1500–1660.* New York: Columbia University Press, 1987.

Camden, Charles Carroll. *The Elizabethan Woman.* Houston: Elsevier Press, 1952; rev. ed., Mamaroneck, N.Y.: P. P. Appel, 1975.

Cannon, Mary Agnes. *The Education of Women during the Renaissance.* Washington, D.C.: National Capitol Press, 1916; Westport, Conn.: Hyperion Press, 1981.

Carroll, Berenice A., ed. *Liberating Women's History: Theoretical and Critical Essays.* Urbana: University of Illinois Press, 1976.

Cioni, Maria L. "The Elizabethan Chancery and Women's Rights." In *Tudor Rule and Revolution: Essays for G. R. Elton from His American Friends,* edited by DeLloyd J. Guth and John W. McKenna, 159–82. Cambridge: Cambridge University Press, 1982.

———. *Women and Law in Elizabethan England, with Particular Reference to the Court of Chancery.* New York: Garland, 1985.

Clark, Alice. *Working Life of Women in the Seventeenth Century.* London: Routledge and Kegan Paul, 1982.

Cleaver, Robert. *A Godly Form of Household Government: for the Ordering of Private Families.* London, 1612.

Clinton, Elizabeth. *The Countess of Lincoln's Nursery.* London, 1622.

Coward, Rosalind. *Patriarchal Precedents: Sexuality and Social Relations.* London: Routledge and Kegan Paul, 1983.

Darcie, Abraham. *The Honor of Ladies: or, a True Description of their Noble Perfections.* London, 1622.

Davies, Kathleen M. "Continuity and Change in Literary Advice on Marriage." In *Marriage and Society: Studies in the Social History of Marriage,* edited by R. B. Outhwaite, 58–80.

———. "The Sacred Condition of Equality—How Original Were Puritan Doctrines of Marriage?" *Social History* 5 (1977): 563–80.

Davis, Natalie Zemon. *Society and Culture in Early Modern France: Eight Essays.* Stanford: Stanford University Press, 1975.

Delany, Sheila. *Writing Woman: Women Writers and Women in Literature—Medieval to Modern.* New York: Schocken Books, 1983.

A Discourse of the Married and Single Life, Wherein, by Discovering the misery of the One, is Plainly Declared the Felicity of the Other. London, 1621.

Donnison, Jean. *Midwives and Medical Men: A History of Inter-Professional Rivalries and Women's Rights.* New York: Schocken Books, 1977.

Dove, John. *Of Divorcement: A Sermon Preached at Paul's Cross the Tenth of May, 1601.* London, 1601.

Dubrow, Heather. *A Happier Eden: The Politics of Marriage in the Stuart Epithalamium.* Ithaca: Cornell University Press, 1990.

DuCastel, Christine (de Pisan). *Here Beginneth the Book of the City of Ladies.* London, 1521.

Dunn, Catherine M. "The Changing Image of Woman in Renaissance Society and Literature." In *What Manner of Woman: Essays on English and American Life and Literature,* edited by Marlene Springer, 15–38. New York: New York University Press, 1977.

Dusinberre, Juliet. *Shakespeare and the Nature of Women.* New York: Macmillan, 1975.

Eccles, Audrey. *Obstetrics and Gynaecology in Tudor and Stuart England.* Kent, Ohio: Kent State University Press, 1982.

Einstein, Lewis. *Tudor Ideals.* 1921. Reprint. New York: Harcourt, Brace, and Co., 1962.

Eliot, Vivian Brodsky. "Single Women in the London Marriage Market: Age, Status, and Mobility. 1598–1619." In *Marriage and Society: Studies in the Social History of Marriage,* edited by R. B. Outhwaite, 81–100.

Elshtain, Jean Bethke. *Public Man, Private Woman: Women in Social and Political Thought.* Princeton: Princeton University Press, 1981.

Elyot, Sir Thomas. *The Defense of Good Women.* London, 1545.

Emmison, F. G. *Elizabethan Life: Disorder.* Chelmsford: Essex County Council, 1970.

———. *Elizabethan Life: Morals and the Church Courts.* Chelmsford: Essex County Council, 1973.

Fahy, Conor. "Three Early Renaissance Treatises on Women." *Italian Studies* 12 (1965): 350–55.

Fell, Margaret. *Women's Speaking Justified.* London, 1666.

Ferguson, Moira, ed. *First Feminists: British Women Writers, 1578–1799.* Bloomington: Indiana University Press; Old Westbury, N.Y.: Feminist Press, 1985.

Fettiplace, Elinor. *Elinor Fettiplace's Receipt Book: Elizabethan Country House Cooking*, edited by Hilary Spurling. New York: Viking, 1987.

Figes, Eva. *Patriarchal Attitudes: Women in Society*. 1970. Reprint. London: Virago, 1981.

Filmer, Robert. *Patriarcha and Other Political Works of Sir Robert Filmer*, edited by Peter Laslett. Oxford: Basil Blackwell, 1949.

Fitz, L. T. "What Says the Married Woman? Marriage Theory and Feminism in the English Renaissance." *Mosaic* 13 (1980): 1–22.

Forbes, Thomas R. *The Midwife and the Witch*. New Haven: Yale University Press, 1966.

———. "The Regulation of English Midwives in the Sixteenth and Seventeenth Centuries." *Medical History* 8 (July, 1964): 235–44.

Fraser, Antonia. *The Weaker Vessel: Woman's Lot in Seventeenth-Century England*. New York: Random House, 1984.

Garanderie, M. M. de la. "Le Féminisme de Thomas More et d'Erasme." *Moreana* 10 (1966): 23–29.

Garber, Marjorie, ed. *Cannibals, Witches, and Divorce: Estranging the Renaissance*. Baltimore: The Johns Hopkins University Press, 1987.

Gataker, Thomas. *A Good Wife God's Gift*. London, 1623.

Gibson, Anthony. *A Woman's Worth, Defended Against all the Men in the World*. London, 1599.

Gilbert, Sandra, and Susan Gubar. "Sexual Linguistics: Gender, Language, Sexuality." *New Literary History* 16 (1985): 515–43.

Gillis, John R. *For Better, for Worse: British Marriages, 1600 to the Present*. Oxford: Oxford University Press, 1985.

Goreau, Angeline, E., ed. *The Whole Duty of a Woman: Female Writers in Seventeenth Century England*. Garden City, N.Y.: Dial Press, 1985.

Gosynhill, Edward. *The Praise of All Women*. [1542?].

Gouge, William. *Of Domestical Duties*. London, 1622.

Goulianos, Joan, ed. *By a Woman Writt: Literature from Six Centuries by and about Women*. Indianapolis: Bobbs-Merril, 1973.

Greaves, Richard L. *Society and Religion in Elizabethan England*. Minneapolis: University of Minnesota Press, 1981.

Greco, Norma, and R. Novotny. "Bibliography of Women in the English Renaissance." *University of Michigan Papers in Women's Studies* 1 (1974): 29–57.

[Greenham, Richard]. *A Godly Exhortation and Fruitfull Admonition to Virtuous Parents and Modest Matrons*. London, 1584.

Greenhut, Deborah G. "Persuade Yourselves: Women, Speech, and Sexual Politics in Tudor Society." *Proteus* 3 (Fall, 1968): 42–48.

Griffith, Matthew. *Bethel: or, a Form for Families*. London, 1633.

Guillemeau, James. *Child-birth or, the Happy Delivery of Women*. London, 1612.

Hageman, Elizabeth H. "Recent Studies in Women Writers of the English Seventeenth Century (1604–1674)." *English Literary Renaissance* 18 (Winter, 1988): 138–67.

———. "Recent Studies in Women Writers of Tudor England, Part I: Women Writers, 1485–1603, Excluding Mary Sidney, Countess of Pembroke." *English Literary Renaissance* 14 (Autumn, 1984): 409–26.

Hair, Philip E. H. "Bridal Pregnancy in Earlier Rural England Further Examined." *Population Studies* 24 (1970): 59–70.

———. "Bridal Pregnancy in Rural England in Earlier Centuries." *Population Studies* 20 (1966): 233–43.

Hamilton, Roberta. *The Liberation of Women: A Study of Patriarchy and Capitalism.* London: G. Allen and Unwin, 1978.

Hannay, Margaret P., ed. *Silent But for the Word: Tudor Women as Patrons, Translators, and Writers of Religious Works.* Kent, Ohio: Kent State University Press, 1985.

Harrington, William. *The Commendations of Matrimony with the Impediments.* London, 1515.

Heale, William. *An Apology for Women, or An Opposition to Mr. Dr. G. his Assertion . . . That it was Lawfull for Husbands to Beat their Wives.* Oxford, 1609.

Henderson, Katherine Usher, and Barbara F. McManus, eds. *Half Humankind: Contexts and Texts of the Controversy about Women in England, 1540–1640.* Urbana: University of Illinois Press, 1985.

Heywood, Thomas. *A Curtain Lecture: As it is Read by a Country Farmer's Wife to her Good Man.* London, 1637.

Hill, Christopher. *Society and Puritanism in Pre-Revolutionary England.* London: Secker and Warburg, 1964.

Hoffer, Peter C., and N. E. H. Hull. *Murdering Mothers: Infanticide in England and New England, 1558–1803.* New York: New York University Press, 1981.

Hogrefe, Pearl. "Legal Rights of Tudor Women and their Circumvention by Men and Women." *Sixteenth Century Journal* 3 (1972): 97–105.

———. *Tudor Women: Commoners and Queens.* Ames: Iowa State University Press, 1975.

———. *Women of Action in Tudor England.* Ames: Iowa State University Press, 1977.

Hole, Christina. *English Home-Life, 1500–1800.* London: Batsford, 1949.

———. *The English Housewife in the Seventeenth Century.* London: Chatto and Windus, 1953.

H[ooke], Chr[istopher]. *The Child-birth or Woman's Lecture.* London, 1590.

Houlbrooke, Ralph A. *The English Family 1450–1700.* London: Longman, 1984.

———. "The Making of Marriage in Mid-Tudor England: Evidence from the Records of Matrimonial Contract Litigation." *Journal of Family History* 10 (1985): 339–52.

Hull, Suzanne W. *Chaste, Silent and Obedient: English Books for Women 1475–1640.* San Marino, Calif.: Huntington Library, 1982.

Hyrde, Richard. "A Plea for Learned Women: 1 October, 1524." *Moreana* 13 (Feb., 1967): 5–24.

Ingram, Martin. *Church Courts, Sex, and Marriage in England, 1570–1640.* Cambridge: Cambridge University Press, 1987.

———. "The Reform of Popular Culture? Sex and Marriage in Early Modern England." In *Popular Culture in Seventeenth-Century England,* edited by Barry Reay, 129–65.

————. "Spousals Litigation in the English Ecclesiastical Courts, c. 1350–c. 1640." In *Marriage and Society: Studies in the Social History of Marriage,* edited by R. B. Outhwaite, 35–67.

Irwin, Joyce L., ed. *Womanhood in Radical Protestantism: 1525–1675.* Lewiston, N.Y.: E. Mellen Press, 1979.

Jardine, Lisa. "Cultural Confusion and Shakespeare's Learned Heroines: 'These are old paradoxes.' " *Shakespeare Quarterly* 38 (1987): 1–18.

————. *Still Harping on Daughters: Women and Drama in the Age of Shakespeare.* Sussex: Harvester Press, 1983.

Joceline, Elizabeth. *The Mother's Legacy to her Unborn Child.* London, 1624.

Johnson, James T. *A Society Ordained by God: English Puritan Marriage Doctrine in the First Half of the Seventeenth Century.* Nashville: Abingdon Press, 1970.

Jordan, Constance. "Feminism and the Humanists: The Case of Sir Thomas Elyot's *Defence of Good Women.*" In *Rewriting the Renaissance,* edited by Margaret W. Ferguson, Maureen Quilligan, and Nancy J. Vickers, 242–53. Chicago: University of Chicago Press, 1986.

————. *Renaissance Feminism: Literary Texts and Political Models.* Ithaca: Cornell University Press, 1990.

Kaufman, Gloria. "Juan Luis Vives on the Education of Women." *Signs* 3 (Summer, 1978): 891–97.

Kelly(-Gadol), Joan. *Women, History, and Theory: the Essays of Joan Kelly.* Chicago: University of Chicago Press, 1984.

Kelso, Ruth. *Doctrine for the Lady of the Renaissance.* Urbana: University of Illinois Press, 1956. Reprint with Foreword by Katharine M. Rogers. 1978.

Kinney, Arthur, ed. "Women in the Renaissance." *English Literary Renaissance* 14 (Autumn, 1984).

————. "Women in the Renaissance II." *English Literary Renaissance* 18 (Winter, 1988).

Klein, Joan Larsen. "Women and Marriage in Renaissance England: Male Perspectives." In *Topic: 36 The Elizabethan Woman,* edited by Anne Parten, 20–37. Washington, Penn.: Washington and Jefferson College, 1982.

Knox, John. *The First Blast of the Trumpet Against the Monstrous Regiment of Women.* [Geneva], 1558.

Laslett, Peter. *Family Life and Illicit Love in Earlier Generations: Essays in Historical Sociology.* Cambridge: Cambridge University Press, 1977.

————. *The World We Have Lost: Further Explored.* 3d ed. New York: Macmillan, 1984.

Laslett, Peter, Karla Oosterveen, and Richard M. Smith, eds. *Bastardy and Its Comparative History.* London: Edward Arnold Ltd.; Cambridge, Mass.: Harvard University Press, 1980.

Latt, David J. "Praising Virtuous Ladies: The Literary Image and Historical Reality of Women in Seventeenth-Century England." In *What Manner of Woman: Essays on English and American Life and Literature,* edited by Marlene Springer, 39–64. New York: New York University Press, 1977.

Leites, Edmund. "The Duty to Desire: Love, Friendship, and Sexuality in Some Puritan Theories of Marriage." *Journal of Social History* 15 (1979): 383–408.

Levine, David. *Family Formation in an Age of Nascent Capitalism.* New York: Academic Press, 1977.

Levine, David, and Keith Wrightson. "The Social Context of Illegitimacy in Early Modern England." In *Bastardy and Its Comparative History,* edited by Peter Laslett, Karla Oosterveen, and Richard M. Smith, 158–75.

Little, David. *Religion, Order and Law: A Study in Pre-Revolutionary England.* Oxford: Basil Blackwell, 1969.

Littleton, His Treatise of Tenures, in French and English, edited by T. E. Tomlins. 1841. Reprint. New York: Russell and Russell, 1970.

MacDonald, Michael. *Mystical Bedlam: Madness, Anxiety, and Healing in Seventeenth Century England.* Cambridge: Cambridge University Press, 1981.

———. "Women and Madness in Tudor and Stuart England." *Social Research* 53, 2 (1986): 261–81.

MacFarlane, Alan. *The Family Life of Ralph Josselin, a Seventeenth-Century Clergyman: An Essay in Historical Anthropology.* Cambridge: Cambridge University Press, 1970.

———. "Illegitimacy and Illegitimates in English History." In *Bastardy and Its Comparative History,* edited by Peter Laslett, Karla Oosterveen, and Richard M. Smith, 71–85.

———. *Marriage and Love in England: Modes of Reproduction 1300–1840.* Oxford: Basil Blackwell, 1986.

———. *The Origins of English Individualism: The Family, Property and Social Transition.* Oxford: Basil Blackwell, 1978.

———. *Witchcraft in Tudor and Stuart England: A Regional and Comparative Study.* London: Routledge and Kegan Paul, 1970.

Maclean, Ian. *The Renaissance Notion of Woman: A Study in the Fortunes of Scholasticism and Medical Science in European Intellectual Life.* Cambridge: Cambridge University Press, 1980.

MacLennan, Hector. "A Gynaecologist Looks at the Tudors." *Medical History* 11 (1967): 66–74.

Mahl, Mary R., and Helene Koon, eds. *The Female Spectator: English Women Writers before 1800.* Bloomington: Indiana University Press, 1977.

Manley, Lawrence. *London in the Age of Shakespeare: An Anthology.* London: Croom Helm, 1986.

Markham, Gervase. *The English Housewife,* edited by Michael R. Best. Kingston, Ontario: McGill-Queen's University Press, 1986.

Martindale, Joanna, ed. *English Humanism: Wyatt to Cowley.* London: Croom Helm, 1985.

Masek, Rosemary, "Women in an Age of Transition, 1485–1714." In *The Women of England from Anglo-Saxon Times to the Present: Interpretive Bibliographical Essays,* edited by Barbara Kanner, 138–82. Hamden, Conn.: Archon Books, 1979.

Menefee, Samuel Pyeatt. *Wives for Sale: An Ethnographic Study of British Popular Divorce.* New York: St. Martin's Press, 1981.

Middleton, Chris. "Patriarchal Exploitation and the Rise of English Capitalism." In *Gender, Class and Work,* edited by Eva Gamarnikow, David Morgan, June Purvis, and Daphne Taylorson, 11–27. London: Heinemann, 1983.

Neely, Carol Thomas. *Broken Nuptials in Shakespeare's Plays.* New Haven: Yale University Press, 1985.

Niccholes, Alexander. *A Discourse, of Marriage and Wiving.* London, 1615.

Notestein, Wallace. "The English Woman 1580–1650." In *Studies in Social History Presented to G. M. Trevelyn,* ed. J. H. Plumb, 69–107. London: Longmans, Green and Co., 1955. Reprint. Freeport, N.Y.: Books for Libraries Press, 1969.

Outhwaite, R. B., ed. *Marriage and Society: Studies in the Social History of Marriage.* New York: St. Martin's Press, 1981.

Parten, Anne, ed. *Topic: 36 The Elizabethan Woman.* Washington, Penn.: Washington and Jefferson College, 1982.

Platt, Hugh. *Delights for Ladies, to Adorn their Persons, Tables, Closets, and Distillatories.* London, [1600?].

Pleasant Quips for Upstart Newfangled Gentlewomen. London, 1595.

Plowden, Alison. *Tudor Women: Queens and Commoners.* New York: Atheneum, 1979.

Pollock, Linda A. *Forgotten Children: Parent-Child Relations from 1500–1900.* Cambridge: Cambridge University Press, 1983.

Powell, Chilton Latham. *English Domestic Relations 1487–1653: A Study of Matrimony and Family Life in Theory and Practice as Revealed by the Literature, Law and History of the Period.* New York: Columbia University Press, 1917. Reprint. 1972.

[Prichard, Thomas]. *The School of Honest and Virtuous Life.* London, [1579].

Prior, Mary, ed. *Women in English Society, 1500–1800.* London: Methuen, 1984.

Quaife, G. R. *Wanton Wenches and Wayward Wives: Peasants and Illicit Sex in Early Seventeenth Century England.* New Brunswick, N.J.: Rutgers University Press, 1979.

Radcliff-Umstead, Douglas. *The Roles and Images of Women in the Middle Ages and Renaissance.* University of Pittsburgh Publications on the Middle Ages and the Renaissance, 3. Pittsburgh: University of Pittsburgh Center for Medieval and Renaissance Studies, 1975.

———, ed. *Human Sexuality in the Middle Ages and Renaissance.* University of Pittsburgh Publications on the Middle Ages and the Renaissance, 4. Pittsburgh: University of Pittsburgh Center for Medieval and Renaissance Studies, 1978.

Reay, Barry, ed. *Popular Culture in Seventeenth-Century England.* London: Croom Helm, 1985.

Reynolds, Myra. *The Learned Lady in England 1650–1760.* New York: Houghton, 1920.

Rich, Barnaby. *The Excellency of Good Women.* London, 1613.

———. *My Lady's Looking Glass.* London, 1616.

Rogers, Daniel. *Matrimonial Honor.* London, 1642.

Rogers, Katharine. *The Troublesome Helpmate: A History of Misogyny in Literature.* Seattle: University of Washington Press, 1966.

Rose, Mary Beth. *The Expense of Spirit: Love and Sexuality in English Renaissance Drama.* Ithaca: Cornell University Press, 1988.

————, ed. *Women in the Middle Ages and the Renaissance: Literary and Historical Perspectives.* Syracuse, N.Y.: Syracuse University Press, 1986.

Rosen, Barbara. *Witchcraft.* London: Edward Arnold, 1969. 2d ed. New York: Taplinger, 1972.

Rowbotham, Sheila. *Hidden from History: Rediscovering Women in History from the Seventeenth Century to the Present.* New York: Pantheon Books, 1974.

————. *Women, Resistance, and Revolution.* New York: Pantheon Books, 1972.

Ruether, Rosemary, ed. *Religion and Sexism: Images of Women in the Jewish and Christian Traditions.* New York: Touchstone Books, 1974.

Sachs, Hannelore. *The Renaissance Woman.* Trans. Marianne Herzfield. New York: McGraw-Hill, 1971.

Samaha, Joel. "Gleanings from Local Criminal Court Records: Sedition amongst the 'Inarticulate' in Elizabethan Essex." *Journal of Social History* 8 (Summer, 1975): 61–79.

Schnucker, Robert V. "Elizabethan Birth Control and Puritan Attitudes." *Journal of Interdisciplinary History* 5 (Spring, 1975): 655–68.

Schochet, Gordon J. *Patriarchalism in Political Thought: The Authoritarian Family and Political Speculation and Attitudes Especially in Seventeenth-Century England.* New York: Basic Books, 1975.

Schucking, Levin Ludwig. *The Puritan Family: A Social Study from the Literary Sources.* 1st German ed., 1929. Translated by Brian Battershaw. London: Routledge and Kegan Paul, 1969.

Shapiro, Susan C. "Feminists in Elizabethan England." *History Today* 27 (Nov., 1977): 703–11.

Sharpe, J. A. *Crime in Early Modern England, 1550–1750.* London: Longman, 1984.

————. *Crime in Seventeenth-Century England: A County Study.* Cambridge: Cambridge University Press, 1983.

————. *Early Modern England: A Social History, 1550–1760.* London: E. Arnold, 1987.

————. "Plebian Marriage in Stuart England: Some Evidence from Popular Literature." *Transactions of the Royal Historical Society* 36 (1986): 69–90.

————. "Reading History . . . from Below: Tudor and Stuart England." *History Today* 36 (Dec., 1986): 46–48.

Shepherd, Simon, ed. *The Women's Sharp Revenge: Women Pamphleteers in the Renaissance.* New York: St. Martin, 1985.

Sizemore, Christine W. "Early Seventeenth-Century Advice Books: The Female Viewpoint." *South Atlantic Bulletin* 41, 1 (1976): 41–48.

Slater, Miriam. *Family Life in the Seventeenth Century: The Verneys of Claydon House.* London: Routledge and Kegan Paul, 1984.

————. "The Weightest Business: Marriage in an Upper-Gentry Family in Seventeenth-Century England." *Past and Present* 72 (1976): 25–54.

Smith, Henry. *A Preparative to Marriage.* London, 1591.

Smith, Hilda L. "Gynecology and Ideology in Seventeenty-Century England." In *Liberating Women's History,* edited by Berenice A. Carroll, 97–114. Urbana: University of Illinois Press, 1976.

————. *Reason's Disciples: Seventeenth-Century English Feminists.* Urbana: University of Illinois Press, 1982.

Snawsel, Robert. *A Looking Glass for Married Folks.* London, 1610.

Sowernam, Esther [pseud.]. *Esther Hath Hang'd Haman: or An Answer to a Lewd Pamphlet, entitled The Arraignment of Women.* London, 1617.

Speght, Rachel. *A Mousell for Melastomus.* London, 1617.

Springer, Marlene, ed. *What Manner of Woman: Essays on English and American Life and Literature.* New York: New York University Press, 1977.

Stenton, Doris Mary. *The English Woman in History.* New York: Macmillan; London: Allen and Unwin, 1957.

Stock, Phyllis. *Better Than Rubies: A History of Women's Education.* New York: Putnam, 1978.

Stockwood, John. *A Bartholmew Fairing for Parents.* London, 1589.

Stone, Lawrence. *The Causes of the English Revolution 1592–1642.* London: Routledge and Kegan Paul, 1972.

————. *The Crisis of the Aristocracy, 1558–1641.* Oxford: Oxford University Press, 1965.

————. *The Family, Sex, and Marriage in England, 1500–1800.* London: Weidenfeld & Nicolson, 1977.

————. "The Rise of the Nuclear Family in Early Modern England: The Patriarchal Stage." In *The Family in History,* edited by Charles E. Rosenberg, 13–57. Philadelphia: University of Pennsylvania Press, 1975.

Swetnam, Joseph. *The Arraignment of Lewd, Idle, Froward, and Unconstant Women.* London, 1615.

Swinburne, Henry. *A Treatise of Spousals.* London, 1686.

Tasso, Torquato. *The Householder's Philosophy.* Trans. T. K[yd]. London, 1588.

Tavard, George H. *Woman in Christian Tradition.* Notre Dame: University of Notre Dame Press, 1973.

Taylor, Thomas. *A Good Husband and a Good Wife: Laid Open in a Sermon.* London, 1625.

Thickstun, Margaret Olofson. *Fictions of the Feminine: Puritan Doctrine and the Representation of Women.* Ithaca: Cornell University Press, 1988.

Thomas, Keith Vivian. "The Double Standard." *Journal of the History of Ideas* 20 (Apr., 1959): 195–216.

————. *Man and the Natural World 1500–1800.* London: Allen Lane, 1983.

————. *Religion and the Decline of Magic.* New York: Charles Scribner's Sons, 1971.

————. "Women and the Civil War Sects." *Past and Present* 13 (1958): 42–62.

Thompson, Roger. *Women in Stuart England and America: A Comparative Study.* London: Routledge and Kegan Paul, 1974.

Tilney, Edmund. *A Brief and Pleasant Discourse of Duties in Marriage Called the Flower of Friendship.* London, 1568.

Todd, Margo. "The Spiritualized Household." In *Christian Humanism and the Puritan Social Order,* 96–117. Cambridge: Cambridge University Press, 1987.

Topsell, Edward. *The House-holder; or, Perfect Man.* [London], 1610.

Torshell, Samuel. *The Woman's Glory.* London, 1645.

Towler, Jean, and Joan Bramall. *Midwives in Society and History.* London: Croom Helm, 1986.

Travitsky, Betty, ed. *The Paradise of Women: Writings by Englishwomen of the Renaissance.* Westport, Conn.: Greenwood Press, 1981.

[Tuvil, Daniel]. *Asylum Veneris, or A Sanctuary for Ladies.* London, 1616.

Underdown, D. E. "The Taming of the Scold: The Enforcement of Patriarchal Authority in Early Modern England." In *Order and Disorder in Early Modern England,* edited by Anthony Fletcher and John Stevenson, 116–36. Cambridge: Cambridge University Press, 1985.

Utley, Francis Lee. *The Crooked Rib.* Columbus: Ohio State University Press, 1944.

Warnicke, Retha M. *Women of the English Renaissance.* Westport, Conn.: Greenwood Press, 1983.

Watson, Foster. *Vives and the Renaissance Education of Women.* New York: Longmans, Green and Co., 1912. Reprint. New York: Kelly, 1972.

Wedlocke, Walter. *A Little Treatise Called the Image of Idleness.* London, [1555?].

Weinstein, Minna F. "Reconstructing Our Past: Reflections on Tudor Women." *International Journal of Women's Studies* 1 (Mar.–Apr., 1978): 113–40.

Weston, C. C., and J. R. Greenberg. *Subjects and Sovereigns: The Grand Controversy over Legal Sovereignty in Stuart England.* Cambridge: Cambridge University Press, 1981.

Whately, William. *A Bride-bush, or a Wedding Sermon.* London, 1616.

Wiesner, Merry E. *Women in the Sixteenth Century: A Bibliography.* Sixteenth-Century Bibliography, 23. St. Louis: Center for Information Research, 1983.

Willoby, Henry. *Willoby his Avisa. Or the True Picture of a Modest Maid.* London, 1594.

Wilson, Derek. *A Tudor Tapestry: Men, Women and Society in Reformation England.* Pittsburgh: University of Pittsburgh Press, 1972.

Wilson, Katharina M., ed. *Women Writers of the Renaissance and Reformation.* Athens: University of Georgia Press, 1987.

Woodbridge, Linda. *Women and the English Renaissance: Literature and the Nature of Womankind.* Urbana: University of Illinois Press, 1984.

Wright, Louis B. *Middle-Class Culture in Elizabethan England.* Ithaca, N.Y.: Cornell University Press, 1935.

———. "The Reading of Renaissance English Women." *Studies in Philology* 28 (1931): 671–88.

Wrightson, Keith. *English Society 1580–1680.* London: Hutchinson, 1982.

Wrightson, Keith, and David Levine. *Poverty and Piety in an English Village: Terling 1525–1700.* New York: Academic Press, 1979.

Wrigley, Edward Anthony, and R. S. Schofield. *The Population History of England, 1541–1871: A Reconstruction.* Cambridge, Mass.: Harvard University Press, 1981.

Xenophon. [Economicus]. *Treatise of an Household.* Trans. G. Hervet. London, 1532.

Yates, Francis A. *Astraea: The Imperial Theme in the Sixteenth Century.* London: Routledge and Kegan Paul, 1975. Reprint. New York: Methuen, 1985.

Yost, John K. "The Value of Married Life for the Social Order in the Early English Renaissance." *Societas* 6 (Winter, 1976): 25–39.

Index

Headings and subheadings generally follow the usage of the authors in this collection.

Lovers: deceptions of, 109–10
Lucas, Edward Verrall, 208n1
Lucretia (Lucrece): chaste mind of, 107, 125; rape of, 55; slew herself, 272–73; mentioned, 85
Lust(s): in marriage, is adultery, 130, 170; not to be satisfied in marriage, 5
Luther, Martin, 12, 68
Lycurgus, 75

McCutcheon, Elizabeth, xivn5
Macfarlane, Alan, xivn6
McManus, Barbara F., 291n4
Maids: loss of virginity results in ostracism and death, 105–6; love of men leads to vice and near madness, 109; must be virgin in mind and soul as well as body, 103–4; reputation of, easily destroyed, 109; should allow parents to choose husband, 110–12; should avoid company and feasts, 109; (and young men) should fast to suppress lust, 107–8; should learn if they can, 101; should love God and parents, 110; virginity is protection from rapists and evildoers, 104; virgins, brides of Christ, 104. *See also* Chastity; Gentlewomen; Virginity; Women
Man: end of creation of, 141. *See also* Men
Margolin, J.-C.: edited *Encomium Matrimonii*, 66, 69nn2, 4, 71–72n9, 93n16
Marriage: adultery in, 134; barrenness in, 170; based on Scripture, 3; bastards in, 171; benefits of, 135; better than celibacy, 67, 80, 152, 158; bondage with freedom in, 85; at Cana, 72, 74; carnal copulation in (marriage duties of), fair and holy, 79, 169–70; carnal copulation in, (marriage duties of), no sin, 67, 78–79, 152, 159, 161n40, 169–70; carnal copulation in, without sin only when conception is intended, 99, 131; children in, 7, 8, 78, 83–84, 86–87, 123, 170, 293, 300; of clergy, should be (is) permitted, 80, 159; commanded by God, 123; companionate, 82–83, 99, 111–12, 123,

127–28, 135, 152–53, 168, 169, 171, 172, 302; consent of both parties, a requirement of, 164; consummation of, 165, 166–67; contract of, by words in the present tense, 34, 35–36, 160, 160n34; defined, 157–58; duties of, 167–68, 169; few incommodities in, 85; free to all men, 156, 159; gifts not necessary to, 37; happiness in, 82–83; heresy or not to prefer over celibacy, 90, 95; honored in Hebrew law, 75; an indifferent thing, 158; instituted (sanctified, ordained) in Paradise, 5, 8, 66, 73, 79, 154, 158; jealousy in, 84–85; legal consequences of, if not consummated, 45; love in, 172; man is as reason in, and woman as body, 115; may be contracted by rapist if victim is willing, 36; means to avoid fornication, 158–59; most holy (best) kind of life, 80, 85–86, 94; most holy sacrament, 66, 72, 73, 76; necessity of prayer in, 15, 16–17, 25; nonessential requirements of (accidents of), 162; nothing more honest than, 72; one flesh (one person), 9, 23, 124, 133, 157, 158, 162, 171, 172, 252; one flesh in law, 32; one flesh only after marriage is consumated, 45–46; ordained by God, 4, 8, 73; parents' consent necessary to (in sight of God), 152, 156, 164, 165, 166–67; partners in, may reconcile after one has committed adultery, 171; partners should be of like age and condition, 163; Patriarchs approved of, 78–79; pleasure and happiness in, 82–83; procreation the end of, 37, 75, 80, 123, 131, 158; public celebration of required, 45; reasons for, 4, 5, 13–14, 78–79; remedy of sin, 159; requirements of (essential signs of), 161–62, 164; sexual abstinence in, 99, 131; sexual relationships in, 178; should be consumated, 46; Socrates approved of, 78; a spiritual conjunction, 166; "sure-making" of, 164; subjection of wives in, *see* Wife; type of Christ and his church, 170. *See also* Gentlewomen; Housewife; Husband; Widow; Wife; Women

A Note on the Author

JOAN LARSEN KLEIN received her B.A. from the University of Michigan, and her M.A. and Ph.D. in English literature from Harvard University. She has published articles on Spenser, Shakespeare, and Milton. She has taught since 1970 in the Department of English at the University of Illinois at Urbana-Champaign.